Unstructured Content

Unstructured Content

Edited by
PETER VAN ELSWYK
DIRK KINDERMANN
CAMERON DOMENICO KIRK-GIANNINI
ANDY EGAN

Great Clarendon Street, Oxford, OX2 6DP,
United Kingdom

Oxford University Press is a department of the University of Oxford.
It furthers the University's objective of excellence in research, scholarship,
and education by publishing worldwide. Oxford is a registered trade mark of
Oxford University Press in the UK and in certain other countries

© Oxford University Press 2025

The moral rights of the authors have been asserted

All rights reserved. No part of this publication may be reproduced, stored in a retrieval system,
transmitted, used for text and data mining, or used for training artificial intelligence, in any form or
by any means, without the prior permission in writing of Oxford University Press, or as expressly
permitted by law, by licence or under terms agreed with the appropriate reprographics rights
organization. Enquiries concerning reproduction outside the scope of the above should be sent
to the Rights Department, Oxford University Press, at the address above.

You must not circulate this work in any other form
and you must impose this same condition on any acquirer

Published in the United States of America by Oxford University Press
198 Madison Avenue, New York, NY 10016, United States of America

British Library Cataloguing in Publication Data
Data available

Library of Congress Control Number: 2024942571

ISBN 9780198823551

DOI: 10.1093/9780191862175.001.0001

Printed and bound in the UK by
Clays Ltd, Elcograf S.p.A.

Links to third party websites are provided by Oxford in good faith and
for information only. Oxford disclaims any responsibility for the materials
contained in any third party website referenced in this work.

The manufacturer's authorised representative in the EU for product safety is
Oxford University Press España S.A. of El Parque Empresarial San Fernando de Henares,
Avenida de Castilla, 2 – 28830 Madrid (www.oup.es/en or product.safety@oup.com).
OUP España S.A. also acts as importer into Spain of products made by the manufacturer.

Contents

List of Contributors — vii
Unstructured Content: Introduction — ix
Peter van Elswyk, Cameron Domenico Kirk-Giannini,
Andy Egan and Dirk Kindermann

PART 1 ENRICHING THE POSSIBLE WORLDS APPROACH

Minimal Rationality and the Web of Questions — 3
Daniel Hoek

Commitment Issues in the Naive Theory of Belief — 42
J. Robert G. Williams

Expressivism and Propositions — 62
Robert Stalnaker

PART 2 TRUTHMAKER-STYLE APPROACHES

A Theory of Partial Truth — 83
Kit Fine

Relevance without Minimality — 109
Stephen Yablo

Outline of an Object-Based Truthmaker Semantics for Modals and Propositional Attitudes — 135
Friederike Moltmann

PART 3 ASSESSING UNSTRUCTURED APPROACHES

Unstructured Content — 167
Jeffrey C. King

Attitudes and Propositions — 192
John Perry

Fregean Particularism   201
Susanna Schellenberg

In Defence of Fregean That-Clause Semantics   234
Katharina Felka and Alex Steinberg

General Index   253
Name Index   256

List of Contributors

Andy Egan is Professor, Philosophy, Rutgers University, New Brunswick, NJ, USA.

Katharina Felka is Assistant Professor, University of Graz, Austria.

Kit Fine is Professor, Philosophy, New York University, USA.

Daniel Hoek is Assistant Professor of Philosophy, Department of Philosophy, Virginia Tech, USA. https://orcid.org/0000-0002-5331-2409.

Dirk Kindermann is Assistant Professor (fixed-term), Institute of Philosophy, University of Vienna, Vienna, Austria.

Jeffrey C. King is Distinguished Professor, Department of Philosophy, Rutgers University, New Brunswick, NJ, USA.

Cameron Domenico Kirk-Giannini is Assistant Professor of Philosophy, Rutgers University–Newark, Newark, NJ, USA.

Friederike Moltmann is research director, CNRS-Université Côte d'Azur, Nice, France. https://orcid.org/0000-0003-3269-8186.

John Perry is Professor Emeritus of Philosophy, Stanford University, Stanford, CA, USA, and Professor Emeritus, Philosophy, University of California, Riverside, USA. https://orcid.org/0000-0002-3689-3731.

Susanna Schellenberg is Distinguished Professor of Philosophy and Cognitive Science, Rutgers University, New Brunswick, NJ, USA.

Robert Stalnaker is Professor emeritus, Massachusetts Institute of Technology, Cambridge, MA, USA.

Alex Steinberg is an independent researcher.

Peter van Elswyk is Assistant Professor, Philosophy Department, Northwestern University, Evanston, IL, USA.

J. Robert G. Williams is Professor of Theoretical Philosophy University of Leeds, UK. https://orcid.org/0000-0003-4831-2954.

Stephen Yablo is Professor of Linguistics and Philosophy, Massachusetts Institute of Technology, Cambridge, MA, USA. https://orcid.org/0000-0002-9486-8323.

Unstructured Content

Introduction

*Peter van Elswyk, Cameron Domenico Kirk-Giannini,
Andy Egan and Dirk Kindermann*

Why posit propositional contents?[1] The usual answer is that the existence of such contents is mandated by our leading theories. We can divide the theoretical roles that propositions are needed to play into three categories: linguistic, logical, and cognitive (van Elswyk 2023). The following list illustrates some of these roles:

(I). Be the meanings of declarative sentences
(II). Be the designata of linguistic expressions
(III). Be the contents of illocutionary acts
(IV). Be the relata of entailment relations
(V). Be the bearers of alethic properties
(VI). Be the bearers of modal properties
(VII). Be the objects of cognitive attitudes
(VIII). Be the contents of perception

A theory of propositional contents, then, needs to perform two explanatory tasks: specify what propositions are, and elucidate how propositions perform roles like (I) through (VIII). An anti-realism about propositions has a different task. It needs to specify what performs each role as opposed to a proposition and/or explain why the roles are not needed by theories of language, logic, and cognition.

Theories of propositions can broadly be divided into four kinds: primitivist, act-typic, structured, and unstructured. *Primitivist theories* take propositions to be unanalyzable entities (Bealer 1998, Merricks 2015, *a.o.*). According to the primitivist, propositions cannot be analyzed as having parts or assimilated to a more familiar ontological category (e.g. sets, sums, collections, act types). Instead, they are sui generis objects. *Act-type theories* take propositions to be the types that correspond to cognitive acts of representing objects as being a certain way (Hanks 2015, Soames 2015, *a.o.*). *Structured theories* regard propositions as entities which have parts or constituents that are put together in a particular way (Salmon 1986, Soames 1987, King 2007, *a.o.*). Typically, the parts or constituents

---

[1] Throughout, we use the terms *propositions*, *contents*, and *propositional contents* interchangeably.

involve an object and a property or relation instantiated by that object. Theories differ on how they are glued together, metaphysically speaking. Finally, *unstructured theories* identify propositions with sets or collections of truth-supporting circumstances (Stalnaker 1984, Lewis 1986, *a.o.*). By *truth-supporting circumstances*, we leniently mean worlds, situations, facts, events, and whatever else is a maximal or non-maximal way things are at which statements are true.

This collection of essays is about unstructured theories of propositions. Recent years have seen considerable attention given to rival theories. An assumption that is occasionally detectable in such literature is that unstructured theories have been relegated to the dustbin of history. But this assumption merits investigation, especially given the ubiquity of unstructured theories in cognate fields like linguistics. The original essays in this volume explore the prospects of the unstructured conception of propositions. Before introducing what's to come, though, we will briefly survey work on unstructured theories. Doing so will situate the volume's essays and help illustrate the initial plausibility of unstructured theories, especially when it comes to performing theoretical roles like (I) to (VIII).

I. The Linguistic Roles

A natural starting place for our discussion is the work of Richard Montague. Montague conceived of natural language—its syntax and semantics—as a branch of mathematics rather than psychology. He dismissed "the contention that an important theoretical difference exists between formal and natural languages" (1968 [1974], 188). Natural language could therefore be investigated with the formal precision facilitated by mathematics. To this end, Montague developed a formal system that borrowed from set theory, logic, algebra, and model theory. This system enabled him to model English in a way that overcame a number of limitations of earlier proposals.

An extensional semantics contains an interpretation function that assigns *semantic values* to expressions of natural language. But that interpretation function is limited in what objects can be semantic values. It can only assign two types of objects—entities and truth-values—and functions to and from those objects. By itself, this enables what we can call *functional compositionality* (Cresswell 2002, 645). Every simple expression is assigned one of the basic objects or a function between them, and the meaning of every complex expression is the semantic value that results from applying the function from one component to the semantic value of the other component. For illustration, consider (9). The name *Sonia* can be understood as denoting an entity and the verb *sneezed* can be understood as denoting a function from objects to truth-values.

(I) Sonia sneezed.

What (1) denotes on the extensional proposal is therefore a truth-value. The shortcoming of this approach is, as Thomason (1974, 43) put it, that there is "no way of linking expressions to semantic values other than [through] the relation of denotation." As a result, an extensional semantics cannot explain intensional phenomena, as illustrated by the fact that (1) has the same semantic value as every other true sentence.

Montague's way of overcoming this problem involved the bits that his system borrowed from model theory. Montague relativized the interpretation function so that it did not assign semantic values full stop, but rather semantic values were assigned relative to a variety of factors. The most obvious factor was a model. But the model-theoretic component of his system also enabled him to explain intensionality as another relativity of the interpretation function. It could now be sensitive to indices like worlds or times. That made the interpretation function a more complex function. Instead of being just a function from an expression of natural language to a denotation, it became a function from an expression of natural language *and* indices to a denotation. Expressions could thereby be linked to semantic values via intensions, or the indices of the interpretation function.

Consider (1) again. Though its final denotation is still a truth-value, that denotation is relative to one or more indices. We can therefore characterize (1) by the set of indices where it is true. For example, assume that the interpretation function is sensitive to a world. Then the characteristic set for (1) is just the set of those worlds where (1) is true. That ensures that (1) no longer has the same semantic value as every other true sentence. Sentences will differ according to what worlds are in that set. What results is a conception of content according to which the content of a sentence is a set of possible worlds.

An unstructured theory of content is therefore the natural result of intensionalizing a semantics that (*a*) is functionally compositional, and (*b*) posits only entities and truth-values as basic entities. Though many of the idiosyncrasies of Montague's system have fallen away as formal semantics has matured, functional compositionality remains the primary notion of compositionality (Heim and Kratzer 1998, 13). Since that is the conception of compositionality that has animated much of the advances made by formal semantics, to abandon it is to abandon what semanticists use to illuminate natural languages. Accommodating functional compositionality is therefore a key virtue of unstructured theories. As Pickel (2019) details, structured theories like those offered by Salmon (1986), Soames (1987), and King (2007) give up functional compositionality, and there is no prima facie reason to think that the semantic theories they enable can perfectly replicate what has done in linguistics by theories with functional compositionality. So when it comes to a theoretical role like (I), unstructured theories in a Montagovian lineage have an upside.

This is not to claim that an unstructured conception of content is forced if one adopts functional compositionality. As flagged above, an unstructured conception is the natural result if we also start with the assumption that the only basic objects are entities and truth-values. We can perhaps ditch this assumption to treat propositions as basic objects alongside entities and truth-values (Thomason 1980, Muskens 2004, Pickel 2019). Pickel (2019) argues that a structured conception of propositions is compatible with functional compositionality if we take this route. However, we want to highlight that the way a proposition fulfills a theoretical role like (I) turns on complex decision-points regarding how to set-up the architecture of a semantic theory. An unstructured conception has historically navigated these decision-points with ease in contrast to the competition.

Another central linguistic role is (III): being the content of an illocutionary act. If we draw the familiar distinction from Frege between the *content* and *force* of an utterance, then a theoretical role emerges wherein a proposition is what we forcefully present with the performance of an illocutionary act. We can therefore look to what we do with propositions to better understand what they are. On this front, Stalnaker (1978, 2002) has proposed that the speech act of assertion—the default act associated with the use of a declarative—has an essential effect. If the proposition asserted by a speaker is accepted by conversational participants, then that proposition becomes *common ground*. Here, the common ground is understood as a set of propositions that participants commonly accept. Though in principle a set of propositions can be a set of whatever entity propositions are, Stalnaker adopts an unstructured theory. That has a useful outcome. If we treat propositions as sets of truth-supporting circumstances like worlds, then we can perform set-theoretic operations on the common ground. For example, we can take the intersection of every proposition in the common ground. This intersection forms what Stalnaker calls the *context set*, a set of worlds that are the "live options" for being the actual world. Inquiry can then be understood as narrowing down the context set. We know everything there is to know when the context set contains only the actual world.

The context set has proven a very useful idea for work in semantics and pragmatics. An unstructured conception of propositions plays an important role in this usefulness. For example, consider a traditional semantics for interrogatives on which they denote sets of propositions (Hamblin 1973). If propositions are sets of worlds, a question denotes a set of sets of worlds. A question can therefore be understood as a partition over worlds (Groenendijk and Stokhof 1984). From there, we can take the illocutionary effect of a question to partition the context set. Unlike an assertion, which proposes to shrink the context set by adding a proposition to the common ground, a question structures the context set.

Once again, the fruitfulness of the unstructured conception does not mandate its adoption. One may, as King (2007) does, take structured propositions to determine sets of worlds. A similar proposal may perhaps be offered by primitivist and act-type theories. Then we can still arrive at the context set and put it to theoretical use; the context set is just not strictly speaking an intersection of the propositions in the common ground. But, still, the point remains that an unstructured conception offers an elegantly integrated account of how a proposition fulfills the linguistic roles.

II. The Logical Roles

Some sentences are true, while others are false. More than that, some sentences seem to be true contingently (e.g. *Napoleon was defeated at Waterloo*), while others seem to be true necessarily (e.g. *Seven is a prime number*). And some sentences seem to guarantee the truth of other sentences. For example, the truth of the sentence *Seven is a prime number* seems to guarantee the truth of the sentence *There are prime numbers*. What can be said about sentences can also be said about assertions and mental states like belief. They too can be described as true contingently or necessarily and guarantee the truth of other assertions or beliefs.

These facts about sentences, assertions, and mental states are typically explained by appealing to propositions: sentences, assertions, and mental states are true or false, have modal properties, and enter into relationships of entailment with each other because they express propositional contents which themselves have alethic and modal properties and enter into entailment relations with one another. According to this kind of approach, it is propositional contents which have these properties essentially. Since propositions perform the logical roles (IV), (V), and (VI), and propositions are expressed by sentences, illocutionary acts like assertion, and cognitive attitudes like belief (e.g. they perform roles (I), (III), and (VII)), the latter inherit the properties form propositions.

Unstructured theories of content have an especially simple story to tell about how propositions come to have the logical properties they do (Stalnaker 1984, Lewis 1986, *a.o.*). Consider first having alethic properties, or theoretical role (V). If propositions are sets of truth-supporting circumstances like worlds, then we can say that what it takes for a proposition to be true at a circumstance like a world is just for that world to be in the set which constitutes the proposition. Correspondingly, we can say that what it takes for a proposition to be false at a circumstance is for that circumstance *not* to be in the set which constitutes the proposition. Since every proposition partitions the set of all possible circumstances into those which it contains and those which it does not contain, the unstructured theory of propositions guarantees the truth of the desirable principle that every proposition is either true or false.

Once we have told an unstructured story about alethic properties, it becomes possible to account for modal properties and entailment relations—i.e. performing roles (IV) and (VI)—in a straightforward way using the tools of set theory. A proposition is necessary if it is true in every possible circumstance. Thus a necessary proposition is the union of all other propositions. Correspondingly, a proposition is contradictory if it is false at every circumstance. Thus the contradictory proposition is the intersection of all other propositions, which is just the empty set of circumstances. A proposition is contingent just in case it is true at some but not all circumstances—that is, just in case it contains some but not all truth-supporting circumstances.

If one proposition entails another, it guarantees its truth. On the unstructured picture, entailment can be thought about in terms of containment. Consider a proposition P consisting of some set S of circumstances. P entails another proposition Q just in case Q must be true at any circumstance where P is true. This condition obtains just in case P is a subset of Q: any circumstance where P is true (that is, any member of P) is also a member of every superset of P (that is, a circumstance where that superset is true).

Act-type, structured, and primitivist theories of propositions cannot appeal directly to the resources of set theory to explain the logical properties of propositions in the same way as the unstructured view. Of course, other theories could posit a function mapping propositions to sets circumstances like possible worlds and then define the logical properties of propositions as above. But this introduces a layer of complexity that the unstructured view avoids. It can help itself immediately to the resources of set theory.

III. The Cognitive Roles

Attitudes like belief, desire, hope, and regret have content. It is natural to take this content to be the same content as what performs some of the other theoretical roles. When a speaker uses a declarative sentence to perform an assertion and an addressee believes what is asserted to them, for example, the same content is presumably what is asserted and then believed. What performs roles (I) and (III) is what performs role (VII). This natural step is convenient, too. It allows for a straightforward interface between theories in philosophy of language and nearby theories in philosophy of mind.

Propositional attitudes are representational mental states. They represent how things are. An unstructured theory of propositions offers a way to understand the nature of such representation. Since propositions as the objects of attitudes are sets of possibilities, representation is accounted for as a way of distinguishing between possibilities (Stalnaker 1984). Representation is possibility-carving. To believe P is to take a stand on how things are, and to take a stand on how things are is to rule out the not-P ways for things to be. Desire, similarly, is a matter of distinguishing between possibilities, by favoring some possibilities over others (Heim 1992). We then treat belief, desire, hope, and regret as relations between a subject and a set of circumstances or a region of a possibility space.

A virtue of how an unstructured theory of content cashes out the nature of representation is its minimality. It follows rather effortlessly from treating propositional contents as sets of truth-supporting circumstances. Such minimality is a frequently cited selling point for unstructured content. Whether one is initially attracted to a possibility-carving picture of representation, it's independently plausible that whatever else the objects of propositional attitudes do, they *at least* distinguish between possibilities. If we can get by with saying that that's what such attitudes do, we are left with a theoretical framework that avoids unnecessary commitments. Minimality plays nicely with multiple realizability, too. If we are trying to explain how attitudes like belief represent generally rather than how belief as realized in humans represents, it's valuable to have an account that's minimal. It allows us to avoid building extra assumptions into our analysis of what was supposed to be a very general, massively multiply realizable phenomenon.

A possibility-carving approach to representation fits elegantly with a functionalist account of mental states. To illustrate, here's a first pass at a functionalist account of belief: A belief that P is a state that (a) indicates that P, and (b) tends, together with a desire that Q, to cause behavior that would bring about Q if P were true. This kind of functionalist account will work best with coarse-grained contents. It will be insensitive to finer-grained distinctions (Stalnaker 1984, Parikh 2008). Here are a few examples. If getting on the train moving with an average speed of 80 mph will get me to the meeting on time, getting on the train moving with an average speed of 129 kph will, too. Likewise, water at 212 degrees Fahrenheit causes exactly the same kinds of burns as water at 100 degrees Celsius. As such, the kinds of causal relations that will be the bread and butter of a functionalist account of the mind look to be sensitive only to coarse-grained content, and not to the sorts of distinctions that would distinguish moving at 80 mph from moving at 129 kph, or having temperature 212 degrees Fahrenheit from having temperature 100 degrees Celsius.

IV. Challenges

Theories of propositions face metaphysical challenges. These challenges typically sort into two categories. The first category concerns the theoretical roles. Once a proposition has been identified with something, it is a further question whether that something can perform the various roles or at least a proper subset of them. If that something cannot, there is good cause to doubt that a proposition is that thing as opposed to something else. The second category concerns identity and distinctness. As Quine (1960, 200) famously quipped, "little sense has been made of the term ["proposition"] until we have before us some standard of when to speak of propositions as identical and when as distinct." A successful theory of propositions will offer some standard that distinguishes between distinct propositions and between propositions and non-propositions. If it cannot, we again have cause to look elsewhere.

Incredulity is regularly expressed that propositions qua sets of truth-supporting circumstances can meet the first challenge. For example, Bealer (1998, 2) writes: "most of us have difficulty honestly believing that the very propositions we believe and assert are really functions or...sets." The most common argument advanced along these lines maintains that, to perform the roles, propositions must non-accidentally represent objects as being a certain way (Plantinga 1987, Jubien 2001, Soames 2014, Merricks 2015, *a.o.*). Only representations can be true or false, be believed, be asserted, and so forth. But sets do not represent anything non-accidentally or otherwise; they are not representational entities. So sets of truth-supporting circumstances cannot be propositions.

Various responses to this argument have been offered. One response is to deny that propositions are representational entities. Though the question of whether propositions are representational is a common point of disagreement between those who favor an unstructured theory and those who do not, it is a separate issue. Accordingly, some deny that propositions are representational even while remaining neutral on what propositions are, or while denying that propositions are sets of truth-supporting circumstances (Speaks 2014, Brown 2021). Another response is to argue that *interpreted* sets can be representational (Lewis 1986, Heller 1998). Still another kind of response is to argue that the right kind of truth-supporting circumstances can be representational. For example, Charlow (2015) takes unstructured content to be representational if the elements of the set include a *perspective*. So sets of centered worlds are representational, even if sets of worlds are not.

Where unstructured theories draw the most criticism is with respect to the second challenge of correctly individuating propositions. Suppose the proposition expressed by a sentence is the set of worlds in which the sentence is true. Then an unstructured theory treats two sentences as expressing the same proposition when those sentences are true in all the same worlds. But this identification appears to get things wrong. Consider this pair of mathematical sentences:

(II) $2 + 2 = 4$.
(III) $\sqrt{49} = 7$.

As necessary truths, these sentences are true in all the same worlds. So if the proposition expressed by a sentence is the set of worlds in which the sentence is true, (2) and (3) are equated. Consider two more:

(IV) Sonia sneezed.
(V) Sonia sneezed and $\sqrt{49} = 7$.

Neither (4) nor (5) is a necessary truth. But, even still, these sentences are true in all the same worlds. (The proposition expressed by (5) is just a proper subset of the proposition expressed by (3).) So (4) and (5) are rendered equivalent too. Consider a final pair:

(VI) The groundhog burrowed under the fence.
(VII) The woodchuck burrowed under the fence.

"Groundhog" and "woodchuck" are equivalent terms for the same waddling rodent. As such, (6) and (7) are true in all the same worlds. An unstructured theory looks like it is committing to their equivalence too.

These unwanted equivalences can be developed into an objection in different ways. One might add that these equivalences are intuitively incorrect and leave the problem there. Another way to develop the equivalences into an objection is to consider how these equivalences interact with the other theoretical roles propositions are alleged to play. Consider (VII), or being the object of an attitude like belief. Some develop these equivalences into an objection by noting that people can seemingly believe the proposition expressed by one member of the pairs above without believing the other (Soames 1987, Richard 1990, King 2007). Still another way to develop the equivalences into an objection is to return to the issue of representationality again. For example, Merricks (2015) argues that the pairs above *represent* things differently. (4) represents Sonia as being a certain way whereas (5) does more than that. It represents Sonia as being a certain way and $\sqrt{49}$ as being a certain way. But these are different representations.

However these unwanted equivalences are developed into an objection, most opponents to an unstructured theory cite this problem as the decisive problem. It is no wonder, then, that a wide array of responses to the problem have been offered. We highlight a few common ones. The first response is to argue that such equivalences are not as unwanted as they may initially seem. For example, Stalnaker (1987, 24), focusing on role (VII) (being the object of cognitive attitudes), maintains that "the identity conditions for the objects of desire and belief are correctly determined by the possible-world account of propositions" because they do not distinguish the propositions expressed by the above pairs. Our earlier discussion of how unstructured content works well with certain functionalist approaches to mental states is relevant here.

Another option is to tinker with what the truth-supporting circumstances are. Suppose there are possible worlds and *impossible worlds*. The latter can be glossed as ways things cannot be, or worlds where the laws of logic do not hold. With such worlds, some argue that unwanted equivalences can be avoided (Ripley 2012, Berto and Jago 2019, *a.o.*). For example, (2) and (3) may be true in all the same possible worlds but remain distinct because they are not true in all the same impossible worlds. Another option is to work with truth-supporting circumstances that are partial or incomplete. Barwise and Perry's (1983) situation semantics provides an important example of this route. Truthmaker semantics, which this volume contains numerous essays about, can be understood as descending from this tradition of working with non-maximal circumstances.

A final common suggestion is that minds are fragmented in what they believe (Lewis 1982, Stalnaker 1984, Braddon-Mitchell and Jackson 2007, Yalcin 2018, a.o.). Suppose the total state of an agent's beliefs is not integrated. Instead, there are belief *states*: different compartmentalized clusters of belief. Then an agent may count as believing (6) but not (7) by virtue of having the proposition that sentence (6) expresses in the belief state that is active relative to questions about groundhog behavior but not in the belief state that is active in response to woodchuck behavior. Whether fragmentation helps with the problem of unwanted equivalences is an on-going area of research.

V. Summary of Contributions

We turn now to outlining the essays collected in this volume. These divide naturally into three categories. First, Daniel Hoek, J. Robert G. Williams, and Robert Stalnaker explore ways in which unstructured theories of content which take propositions to be sets of possible worlds can be enriched to provide explanations of a number of interesting semantic and epistemic phenomena. Second, Kit Fine, Stephen Yablo, and Friederike Moltmann develop and apply a more fine-grained unstructured approach which identifies contents with sets of states of affairs or circumstances. Third, Jeffrey King, John Perry, Susanna Schellenberg, Katharina Felka, and Alex Steinberg consider the advantages and disadvantages of unstructured accounts of content as compared with structured accounts.

Enriching the Possible-Worlds Approach

In his contribution, Daniel Hoek develops an unstructured approach to the problem of defining a notion of *minimal rationality*. While fields like decision and game theory often assume that agents are perfectly rational, ordinary people fall far short of this standard: we struggle to ensure that our beliefs are consistent and to understand their logical consequences. In fact, many mundane practices like teaching children arithmetic in grade school would be unintelligible if we were ideally rational. And yet, though they fail to be ideally rational, ordinary people are not completely irrational. The problem of minimal rationality is the problem of characterizing the kind of rationality that everyday people can be expected to have.

At first glance, it may seem that unstructured theories of content are ill-suited to feature in an explanation of minimal rationality. If propositions are identified with sets of possible worlds, then to believe any proposition is to believe its conjunction with any proposition it entails. Thus to believe the axioms of set theory is, ipso facto, also to believe all of their consequences. But while the beliefs of ideal agents might be representable in this way, ordinary people must work to appreciate the consequences of their beliefs. To solve this problem, Hoek augments the unstructured approach with the logical machinery required to model the semantics of questions. When beliefs are understood as question-sensitive, it becomes possible to explain the requirements of minimal rationality as holding only over beliefs which pertain to the same subject matter. This allows Hoek's theory to avoid the traditional problems associated with unstructured views of minimal rationality without having to abandon the unstructured framework.

In his contribution, J. Robert G. Williams is interested in a puzzle about commitment. On the one hand, it is natural to hold that agents can be committed to propositions that they do not believe. This happens, for example, when an agent fails to recognize that a proposition is a consequence of some of her beliefs. On the other hand, because they are not logically omniscient, agents often have beliefs which are logically inconsistent. But then, since an inconsistent set of propositions entails every proposition, it seems that we have to hold that most or all agents are committed to *every* proposition. This consequence threatens to trivialize the idea of commitment, and Williams is interested in developing the resources to avoid it.

To resolve the puzzle about commitment, Williams draws on a structural similarity between theories of commitment and Robert Stalnaker's account of belief as articulated in his 1984 book *Inquiry*. For Stalnaker, agents are belief-related to sets of possible worlds called belief states, and a proposition counts as believed by an agent just in case that proposition is entailed by a belief state to which she is related. Just as a simple theory of commitment threatens to entail that an agent with inconsistent beliefs is committed to every proposition, Stalnaker's account of belief threatens to entail that an agent with inconsistent beliefs believes every proposition. Stalnaker's solution to this problem is to hold that agents can have *fragmented* beliefs: they can be related to multiple internally consistent but jointly incompatible belief states. When this happens, they can believe inconsistent propositions without believing every proposition as long as the inconsistent propositions are located in different fragments. Williams develops a similar strategy for thinking about commitment: beliefs can either be *co-believed* or not, and an agent is committed to the consequences of a set of beliefs only if those beliefs are co-believed.

In his contribution, Robert Stalnaker considers the best way to understand expressivism as a semantic thesis about normative discourse. Focusing on the expressivist framework of Alan Gibbard, he outlines two possible philosophical interpretations of the formalism required to solve the Frege-Geach problem. According to the first interpretation, favored by Stalnaker but rejected by Gibbard, the expressivist is in the business of specifying in a mind-independent way the set of possible normative contents which can be expressed in language and then explaining why certain sentences or speech acts express the normative contents they do. On this interpretation, the project of the expressivist is structurally similar to the project of the semanticist interested in factual discourse: to interpret factual discourse, the semanticist first specifies in a mind-independent way a set of possible contents (truth conditions) and then associates them with certain sentences or speech acts. According to the second interpretation, the order of explanation goes the other direction: first the expressivist posits a taxonomy of possible states of mind; only afterwards is it possible to talk about the contents of mental states. Stalnaker argues that there are insurmountable difficulties associated with the project of understanding content in terms of mental states.

A second locus of disagreement between Stalnaker and Gibbard concerns the nature of truth. Stalnaker shows how a possible-worlds framework can be used to define both a notion of relative truth (truth at a world) and a notion of absolute truth (truth at the actual world). Since Gibbard accepts a deflationary account of truth, he rejects the second notion. But, Stalnaker argues, one consequence of rejecting the notion of absolute truth is that Gibbard lacks the resources to distinguish his expressivist theory from non-natural moral realism. An expressivist theory which preserves a notion of absolute truth is not subject to this problem. In the final section of his contribution, Stalnaker sketches a way to integrate recent expressivist accounts of epistemic modals with Gibbard's framework.

Truthmaker-Style Approaches

In his contribution, Kit Fine develops a semantical account of partial truth based on the truthmaker framework. The account is meant to capture the idea that the facts can favor the truth of a proposition in some important sense without actually making it true. Beyond its intrinsic interest, developing a framework for reasoning about partial truth can help advance the project of understanding related notions like partial content and verisimilitude.

The semantical account Fine develops is hyperintensional in that it does not always treat logically equivalent propositions as identical, and it makes truth simpliciter neither necessary nor sufficient for partial truth—a partially true proposition need not be true, and a true proposition need not be partially true. In addition to the notion of partial truth, the resources of the truthmaker framework permit Fine to define a number of related notions, including what he calls *part-wise truth* (a proposition is part-wise true if the facts favor its truth *as opposed to* its falsity), and *partial lack of falsity*.

In his contribution, Stephen Yablo develops a theory of the very general concept of the *relevance* of a circumstance to an outcome, where this is understood to subsume such diverse relations as that of a cause to an effect, that of a premise to a conclusion, and that of a reason to the action it favors. He takes as his starting point the minimal sufficiency model of relevance, according to which a circumstance is relevant to an outcome if it forms part of some circumstance that (i) suffices for that outcome and (ii) has no proper part which would also suffice for that outcome. But the minimal sufficiency model encounters problems when one considers certain infinitary cases. Suppose God is pleased just in case he is praised for infinitely many days. If he is in fact praised for infinitely many days, it would seem that each individual day of praise contributes to the outcome that he is pleased. But this cannot be so on the minimal sufficiency model, since every infinite sequence of days has a proper subsequence that is also infinite and so would also suffice for making God pleased.

To solve this problem with the minimal sufficiency model, Yablo appeals to the notion of ways in which a circumstance can obtain. This allows him to define a graded notion of sufficiency, such that a circumstance might have parts which are sufficient for an outcome without being *as* sufficient for that outcome. Having two children, for example, is more sufficient for being a parent than having one child, since the circumstance of being a parent obtains in two ways for a person with two children but only one for a person with one child. Incorporating the idea of graded sufficiency into the minimal sufficiency model gives us the idea that a circumstance is relevant to an outcome if it forms part of some circumstance that (i) suffices for that outcome and (ii) has no proper part which would suffice for that outcome just as fully. This revised theory of relevance makes the right predictions about cases like the praise case. Every day on which God is praised contributes to the outcome that he is pleased because it forms part of an infinite series of praise days that suffices for God to be pleased, such that any smaller infinite series would not suffice for that outcome as fully.

In her contribution, Friederike Moltmann describes and motivates an object-based truthmaker semantics for modals and propositional attitudes. Central to this approach is the idea of modal and attitudinal *objects*, like obligations and judgments, which have truth or satisfaction conditions. Moltmann envisions a truthmaker-type semantics compositionally assigning truth or satisfaction conditions to attitudinal objects. This allows her to assign truth conditions to modals and propositional attitudes which treat their prejacents (in the case of modals) or complementizer clauses (in the case of attitudes) as predicates of attitudinal objects. For example, *that P* in *Mary claimed that P* characterizes a property of a claim (an attitudinal object)—namely, that it has the content *that P*. In the case of modals, *John needs to leave* is analyzed as an existential quantification over needs: there is a need, and its content is given by *John to leave*.

Moltmann describes a number of advantages of her framework as compared to traditional views like the relational analysis of propositional attitudes and the quantificational analysis of modals. For example, she argues that an object-based truthmaker semantics is better able than traditional approaches to capture the distinction between heavy and light permissions, and to deal with the possibility of underspecified desire reports. It also avoids certain well-known problems with alternatives. For example, the relational analysis of propositional attitude reports struggles to explain why substituting *the proposition that P* for *that P* in a sentence like *Mary suspects that P* results in infelicity.

Assessing Unstructured Approaches

In his contribution, Jeffrey King re-assesses his reasons for preferring a structured conception of content rather than an unstructured one. King helpfully surveys a number of objections to unstructured views, but he focuses his attention on the problem of unwanted equivalences–that on an unstructured view, propositions that are true in all the same possible worlds are identical. This seems to make bad predictions about the informativeness of utterances of sentences expressing necessary truths, such as "Hesperus is Phosphorus," and about the differences in cognitive significance between sentences like "Hesperus is a planet" and "Phosphorus is a planet." King surveys responses to these problems in the literature (largely due to Robert Stalnaker) and argues that these responses are all beset with their own difficulties: phenomena that they struggle to explain and/or uncomfortable theoretical costs.

In his contribution, John Perry argues that theories of propositional attitudes which construe them as relations to propositions are mistaken: they constitute a "detour" from productive theorizing. Instead of understanding propositional attitudes as relations to propositions, Perry suggests understanding them as structured brain states, where the structure of a given belief is determined by how it is constructed out of small building-blocks which he calls *ideas*. Thinking about beliefs in this way is constructive, he believes, because it allows us to distinguish between two senses in which beliefs have truth conditions. A belief's *referential* truth conditions are the conditions we get by holding fixed both its structure and the referents of its constituent ideas. A belief's *reflexive* truth conditions are the conditions we get if we do not hold fixed the referents of its constituent ideas. To use Perry's example, the referential truth conditions of 'Mogadishu is the capital of Somalia' determine that the sentence is true just in case Mogadishu is the capital of Somalia, whereas its reflexive truth conditions determine that it is true just in case the referent of 'Mogadishu' and the referent of 'Somalia' stand in the relation expressed by 'is the capital of'. This example is linguistic rather than attitudinal, but Perry holds that a similar distinction can be drawn when we consider the attitudes. This distinction is important, moreover, because we care mostly about referential truth conditions when our goal is to convey information about the world and mostly about reflexive truth conditions when our goal is explanatory.

Treating beliefs as structured brain states does not mean that we must abandon talk of propositions altogether, however. Perry is friendly to the idea that brain states can be mapped to the propositions which characterize their truth conditions. However, he believes that the mapping is more complex than might naively be expected. Individuals believe via *notions*, which capture the ways in which they think about things in the world, and the notions via which an individual believes a content are not always immediately obvious from the natural language sentence we use to report the belief.

In her contribution, Susanna Schellenberg develops a theory of perception (*Fregean particularism*) designed to vindicate two common claims: first, that perceptions, illusions, and hallucinations can have the same phenomenal character; second, that the state of perceiving a particular object is partially constituted by that object, so that one could not be in the very same state without perceiving that object. On Schellenberg's view, perceptions are formed by the exercise of perceptual capacities for singling out objects in the perceiver's environment and have object-dependent contents. This is because the contents of such perceptions are made up of Fregean modes of presentation, where these are construed in a *de re* way so that no mode of presentation of an object *o* could be the content of a perception of anything other than *o* itself.

The fact that no perceptual experience of anything other than *o* could have the same content as a perceptual experience of *o* explains why, on Schellenberg's view, the state of perceiving an object is partially constituted by that object. But how can it be that perceptions, illusions, and hallucinations sometimes have the same phenomenal character? While Schellenberg holds that the content of an illusion or a hallucination is "gappy" in the sense that there are no objects for the Fregean modes of presentation to pick out, she also holds that the phenomenal character of a state is not determined by its content. So, while illusions and hallucinations are defective states which cannot be assigned accuracy conditions, they have the same cognitive structure as veridical perceptual states because they are formed by exercising the same perceptual capacities. It is this cognitive structure, rather than content, which accounts for the phenomenal character of a state.

In their contribution, Katharina Felka and Alex Steinberg consider a problem for structured accounts of content articulated by Stephen Schiffer (2003) and Adam Pautz (2008). The problem has to do with the idea of *reference shift*—that is, the idea that material embedded in the complementizer clauses of propositional attitude ascriptions must function semantically to refer to something other than what it refers to in unembedded contexts. Focusing in particular on Frege's theory of content, Felka and Steinberg state the problem as follows: If 'Hesperus' in the sentence 'Ben believes that Hesperus is a planet' refers not to Venus but rather to the sense associated with the lexical item 'Hesperus', and if existential quantification works in the normal way, then the sentence 'There is something such that Ben believes that it is a planet' would seem to be true just in case there is a sense which Ben believes to be a planet. But, unless Ben is a peculiar individual indeed, he would never mistake a concept for a planet. So it seems that certain intuitively true sentences are predicted to be false by theories that posit reference shift.

Felka and Steinberg suggest that the best response to this kind of argument for proponents of reference shift is to hold that the value of a variable relative to an assignment function shifts in propositional attitude ascriptions just like the value of any other kind of expression. In particular, they propose that a variable embedded in an attitude ascription indefinitely denotes all of the senses which pick out its referent. They then show how this proposal can be integrated with a semantics for attitude ascriptions to yield intuitive truth conditions for sentences like 'There is something such that Ben believes it is a planet'.

References

Barwise, J. and J. Perry. 1983. *Situations and Attitudes*. Cambridge, MA: MIT Press.
Bealer, G. 1998. "Propositions." *Mind* 107(425): 1–32.
Berto, F. and M. Jago. 2019. *Impossible Worlds*. Oxford: Oxford University Press.
Braddon-Mitchell, D. and Jackson, F. 2007. *The Philosophy of Mind and Cognition: An Introduction*. London: Blackwell.
Brown, T. 2021. "Propositions are not representational." *Synthese* 199(1–2): 1–16.
Charlow, N. 2015. "Prospects for an expressivist theory of meaning." *Philosopher's Imprint* 15(23): 1–43.
Cresswell, M. J. 2002. "Why propositions have no structure." *Noûs* 36: 643–62.
van Elswyk, P. 2023. "The linguistic basis for propositions." In *Routledge Handbook of Propositions*, ed. C. Tillman, 57–78. Routledge.
Groenendijk, J. A. G., and Stokhof, M. J. B. 1984. Studies on the semantics of questions and the pragmatics of answers (PhD Thesis). Amsterdam: Universiteit van Amsterdam.
Hamblin, C. 1973. "Questions in Montague English." *Foundations of Language* 10(1): 41–53.
Hanks, P. 2015. *Propositional Content*. Oxford: Oxford University Press.
Heim, I. 1992. "Presupposition projection and the semantics of attitude verbs." *Journal of Semantics* 9(3): 183–221.
Heim, I. and Kratzer, A. 1998. *Semantics in Generative Grammar*. Malden: MA: Blackwell Publishers.
Heller, M. 1998. "Property counterparts in ersatz worlds." *Journal of Philosophy* 95: 293–316.
Jubien, M. 2001. "Propositions and the objects of thought." *Philosophical Studies* 104: 47–62.
King, J. 2007. *The Nature and Structure of Content*. Oxford: Oxford University Press.
Lewis, D. 1982. "Logic for equivocators." *Noûs* 16(3): 431–41.
Lewis, D. 1986. *On the Plurality of Worlds*. Oxford: Blackwell.
Merricks, T. 2015. *Propositions*. Oxford: Oxford University Press.
Montague, R. 1974. *Formal Philosophy: Selected Papers of Richard Montague*, ed. R. Thomason. New Haven: Yale University Press.
Muskens, R. 2004. "Sense and the computation of reference." *Linguistics and Philosophy* 28(4): 473–504.

Parikh, R. 2008. "Sentences, belief and logical omniscience, or what does deduction tell us?" *Review of Symbolic Logic* 1(4): 459–76.

Pickel, B. 2019. "Structured propositions in a generative grammar." *Mind* 510: 329–66.

Plantinga, A. 1987. "Two concepts of modality: modal realism and modal reductionism." *Philosophical Perspectives* 1: 189–231.

Quine, W.V.O. 1960, *Word and Object*, Cambridge, MA: MIT Press.

Richard, M. 1990. *Propositional Attitudes: An Essay on Thoughts and How We Ascribe Them*. Cambridge: Cambridge University Press.

Ripley, D. 2012. "Structures and circumstances: two ways to fine-grain propositions." *Synthese* 189: 97–118.

Russell, B. 1910. "On the nature of truth and falsehood." In *Philosophical Essays*, 147–59. London: Longmans, Green & Co.

Salmon, N. 1986. *Frege's Puzzle*. Cambridge, MA: MIT Press.

Schiffer, S. 2003. *The Things We Mean*. Oxford: Clarendon Press.

Stalnaker, R. 1978. "Assertion." In *Pragmatics*, ed. P. Cole, vol. 9, 315–32. New York: New York Academic Press.

Stalnaker, R. 1984. *Inquiry*. Cambridge, MA: MIT Press.

Stalnaker, R. 2002. "Common ground." *Linguistics and Philosophy* 25: 701–21.

Soames, S. 1987. "Direct reference, propositional attitudes, and semantic content." *Philosophical Topics* 15: 47–87.

Soames, S. 2014. "Why the Traditional Conceptions of Propositions Can't Be Correct" and "Cognitive Propositions." In *New Thinking About Propositions*, eds J. C. King, S. Soames, and J. Speaks. Oxford: Oxford University Press.

Soames, S. 2015. *Rethinking Language, Mind, and Meaning*. Princeton: Princeton University Press.

Stalnaker, R. 1987. *Inquiry*. Cambridge, MA: MIT Press.

Thomason, R. 1974. "Introduction." *Formal Philosophy: Selected Papers of Richard Montague*, ed. R. Thomason, 1–69. New Haven: Yale University Press.

Thomason, R. 1980. "A model theory for propositional attitudes." *Linguistics and Philosophy* 4(1): 47–70.

Yalcin, S. 2018. "Belief as question-sensitive." *Philosophy and Phenomenological Research* 97(1): 23–47.

PART 1
ENRICHING THE POSSIBLE WORLDS APPROACH

Minimal Rationality and the Web of Questions

Daniel Hoek

Both ordinary and theoretical explanations of human and animal behaviour tend to turn on the assumption that the agent in question has coherent, rational beliefs. What does that assumption amount to, exactly? *Ideal* rationality, the standard typically assumed in doxastic logic and game theory, requires an agent to have perfectly consistent beliefs, and to be logically omniscient in the sense that their beliefs are closed under entailment. But while this can be a useful idealization, ideal rationality is often more than we need to assume, and in some cases it is clearly too much. For example, the purchase of a calculator only makes sense if the buyer is *not* ideally rational. And if we are trying to understand the behaviour of someone who is attempting to solve a Rubik's cube, the assumption of ideal rationality is a non-starter: an ideally rational agent would instantly know how to solve the cube, simply by observing its scrambled state. To really achieve ideal rationality would require instantaneous computational powers and an infinite memory. Ordinary, finite creatures like ourselves not only fall short of that ideal: we do not even come anywhere close.

So there is a theoretical need for a less demanding, more realistic standard of doxastic rationality. This need arises in philosophy and a range of other disciplines where belief-based explanations of behaviour play a role, such as psychology, economics, legal theory, political theory and computer science. This lower standard should be attainable, and for the most part attained, by real-world believers like ourselves, with finite cognitive and computational resources. But it should still be high enough to sustain ordinary and theoretical belief-based explanations of behaviour.

An early advocate for such a lowered standard of rationality was Christopher Cherniak (1986). His outline for a theory of what he dubbed *minimal* rationality will be our starting point here. It goes roughly like this. A minimally rational subject may not see every consequence of their beliefs, but they do generally see the *direct* consequences. And while their beliefs may contain inconsistencies, a minimally rational believer avoids *blatant* inconsistencies. Cherniak's account also has an important dynamic aspect: when the need arises, minimally rational agents reliably make straightforward deductive inferences from their beliefs. But the more difficult an inference gets, and the more cognitive resources it requires, the less likely a subject is to perform it.

In developing this view, the challenge is to flesh out the operative notions of a *direct* consequence, a *blatant* inconsistency and the *difficulty* of a deductive inference in ways that steer clear of both triviality and over-idealization. If we render the notion of minimal rationality too weak, it ceases to have predictive or explanatory value. But if we make it too strong, it could collapse into ideal rationality or something uncomfortably close. There are strong pressures from both sides, which makes this a notoriously difficult balance to strike.

In this chapter, I show that a simple, intuitive solution to this challenge naturally suggests itself once we take on board a conception of belief advocated by Seth Yalcin (2011, 2018) and others: namely the view that the contents of our beliefs are answers to specific questions, and not undirected pieces of information. On the account of minimal rationality I will propose, minimally rational beliefs are linked together by their *thematic* connections rather than their entailment relations. On this view, a minimally rational subject's beliefs are not perfectly integrated like those of an ideally rational subject. But neither are they partitioned into isolated compartments, as in fragmentation theories of belief. Rather, a distinctive and I think cognitively plausible picture of doxastic states arises, according to which an agent's views are indirectly connected to one another in a *web of questions*.

The approach I take here is rooted in an unstructured or non-syntactic view of belief content. This is a departure from the norm. At least in the philosophy literature,[1] nearly all extant accounts of minimal or bounded rationality are built on the assumption that belief contents are imbued with syntactic structure. Given that state of affairs, one could be forgiven for thinking that it is impossible to articulate a plausible notion of minimal rationality unless one embraces the view that belief contents are syntactically structured. This contributes to the impression that unstructured views of belief content only apply to heavily idealized subjects, and are inadequate for more realistic contexts, where notions like minimal rationality become important.

One core aim of this chapter is to help dispel that impression. As I will argue, the theory of minimal rationality proposed here holds its own against the syntax-based competition, and even has some clear advantages. It is more elegant and principled, and makes a sharp division between minimal rationality and irrationality, rather than leaving that boundary arbitrary or vague. I agree that the sets-of-worlds view of belief contents makes an inauspicious starting point for a

---

[1] Computer science has the awareness-based strategy of Fagin and Halpern (1988). See also Sim (1997), Franke and de Jager (2011), Egré and Bonnay (2012), Fritz and Lederman (2015), Schipper (2015). This approach is not essentially syntactic, and it has affinities with my proposal below. But it cannot capture the notion of minimal rationality I am aiming for here, because it precludes the possibility of rational inconsistencies (see Section II below).

theory of minimal rationality. But in this chapter I hope to show that this critique does not carry over to the new crop of theories of hyperintensional unstructured propositions, such as the views articulated in Yablo (2014), Fine (2016, 2017), Ciardelli, Groenendijk and Roelofsen (2019), and the present volume.

The first half of the chapter concerns the *static* aspects of minimal rationality. Sections I and II describe the more-or-less familiar difficulties one encounters when trying to combine an intensional, sets-of-worlds account of belief content with the notions of a direct consequence or a blatant inconsistency. This takes the form of two puzzles about minimal rationality: one about closure and one about consistency. In light of those difficulties, Section III proposes a hyperintensional notion of belief contents, and outlines a natural account of minimal, static rationality on this basis. Section IV then revisits the two puzzles we started with, explaining how the new account resolves them both.

The second half of the paper is about the dynamic aspect of minimal rationality. Section V introduces a third puzzle about minimal rationality. It argues that the intensional, sets-of-worlds view of belief content faces serious difficulties in making sense of the observation that some deductive inferences are harder to perform than others. Section VI shows how we can understand deductive inquiry as a question-guided endeavour, an idea that flows naturally from the account of minimally rational belief states developed in the first half of the paper. Section VII shows how this model makes sense of the distinction between easy and difficult deductive inferences, identifying three cognitive obstacles that are captured by the model: *conceptual* barriers that prevent us from asking certain "novel" questions, *computational* limitations that prevent us from asking certain "big" questions, and *strategic* limitations that prevent us from identifying the right question to ask.

I. A Puzzle about Closure

Suppose I am of the opinion that *it is 8:30 pm*. It would be natural to infer from this that apparently, I believe that *it is not 4:30 pm*, and that *it's evening*, and that *it is not yet 9 o'clock*. Or suppose Amy thinks *October 31st will be a warm, cloudy Tuesday*. Then presumably she also thinks that *October 31st is a Tuesday*, that *October 31st will be a warm day* and that *it will be cloudy on October 31st*. Thus our ordinary belief attributions bear out the assumption that when you believe something, you also believe some of its entailments (at least if you are rational). Ideal theories of rationality capture this with the requirement that beliefs are closed under single-premise entailment:

> **Ideal Closure.** Whenever a rational agent believes something, they believe all of its logical consequences. That is, if $\varphi \vDash \psi$, then also $B\varphi \vDash B\psi$.

Here "B" is to be read as "x believes that" where x is an arbitrary rational believer.[2]

But given that our present aim is to capture our ordinary, minimal rationality assumptions, *Ideal Closure* should be rejected. For example, suppose Joe believes that *there are exactly thirteen cartons of eggs in the box (containing a dozen eggs each)*. It does not intuitively follow that Joe believes *there are exactly 156 eggs in the box*: Joe can be (minimally) rational without having bothered to make the calculation. A different sort of counterexample to *Ideal Closure* is emphasized in the literature on attention (e.g. Franke and de Jager 2011). Suppose Emma thinks that *the car keys are nowhere in the house*. Does it follow that she believes that *the car keys are not in the second drawer of the little wooden cabinet by the front door*? The answer seems to be "no": Emma may not have considered that particular possibility. Other counterexamples to *Ideal Closure* involve conceptual limitations, like this one from Stalnaker (1984, 88): King William believed *he could avoid war with France*. But he did not, intuitively, believe that *he could avoid nuclear war with France*. As an eighteenth-century monarch, William lacked the concept of nuclear war.

So a theory of minimal rationality needs a weakening of *Ideal Closure*:

Minimal Closure. Whenever a rational agent believes something, they believe all of its direct consequences. That is, if ψ is a direct consequence of φ, then $B\varphi \vDash B\psi$.

In fleshing out the notion of a "direct" consequence here, we will have to tread carefully: by closing beliefs under direct consequence, we allow in the direct consequences of those direct consequences as well, and their direct consequences. The worry is that we may reach some very indirect consequences in this manner. It is a familiar fact that even very remote consequences can often be reached through a long sequence of simple steps. So before you know, *Minimal Closure* collapses back into *Ideal Closure*.

But such a collapse is not inevitable. The key is to identify a notion of direct consequence that is transitive. As long as any direct consequence of a direct consequence of φ is itself already a direct consequence of φ, we stay out of trouble. That way, there is no risk of finding any indirect consequences amongst the direct consequences of the direct consequences. Following Cherniak, we might think of deductive inferences as carrying a certain cognitive cost. The very easiest inferences do not carry any cost. Instances of the Reiteration rule $\varphi \therefore \varphi$ should make for uncontroversial examples. This "inference" requires no effort at all: if you

---

[2] The schema "if $\varphi \vDash \psi$, then also $B\varphi \vDash B\psi$" is validated by a range of logics of belief, and also by the standard natural language semantics for belief reports (e.g. Heim and Kratzer 1998, ch. 12). A version of the Puzzle about Closure arises in both contexts, though the schema means subtly different things in each one: the schematic letters range over different sentences, and different notions of entailment are in play. See appendix.

believe its premise, φ, then ipso facto you also believe its conclusion, which is also φ. As long as we are careful to restrict the moniker "direct consequence" to such zero-cost inferences, the feared collapse will not occur. For though a long sequence of low-cost steps can add up to a costly procedure, a long sequence of zero-cost steps still costs nothing (cf. the treatment of System I inferences in Solaki et al. 2021).

For a non-trivial *Minimal Closure* condition, some inference patterns besides Reiteration must be counted as direct. Cherniak conjectures that conjunction eliminations are the easiest kind of inference—that is, inferences of the form $(\varphi \wedge \psi) \therefore \varphi$ (Cherniak 1986, 28). So conjunction eliminations should count as direct, zero-effort inferences if any inferences do.[3] To appreciate the intuitive pull of this suggestion, just consider a few examples: if Jill believes that *tigers and zebras are striped*, it seems to follow that she believes *tigers are striped*. And if she thinks *John is nasty, brutish and short*, clearly she believes that *John is short*.

The intuition that belief is closed under conjunction elimination is widely attested (see Dretske 1970, Vardi 1986, Jago 2013, Fine 2016, Hawke 2016, Yablo 2017). Like reiterations, conjunction elimination is so straightforward that it seems questionable whether it is properly speaking an inference at all, or really just repetition of what was already said. As Yablo likes to put it: anybody who believes $(\varphi \wedge \psi)$ *already* believes φ (Yablo 2014, 116). Note also that conjunction elimination is transitive in the desired way. By positing that a minimally rational agent believes the conjuncts of their beliefs, we do not risk letting in anything unforeseen: the conjuncts of the conjuncts of a sentence are themselves also conjuncts of the whole sentence.

So it is plausible that, if there are non-trivial direct inferences at all, conjunction eliminations should be amongst them. Intuitively, inferences just do not get more immediate than this. If we take that idea on board, then any non-trivial *Minimal Closure* condition should entail the following:

Closure under Conjunction Elimination. When a rational agent believes a conjunction, they also believe its conjuncts. That is, $B(\varphi \wedge \psi) \vDash B\varphi$ and $B(\varphi \wedge \psi) \vDash B\psi$.

Summing up, we want a *Minimal Closure* constraint that is intermediate in strength between *Closure under Conjunction Elimination* and *Ideal Closure*. Or in other words, we are aiming for an account of rationality that endorses *Closure under Conjunction Elimination* but rejects *Ideal Closure*.

---

[3] I will assume that some non-trivial inferences are zero-effort and automatic. But I should say that Cherniak himself vacillates a little on this point: some remarks clearly imply that bottom-rung, maximally easy inferences are totally automatic, while others suggest they are merely low-effort (see esp. §1.4 and §2.6–7 of Cherniak 1986).

The Puzzle about Closure arises when trying to combine these desiderata with the traditional unstructured view of belief as a relation between agents and sets of possible worlds, or indeed any view of belief that endorses the following venerable principle of doxastic logic:

Intensionality. If two propositions are logically equivalent, agents believe one just in case they believe the other: if $\varphi \dashv\vDash \psi$, then $B\varphi \dashv\vDash B\psi$.

The problem is that, given *Intensionality*, *Closure under Conjunction Elimination* is equivalent to *Ideal Closure*. For if φ entails ψ, then φ is equivalent to $(\varphi \wedge \psi)$. So on an intensional view, believing φ comes to the same thing as believing $(\varphi \wedge \psi)$. But then you can infer ψ from φ using conjunction elimination. Given *Intensionality*, all single-premise inferences are instances of conjunction elimination. Thus we cannot reject *Ideal Closure* if we accept both *Intensionality* and *Closure under Conjunction Elimination*. The Puzzle about Closure is the resulting trilemma between rejecting *Intensionality*, rejecting *Closure under Conjunction Elimination* and accepting *Ideal Closure* (this problem is discussed, in one form or other, in Hawthorne (2009), Kripke (2011), Fine (2013), Hawke (2016) and Yablo (2017)).

To maintain *Intensionality* in the face of this puzzle, one has to give up the hope of finding a *Minimal Closure* constraint of the kind we just envisioned. For if you embrace the view that conjuncts are direct consequences, you are forced to say that *every* entailment is a direct consequence. That view endorses *Ideal Closure* for minimally rational subjects, which is problematic in view of the abundance of apparent counterexamples. On the other hand, if you think conjuncts are not direct consequences, then it is hard to see what direct inferences could plausibly remain: intuitively speaking, it does not get easier than conjunction elimination. Either way, there is no space for a *Minimal Closure* principle that occupies a comfortable middle ground between *Ideal Closure* and triviality, because *Intensionality* obliterates the distinction between direct and remote consequences. If you take the demand for a notion of minimal rationality seriously, that is a strong reason to reject *Intensionality*.

However, rejecting *Intensionality* is not, by itself, enough to solve the puzzle. For in fairness to the intensional view of belief, it must be said that its "structured" competitors do not directly shed any great light on the distinction between direct and remote consequences either. Syntax-based views of doxastic rationality typically understand rationality as the result of a series of syntactic operations on a belief state. Belief states here are either modelled as a set of sentences or syntactically structured propositions (a *belief box*), or as a set of logically impossible worlds, where those worlds are in turn sets of sentences.[4] Bounded or minimal

---

[4] Shouldn't sets of impossible worlds be classified as unstructured contents? The superficial similarity with sets of possible worlds suggests as much, but that appearance is misleading. See for

rationality is the product of applying deductive inference rules of limited difficulty to such a set, involving sentences of limited length, using a limited number of reasoning steps, etcetera. On this picture, ideal rationality is the theoretical limit of the process, where all inferences have been made. Proposals in this tradition include Cherniak's theory, Eberle (1974), Moore and Hendrix (1979), Konolige (1986), Gaifman (2004), Bjerring and Skipper (2019) and Solaki, Berto and Smets (2021); other syntactic approaches are based on non-classical logic, including Cresswell (1975, 1985), Levesque (1984) and Fagin, Halpern and Vardi (1995).

Views like these can easily capture *Closure under Conjunction Elimination* without collapsing into *Ideal Closure*. The problem is where to take it from there. What other inferences are direct? Is the inference from $(\varphi \vee \psi)$ to $(\psi \vee \varphi)$ direct? What about the inference from $(\varphi \supset \psi) \wedge \varphi$ to ψ? Even if it is clear from the outset that all sorts of boundaries can be drawn here, the view gives us no guidance about which boundary to pick. For this reason, syntactic accounts of minimal closure tend to involve a good amount of arbitrariness or vagueness. Moreover, views in this tradition are maladapted to capture the intuition that, say, *It's evening* is a direct consequence of *It's 8:30 pm*. Sentences do not in general seem to bear any simple, uniform syntactic relationship to their direct consequences.

Ideally, we would like a solution to the Puzzle about Closure that yields some insight into minimal rationality and gives us some principled guidance on how a *Minimal Closure* principle should be formulated. If that is our aim, then simply rejecting *Intensionality* does not cut it: what we need in its place is a view of belief contents that, unlike the intensional and syntactic views, does something to illuminate the relation that propositions bear to their direct consequences.

II. A Puzzle about Consistency

Suppose Joe knows *he has to go to Sarah's birthday party*. And he also knows that *Sarah's birthday is this Wednesday*. But he has not put two and two together yet to form the belief that his Wednesday night is taken. Consequently, when that question arises, he consults his diary. The diary tells him *he has Wednesday evening free*, and Joe comes to believe that too. If Joe retained his beliefs about Sarah's birthday, his beliefs have now become inconsistent. In this way, deductive limitations inevitably make one vulnerable to inconsistency too.[5] That is not to say we

---

instance Jago (2015) on the similarity between impossible worlds-based and Russellian accounts of propositions. Unlike possible worlds, impossible worlds are typically characterized as collections of sentences, and views like Jago (2013), Bjerring and Skipper (2019) and Solaki et al. (2021) rely heavily on the syntactic character of impossible worlds.

[5] In fact, this example involves two failures of deductive closure: first, a failure to form the belief that Wednesday night is taken, and later a failure to appreciate that if his Wednesday night were really free, it would follow that Joe did not have to go to Sarah's birthday party on Wednesday.

believe straight-up contradictions. For instance, in Joe's case, it would not be intuitively correct to say he believes that *he has Wednesday evening free even though he has to go to Sarah's birthday party then.*

So while any plausible theory of minimal rationality must countenance the possibility of inconsistent beliefs, that does not mean anything goes. Minimally rational agents may not be immune to inconsistency, but we do want to rule out *blatant* inconsistencies. As Cherniak argues, minimal rationality must license inferences about the beliefs a subject *lacks* on the basis of the beliefs they *have* (Cherniak 1986, §1.5). So we should reject *Ideal Consistency* but accept *Minimal Consistency*:

Ideal Consistency. A rational agent's beliefs are consistent. That is, if $\varphi_1, \varphi_2, \ldots, \varphi_n \models \bot$, then $B\varphi_1, B\varphi_2, \ldots, B\varphi_{n-1} \models \neg B\varphi_n$.

Minimal Consistency. Rational agents do not believe blatant inconsistencies: if $\varphi_1, \varphi_2 \ldots \varphi_n$ are blatantly inconsistent, then $B\varphi_1, B\varphi_2, \ldots, B\varphi_{n-1} \models \neg B\varphi_n$.

Given that a rational agent has a particular belief, *Minimal Closure* allows us to make inferences about what other beliefs they must have. *Minimal Consistency*, on the other hand, is supposed to license conclusions about what beliefs they must lack. To flesh out the *Minimal Consistency* principle, the notion of a "blatant" inconsistency must be analysed.

To begin with, the discussion above suggested that outright contradictions cannot be rationally believed, and should be counted as blatant inconsistencies. Then *Minimal Consistency* entails:

Avoidance of Contradictions. Rational agents do not believe contradictions. That is, if $\varphi \models \bot$, then $\models \neg B\varphi$.

But this principle alone does not yet ground inferences about the beliefs an agent lacks from the beliefs they have. For that, we have to ask when inconsistencies between multiple beliefs count as blatant. Cherniak suggests *contradictories* are examples of this kind (i.e. a proposition and its negation). That is, if a minimally rational person believes φ, they do not believe $\neg\varphi$ as well (p. 16). As with conjunction elimination, Cherniak's intuition about contradictories is widely shared (in particular, the notions of minimally rational belief of Vardi 1986, Jago 2013 and Solaki et al. 2021 underwrite this principle.) So plausibly, *Minimal Consistency* should also entail the following principle:

Avoidance of Contradictories. Rational agents do not believe contradictories: $B\varphi \models \neg B\neg\varphi$.

The Puzzle about Consistency arises from the tension between this conception of minimal consistency and another venerable principle of doxastic logic:

Ideal Adjunction. If a rational agent believes some things, they also believe their conjunction. That is: $B\varphi, B\psi \vDash B(\varphi \wedge \psi)$.

If we assume *Ideal Adjunction*, then *Ideal Consistency* is equivalent to *Avoidance of Contradictions*. For suppose an agent believes the inconsistent propositions $\varphi_1, \varphi_2, \ldots, \varphi_n$. Then given *Ideal Adjunction* they would also believe $(\varphi_1 \wedge \varphi_2 \wedge \ldots \wedge \varphi_n)$, which is a contradiction.[6] Thus accepting *Ideal Adjunction* makes it impossible to formulate a *Minimal Consistency* condition that is intermediate in strength between *Ideal Consistency* and *Avoidance of Contradictions*. In Section I we saw that *Intensionality* collapses the distinction between *Ideal* and *Minimal Closure*, and the distinction between proximate and remote consequences. In a similar way, *Ideal Adjunction* collapses the distinction between *Ideal* and *Minimal Consistency*, and the distinction between blatant and hidden inconsistencies.

Consequently, just as the theoretical demand for *Minimal Closure* casts doubt on *Intensionality*, so the need for *Minimal Consistency* casts doubt on *Ideal Adjunction*.[7] This doubt is reinforced by the fact that cases of conflicting beliefs typically make for intuitive counterexamples to *Ideal Adjunction*. For instance, suppose I believe that Ann will come to the party even though I know that Tom was also invited and that Ann avoids Tom like the plague. If someone were to point this out, I would revise my belief that Ann will come. But as things stand, I have the belief that Ann will come, and the belief that Tom will come, but I intuitively lack the belief that Ann and Tom will both come.

A popular response to the Puzzle about Consistency is the fragmentation theory of belief (Lewis 1982, Stalnaker 1984, 1999, §6 of Fagin and Halpern 1988, Egan 2008, Greco 2015, Pérez Carballo 2016, Yalcin 2018, 2021, Borgoni, Kindermann and Onofri 2021, Elga and Rayo 2021, 2022). According to this view, *Ideal Adjunction* is false because our beliefs are divided into distinct, compartmentalized belief systems. Each fragment is individually consistent, and the conjunctions of beliefs within a single fragment are believed. But if the belief that φ is part of one fragment and the belief that ψ is part of another, then the belief $(\varphi \wedge \psi)$ need not be part of any fragment.

The fragmentation view accepts *Avoidance of Contradictions* while denying *Ideal Consistency*. So it has a *Minimal Consistency* condition of sorts. But I think

---

[6] For simplicity, I'm ignoring the case of infinitary inconsistencies, as well as infinitary conjunctions.
[7] The case against *Ideal Adjunction* is admittedly less clear-cut than the case against *Intensionality*, because the status of contradictions as blatant inconsistencies is intuitively less secure than the status of conjuncts as direct consequences. In particular, you could have a view of blatant inconsistency that rules in some contradictions but not others. Such an account could combine a commitment to *Ideal Adjunction* with a non-trivial *Minimal Consistency* constraint that entails *Avoidance of Contradictories*, say, but not *Avoidance of Contradictions*. But that way out of the puzzle is not available if you endorse *Ideal Closure*, as many of the fragmentation theorists cited below do. Given *Ideal Adjunction* and *Ideal Closure*, any agent with inconsistent beliefs believes every proposition. That makes *Ideal Consistency* equivalent to *Avoidance of Contradictories* and to any other non-trivial consistency constraint you might come up with.

this condition is too weak to make for a satisfactory solution to the puzzle. In particular it does not do justice to Cherniak's idea that what we know about the beliefs someone *has* normally tells us something about the beliefs they *lack*. By design, the fragmentation view does not sustain any such inferences. The beliefs in different fragments are compartmentalized and do not constrain one another. So switch fragments, and all bets are off. In particular, a fragmentation account of rational belief does not sustain *Avoidance of Contradictories*: a fragmented agent may believe φ and simultaneously believe $\neg\varphi$ as part of some other fragment. So a truly fragmented agent is not minimally rational in Cherniak's sense.[8]

One could add a stipulation that belief fragments are to be pairwise consistent. That formal fix does give you *Avoidance of Contradictories*, but it seems rather ad hoc. The move also goes against the spirit of the fragmentation view: how are the fragments supposed to stay pairwise consistent if they are compartmentalized? Furthermore, once you allow such add-on stipulations, we get perhaps more freedom than we want. Why stop at pairwise consistency, for instance? What about a constraint that any four fragments need to be mutually consistent? Or any five? Again, a more satisfactory solution to the Puzzle about Consistency would yield insight into minimal rationality, and provide some guidance on how to explicate the intuitive notion of a blatant inconsistency.

III. Question-Directed Beliefs

In this section, I give an outline of a simple new theory of static minimal rationality that addresses our Puzzles about Closure and Consistency, yielding precise notions of direct consequence and blatant inconsistency. The starting point for my account is a view of cognitive content that has been defended by Seth Yalcin (2011, 2018) and many others on a range of philosophical, linguistic and psychological grounds: namely the view that the objects of belief are answers to specific questions, instead of undirected pieces of information about the world.[9]

---

[8] This relates to a deeper worry about the idea of using fragmentation to capture minimal rationality. The choices of a fragmented agent are guided by different fragments on different occasions (Elga and Rayo 2021). Even if their beliefs are assumed to stay fixed, the beliefs that guide an agent now are not guaranteed to be in effect in five minutes: the agent could switch their active fragment in the interval. For this reason, fragmentation threatens to undermine the very coherence that Cherniak's notion of minimal rationality was specifically designed to capture (cf. Norby 2014).

[9] Defences include Dretske (1970), Schaffer (2007), Egré and Bonnay (2012), Blaauw (2013), Koralus and Mascarenhas (2013, 2018, Yablo (2014, ch. 7), Ciardelli and Roelofsen (2015), Fritz and Lederman (2015), Pérez Carballo (2016), Friedman (2017), Bledin and Rawlins (2020), Drucker (2020) and Holguín (2022). The main development from Yalcin's question-sensitive theory of belief to the account below is the addition of coherence constraints between agents' answers to different questions. Being a fragmentation theorist, Yalcin posits no such constraints (see also Yalcin 2021). Another difference is that for Yalcin, the contents of beliefs are still sets of worlds, and not question-directed propositions. Yalcin (2018) draws explicit attention to the fact that his account still validates *Intensionality*, which he labels "*Closure under Necessarily Equivalence*". Yalcin does in effect

According to that view, believing that *Paul is going to Paris **next week*** in answer to the question *When is Paul going to Paris* is not the same thing as believing that *Paul is going to **Paris** next week* in answer to the question *Where is Paul going next week*. These beliefs have the same truth conditions, but answer different questions. Likewise, the belief that *Either emus can fly or they can't* is distinct from the intensionally equivalent belief that *Either it is snowing or it isn't* because those beliefs answer different questions: *Can emus fly* versus *Is it snowing*. In belief reports, these distinctions are sometimes marked using word choice or focus.

To distinguish those hyperintensional belief contents from other kinds of propositions, I will call them *quizpositions*, short for question-directed propositions. We will model questions as partitions of logical space (in the tradition of Hamblin 1958, Lewis 1982, Groenendijk and Stokhof 1997):

Def. 1. A *(partition) question* Q is a partition of logical space Ω. The cells $q \in Q$ of this partition are called Q-**cells**. When two worlds w and v share a Q-cell, we write $w \sim_Q v$. Any set of Q-cells $A \subseteq Q$ is an *answer* to Q.

Def. 2. A *question-directed proposition* or *quizposition* is an ordered pair $\langle Q, A \rangle$, also denoted A^Q, consisting of the partition question Q that A^Q is said to be *about*, and some answer $A \subseteq Q$. The quizposition A^Q is *true* at a Q-cell q if and only if $q \in A$, and it is *true* at a world w if and only if $w \in \cup A$.

The singleton sets $\{q\} \subseteq Q$ are *complete* answers to the question Q; all other non-empty subsets of Q represent *partial* answers. For instance, *There are fewer than ten people in the room* is a partial answer to the question *How many people are there in the room*. Any question Q has a tautologous answer Q and an absurd answer $\emptyset$; the corresponding quizpositions are written Q^Q and $\bot^Q$.

How does the move from intensional propositions to quizpositions help us formulate a principled notion of minimal rationality? Let me briefly sketch an answer. The intensional, sets-of-worlds account of belief explicates belief in terms of our ability to rule out ways the world might be. This picture ignores the role of another, prior cognitive ability: namely the ability to distinguish between various possibilities in the first place. In taking beliefs to be sets of possible *worlds*, the traditional account in some sense presupposes that believers individuate possibilities maximally finely, and have already made every distinction there is to make.

The question-directed view of belief eliminates that idealization. It holds that, prior to forming a contingent belief, a subject must conceptualize the relevant possibilities. If a question Q has four cells, say, one can come to believe the quizposition A^Q only after first distinguishing those four possibilities. Forming a view

---

address the Puzzle about Closure. But his solution is to accept *Intensionality* and to reject *Closure under Conjunction Elimination*: on Yalcin's account, one can believe $A \wedge B$ in answer to $Q \wedge R$ without believing A in answer to Q.

on a given question is itself a substantive cognitive achievement, which takes mental resources and requires developing a certain connection or sensitivity to the corresponding aspect of what the world is like. This makes it natural to assume that doxastic rationality does not require us to ask particular questions, any more than it requires us to give particular answers: it can only constrain how our views on questions we do grasp should cohere with one another. By following that line of thought, a picture will emerge of a minimally rational believer whose deductive achievements and limitations can be systematically understood in terms of the possibilities they have and have not distinguished, and the questions they have and have not asked.

Question Mereology

In natural language, interrogatives can be conjoined in the same way as declarative sentences. This naturally gives rise to a notion of question *conjunction* and the related notion of question *parthood*, both of which will be important for my account. Consider for example the conjunctive question *How many stars are there and how many planets are there*. One complete answer to that question is *exactly twenty-five stars and three planets*, and in general any complete answer to the conjunctive question is a conjunction of a complete answer to *How many stars are there* and a complete answer to *How many planets are there*. Generalizing that pattern, we get the following definition:

Def. 3. The **conjunction** of two questions Q and R, written QR, is the question

$$QR := \{(q \cap r) : q \in Q \text{ and } r \in R\} \setminus \{\emptyset\}$$

QR is the partition such that $w \sim_{QR} v$ if and only if $w \sim_Q v$ and $w \sim_R v$.

Not every partial answer to QR is a conjunction of an answer to Q and an answer to R: for instance, one partial answer to *How many stars and planets there are* is *There are more planets than stars*.

Note that Q and R are both *coarser* partitions than QR, in the sense that each Q-cell and each R-cell is a union of smaller QR-cells (in fact, QR is just the coarsest common refinement of Q and R). The notion of question *parthood* is a generalization of the relation question conjuncts bear to their conjunction:

Def. 4. One question Q **contains** (or is **at least as big as**) another question R if and only if every R-cell is a union of Q-cells. We say R is **part of** Q if and only if Q contains R. Equivalently, R is part of Q just in case $w \sim_R v$ whenever $w \sim_Q v$.

Note that Q contains R if and only if $QR = Q$. Big questions draw more distinctions between possibilities than the questions they contain. Less abstractly, one

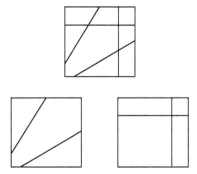

Figure 1 Question parthood and question conjunction

question is part of another if it has to be resolved to get a complete answer to the bigger question. For instance, *What month is it* is part of *What date is it* and *What street does Jess live on* is part of *What is Jess's address*. The trivial question {Ω}, drawing no distinctions at all, is part of every question.

Figure 1 below provides a visual illustration. Each square represents a question: a partition of logical space. The question at the top makes more distinctions than those displayed below it, and so it *contains* those questions as parts. In fact, since it is the smallest (most coarse-grained) question to contain both of them as parts, it is the conjunction of the smaller questions.

A conjunction of question parts is itself always a part. Hence the common parts of any two given questions are closed under conjunction, so that there is always a greatest common part:

Def. 5. The **overlap** of two questions Q and R is the biggest question that is part of Q and also part of R. Two questions **overlap** if and only if their overlap is not {Ω}. Otherwise they are **disjoint**.

For instance, the question *What are the capitals of Europe* overlaps *What are the capitals of Asia*, and their overlap is the question *What are the capitals of Turkey and Russia*. Any answer to the latter question is a partial answer to both of the bigger questions (assuming for the sake of the example that it is not contingent what the countries of Asia and Europe are). In general, the more (partial) answers two questions have in common, the more they overlap, and two questions do not overlap at all if they do not have contingent partial answers in common.

Minimally Rational Answers

An answer to a big question also answers all of its parts. A view on *What date it is* says something about *What month it is* and something about *What day of the month it is*. So given the view that beliefs *are* answers to questions, it is natural to expect that an agents' beliefs about a question should harmonize with their beliefs about the parts:

> **Harmonic Parts.** If a rational agent has beliefs about Q, then they have *matching* beliefs about every part R of Q: that is to say, they believe all and only those quizpositions about R that are entailed by their beliefs about Q.

This is a pretty intuitive constraint. An agent's view about the whole includes and reflects their views about the parts. So if you believe *It is the 13th of March* (in answer to *What date is it*), plausibly you also believe that *it is March* (in answer to *What month is it*). And if I am unsure whether *It is the 13th of March or April*, it intuitively follows that I must also be unsure whether *It is March or April*.

Recall that the trivial question $\{\Omega\}$ is part of every other question. So it follows from *Harmonic Parts* that if an agent believed the trivial absurdity $\perp^{\{\Omega\}}$, they would have inconsistent beliefs about every question to which they had an answer. To exclude that possibility, we will assume that minimally rational agents cannot be in such a state:

> **Non-Absurdity.** Rational agents do not believe $\perp^{\{\Omega\}}$.

That completes the account of static minimal rationality I want to propose: at a given time, an agent has minimally rational beliefs if they satisfy *Harmonic Parts* and *Non-Absurdity*. In Section IV below, I show how this account yields attractive *Minimal Closure* and *Minimal Consistency* conditions.

Harmonic Parts and *Non-Absurdity* are limited constraints that are in principle attainable by a finite reasoner whose beliefs concern questions with finitely many cells. They only require the agent to integrate a given belief with beliefs related to it, rather than with all other beliefs. I will seek to make it plausible that, besides being attainable in principle, ordinary agents for the most part also meet these constraints in practice (by "ordinary agents" I have in mind normal adult human beings, say).

At the same time, *Harmonic Parts* and *Non-Absurdity* impose a greater amount of coherence on an agent's beliefs than meets the eye. Let me explain why. An ordinary agent presumably has views on a wide variety of questions. Wherever those questions overlap, *Harmonic Parts* directly constrains the relationship between an agent's views on those questions: if a minimally rational agent has beliefs on questions Q and R which share a part S, then their beliefs on Q and R must entail all and only the same answers to S. For instance, minimally rational views about *How old Alice and Bob are* and about *How old Bob and Carmen are* must always coincide on the issue of Bob's age.

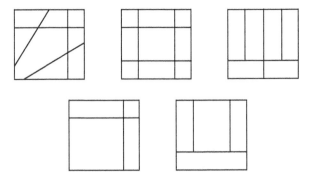

Figure 2 A daisy-chain of overlapping questions

The theory also forges indirect links between the agent's views on disjoint questions. The reason is that those views may be connected through one or more daisy-chains of background beliefs about overlapping questions. Figure 2 illustrates this. The questions on the top left and top right are disjoint: they do not make any of the same distinctions. Nonetheless, they each overlap with the question in the middle: the shared parts are shown underneath. The questions addressed by an agent's beliefs can thus form a complex mereological structure, naturally described as a web: hence the *web of questions*. Broadly speaking, an agent's views on some questions become better integrated and more coherent the more connected those questions are within the agent's web. And while some questions may be more interconnected than others, few if any will be entirely isolated from the overall web.

In this way, *Harmonic Parts* and *Non-Absurdity* impose substantial yet attainable constraints on minimally rational beliefs. Thus the present account aims to do justice to Cherniak's observation that "the assumption that the agent can make quite complex inferences from his beliefs is crucial to our pretheoretical attributions of psychological states in everyday situations" (p. 28).[10]

IV. Direct Consequences and Blatant Contradictions

We now have a simple theory of static minimal rationality. This section explains how this theory addresses the Puzzles about Closure and Consistency. In particular, I isolate the *Minimal Closure, Minimal Adjunction* and *Minimal Consistency*

---

[10] Still, are these constraints strong enough to sustain our ordinary belief-based explanations and predictions of behaviour and decision-making, the way Cherniak envisioned? I think so, but admittedly the matter requires more attention than I can give it here. I say a good deal more in Hoek (2022), which approaches the problem of logical omniscience from a practical angle.

conditions entailed by the theory. This yields sharply defined notions of a *direct consequence* (the sort of consequence any minimally rational agent can see), and of a *blatant* inconsistency (the sort of inconsistency any minimally rational agent will avoid).

Minimal Closure

Section I hypothesized that minimally rational agents believe the *direct* consequences of their beliefs, including the conjuncts of every conjunction they believe. To appreciate what that implies in the present context, we first need to define quizposition conjunction. Given our definition of question conjunction, there is only one sensible way to do this:

> *Def. 6.* The **conjunction** of a Q-answer A and an R-answer B, written AB, is the QR-answer $\{ (a \cap b) : a \in A \text{ and } b \in B \} \setminus \{\emptyset\}$. The conjunction of the quizpositions A^Q and B^R, written AB^{QR} or $A^Q \wedge B^R$, is the quizposition $\langle QR, AB \rangle$.

A quizposition conjunction makes just enough distinctions between possible worlds to make every distinction that its conjuncts make, and rules out just enough possibilities to rule out every possibility that its conjuncts rule out.

This yields a notion of propositional (quizpositional) *parthood* comparable to that of Yablo (2014) and Fine (2017). Just as question parthood is the relation that question conjuncts bear to a conjunctive question, quizposition parthood is the relation quizposition conjuncts bear to their conjunction. That is, one quizposition is part of another if it makes fewer distinctions and rules out fewer possibilities:

> *Def. 7.* A quizposition A^Q **contains** a quizposition B^R, or B^R is **part of** A^Q, if and only if Q contains R and A entails B (that is, $\cup A \subseteq \cup B$).

As in the case of questions, one quizposition contains another just in case the conjunction is equal to the whole. That is to say, A^Q contains B^R if and only if $AB^{QR} = A^Q$. Not every part is an explicit conjunct. For instance, the quizposition *Gold is a soft yellow metal* (in answer to *What are the properties of gold*) contains the quizposition *Gold is yellow* (in answer to *What is the colour gold*). And *Fred's phone number starts with a four*, in answer to *What is the first digit of Fred's phone number*, is part of *Fred's phone number is 49753*, in answer to *What is Fred's phone number*.

If the objects of belief are intensional, $B\varphi \dashv\vdash B(\varphi \wedge \psi)$ just in case φ entails ψ: that is why *Closure under Conjunction Elimination* collapses into *Ideal Closure* in an intensional context. But on the quizpositional account of belief, $B\varphi \dashv\vDash B(\varphi \wedge \psi)$ just in case φ and $(\varphi \wedge \psi)$ express the same quizposition, which happens just in case φ contains ψ as a part. So in the present setting, *Closure under Conjunction Elimination* yields the following principle:

Closure under Parthood. Whenever a rational agent believes something, they believe all of its parts. So if $\varphi \leq \psi$, then $B\varphi \vDash B\psi$.

Here the notation "$\varphi \leq \psi$" abbreviates "the quizposition expressed by φ contains the quizposition expressed by ψ".[11] *Closure under Parthood* is precisely the *Minimal Closure* principle we get from the present theory: it is a straightforward consequence of *Harmonic Parts*. Yablo (2014, ch. 7) and Hawke (2016) have defended an analogous closure principle for knowledge.

Intuitively, *Closure under Parthood* covers precisely the sort of automatic inferences we want a *Minimal Closure* condition to capture. For instance, it is immediately plausible that believing that *gold is a soft yellow metal* implies believing *gold is yellow*. Likewise, believing that *Mary lives on 15 Baker Street* seems to involve believing that *Mary lives on Baker Street*. Or suppose I ask myself *What time is it*, and take a look at my watch: as I find out *It's three forty-five*, I also acquire the belief that it is *not yet four o'clock*.

More tellingly still, as Yablo points out, *Closure under Parthood* yields intuitively compelling explanations for the failures of *Ideal Closure*. For instance, believing that *The wall is blue* does not entail believing *Either the wall is blue or there is something wrong with the lights*, because the latter belief involves consideration of a bigger question, *What colour is the wall and what is the condition of the lights*. Believing *Zed is a zebra* does not entail believing *Zed is not a cleverly disguised mule*, because only the latter belief is about disguise. King William believed that *England could avoid war with France* but not that *England could avoid nuclear war with France*, because the latter belief answers a question no one in the eighteenth century was even able to pose (cf. Yalcin 2011, §8). And we can begin to see, faintly, why believing the second-order Peano axioms does not entail believing that there are infinitely many primes. None of those axioms say anything about primes, or about how many there are.

---

[11] This gloss of "$\leq$" corresponds to an understanding of the statement "if $\varphi \leq \psi$, then $B\varphi \vDash B\psi$" as a schema in which φ and ψ range over English declarative sentences, and "B" abbreviates ⌜α believes that⌝. Like *Ideal Closure*, *Closure under Parthood* can also be understood as a property of a logic of belief. In that context, "$\leq$" expresses the relation of *analytic entailment*, or parthood under every interpretation (cf. Fine 2016). That relation can be characterized axiomatically, as in Goodman (2019). For a semantics that validates *Closure under Parthood* and the other principles of minimal rationality advocated here, see appendix.

Minimal Adjunction

Before moving on to the Puzzle about Consistency, it will be helpful to discuss where the present theory leaves closure under adjunction. Since any question Q is part of itself, it follows from *Harmonic Parts* that an agent believes all and only those quizpositions about Q that are entailed by their beliefs about Q. In particular, that implies that minimally rational agents believe the conjunction of all their beliefs about a given question. So:

Internal Adjunction. A rational agent believes the conjunction of all their beliefs about any particular question. That is, if $\varphi \approx \psi$, then $B\varphi, B\psi \vDash B(\varphi \wedge \psi)$.

Here the notation "$\varphi \approx \psi$" abbreviates "the quizpositions expressed by φ and ψ are about the same question". Let us say an agent's *view* about a given question Q is the conjunction of all their beliefs about Q. Together, *Internal Adjunction* and *Closure under Parthood* tell us that a rational agent with beliefs about Q believes all and only those quizpositions about Q that their view on Q entails.

Suppose an agent has a view V^Q on Q. Now consider any part R of Q. *Closure under Parthood* says that the agent believes every quizposition about R that V^Q entails. The other half of *Harmonic Parts* is the converse: the minimally rational agent believes *only* those quizpositions about R that V^Q entails. This is encoded in the following *Minimal Adjunction* principle:

Partial Adjunction. Rational agents' beliefs on any part of a question are incorporated into their view about the whole question. That is, if $\varphi \approx (\varphi \wedge \psi)$, then $B\varphi, B\psi \vDash B(\varphi \wedge \psi)$.

Internal Adjunction is a consequence of *Partial Adjunction*.

For an intuitive motivation of *Partial Adjunction*, consider situations where a rational agent is unsure about the conjunction in question. In such cases, it intuitively follows that they must be unsure about the relevant conjunct too. For example, suppose you believe Beth's house number is 22, but are unsure whether she lives on *22 Broad Street or 22 High Street*. It seems to follow that you must be unsure about *What street Beth lives on*. Contrapositively, if you firmly believed *Beth lives on Broad Street*, that belief would settle your view on *What Beth's address is*. Likewise, if you are unsure whether John's phone number is *76453* or *86453*, you are unsure about the first digit. If you believe *Bismuth is either a hard, reddish metal or a soft, blueish metal* but are unsure which it is, then you are uncertain about both the hardness and the colour of bismuth. And so on. *Partial Adjunction* makes systematic sense of these intuitions. As with *Closure under Parthood*, this constraint is not just attainable in principle. It is at least *prima facie* plausible that ordinary, finite agents for the most part attain it.

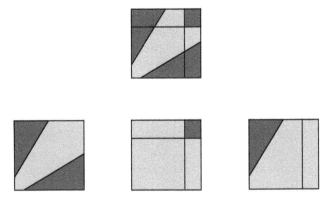

Figure 3 The view about the whole determines the views about the parts

Taken together, *Closure under Parthood* and *Partial Adjunction* are equivalent to *Harmonic Parts*: when R is part of Q, a rational agent with a view on Q believes all and only those quizpositions about R that their view on Q entails. So on the present theory, a minimally rational agent's view on Q completely determines their view on every Q-part R. More specifically, if V^Q is their view on Q, the agent's view on R is the strongest quizposition about R entailed by V^Q.

Figure 3 above illustrates the principle. Each square represents a quizposition. The black lines make a partition representing a question (as before): this is the inquisitive component of the quizposition. The colouring represents its informational component: light grey marks the cells where the quizposition is true and a darker grey the cells where it false. The three quizpositions displayed at the bottom are part of the quizposition at the top: they are weaker, and make fewer distinctions. More specifically, they each rule out all and only those answers ruled out by the view at the top. So if the top quizposition represents a minimally rational agent's view on some big question, then the quizpositions displayed underneath are the views this agent must hold about its component questions.

Minimal Consistency

Now we are ready to address the Puzzle about Consistency. Let me start by checking that from *Harmonic Parts* and *Non-Absurdity*, we can recover *Avoidance of Contradictions* and *Avoidance of Contradictories*. To evaluate the latter principle, we need to define quizposition negation:

Def. 8. The **negation** of a quizposition A^Q, written $\neg A^Q$, is the quizposition $\langle Q, Q \backslash A \rangle$.

From *Harmonic Parts*, we get that agents believe both A^Q and $\neg A^Q$ just in case they believe $\bot^Q$. Now since $\{\Omega\}$ is part of any question Q, $\bot^{\{\Omega\}}$ is always part of $\bot^Q$, and thus *Non-Absurdity* rules out belief in contradictions and also belief in contradictories.

More generally, the theory has it that an agent cannot have inconsistent beliefs about a particular question Q, since those would always adjoin to $\bot^Q$. This accords pretty well with our pre-theoretical intuitions. If I am at all rational, I cannot both be convinced that *my coat is red all over* and also that *it is blue all over*. If I believe *I left the keys in the car*, I do not think *the keys are in my pocket*. If I look at the clock on the wall to discover *it is 3 o'clock*, I am forced to discard the belief that *it is 2:30*. And so on. The pattern extends beyond pairwise consistency. It would be odd if you were certain that *Montesquieu was either a novelist, an architect or a banjo player*, while also being convinced that *he was definitely not a novelist*, that *he was definitely not an architect* and that *he was definitely not a banjo player*.

So question-internal inconsistencies are blatant inconsistencies. Are all blatant inconsistencies question-internal? Given *Closure under Parthood*, the answer must be "no". For instance, consider the belief *Jill and Jack are over twenty-one* and the belief *Jane and Jill are under eighteen*. These quizpositions concern different questions: *How old are Jill and Jack* and *How old are Jane and Jill* respectively. And yet these two beliefs are blatantly inconsistent, both intuitively speaking and according to the theory. For the two questions overlap on the question *How old is Jill*; and it is part of the first quizposition that *Jill is over twenty-one* and part of the second quizposition that *Jill is under eighteen*; and those parts make a question-internal inconsistency. So you cannot believe both of the wholes either.

Generalizing from this, minimally rational beliefs about overlapping questions cannot contradict each other on the overlap. That gives us the following *Minimal Consistency* constraint:

Partial Consistency. A rational agent's beliefs agree on any question. If $\varphi_1 \approx ... \approx \varphi_n$, and $\varphi_1, \varphi_2, ..., \varphi_n \vDash \bot$, and for any i, $\psi_i \leq \varphi_i$, then $B\psi_1, B\psi_2, ..., B\psi_{n-1} \vDash \neg B\psi_n$.

So a *blatant* inconsistency arises whenever overlapping quizpositions contradict one another on a question in the overlap. When some quizpositions are inconsistent but not blatantly so, we can speak of an *opaque* inconsistency. The two quizpositions at the top of Figure 4 above are opaquely inconsistent. They are inconsistent because there is no point in logical space at which both are true. And they overlap, because they make some of the same distinctions. But nevertheless

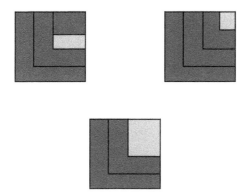

Figure 4 Opaque inconsistency between views on overlapping questions

they agree about the answer to the overlapping part, displayed underneath. So these beliefs are not blatantly inconsistent, and the present theory admits such combinations of views.

Let's look at a more concrete example. Here are three opaquely inconsistent quizpositions:

1) *I have Wednesday free* in answer to *What do I have to do on Wednesday?*
2) *I have to go to Sarah's birthday party* in answer to *Do I have to go to Sarah's birthday?*
3) *Sarah's birthday party is on Wednesday* in answer to *When is Sarah's birthday party?*

Quizpositions (1–3) are about non-overlapping questions, so they are opaquely inconsistent. Now if you conjoin all three with *Today is Monday*, the three resulting conjunctions (1*–3*) overlap, but they are still opaquely inconsistent. That's because drawing attention to what day it is does nothing to reveal the inconsistency between (1–3). While (1*–3*) overlap on the question *What day is it today*, they all agree on the overlapping part: the inconsistency lies elsewhere.

By contrast, if we conjoin (1) and (3), and also conjoin (2) and (3), then we do get a blatant inconsistency, both intuitively speaking and according to the theory:

4) *I have Wednesday free and Sarah's birthday party is on Wednesday.*
5) *Sarah's birthday party is on Wednesday and I have to go to Sarah's birthday party.*

Quizpositions (4) and (5) overlap on the polar question *Do I have to go to Sarah's birthday party on Wednesday or not?*, and directly contradict each other there, answering *No* and *Yes* respectively. So *Partial Consistency* rules out this pair of views. In this way, deductive inferences may reveal inconsistencies: with two adjunctions, we went from an opaque to a blatant contradiction.

Here is a more interesting example of an opaque inconsistency between overlapping questions. Let *H*, *N* and *C* be the questions *How tall is Hob*, *How tall is Nob* and *How tall is Cob* respectively. Then these three quizpositions are opaquely inconsistent, even though they all overlap one another:

6) *Hob is taller than Nob*, in answer to *HN*.
7) *Nob is taller than Cob*, in answer to *NC*.
8) *Cob is taller than Hob*, in answer to *CH*.

This example is reminiscent of the opaque inconsistency observed in a Penrose triangle or an Escher print (Figure 5). Such images initially appear consistent, since any sufficiently small region provides a consistent representation of part of the world, just as (6), (7) and (8) are each consistent answers to their respective questions. In both cases, these consistent representations are not compartmentalized. On the contrary, they all overlap with one another, and you cannot draw sharp boundaries between them. Yet they do not add up to a consistent representation of how things are.

This is clearly very different from the account of inconsistent belief given by fragmentation theorists. On that account, inconsistency arises when discrete, independent doxastic representations offer directly contradictory views of the world. It may be that this kind of belief fragmentation occurs in people who have split brains or dissociative personalities. But those cases are pathological and plausibly fall short even of minimal rationality. I contend that the present account paints a more realistic picture of inconsistent belief as it arises in non-pathological subjects, as a consequence of ordinary failures of logical omniscience.

Figure 5 A penrose triangle and detail of M. C. Escher's "waterfall"

V. A Puzzle about Deductive Inference

Taken together, the principles of minimal rationality defended above yield a new definition of rational belief states. The standard definition of a rational belief state, exemplified by Jaakko Hintikka's (1962) model of rational belief, runs like this:

> *Def. 9.* An ***ideal belief state*** is a non-empty set **I** of intensional propositions (that is, sets of worlds) subject to these three conditions:
>
> ➢ *Ideal Closure*: If p entails q and $p \in$ **I**, then $q \in$ **I**.
> ➢ *Ideal Adjunction*: If $p, q \in$ **I**, then $(p \wedge q) \in$ **I**.
> ➢ *Ideal Consistency*: $\bot \notin$ **I**.

This definition uses a simplified statement of *Ideal Consistency*: conditional on *Ideal Adjunction*, the consistency of **I** is equivalent to $\bot \notin$ **I**.

The analogous definition for a minimally rational belief state replaces each clause in the definition of an ideal belief state with its minimal analogue:

> *Def. 10.* A ***minimally rational belief state*** is a non-empty set **B** of quizpositions subject to the following three conditions:
>
> ➢ *Closure under Parthood*: If A^Q contains B^R and $A^Q \in$ **B**, then $B^R \in$ **B**.
> ➢ *Partial Adjunction*: If Q contains R, and $A^Q, B^R \in$ **B**, then $AB^Q \in$ **B**.
> ➢ *Partial Consistency*: $\bot^{\{\Omega\}} \notin$ **B**.

Again, this definition uses a simplified consistency clause. Conditional on the first two clauses, *Partial Consistency* is equivalent to $\bot^{\{\Omega\}} \notin$ **B** (*Non-Absurdity*).

Perhaps the most exciting aspect of this new account of belief states is the way it allows us to theorize systematically about deductive inferences. A deductive inference is the formation of a new belief on the basis of extant beliefs that entail it. Ideal belief states preclude the very possibility of such transitions, because they are already deductively closed. *Intensionality* is by itself compatible with failures of deductive closure, as witnessed by the fragmentation view discussed above, as well as by the neighbourhood models of Montague (1970) and Scott (1970). But any intensional view individuates inferences very coarsely, and that makes it difficult to form a realistic picture of deductive reasoning on an intensional basis. To bring that out, this section turns to another question Cherniak raised: what makes some deductive inferences more difficult than others?

As I mentioned at the beginning of the chapter, Cherniak holds that minimal rationality has a dynamic aspect. For Cherniak, minimal rationality not only requires that you have fairly cogent beliefs, but also that you make sensible inferences from those beliefs when the need arises. Of course there is a limit on what can reasonably be demanded. Cherniak holds that the complexity of the deductive inferences that a subject can reliably be expected to make depends on the time and cognitive resources that are available for thinking about the issue at hand.

Common sense offers some guidance about which deductions require greater cognitive resources: the inference from the truth of the Peano axioms to the truth of Fermat's last theorem, for instance, was extremely difficult. It was much harder than the inference from the clue entries of a simple Sudoku to its solution. Solving a Sudoku, in turn, is harder than performing an instance of universal instantiation. However, to render this aspect of Cherniak's view predictive, we need something more systematic than those case-by-case judgments. We need some independent handle on what makes particular inferences more or less difficult. Ideally, this would allow us to order deductive inferences by difficulty in a hierarchy, and this is what Cherniak envisaged.

However, *Intensionality* makes it very difficult to make sense of Cherniak's vision. In the case of single-premise inferences, we have already seen why: modulo *Intensionality*, every valid single-premise inference is an instance of Conjunction Elimination. That would make Conjunction Elimination the hardest single-premise inference rule there is, since it subsumes all the others. Putting it differently, given *Intensionality*, every single-premise inference is as easy as a Conjunction Elimination. That leaves no space for any interesting hierarchy in the domain of single-premise inferences.

An analogous issue arises for multi-premise inferences. Assuming *Intensionality*, every deductively valid inference is an instance of the following inference rule:[12]

Recombination. $(\varphi_1 \wedge \psi_1), (\varphi_2 \wedge \psi_2), \ldots, (\varphi_n \wedge \psi_n) \therefore (\varphi_1 \wedge \varphi_2 \wedge \ldots \wedge \varphi_n)$

Intuitively, the Recombination rule looks like a trivial inference: it simply reasserts some conjuncts in the premises. Nonetheless, given *Intensionality*, Recombination encompasses everything from the humblest modus ponens to the highest flights of human reason. You could say *Intensionality* puts a ceiling on how difficult a deductive inference can be, and that ceiling looks uncomfortably low. On the face of it, *Intensionality* forces the bizarre conclusion that every deductive argument ever made is really only a repetition of some judiciously

---

[12] *Proof.* To show: if $\alpha_1, \alpha_2, \ldots \alpha_n \vDash \beta$, then the inference from $\alpha_1, \alpha_2, \ldots \alpha_n$ to β is an instance of *Recombination*, modulo *Intensionality*. To see this, simply substitute $\varphi_i = (\beta \vee \alpha_i)$ and $\psi_i = \alpha_i$. For note $\alpha_i =\!\!\Vdash (\varphi_i \wedge \psi_i)$, and because of distributivity, we have $\beta =\!\!\Vdash \beta \vee (\alpha_1 \wedge \alpha_2 \wedge \ldots \wedge \alpha_n) =\!\!\Vdash (\beta \vee \alpha_1) \wedge (\beta \vee \alpha_2) \wedge \ldots \wedge (\beta \vee \alpha_n) = (\varphi_1 \wedge \varphi_2 \wedge \ldots \wedge \varphi_n)$.

selected premises. If one accepts this, it is hard to make sense of Cherniak's hierarchy in the case of multi-premise inferences, too. The Puzzle about Deductive Inference is the question of how we are to resolve the resulting tension between *Intensionality* and the undeniable fact that deductive accomplishments often require considerable effort.

Arguably, the intensionalist's prospects for explaining the effort involved in multi-premise inferences are a little better than for single-premise inferences. That is because the Recombination rule involves *adjunction* (conjunction introduction) as well as conjunction elimination. And amongst advocates of fragmentation theories, there is a tradition holding that conjoining separated beliefs into a single conjoined belief can be a non-trivial problem. As Stalnaker (1984) writes: "There may be propositions which I would believe if I put together my separate [fragments] of belief, but which, as things stand, hold in none of them. These are the propositions that may be discovered by a purely deductive inquiry" (p. 85). If that is right, and adjunction is what takes cognitive effort, then Recombination is more difficult if it involves more adjunctions. Could this be the hierarchy Cherniak envisioned? Could adjunction be the intensionalist's Archimedean point, the one source of friction that will put a distance between obvious and remote consequences?

Probably not. Deriving the commutativity of multiplication from the second-order Peano axioms requires eight adjunctions, since there are nine axioms. Deriving Fermat's last theorem? Again, eight. The Goldbach Conjecture? Eight again, if it is true. Simply counting the number of adjunctions made is clearly no guide to the impressiveness of a deductive accomplishment. Perhaps we can instead distinguish easy and difficult adjunctions. According to Stalnaker, adjunction "may require only a routine calculation, or it may be a challenging and creative intellectual task" (1984, p. 84). Still, there is apparently no way of anticipating, in any given case, which it is. To get at the Goldbach Conjecture, nine beliefs must be conjoined: (*Peano Axiom 1* ∨ *Goldbach Conjecture*),..., (*Peano Axiom 9* ∨ *Goldbach Conjecture*). Which of these adjunctions is it that has baffled the world's greatest mathematicians for three centuries?

The fragmentation theorist's project of reducing all deductive reasoning and information processing to adjunction undeniably has a certain heroic charm. But if we take it seriously, this vision of inference quickly begins to look very implausible (cf. Jago 2014, §2.5). Even if the reader does not agree that the intensional view renders the cognitive distinctions we are after more puzzling, I hope I have said enough to persuade them that the intensional view does not *help* dissolve the mystery either. As with the two puzzles about static rationality, what we are really looking for in a solution to this Puzzle about Deduction is a view of belief that makes some progress on the question we started off with. That is, we want a view that yields clarification on what it is that makes deductive inferences challenging.

In the remaining two sections, I will try to show how the question-based view of minimal rationality meets that demand.

VI. Tautological Belief Updates

In this section, we will make a foray into the dynamics of minimally rational belief, by defining belief updates for minimally rational belief states. This yields the notion of a *tautological* belief update, which gives us a natural way to model some deductive inferences. In Section VII, I will then discuss three sources of cognitive difficulty that arise in performing these updates and relate those observations to experimental findings from psychology.

Belief Updates

The basic dynamic notion in regular doxastic logic is that of an informational update, representing the way an ideally rational subject acquires new beliefs. Given a belief state I and a new proposition p, the updated state $I + p$ is the smallest set of propositions closed under entailment and adjunction that has $I \cup \{p\}$ as a subset. $I + p$ is only a belief state when p is consistent with I. To adopt a belief that is inconsistent with their prior beliefs, an ideal agent would first have to revise their beliefs.

Quizpositional updates can be defined in an exactly analogous way. Call a set of quizpositions **harmonic** just in case it is closed under parthood and partial adjunction (that is, just in case anyone who believed just those quizpositions would satisfy *Harmonic Parts*).

> *Def. 11.* The **update** of a harmonic set of quizpositions **B** by a quizposition A^Q, written $\mathbf{B} + A^Q$, is the smallest harmonic set containing $\mathbf{B} \cup \{A^Q\}$.

Since the set of all quizpositions is harmonic, $\mathbf{B} \cup \{A^Q\}$ always has a harmonic superset. Since any intersection of harmonic sets is itself harmonic, $\mathbf{B} \cup \{A^Q\}$ always has a minimal harmonic superset. So $\mathbf{B} + A^Q$ is always well defined.

As in the ideal case, the result of a quizpositional update is not always a belief state. Since minimal rationality allows for inconsistency, updating by a quizposition that is inconsistent with the anterior state need not be a problem. But if the update fails to preserve *Partial Consistency*, some sort of belief revision will be needed before the update can be performed (cf. Berto 2019). For present purposes, we will set such difficult cases aside, focusing on updates that do preserve *Partial Consistency*.

Tautological Updates

Updating an ideal belief state with a necessary truth leaves the state unaffected. But updating a minimally rational belief state with a necessarily true quizposition Q^Q can yield new beliefs, including new contingent ones. Drawing new distinctions enriches your prior views, bringing them to bear on larger questions with more parts. For instance, you can get from *England will avoid war with France* to the conclusion that *England will avoid nuclear war with France* by drawing a distinction between nuclear war and other kinds of war. New questions can also link previously separated views. For instance, to get from *Hob is five foot five* and *Nob is five foot six* to the conclusion *Nob is taller than Hob*, you need to ask *How tall Hob and Nob are*: that question brings both pieces of information together into a single view. Since tautological updates only yield new beliefs that are entailed by the subject's prior beliefs, they make a natural model of deductive inference.

To see how this works, let me go through the two examples just mentioned in more detail. Let E be the polar question *Will England have a war with France or not*. Now suppose Mary's belief state $\mathbf{B}_m$ contains the quizposition A^E, that *England will avoid war with France*. Let F be the tripartite question *Will England have a nuclear war with France or some other kind of war or no war at all*: this question contains E. The tautologous answer to F is F^F, that *Either England will have a nuclear war with France or some other kind of war or no war at all*. If Mary has the ability to distinguish the possibility of nuclear war with France from other kinds of war, she can reason her way from the prior belief state $\mathbf{B}_m$ to the state $\mathbf{B}_m + F^F$. Besides the quizposition A^E, the posterior state $\mathbf{B}_m + F^F$ includes a view on the new question F. Because $\mathbf{B}_m + F^F$ is harmonic, and the question F contains E, the view on F in $\mathbf{B}_m + F^F$ must rule out every F-possibility incompatible with A^E. In particular, the view rules out the possibility of nuclear war, and so $\mathbf{B}_m + F^F$ is bound to include the quizposition B^F, *England will avoid nuclear war with France*.

For the second example, let H and N stand for the questions *How tall is Hob* and *How tall is Nob*. Cob's belief state $\mathbf{B}_c$ includes the following two quizpositions:

V^H: *Hob is five foot five.*

S^N: *Nob is five foot six.*

Suppose Cob now forms a view on the conjunctive question HN for the first time: *How tall are Hob and Nob*. Then he transitions from his anterior state $\mathbf{B}_c$ to the belief state $\mathbf{B}_c + HN^{HN}$. To preserve harmony, Cob's newly acquired view on HN must exclude the possibilities excluded by V^H, as H is part of HN. By the same token, the view will exclude every possibility excluded by S^N, since N is also part of HN. Thus $\mathbf{B}_c + HN^{HN}$ contains VS^{HN}, the conjunction of V^H and S^N. So this tautological update effectively amounts to adjoining Cob's views on H and N. Now the quizposition:

T^{HN}: *Nob is taller than Hob.*

is part of VS^{HN}. So because of *Closure under Parthood*, $T^{HN} \in \mathbf{B}_c + HN^{HN}$.

As described at the end of Section III above, the beliefs of a minimally rational agent form a web of interconnected views. For this reason, the effects of a belief update need not be restricted to views on questions that are directly related to the new quizposition. For instance, given suitable background beliefs in $\mathbf{B}_c$, the realization that *Nob is taller than Hob* might be accompanied by the realization that *Gob is taller than Hob* too, which could in turn affect Cob's opinion about *How tall Gob is*, even though the latter question is disjoint from the question *HN* we updated with.

Figure 6 below illustrates the abstract situation. Here we start out with a belief state containing views on Q_0, R and S, and then perform a tautological update to refine the first of these questions, Q_0, to Q_1. The resulting view A_1^{Q1} has the same truth conditions as A_0^{Q0}. However, the new question Q_1 that this view addresses overlaps with R, and A_1^{Q1} rules out some cells in the overlapping part. Consequently, the update strengthens the agent's view on R from B_0^R to B_1^R to preserve harmony. This change in view about R in turn strengthens the agent's view on the question S, which also overlaps with R. Thus the update by Q_1^{Q1} causes a change in view about S, even though the new question Q_1 does not overlap with S. In the same way, the update could percolate further down the daisy chain, spreading through the agent's web of questions. In this way, a tautological update with Q_1^{Q1} can in principle affect the agent's view on all kinds of questions that are linked only indirectly to Q_1.

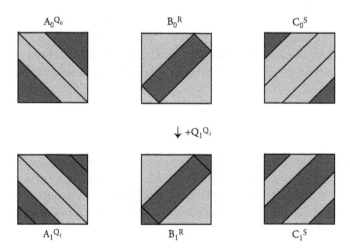

Figure 6 A tautological update on overlapping views

So on the present model, the acquisition of new tautologous beliefs can lead to all sorts of new contingent beliefs, including beliefs about questions that are pretty remote from the question the new tautology directly addresses. We can think of tautological updates as modelling what happens when an agent poses a new question for the first time, where to "pose" a question Q is to acquire a view about Q. The mapping $I \mapsto I + Q^Q$ is the natural formalization of this idea: its output $I + Q^Q$ is the smallest extension of the information state I that includes a view about Q.

This idea of deductive inquiry as a question-guided endeavour has a precedent in the slave boy from Plato's *Meno* (compare also Pérez Carballo 2016, Friedman 2017). Guided by the questions that Socrates asks him, the boy reasons his way to the conclusion that the diagonal of a square of size one is equal to the side of a square of size two. At the outset, the boy already has all the basic geometric intuitions he needs to figure this out. But he only arrives at the right conclusion after thinking through Socrates' strategically posed questions.

There are limitations to this paradigm. Tautological updates are a neat model for simple deductive inferences, but not every deduction can be modelled using tautological updates alone. For instance, the hypothetical reasoning in a proof by cases or in a reductio ad absurdum appears to involve the tentative addition of a piece of information to the subject's stock of beliefs (cf. Staffel 2021). Moreover, as discussed in Section V, deductive inference can bring to light an inconsistency in the reasoner's beliefs, and force them to discard one of their prior beliefs. In cases like that, the deductive process involves belief revisions as well as updates.

VII. Three Kinds of Hard Questions

As the story of Socrates and the slave boy illustrates, human beings can increase their knowledge by posing new questions, rather than acquiring new information. But that ability is not unlimited. In this section, I discuss three different kinds of limits on our question-posing ability, each of which captures a different cognitive barrier curbing our deductive abilities. Bounds on our ability to pose *novel* questions capture our *conceptual* limitations. Bounds on our ability to pose very *large* questions capture our *computational* limitations. And finally, bounds on our ability to identify *good* questions capture our *strategic* limitations.

Novel Questions

In distinguishing between possibilities, we draw on our conceptual resources and world knowledge. Limitations in those resources limit what questions we can pose. One illustration of this point has come up a few times already: King William believes he can avoid war with France. And as we saw in the last section, this means he is only a tautological update away from believing that he can avoid nuclear war with France. However, William is in no position to form a view on the question *Will England have a nuclear war with France*. The reason is that William lacks the requisite conceptual resources: he does not know what a nuclear war is (for a detailed discussion of this point see also Yalcin 2011, §§6–8).

Concepts might also facilitate the posing of new questions in cases where the subject does already have the ability to distinguish the relevant possibilities. One possible example is suggested in Pérez Carballo (2016). The Königsberg Bridges problem asks whether it is possible to take a roundtrip through the city of Königsberg that crosses each of its seven bridges exactly once. In Pérez Carballo's telling, Euler solved this problem by first posing a new question: *What is the graph-theoretic representation of the bridges and landmasses of Königsberg?* Each cell of this question is just an intensional proposition about the layout in the city, so that each one of these possibilities could also be described by someone who lacked the concept of a graph. Still, having the concept of a graph certainly makes it much easier to partition the possibilities in this particular way, and it may well be essential.

Big Questions

I have a terrible sense of direction. When I am new in a city, I will figure out how to get from the hotel to the central square, say, and how I can get from the central square to the museum or the river bank, and from the museum to the restaurant. But having gathered all that information, I still will not be able to work out a halfway efficient route back from the restaurant to the hotel. Without a map, the safe option is just to retrace my steps: return to the museum, then back to the central square, then to the hotel. Else I will probably get lost. My friend is different. Given the exact same information, she will identify the shortest way back in a heartbeat, even if it runs through a neighbourhood she has never seen before.

Maybe my friend has a better memory for these things than I do. But what is more important is the way she puts all the information together. My web of beliefs about the city's geography is a chaotic patchwork of partially overlapping little maps, patched up with landmarks, mnemonics and other crutches. I only have answers to small, local questions about the city's geography, none of which have any bearing on unexplored areas. My friend, on the other hand, sees the bigger picture. Her views are more robustly connected because she has global views about the overall layout of the city that integrate her detailed views about the small parts. This puts her in a position to see we have walked in a big circle, and that the hotel is just a few blocks away. Her geographical beliefs answer bigger questions and are better linked together.

Maintaining a high level of integration between geographical beliefs is a nontrivial cognitive skill: my friend is better at it than I am. The skill can be improved with practice. London cab drivers are an extreme example. Over three to four years of intensive training for a harrowing exam called *The Knowledge*, they acquire the ability to efficiently deploy a vast amount of detailed geographical information in order to determine the fastest route from one place in London to another. It has been shown that in successful trainees, this learning process results in a significantly enlarged posterior hippocampus (Maguire et al. 2000, Maguire and Woollett 2011). This is a remarkable illustration of the way that neuroplasticity allows human beings to go beyond their innate cognitive endowments. At the same time, the discovery that this requires additional grey matter implies that there is a limit to how far our abilities can be stretched. There is only so much new grey matter one can acquire, if only because there is a finite amount of space in a human skull.

Minimally rational agents see more consequences of their beliefs as they bring their views to bear on bigger questions, and as their views become better connected to other questions in the web. The more an agent's views are connected, the better information is distributed across the web, and the easier it is to recall. But there is a limit to the number of questions a finite agent can have views about, and also to the size of the questions. This limitation puts ideal rationality out of reach for us mere mortals: a minimally rational agent who had views on every question would be ideally rational, in that their beliefs would satisfy *Ideal Closure*, *Ideal Adjunction* and *Ideal Consistency*.[13]

Tautological updates take effort because they enlarge a believer's web of questions and require the integration of beliefs on different questions. Sometimes, a small question can already produce a sweeping cognitive change. But adding bigger questions with more parts is always more demanding: bigger questions contain the smaller ones as parts, making more distinctions and forging more connections. We have been thinking of parts as "free" consequences, which are believed without additional cogitation. But that is just to say that no cogitation *beyond* the acquisition of a belief in the whole is needed to believe the parts. The flip-side is that acquiring beliefs with many parts is hard, because it is a precondition for doing so that you acquire beliefs about the parts as well.

---

[13] *Proof.* Suppose Laplace is a minimally rational agent with views on every question. Then Laplace's beliefs satisfy *Ideal Closure*. For suppose she believes A^Q, and suppose A^Q entails B^R. Since she has a view on QR, harmony demands she must believe AR^{QR}, which contains B^R as a part. So she believes B^R. Laplace's beliefs also satisfy *Ideal Adjunction*. For suppose she believes A^Q and B^R. She has a view on QR, so by harmony she believes AR^{QR}, QB^{QR}, and therefore AB^{QR}. Finally, Laplace's beliefs satisfy *Ideal Consistency*. If not, by *Ideal Adjunction*, she would believe $\perp^Q$ for some Q and thus, by harmony, believe $\perp^{\{\Omega\}}$.

Good Questions

A good question can be hard to find. Since any tautological update requires cognitive effort to process, and resources are limited, we cannot look into *every* possible question. Consequently, when we engage in deductive reasoning, we inevitably make choices about which questions to look into. Sometimes, the hardest part of a deduction is not the update itself but knowing which update to perform. Hitting on the right question may require insight or luck. In the *Meno*, Socrates' strategic questioning helps the slave boy precisely because it relieves him of the most creative part of the deductive process.

Here is an example taken from the psychology literature to illustrate the point (Levesque 1986, Toplak and Stanovich 2002). Based on the following three pieces of information, can you say whether or not an unmarried person is looking at a married person?

9) Jack is looking at Kate and Kate is looking at George.
10) Jack is unmarried.
11) George is married.

Take a moment to picture the situation and think it through.

In Toplak and Stanovich's survey, 86% of subjects answered that the correct answer cannot be determined on the basis of the information provided. But as a matter of the fact it can. This becomes easy to see once you are given the following hint:

12) Either Kate is married or she is unmarried.

Once those two possibilities are separated, the answer becomes clear. If Kate is married, then Jack is an unmarried person looking at a married person, because Jack is looking at Kate. If Kate is unmarried, then she herself is an unmarried person looking at a married person, because she is looking at George. It is striking how an instance of the law of the excluded middle transforms an otherwise elusive inference into a no-brainer. This makes (12) an unusually simple and elegant example of an informative tautology.

We can account for this as follows. Conjoining the three given premises (9–11) is insufficient to arrive at the conclusion that an unmarried person is looking at a married person. But this conclusion *is* a direct consequence of the conjunction of (9–12). To see this, associate premises (9), (10) and (11) with the quizpositions A^L, B^J and C^G respectively, where:

L: Out of Jack, Kate and George, who is looking at whom?
J: Is Jack married?
G: Is George married?

The task confronts subjects with something like the following question:

Q: *Who out of Jack, Kate and George is unmarried? And who is looking at a married person?*

And the target conclusion is:

D^Q: *One of Jack, Kate or George is an unmarried person looking at a married person.*

In approaching this problem, the natural first step is to try to picture the situation, putting all the given information together into a single representation. This can be modelled as an update with the tautologous quizposition LJG^{LJG}, which takes a state in which A^L, B^J and C^G are believed individually to a state where their conjunction ABC^{LJG} is also believed. However, doing this is not sufficient. The conjunction ABC^{LJG} entails the conclusion D^Q. But because Q is not part of *LJG*, it does not *contain* D^Q as a part. A further step is required to get from the belief ABC^{LJG} to the conclusion D^Q.

Other attempts to get at the answer also fail to work in this case. For instance, it is natural to break up Q into simpler questions: *Is Jack an unmarried person looking at a married person, Is Kate an unmarried person looking at a married person* and *Is George an unmarried person looking at a married person*. ABC^{LJG} fails to settle the first two questions, and entails a negative answer to the latter. These discouraging results would reasonably lead one to conclude that the given information is insufficient to settle Q. Plausibly, that is where the inquiry ends for most of Toplak and Stanovich's respondents.

We can only get at the target conclusion by making a further distinction. We need to separate two possibilities that *LJG* joins together: namely the possibility that *Jack and Kate are unmarried and only George is married*, and the possibility that *only Jack is unmarried and Kate and George are married*. Separating these two scenarios involves conjoining ABC^{LJG} with the content of (12), *Either Kate is married or not*. This is the tautologous quizposition K^K, where:

K: *Is Kate married?*

After that further adjunction, the subject's overall view of the situation is $ABCK^{LJGK}$; and since *LJGK* does contain Q as a part, it follows that they now believe the target conclusion D^Q as well.

There is some amount of cognitive effort involved in making the extra distinction that takes you from ABC^{LJG} to $ABCK^{LJGK}$. But the students Toplak and Stanovich interviewed could all have made this further reasoning step if prompted. The explanation for why they mostly failed to do so does not lie in the intrinsic difficulty of this update. Rather, the students must have *overlooked* the question *K* for some reason. It may be that it did not occur to them: there is experimental evidence that reasoners are better at *recognizing* a good question when it is presented to them than they are at coming up with good questions on their own (Rothe, Lake and Gureckis 2018). It is also possible that they did consider the question, but made an *a priori*, metacognitive judgment that it was not worth looking into.

In this particular context, two factors may contribute to that decision. Firstly, the fact that they were not given information about Kate's marital state could be taken as an indication that this issue is irrelevant. There is independent evidence that reasoners are generally reluctant to think through a question when they know in advance that the answer is unknown (Tversky and Shafir 1992, Shafir 1994). Secondly, the fact that other lines of inquiry do not resolve the matter may have given rise to an overriding impression that further cogitation was pointless.

Because we cannot ask every question, we inevitably need heuristics to decide which questions to ignore and which to consider, and those must be prior to actually thinking through the questions. For instance, conjoining ABC^{LJG} with the tautology *Either George owns a sloop or he does not* also makes some new consequences available. But since you know *a priori* that those consequences will be of no help in resolving the task at hand, you would never look into that question: it is safely ignored. In the case at hand, the question *K* apparently does not appear fruitful to most people, although that appearance is misleading.

No doubt, these last two sections have raised as many questions about deductive inference as they answered. How do we model belief revision in this context? Can we give an informative quantitative measure of the difficulty of a given tautological update? How do reasoners assess the interest of a question prior to updating? But I hope I have said enough to show that the present account of minimally rational belief states gives us a systematic framework in which these and other theoretical questions about deduction can be fruitfully discussed, and relative to which experimental results about deductive inference can be sensibly interpreted. And because the old, intensional account of belief contents was ill-adapted to those tasks, this development opens up a whole new domain of inquiry for unstructured conceptions of belief content.[14]

---

[14] I originally wrote this chapter during a postdoc at Princeton in 2019. There have been some minor changes and improvements since. I would like to thank Anthia Solaki for the conversation that introduced me to Cherniak's work. Thanks also to Justin Bledin, David Chalmers, Cian Dorr, Paul Egré, Kit Fine, Simon Goldstein, Jordan MacKenzie and David Thorstad for their comments on earlier drafts. Thanks to Dane Stocks for editorial assistance.

Appendix: Belief Reports

Section IV above articulated and defended three general principles of minimally rational belief: *Closure under Parthood*, *Partial Adjunction* and *Partial Consistency*. My official interpretation of these principles is as schemata that range over English sentences, using the following abbreviations:

∧, ∨, ¬	and, or, not
Bφ	α believes that φ
$\varphi \vDash \psi$	φ semantically entails ψ
$\varphi \leq \psi$	the quizposition φ expresses contains the quizposition ψ expresses
$\varphi \approx \psi$	the quizpositions φ and ψ express are about the same question [or alternatively: $\varphi \leq (\psi \vee \neg\psi)$ and $\psi \leq (\varphi \vee \neg\varphi)$]

For instance, *Closure under Parthood* says, in unabbreviated form, that if the quizposition expressed by φ contains the quizposition expressed by ψ, then ⌜α believes that φ⌝ entails ⌜α believes that ψ⌝. This appendix provides a semantics of belief reports that validates these schemata, while also invalidating *Ideal Closure*, *Ideal Adjunction* and *Ideal Consistency*.

For the reasons explained in Section I, this is impossible if the only meaning we assign the prejacent of a belief report is its truth conditions. So we shall assume declarative sentences are also associated with a compositionally determined question. There is independent linguistic motivation for such an approach, and there are in fact numerous well-developed semantic frameworks on the market that do something like this, notably alternatives semantics (Rooth 1992), truthmaker semantics (Van Fraassen 1969, Yablo 2014, Fine 2017), and inquisitive semantics (Ciardelli et al. 2019).

Let us write [φ] for the question assigned to φ and ⟦φ⟧ for the quizposition expressed by φ (the question-answer pair). The semantic clauses for negation, conjunction and disjunction can be given in terms of the corresponding quizpositional operations, as defined in Section III:

$$⟦\text{not } \varphi⟧ = \neg⟦\varphi⟧$$
$$⟦\varphi \text{ and } \psi⟧ = ⟦\varphi⟧ \wedge ⟦\psi⟧$$
$$⟦\varphi \text{ or } \psi⟧ = ⟦\varphi⟧ \vee ⟦\psi⟧ = \neg(\neg⟦\varphi⟧ \wedge \neg⟦\psi⟧)$$

What about atomic sentences π? The simplest course is to let [π] be the polar question $\{p, \neg p\}$, where p is the set of worlds at which π is true. But we can do better if we take a suggestion from Yalcin (2011), and assume that the question component incorporates the focus alternatives of the sentence: if the set of focus alternatives of π is any set of intensional propositions A, define [π] as the coarsest partition question such that each proposition in A is a union of [π]-cells. For our purposes, the advantage of this approach is that it lets us capture parthood relations between atomic sentences. For instance, the quizposition expressed by "Jill's birthday is in *April*" is part of that expressed by "Jill's birthday is on *April 15th*". Sentences often have a contextually inferred focus even when they lack any audible or typographical stress (Breen 2014). But if an atomic sentence π lacks focus alternatives altogether, we can revert to the default, polar option for [π].

Now for the semantics of "believe". Since we are giving a quizpositional semantics, we will need to specify what question is answered by a sentence of the form "Jake believes that φ". I suggest the natural candidate is the question *What are Jake's beliefs about Q?*, where Q is the question the prejacent φ is about. Let's do this in steps. First, to zero in on the relevant set of beliefs, let us define:

$$\text{DOX}(x, Q, w) = \{A^R \in \mathbf{B}_{x,w} : R \text{ is part of } Q\}$$

where $\mathbf{B}_{x,w}$ is the inquisitive belief state of agent x at world w. Next, let $\Theta(x, Q)$ be the partition induced by the following equivalence relation on worlds: $w \sim v$ iff $\text{DOX}(x, Q, w) = \text{DOX}(x, Q, v)$. Finally, we specify the clause for "believe" as follows (where α names x):

[α believes that φ] $= \Theta(x, [\varphi])$

⟦α believes that φ⟧ $= \langle \Theta(x, [\varphi]), \{ t \in \Theta(x, [\varphi]) : \forall w \in t, ⟦\varphi⟧ \in \text{DOX}(x, [\varphi], w) \} \rangle$

This semantics validates *Closure under Parthood*, *Partial Adjunction* and *Partial Consistency*, and hence also *Closure under Conjunction Elimination*, *Avoidance of Contradictions* and *Avoidance of Contradictories*. At the same time, *Ideal Closure*, *Intensionality*, *Ideal Adjunction* and *Ideal Consistency* are all invalidated.

Other notable validities under this semantics include the following:

Closure under Material Modus Ponens. $B\varphi, B(\neg\varphi \vee \psi) \vDash B\psi$.

Strong Avoidance of Contradictories. If $\varphi =\!\!\vDash \psi$, then $B\varphi \vDash \neg B\neg\psi$.

Closure under Embedded Parthood. If $\varphi \leq \psi$, then $BB\varphi \vDash BB\psi$.

Closure under Material Modus Ponens and *Strong Avoidance of Contradictories* further heighten the contrast of the present account with fragmentation theories of belief, which lack non-trivial coherence principles of this sort.

References

Berto, F. 2019. "Simple hyperintensional belief revision." *Erkenntnis* 84(3): 559–75.
Bjerring, J. C. and M. Skipper. 2019. "A dynamic solution to the problem of logical omniscience." *Journal of Philosophical Logic* 48: 501–21.
Blaauw, M., 2013. "Contrastive belief." In *Contrastivism in Philosophy: New Perspectives*, ed. Martijn Blaauw, 88–100. New York: Routledge.
Bledin, J. and K. Rawlins, 2020. "Resistance and resolution: Attentional dynamics in discourse." *Journal of Semantics* 37(1): 43–82.
Borgoni, C., D. Kindermann and A. Onofri (eds). 2021. *The Fragmented Mind*. Oxford: Oxford University Press.
Breen, M. 2014. "Empirical investigations of the role of implicit prosody in sentence processing." *Language and Linguistics Compass* 8(2): 37–50.
Cherniak, C. 1986. *Minimal Rationality*. Cambridge, MA: Bradford Books.
Ciardelli, I. and F. Roelofsen. 2015. "Inquisitive dynamic epistemic logic." *Synthese* 192(6): 1643–87.
Ciardelli, I., J. Groenendijk and F. Roelofsen. 2019. *Inquisitive Semantics*. Oxford: Oxford University Press.
Cresswell, M. 1975. "Hyperintensional logic." *Studia Logica* 34(1): 25–38.

Cresswell, M. 1985. *Structured Meanings*. Cambridge, MA: MIT Press.
Dretske, F. 1970. "Epistemic operators." *Journal of Philosophy* 67(24): 1007–23.
Drucker, D. 2020. "The attitudes we can have." *Philosophical Review* 129(4): 591–642.
Eberle, R. A. 1974. "A logic of believing, knowing, and inferring." *Synthese* 26(3–4): 356–82.
Egan, A. 2008. "Seeing and believing: perception, belief formation and the divided mind." *Philosophical Studies* 140(1): 47–63.
Egré, P. and D. Bonnay. 2012. "Metacognitive perspectives on unawareness and uncertainty." In *Foundations of Metacognition*, ed. M. J. Beran et al. New York: Oxford University Press.
Elga, A. and A. Rayo. 2021. "Fragmentation and information access." In Borgoni, Kindermann and Onofri (eds), 37–53.
Elga, A. and A. Rayo. 2022. "Fragmentation and logical omniscience." *Noûs* 56(3): 716–41.
Fagin, R. and J. Y. Halpern. 1988. "Belief, awareness, and limited reasoning." *Artificial Intelligence* 34: 39–76.
Fagin, R., J. Y. Halpern and M. Y. Vardi. 1995. "A nonstandard approach to the logical omniscience problem." *Artificial Intelligence* 79(2): 203–40.
Fine, K. 2013. "A note on partial content." *Analysis* 73(3): 413–19.
Fine, K. 2016. "Angellic content." *Journal of Philosophical Logic* 45(2): 199–226.
Fine, K. 2017. "A theory of truthmaker content I, II." *Journal of Philosophical Logic* 46(6): 625–702.
Franke, M. and T. de Jager. 2011. "Now that you mention it: awareness dynamics in discourse and decisions." In *Language, Games, and Evolution*, ed. Benz et al., Lecture Notes in Computer Science 6207, 60–91. Berlin: Springer.
Friedman, J. 2017. "Inquiry and belief." *Noûs* 53(2): 296–315.
Fritz, P. and H. Lederman. 2015. "Standard state-space models of unawareness." *Proceedings of TARK*, R. Ramanujam (ed.), 141–58.
Gaifman, H., 2004. "Reasoning with limited resources and assigning probabilities to arithmetical statements." *Synthese* 140(1–2): 97–119.
Goodman, J. 2019. "Agglomerative algebras." *Journal of Philosophical Logic* 48: 631–48.
Greco, D. 2015. "Iteration and fragmentation." *Philosophy and Phenomenological Research* 91(3): 656–73.
Groenendijk, J. and M. Stokhof. 1997. "Questions." In *Handbook of Logic and Language*, ed. J. van Benthem and A. ter Meulen, 1055–1124. Amsterdam: Elsevier.
Hamblin, C. L. 1958. "Questions." *Australasian Journal of Philosophy* 36: 159–68.
Hawke, P. 2016. "Questions, topics and restricted closure." *Philosophical Studies* 173: 2759–84.
Hawthorne, James, 2009. "The Lockean Thesis and the Logic of Belief." In: Franz Huber and Christoph Schmidt-Petri (eds.), *Degrees of Belief*, 49074. Synthese Library: Springer.
Heim, I. and A. Kratzer, 1998. *Semantics in Generative Grammar*. Malden, MA: Blackwell.
Hintikka, J. 1962. *Knowledge and Belief*. Ithaca: Cornell University Press.
Hoek, D. 2022. "Questions in action." *Journal of Philosophy* 119(3): 113–43.
Holguín, B. 2022. "Thinking, guessing and believing." *Philosophers' Imprint* 22(6): 1–25.
Jago, M. 2013. "The content of deduction." *Journal of Philosophical Logic* 42(2): 317–34.
Jago, M. 2014. *The Impossible*. Oxford: Oxford University Press.
Jago, M. 2015. "Hyperintensional propositions." *Synthese* 192(3): 585–601.
Konolige, M. 1986. *A Deduction Model of Belief*. Burlington, MA: Morgan Kaufmann.
Koralus, P. and S. Mascarenhas. 2013. "The erotetic theory of reasoning." *Philosophical Perspectives* 27(1): 312–65.

Koralus, P. and S. Mascarenhas. 2018. "Illusory inferences in a question-based theory of reasoning." In *Pragmatics, Truth, and Underspecification: Towards an Atlas of Meaning*, ed. K. Turner and L. Horn, 300–22. Leiden: Brill.
Kripke, S. A., 2011. "Nozick on knowledge." In *Philosophical Troubles*, 162–224. Oxford: Oxford University Press.
Levesque, H. J. 1984. "A logic of implicit and explicit belief." *AAAI-84 Proceedings*, 198–202.
Levesque, H. J. 1986. "Making believers out of computers." *Artificial Intelligence* 30, 81–108.
Lewis, D. 1982. "Logic for equivocators." *Noûs* 16(3): 431–41.
Maguire, E. A., D. G. Gadian, I. S. Johnsrude, C. D. Good, J. Ashburner, R. S. Frackowiak and C. D. Frith. 2000. "Navigation-related structural change in the hippocampi of taxi drivers." *Proceedings of the National Academy of Sciences USA* 97: 4398–403.
Maguire, E. A. and K. Woollett. 2011. "Acquiring 'the knowledge' of London's layout drives structural brain changes." *Current Biology* 21(24): 2109–14.
Montague, R. 1970. "Universal grammar." *Theoria* 36(3): 373–98.
Moore, R. C. and G. G. Hendrix. 1979. "Computational models of beliefs and the semantics of belief-sentences." Technical Note 187, SRI International, Menlo Park.
Norby, A. 2014. "Against fragmentation." *Thought* 3(1): 30–8.
Pérez Carballo, A. 2016. "Structuring logical space." *Philosophy and Phenomenological Research* 92(2): 460–91.
Rooth, M. 1992. "A theory of focus interpretation." *Natural Language Semantics* 1: 75–116.
Rothe, A., B. M. Lake and T. M. Gureckis. 2018. "Do people ask good questions?" *Computational Brain & Behavior* 1: 69–89.
Schaffer, J. 2007. "Knowing the answer." *Philosophy and Phenomenological Research* 75(2): 383–403.
Schipper, B. C. 2015. "Awareness." In *Handbook of Epistemic Logic*, ed. H. van Ditmarsch et al., 77–146. London: College Publications.
Scott, D. 1970. "Advice on modal logic." In *Philosophical Problems in Logic*, ed. K. Lambert, 143–73. Dordrecht: D. Reidel.
Shafir, E. 1994. "Uncertainty and the difficulty of thinking through disjunctions." *Cognition* 50: 403–30.
Sim, K. M. 1997. "Epistemic logic and logical omniscience: a survey." *International Journal of Intelligent Systems* 12(1): 57–81.
Solaki, A., F. Berto and S. Smets. 2021. "The logic of fast and slow thinking." *Erkenntnis* 86: 733–62.
Staffel, J. 2021. "Transitional attitudes and the unmooring view of higher-order evidence." *Noûs* 57(1): 238–60.
Stalnaker, R. 1984. *Inquiry*. Cambridge, MA: MIT Press.
Stalnaker, R. 1999. "The problem of logical omniscience II." In his *Context and Content*, 255–73. New York: Oxford University Press.
Toplak, M. and K. Stanovich. 2002. "The domain specificity and generality of disjunctive reasoning." *Journal of Educational Psychology* 94(1): 197–209.
Tversky, A. and E. Shafir. 1992. "The disjunction effect in choice under uncertainty." *Psychological Science* 3: 305–9.
Van Fraassen, B. 1969. "Facts and tautological entailments." *Journal of Philosophy* 66(15): 477–87.
Vardi, M. Y. 1986. "On epistemic logic and logical omniscience." *Proceedings of TARK*, ed. J. Y. Halpern, 293–306.
Yablo, S. 2014. *Aboutness*. Princeton, NJ: Princeton University Press.
Yablo, S. 2017. "Open knowledge and changing the subject." *Philosophical Studies* 174(4): 1047–71.

Yalcin, S. 2011. "Nonfactualism about epistemic modality." In *Epistemic Modality*, ed. A. Egan and B. Weatherson, 295–332. New York: Oxford University Press.

Yalcin, S. 2018. "Belief as question-sensitive." *Philosophy and Phenomenological Research* 97(1): 23–47.

Yalcin, S. 2021. "Fragmented but rational." In Borgoni, Kindermann and Onofri (eds), 156–79.

Commitment Issues in the Naive Theory of Belief

J. Robert G. Williams

I. Commitments and Belief

Commitment and Rationality

Ada and Beth are arguing over whether the Butler murdered the Gardener.[1] Beth steadfastly maintains the Butler's innocence. Ada pounces on Beth's latest admission:

> Beth, you just said yourself that whoever was in the toolshed at midnight must have done it. We know it was one of the staff. And we knew that the person in the woodshed was over six feet tall. But remember, the Butler is the only person over six feet tall on the staff. You believe all this! So put the pieces together: it must have been the Butler.

At the point at which Ada makes this intervention, Beth does not believe that the Butler is the murderer. She does, however, believe all the following:

1. The murderer was in the toolshed at midnight.
2. The murderer was one of the staff.
3. The Butler is the only member of staff over six feet tall.
4. The person in the woodshed was over six feet tall.

From these four propositions it *follows* that the Butler is the murderer. Ada, in pointing this out, is revealing to Beth that Beth is already *committed* to believing that the Butler did it.

Beth has several options at this point. She can yield to Ada's pressure and form the belief that the Butler did it. She can give up one of (1–4), making the ensuing commitment go away. She might, perhaps, stubbornly cling to (1–4) but refuse to

---

[1] The research leading to these results has received funding from the European Research Council under the European Union's Seventh Framework Programme (FP/2007–2013)/ERC Grant Agreement n. 312938. It was presented at a Cambridge graduate conference in the philosophy of logic and mathematics, and at a CMM intramural workshop. I thank everyone who has given me comments on the paper, and especially Andy Egan.

live up to her commitments. Failing to live up to your doxastic commitments is a bad thing (it makes you less than perfectly rational), but it is possible.

There's a final option for Beth, but to see it I will shift to a second case. Beth initially doubts that there could be irrational numbers x and y such x^y is rational. Ada gets Beth to accept all the following:

i. $\sqrt{2}$ is an irrational number.
ii. If $\sqrt{2}^{\sqrt{2}}$ is a rational number, then there exist irrational numbers x and y such x^y is rational. (since $x = y = \sqrt{2}$ provides an example).
iii. $\sqrt{2}^{\sqrt{2}^{\sqrt{2}}} = \sqrt{2}^{\sqrt{2} \times \sqrt{2}} = \sqrt{2}^2 = 2$.
iv. If $\sqrt{2}^{\sqrt{2}}$ is not a rational number, then there exist irrational numbers x and y such x^y is rational (since $x = \sqrt{2}$, $y = \sqrt{2}^{\sqrt{2}}$ provides an example).

Ada claims that, since Beth believes (i–iv), Beth is now committed to believe:

R: there exist irrational numbers x and y such x^y is rational.

Beth can now respond:

> (R) is a *classical* consequence of things I believe, but I reject the underlying classical presupposition that a given number is either rational, or not rational. The proposition in question has not been shown to be an *intuitionistic* consequence of what I believe. I'm not convinced it follows from what I believe via rules I accept. So I'm not committed to it.

Ada replies:

> The issue is not what rules of logic you accept. The issue is what the right rules are. The correct logic is classical, and the reasoning I gave you was valid. You are committed to the conclusion, whether you acknowledge that commitment or not.

Ada and Beth agree on the status of the argument according to the two logics in question: the conclusion is a classical but not an intuitionistic consequence of (i–iv). The conversation can now proceed in two ways. Beth can agree with Ada that what matters as far as her commitments go is not what logic she acknowledges, but what the logical facts are. In that case, Ada and Beth will have to agree to disagree about whether Beth is committed to believe R, as a reflex of their disagreement about the One True logic. The other option, however, is that Beth can insist that commitments (what the world must be like, given her beliefs) depend on the logic she acknowledges. If she can convince Ada of this, then Ada will agree with that Beth is not committed to believe R, even while Ada continues to believe R follows from what Beth believes.

The first option is an externalist conception of commitment. The second is an internalist conception. Both are well-defined relations, so the only question is what theoretical role each plays. Elsewhere, I've argued (in effect) that internalist commitment is what matters for rationality (Williams 2017). But I will continue to keep both on the table, since they are subject to a common problem.

The Puzzle of Commitment

Ada accepts classical logic, but the classical rules that she accepts can be chained together in ways that she lacks the time, energy and inclination to run through. The same goes for the intuitionistic rules Beth accepts. So whether we think it is Accepted Logic or the One True Logic that defines commitment, a person's commitments-to-believe can far outstrip what they believe they are committed to. Complex mathematical truths—e.g. of classical or intuitionistic arithmetic—bear witness to the phenomenon.[2]

There is a puzzle about commitments-to-believe that afflicts any computationally bounded creature. Ada believes each of the axioms of classical arithmetic and accepts classical inference rules. She also believes the negation of Fermat's Last Theorem, FLT (perhaps on the basis of some erroneous testimony). What now is she committed to believe?

The axioms of arithmetic that Ada believes entail, via classical rules that Ada accepts, FLT. So the totality of what Ada believes—the axioms and the negation of FLT—form a classically contradictory set. Classical logic also says that any proposition whatsoever follows from a contradictory set of propositions. So in virtue of (perfectly reasonably) believing the axioms and the negation of FLT, Ada is committed to believing any proposition whatsoever. This is so on both the internalist and the externalist conception of commitment-to-believe.

The example exploits a structural vulnerability: if our commitments outstrip what we currently take our commitments to be, it will always be possible for us to make a mistake and believe contrary to our commitments. If Ada had unlimited cognitive resources, she could avoid getting into this situation simply by deriving the consequences of her beliefs and monitoring their consistency. But none of us are like this. Most of us, indeed, have hidden inconsistencies in our beliefs, which

---

[2] In the picture of rationality I defended in my (2017), I was concerned to allow that an agent may not accept any named logic at all, but instead, in a clear-eyed way, be uncertain between then. Perhaps you are like this, being agnostic over whether Ada or Beth has locked onto the right logic. An analogue of the point still remains. One can be committed to believe-under-a-supposition things one doesn't in fact believe-under-that-supposition. *Under the supposition* that classical logic is right, you accept the same rules as Ada does, and so your commitments to believe-under-that-supposition far outstrip your current beliefs-under-that-supposition in ways that you haven't the time, energy or inclination to address.

we try to iron out as they come to light.[3] So if commitment is as I have taken it to be, it seems that most of us are committed to believe absolutely every absurd proposition: that Trump is a great president, that the moon is made of green cheese, that we ourselves do not exist.[4]

So, on the one hand, it does very much seem that our commitments-to-believe things outstrip what we in fact believe. What use would be a theory of commitment on which this was not so? On the other hand, if our commitments explode in the way just sketched, this looks like an utterly undiscriminating, and so useless, notion.

What Is to Be Done

The strategy of this paper is to locate a partner in crime—a theory which faces this kind of puzzle in its rawest form and has grappled with it before. The extant criminal is the theory of belief that Stalnaker laid out in *Inquiry* (1984). Stalnaker's account is highly revisionary in various ways. In particular, if one believes p, and p entails q, then according to Stalnaker one believes q. By contrast, the puzzle above is a puzzle even for a naive theory of belief where no such closure properties are assumed. Since even on the naive theory what we are committed to believe is closed under an appropriate consequence relation, there are structural parallels.

Section II explains Stalnaker's account of belief, concentrating in particular on the foundational picture of the metaphysics of belief that motivates his conception, and the way that his approach allows for inconsistent beliefs.

In Section III, I examine the feasibility of adapting this strategy to solve the commitment problem. I also set out a rival foundational picture, closely related to Stalnaker's, that will avoid Stalnaker's arguments for his revisionary picture of belief. This rival metaphysics is suited to underpin a more naive picture of belief, including the structures needed for an adequate treatment of commitment.

II. Stalnakerology

Stalnaker on Equivalence and Omniscience

Stalnaker argues for the following:

> The most basic belief-relation that an agent stands in is to a "belief state". The content of a belief state is a set of possible worlds (those possibilities that, for all

---

[3] The preface paradox of Makinson (1965) gives one general route to this conclusion.
[4] I am not going to discuss an interesting alternative reaction: to model commitment not with the One True Logic, nor with Accepted Logic, but with some extremely weak special-purpose logic. For an example of this reaction, and references to the background literature, see e.g. Berto (2019).

the agent believes, could be actual). The agent believes a thing if and only if the content of a belief state of theirs entails it.

For all this says, agent may stand in the belief-relation to many belief states. But irrespective of the number of belief states they are in, two striking consequences follow:

* **The Equivalence Property.** If p and q are equivalent (i.e. entail one another) then an agent believes p iff she believes q.
* **The Closure Property.** If q is entailed by p, then an agent believes q if she believes p.

Closure implies Equivalence, and has two more immediate consequences:

* **The Omniscience Property.** If a subject believes anything, then for every necessary truth p, she believes p.
* **The Consistency Property.** If p is any proposition that is not possibly true, then no subject who fails to believe at least one thing believes p.

There seem to be intuitively compelling counterexamples to all of these. Against Equivalence: Lois believes that Clark Kent is sitting in front of her, but she doesn't believe Superman is sitting in front of her. But since Clark Kent is Superman, the proposition that Clark is sitting in front of her entails and is entailed by the proposition that Superman is sitting in front of her. Against the Omniscience Property: Lois doesn't believe Fermat's Last Theorem (FLT). Maybe she explicitly suspends judgement on the question, having not seen a convincing proof. But FLT is necessary, so by Omniscience, she believes it. Against the Consistency Property: Lois may believe, on the basis of testimony or a mistake in reasoning, the negation of Fermat's Last Theorem (or that water is not H2O, or that composition is not universal—substitute in the negation of your favourite necessary truth). Since Closure implies the other properties, it appears to be counterexampled three times over.

As Stalnaker understands belief, the modal concepts (entailment, necessity, possibility) relevant to the account of belief, and which feature in Closure and its siblings, are to be understand as expressing *metaphysical modalities*. For p to entail q is for q to obtain at every metaphysical possibility where p obtains. Some theorists have accepted the letter of the above but advocated an alternative understanding of entailment—perhaps focusing on narrowly logical consequence. This helps around the edges, but it is easy to construct analogous equally compelling counterexamples.

Stalnaker is well aware of the surprising consequences of his theory of belief. He argues that this is accounted for by slack between two distinct things: true *ascriptions* of belief and the facts about the belief-relation itself. What is said when we utter the words "Lois believes that Fermat's Last Theorem" might not be true—even if Lois does indeed stand in the belief relation to the proposition that the statement of Fermat's Last Theorem expresses. The account Stalnaker gives of the way this slack arises will matter to us a great deal—we will look at if further, but for now, let it be a promissory note.

To understand Stalnaker's perspective, the question to ask is this: Why start from a model of belief that obviously has such odd consequences, such that one then has to scrabble around to make a case that it is not immediately refuted? One possible answer that I will not go into here is that this kind of theory of belief (and refinements of it, such as degrees of beliefs as probability functions defined over an algebra of possibilities) has proved theoretically fruitful—in economics, decision theory, linguistics, and so forth. This is a potentially excellent motivation, but exploring it would get us caught up in issues such as: to what extent such theoretical deployments concern ideal rather than real, people? To what extent should the features of these formal models (e.g. entailment) be glossed in the way Stalnaker advocates? Stalnaker's stated motivation in *Inquiry* is rather different. He describes a metaphysics of belief and argues his theory of belief is a consequence of it. The next two subsections explore these arguments.

The Metaphysics of Belief as Motivating Equivalence

Stalnaker (1984) offers a theory of how a naturalistic world can contain content-bearing states. He advocates a "causal-pragmatic picture" of content. I understand this as follows. Let an *interpretation* of an agent be an abstract function which maps "states" of the agent into pairs of attitude-types and contents. Thus relative to an interpretation of Harry, we can say that Harry's state s1 is a belief with content p, and his state s2 is a desire with content q. Then I take it that Stalnaker proposes two conditions for an interpretation I of Harry to be correct:

(a). If I maps s to <belief, p> then s must be something that, optimally, Harry is in only if p, and optimally, he is in that state because of p or something that entails p;
(b). Harry is disposed to act in ways that would tend to satisfy the contents assigned by I to desire states (i.e. those classified by I as desires) at worlds in which the contents assigned by I to belief states (i.e. those classified by I as beliefs) are true.[5]

---

[5] Relevant texts: "To desire that P is to be disposed to act in ways that would tend to bring it about that P in a world in which one's beliefs, whatever they are, were true. To believe that P is to be disposed to act in ways that would tend to satisfy one's desires, whatever they are, in a world in which P (together with one's other beliefs) were true" (op. cit. p. 15). "We believe that P just because we are in

The minimal version of the theory tells us that (a) and (b) are jointly sufficient, as well as necessary, for an interpretation to be correct. Stalnaker emphasizes that this is a first pass at articulating the causal-pragmatic picture and may need refinement. Nevertheless, he treats it as representative when drawing out consequences for belief.

Suppose we accept this view of the correctness of interpretations. Stalnaker then argues that it entails that the content of beliefs can be no more fine-grained than the conditional or causal-explanatory relations that feature in (a) and (b). As an example, consider the content that grass is green. In order to have a belief with this content, it must be that we are in some s such that:

(i) Under optimal conditions, we are in s only if grass is green.
(ii) Under optimal conditions, we are in s because grass is green, or because of something that entails that grass is green.

It follows from (i) and (ii) that:

(iii) Under optimal conditions, we are in s only if grass is green and Fermat's last theorem holds.
(iv) Under optimal conditions, we are in s because grass is green and Fermat's last theorem holds, or because of something that entails that grass is green and Fermat's last theorem holds.

But that is just to say that an interpretation satisfies clause (a) with respect to the content *that grass is green* just in case it does so for the content *that grass is green and Fermat's Last Theorem is true*. Nor will condition (b) knock out the FLT-involving content, since what matters is whether actions performed would promote the satisfaction of certain desires *in certain possible worlds* and the two candidate contents are true at precisely the same set of worlds. Stalnaker puts the situation thus: "We lack a satisfactory understanding, from any point of view, of what it is to believe that P but disbelieve that Q, where P and Q stand for necessarily equivalent propositions" (op. cit. p. 24) His recommendation is that we accept the conclusion: belief states are 'coarse grained', in the sense that they have the content p iff they have the content q, whenever p and q are equivalent.

Stalnaker's argument doesn't turn on the specific details of his account of correct interpretation. The same style of argument can be given for any account that has the form: (a) If I maps s to <belief, p> then $R_1(s,p)$; and (b) If I maps s to

---

a state that, under optimal conditions, we are in only if P, and under optimal conditions, we are in that state because P, or because of something that entails P" (op. cit. p. 18). "Beliefs have determinate content because of their presumed causal connections with the world. Beliefs are *beliefs* rather than some other representational state, because of their connection, through desire, with action. Desires have determinate content because of their dual connection with belief and action" (op. cit. p. 19).

<desire,q> then R_2(s,q), so long as the matrices R_1 and R_2 do not discriminate among necessarily equivalent propositions, i.e. are intentional rather than hyperintensional operators.[6] The counterfactuals, causal-explanatory relations and restricted modals of the causal-pragmatic account have this feature, according to Stalnaker, but so do many of its rivals. Stalnaker's underlying argument is that a good account of correct representation has to be built out of a basic set of "naturalistically respectable" resources, and those resources are intentional rather than hyperintensional. Given that, the coarse-graining conclusion follows as before.[7]

The conclusion of the argument is a form of equivalence, but it is not quite the form I originally laid out. The original principle talked of what the agent believes. The form above concerns the content of belief states that the agent is in. In order to bridge the gap, we need a principle that connects the three-place relation between an agent, a state and its content, to a two-place belief-relation between an agent and a content-believed.

Belief, Belief States and Closure

There are two salient options for connecting the content of belief states to facts about what an agent believes:[8]

(**Pointwise**): An agent believes that p iff they are in some state s, such that s is mapped by the correct interpretation to <belief, the proposition that p>.

(**Holistic**): An agent believes that p iff they are in some state s, such that s is mapped by the correct interpretation to <belief, the proposition that q>, and q entails p.

Either would suffice to complete the argument of the previous section—so in order to finish that argument, we wouldn't need to take a stance. But distinctively, (Holistic) also entails Closure (and so would entail Equivalence, Omniscience,

---

[6] More generally, the constraints take the form: if I maps each s1...si...to <A1,p1>...<Ai,pi>..., respectively, then R*(s1,p1,...si,pi...). Then the argument goes through so long as the relation R* is intentional rather than hyperintensional.

[7] Note that it is consistent with this argument that we can characterize an (extensional) belief relation between an agent's belief state and a structured proposition, conceived as Russellians or Fregeans favour. We may use the extensional belief relation bel(x,y), where y is some object (e.g. a structured proposition) to analyze truths about belief by claiming: x believes that p iff (∃y) (bel(x,y) and y is the proposition that p). But if propositions are Russellian structures or Fregean thoughts the expression "y is the proposition that p" is itself hyperintensional in the sense that substitution of cointensional sentences in the p-position can change its truth value. The Stalnakerian would request a naturalistic analysis of this notion.

[8] For Stalnaker, "the proposition that p" can be characterized modally: it is a set S of possible worlds such that w in S iff were w the case, p. This treatment of course presupposes the conclusion of the coarse-graining argument.

Consistency). I present in this section an argument for Holistic using materials that appear on pp. 82–3 of *Inquiry*—though I'm unsure how close it is to what Stalnaker originally intended.

I want to first show that we must understand clause (b) of the causal-pragmatic account in a very particular way if the account is to work. Recall that for Stalnaker, an agent can be in an inconsistent belief state, that is, it can be the case that there is no possibility at which all the contents of all of Harry's belief states are true together. But now consider again the way Stalnaker characterizes the content of desires:

(b) Harry is disposed to act in ways that would tend to satisfy the contents assigned by I to desire states (i.e. those classified by I as desires) at worlds in which the contents assigned by I to belief states (i.e. those classified by I as beliefs) are true.

Suppose Harry's belief states are inconsistent. Then there are no worlds in which the contents (plural) assigned by I to his belief states are all true. Clause (b) is a counterfactual with an impossible antecedent. Such counterfactuals are standardly treated as vacuously true. Any assignment of desire content whatsoever would therefore satisfy this clause. But obviously some attributions of desire to agents with inconsistent beliefs are correct, and others wrong. Something has gone wrong. To avoid all this, I read clause (b) as follows:

(b*) Harry is disposed to act in ways that would tend to satisfy the content assigned by I to a desire state at worlds in which the contents assigned by I to an associated belief state are true.

This starts with each individual belief state. For Stalnaker, that is always a consistent proposition, so we can non-vacuously look at how the agent acts in worlds where it is true. And now it makes sense, in principle, to fix on a proposition as that one which the agent's actions at those worlds tends to bring about. The proposal is then that that proposition is the content of a desire state paired with the belief state we started with.

With the proposal clarified, consider the following. An agent has an overriding desire for food and raises their hand because they believe each of the following:

(i). A person wearing a red hat will get food if and only if they raise their hand.
(ii). I am wearing a red hat.

It's not true that they act as to satisfy their desires at all worlds in which (ii) is the case (at some of those worlds, people wearing red hats go hungry when they raise their hand). Nor is it the case that they act as to satisfy their desires at all worlds in which (i) is the case (at some of those worlds, they are wearing a blue hat, and so raising their hand is ineffective). So if belief states were conceived to pair one-to-one to beliefs, then Stalnaker's clause (b*) would not work at all. The content of the relevant belief state would have to entail both (i) and (ii). In general, the causal-pragmatic account will only fly if the content of a belief state is a "totalizing" content, entailing the content of all practically relevant beliefs.

The causal-pragmatic account forces us to a totalizing conception of the content of belief states. But then, (Pointwise) would falsely predict that the agent does not believe they are wearing a red hat. So it is the wrong account, and absent any better suggestions, (Holistic) is the way to go. Since (Holistic) entails (Closure) we have here an reason for endorsing (Closure) and the principles it entails independent of the argument given in the last section.

Conclusion to Section II

It would be a pleasant task to pick apart the motivations for (Equivalence) and (Closure) set out in the last two sections and identify loopholes. What conception of belief would we motivated, for example, if we think that counterfactuals with impossible antecedents are not vacuous? And could we avoid (Closure) if we, using the sophisticated resources of Leitgeb (2017), deny the possibility of inconsistent beliefs altogether?

But my concern is to get back to the puzzles about commitment, so I simply finish this section with an observation about the relation between the two arguments discussed in the last two sections. As noted, Equivalence follows from Closure, so the conclusion of the second argument is stronger than the first (their premises are different, though, so it's not the case that the latter supercedes the former). But the first argument has an additional dimension of interest. As mentioned earlier, Stalnaker has a particularly strong version of (Equivalence) and (Closure), on which p entails q when it is metaphysically necessary that either not p, or q. Why not, ask some critics (e.g. Jago 2014), adopt the structure of this account, but make the relevant entailment relation much more demanding? If for example entailment was *analytic* entailment, then (Equivalence) would not have the disturbing Clark Kent-Superman implications, since it's not *analytic* that Clark is Superman. Or perhaps it could be even more demanding, with entailment requiring truth preservation at every *epistemic possibility* for the agent— where an agent's epistemic possibilities might include, for all we have said, worlds that are *logically* impossible. Now, the argument I extracted for Closure via (Holistic) is essentially schematic: an argument for closure of belief under *the relevant notion of entailment, whatever that might be*. So these considerations don't give Stalnaker much leverage against critics who want to preserve the formal structure of his model but implement it with a different modality. The arguments for Equivalence do provide such leverage.

III. Fragmented Commitment, Modified Metaphysics

Having explored Stalnaker's theory of belief and its metaphysical motivations, I now go back to the original, naive picture from which I started. On this view, the beliefs of ordinary agents like us satisfy neither (Equivalence) nor (Closure). In virtue of what we believe, however, we incur commitments to believe other things—and that generated a puzzle, since when we have inconsistent believes (or inconsistent-by-our-own-lights beliefs) then commitment trivializes.

Commitment and Fragmented Belief

Suppose the set B contains all the propositions Harry believes. On the current, naive, conception of belief, B need not be closed under equivalence or entailment, but the set of all the propositions that Harry is committed to believing, C, is closed under entailment (and so equivalence). The relevant conception of entailment under which C is closed will depend on the details of the conception of commitment with which we are working. But C satisfies all four of the properties that on Stalnaker's conception, B itself enjoys.

Stalnaker allows that B contain inconsistent beliefs. Beliefs stand to Stalnakerian belief states in a many-one relation. The set B* of contents of an individual's belief states consists of several individually consistent but potentially mutually inconsistent propositions. B then contains all propositions entailed by any member of B*. B* therefore defines a certain structure over B—dividing it into various overlapping and individually consistent "fragments".

The analogous move for a fan of the naive picture of belief and commitment is to posit a parallel structure of internally consistent/mutually inconsistent fragments of C. We need not follow Stalnaker in thinking of a fragment as defined by something belief-like (with its own representational content)—that is part of Stalnaker's *explanation* of how the structure arises, but it is inessential. The minimal conception of a fragment is that of a space in which some (but not all) of an agent's beliefs are located and interact.

I propose to take nothing away from the naive picture of belief, but I add an additional relation: a relation of co-belief. Strictly, this is a relation between beliefs, but it induces a relation among contents that are believed: contents can be co-believed or not. Maximal clusters of co-believed propositions are the fragments of our mind.

We now re-characterize commitment: we are committed to believe is anything that follows from any collection of co-believed propositions. So long as we never co-believe mutually inconsistent propositions, commitment won't trivialize, even if we believe contradictory things. (There is an additional parameter to be factored in if we go for an internalist conception of commitment—I will set this out later, but for now, let us run with an externalist conception of commitment to keep things simple, so that notions like "consistency" are exogeneous.)

With Stalnaker, I hold that the ideal believer would have a unified mind, where all beliefs are co-believed. This is why it's normatively bad to be inconsistent, even if you do not co-believe the inconsistent propositions. Let us say that we pool two fragments when we come to co-believe all the beliefs in each fragment. The problem with inconsistent beliefs, even if they are in different fragments, is that without changing your mind on one or the other, you cannot pool the relevant two fragments without things going badly wrong—becoming inconsistent within a single fragment.

With the revised account of commitment, it may appear we lose some of the original data. For example, it's pointed out to Harry that he believes p, and that he believes if p then q (and Harry accepts modus ponens). Nevertheless, Harry steadfastly suspends belief on q. This is terrible! And the simple theory of commitment would capture this by saying that Harry was failing to live up to his commitment to believe q. The revised account of commitment only says this in situations in which Harry's two original beliefs are co-believed. The accusation would be, though, that this is too weak. Harry's stance is terrible whether or not he co-believes the premises.

I think the ideal of unity just mentioned can explain what needs to be explained here. Let us divide it into two cases. The first case is Harry's belief that p and belief that if p then q are drawn from two fragments that are wildly inconsistent with one another. Then I am comfortable sticking to my guns: there's no sense in which Harry is committed to believing that q, and suspending may well be the best attitude for him to take. The situation is not a good one for Harry, but that can already be explained by pointing to the inconsistency of the two fragments, and we have already noted having inconsistent fragments is a way of being irrational, given the ideal of a unified mind. Appealing to commitment in this circumstance is redundant.

On the other hand, when two fragments are perfectly compatible with each other, the ideal of unity suggests that prima facie, they should be pooled. We should carefully distinguish between two situations: *that x is committed to p* and *that x would be committed to p if they were as they should be*. When Harry believes p and believes if p then q in two perfectly compatible but distinct fragments, then prima facie this is the case: if Harry were as he should be, he would be committed to q. So prima facie, given that Harry suspends on q, he is either not as he should be, or he is not living up to his commitments. So we have again explained what is out of order in Harry's situation.

There are many cases intermediate between wild inconstancy and perfect compatibility. Sometimes we'd do better to integrate mutually consistent fragments by revising each for a more powerful overall account of the disparate data each reflects, rather than straightforwardly pooling. In situations where we have three jointly inconsistent but pairwise consistent fragments, it is not clear that pooling the pairs helps gets closer to the ideal of integration. So the normative truths about how and when to integrate a fragmented mind is messy. That's one reason for keeping them separate from the clean lines of the theory of commitment; but as we've seen, they can't be ignored.[9]

In endorsing this revised theory of commitment, not everything in the naive picture of belief can be preserved. For the naive picture, taken straight, would tell us that among the things we believe are straightforwardly contradictory propositions (propositions that are inconsistent even by our own lights, though we might not yet realize this). An example would be Lois's belief in the conjunction of the axioms of arithmetic and the negation of Fermat's Last Theorem. To borrow the Stalnakerian solution, then, we might also have to borrow some of his revisionism. And Stalnaker discusses strategies for reanalyzing these cases at length (1984, chs 4 and 5). In the case just mentioned, he denies that we believe the impossible conjunctive proposition—even when we believe the individual conjuncts. To be sure, we would be prepared to utter a conjunctive sentence that expresses this proposition, but even if we concede we believe that the sentence is true, this is not at all the same thing as believing the proposition it expresses.

If we have to follow Stalnaker in the reanalysis of apparent cases of inconsistent beliefs, this would be a significant concession, but it seems to me a price that would be worth paying. It tells us that the naive conception of belief *overgenerates* in some cases, attributing to us beliefs we don't really have. That is very far from the full-fat version of the Stalnakerian picture according to which the naive conception of belief dramatically *undergenerates*. I can live with a certain amount of revisionism around the edges here. I wouldn't want to play the card too often—for example, it seems clear to me that Graham Priest believes various explicit contradictions, without being committed to everything whatsoever. But that is why I favour the more internalized conception of commitment, on which beliefs with individually impossible content are perfectly kosher, as long as they're not impossible *by the lights of rules the agent accepts*.

I will not press the point further here, but I think we might escape even the cost just mentioned. At the end of this essay, I suggest that acceptance-of-rules, just like beliefs, will belong to some fragment of an agent's mentality. So while the agent might accept a rule of explosion, simpliciter, that acceptance need not figure in every fragment of her mentality. This would allow an agent accept classical rules, accept the conjunction of arithmetical axioms and negation of FLT, but deny that the acceptance of explosion and the conjunctive belief are in the same fragment. Indeed, in principle, beliefs that are bundled with no non-structural

---

[9] Thanks to Andy Egan here for questions that led to these paragraphs.

rules at all will contribute nothing at all (beyond themselves) to the agent's commitments. This might be a reasonable description of a belief which is a mere idee fixe, utterly insensitive and isolated from the rest of the agent's cognitive economy.

Co-belief and Rationality

Stalnaker's model of belief is a special case of the co-belief strategy. If we accepted the Stalnakerian picture, a belief that p and a belief that q stand in the co-belief relation when there is some belief state whose content entails both p and q. And we could also accept the definition of commitment to believe—it would just turn out that the picture predicts that we already believe anything we are committed to believe.

If we, as I have suggested, strip away the explanatory framework that supports Stalnaker's implementation of co-belief, the danger will be that the result is just ad hoc, a way to bar the monster of trivializing commitment, without independent motivation or foundation.

The best answer to this would be to find independent theoretical roles that co-belief plays, which would give us confidence that our new terminology picks up on a real doxastic phenomenon. It is very plausible that the theory of *suboptimal rationality* of agents, on the naive conception of belief, will already need to deploy a notion of co-belief. The following example, inspired by one given in Rayo (2013), illustrates this.

Suppose Harry and Sally both believe these four things: the patio is square, that it has one side of 8 metres, another of 7 metres, and its area is 49 metres square. These beliefs are mutually inconsistent (perhaps together with side-premises I have suppressed). Harry, going to the fencing store, buys 28 metres of fencing. Sally buys 30 metres of fencing. They each buy 49 metres worth of paving.

In either case, we can explain and rationalize their behaviour by appealing to subsets of their beliefs. In each case their paving-purchasing is rationalized by the area-belief. Sally's fence-purchasing is rationalized by her beliefs about the length of the long and short side together. Harry's fence-purchasing is rationalized by his beliefs about the length of the short side and his belief about its shape. The problem of course is that in each case we could pick some *other* subset of their beliefs that would rationalize a very different action. The beliefs about the lengths of sides of patio would support more paving. Sally has all the beliefs that led Harry to purchase a different length of fencing, and vice versa.

When an agent's beliefs are perfectly consistent, we don't have to worry about what to ignore when rationalizing behaviour (or indeed, belief formation). But in cases of inconsistency, rival explanations are all in the offing. We *better* rationalize behaviour if we have more structure in description of the agents, so that we can explain Sally's choice to buy 30 *rather than* 28 metres of fencing. Co-belief could do this job for us, by identifying psychological difference between Sally and Harry: Sally co-believes that sides are 8 metres and 7 metres, respectively, Harry does not. Harry co-believes that one side is 7 metres, and that the patio is square, and Sally does not. The contrast in their actions then can be rationalized by the difference in the ways the beliefs they share are differently integrated.

I have not provided a theory of suboptimal rationality that appeals to co-belief. I assert, rather, that there needs to be such a thing. Not surprisingly, the motivations for this echo what some Stalnakerians say about fragmented belief and how it ties to action. But my point is that even on a naive non-Stalnakerian conception of belief, structure beyond belief will be required to explain what acts are or are not rationalized. I reject the accusation, therefore, that it is in any way ad hoc to appeal to co-belief in dissolving our problem of commitment.

Rival Foundations

As we saw in Section II, Stalnaker's theory of belief was motivated by a causal-pragmatic metaphysics of belief. This metaphysics both predicts properties such as Equivalence and Closure, and also found a place for what we are now calling co-belief, the structure that in Stalnaker's framework is provided by the content of the underlying belief states.

I will finish by sketching a different metaphysics of belief, one that is a cousin of Stalnaker's own, but which is compatible both with the naive conception and with a Stalnakerian conception of belief. I will argue that it also provides foundations for co-belief—in a way that other rivals to the causal-pragmatic picture may struggle to do. This rival metaphysics is the form of Radical Interpretation I have developed in detail elsewhere (Williams 2018, 2019).

Like the version of the causal-pragmatic picture I set out earlier, Radical Interpretation starts taking as given a space of abstract interpretations, which for present purposes we take to be assigning attitude-content pairs to states. One among these interpretations is correct (or, if indeterminacy arises, then perhaps a cluster will be co-correct). I will develop it in a way consistent with the naive conception of belief, and so I endorse an analogue of (Pointwise), viz:

(P) Harry believes that p iff Harry is in some state s such that the correct interpretation assigns to s the pair <belief, p>.

The causal-pragmatic metaphysics of belief consisted in two filters that an interpretation I must pass to be counted as correct. To repeat, these were:

> (a) If I maps s to <belief, p> then s must be a state such that: optimally, Harry is in only if p, and optimally, he is in that state because of p or something that entails p;

(b) Harry is disposed to act in ways that would tend to satisfy the contents assigned by I to desire states (i.e. those classified by I as desires) at worlds in which the contents assigned by I to belief states (i.e. those classified by I as beliefs) are true.

I substitute the following:

(RI) I is a correct belief/desire interpretation of x iff I is the belief/desire interpretation which best rationalizes x's dispositions to act in the light of x's experiences.

The facts mentioned on the right-hand side of (RI) are the metaphysical foundations of belief. They include facts about experience, action and the relations of rational update in the light of experience and rational choice in the light of belief and desire. Facts about how a subject is disposed to act were also part of the basis on which Stalnaker grounded belief, in his clause (b). Facts about experience are not appealed to by Stalnaker explicitly. But there is a parallel: the appeal to experience is what does duty for Stalnaker's clause (a).

(Just to briefly motivate this. Consider the belief that all emeralds are green, formed, defeasibly, on the basis of local evidence about the colour of observed emeralds. In any naturalistic, non-representational notion of optimality, such a belief (or any belief state whose content entails it) can exist while some far-flung emeralds are not green. So I think that the causal pragmatic picture overreaches when it tries to use optimal covariation characterize the content of arbitrary beliefs. My strategy, in developing (RI), is to use the kind of naturalistic tradition on which Stalnaker is drawing in (a) to naturalize perceptual evidence, which is an *input* to (RI), and so one of the things that constrains the assignment of beliefs in general. I think similar resources can be deployed to naturalize the content of action-guiding states—basic intentions and the like—which are also appealed to in (RI). See Williams (2019) for the full story).

At a strategic level, to this point (RI) has appealed to the same kind of resources as the causal-pragmatic picture but arranges them differently within the account. The appeal to rationalization however marks a significant departure—but even here there is precedent within the causal-pragmatic picture. Clause (b) of that account is the principle that (on the correct interpretation) one acts so as to realize one's desires given what one believes (= in worlds where the contents of one's belief is true). This is an approximation of a principle of instrumental rationality, and so to satisfy (b) is, at first pass, to be instrumentally rational. But the demand for rationality in (RI) requires much more than this—in order for the account to be tenable, it must pick out a relation of *substantive* rationality. To be substantively rational, the agent needs to possess good reasons for their beliefs and good reasons for acting as they do. Such demands may include but go well beyond the kind of 'structural' patterns of instrumental rationality that the causal-pragmatic picture (b) approximates. Committed naturalizers like Stalnaker will have legitimate worries that the appeal to a body of normative truths about good reasons for belief and action will frustrate their project—and I can offer them little comfort. This is not the causal-pragmatic picture, but a rival.[10]

Relitigating Equivalence and Closure

Stalnaker's argument for Equivalence was based on the naturalistic relations that appear in his (a) and (b) being *intentional* resources. Very roughly: if you say that the content of state b is some p such that in optimal conditions, you would be in b if and only if p, then the condition is met by one proposition if and only if it is met by every proposition necessarily equivalent to it. Throwing in more conditions on p will do no good unless they generate a hyperintentional context which means necessary equivalents can no longer be substituted *salva veritatis*. Stalnaker's bet is that naturalistically acceptable resources will never do the job.

I favour comparable treatments of the content of experience (and of action-guiding states). I think this style of argument does show that their content is coarse-grained. But given (RI), the case of belief and desire is far more delicate. It turns on what theory of rationalization is given.

There are theories of rational belief update and rational choice that work with coarse-grained contents. David Lewis, one source for my (RI), favoured this kind of theory, with the assumption that a Bayesian theory of belief update on which (degrees of) belief have sets of possible worlds as their contents, are updated by coarse-grained facts about what a subject has experienced, and rationalize actions under coarse-grained descriptions (Lewis 1974, 1986). Feed that model of rationality into (RI), and the argument for Equivalence goes through. However, we only get coarse-grained content out because we fed in a coarse-grained theory of rationality. I wish to deny Equivalence, and all I need to do in order to make (RI) compatible with this is feed in an account of rationalization that, just as one would naively think, generates hyperintentional contexts.

Here is one example: it might be that one has good reason to form a belief that a is F when one is in a certain kind of information-link with an object, one which inter alia generates the perceptual content *that a is F*. But one may not have good reason to believe *that b is F* in these same circumstances, even when b and a are

---

[10] Stalnaker can hope to get away with the appeal to (b) because he hopes that the appeal to independent constraints on (a) will have already filtered out deviant interpretations of what the agent believes. The role for (b) is primarily to fix the content of desires. So one of the reasons I feel impelled to put more weight, and make more substantive, the notion of rationality in (RI) is that, as reported above, I am pessimistic about whether any plausible successor to (a) can bear the weight placed upon it. There is a version of radical interpretation that does try to run with a thin notion of rationality (something like the "structural" rationality that I talked about earlier)—but this is in my view demonstrably hopeless, even if we can help ourselves to pretty much as much naturalistically fixed representational content for experience and action as one likes (cf. Williams 2016).

one and the same item, simply because the concept *b* involves a mode of presentation of the item which is tied to a numerically distinct information link. This is all compatible with the claim that the perceptual content itself is coarse-grained—one might indifferently describe the perceptual content as that a is F, or that b is F. The structural point is that justification (believing for good reasons) can involve more than a relation between the (assumed to be coarse-grained) perceptual content and the belief formed in response. Justification can require that the belief be formed *through a certain route* that inter alia involves a state with that perceptual content. There's nothing here that seems particularly outlandish so far as epistemology is concerned. But if things work this way, then the relata of rationalization include, at the belief-end, fine-grained content.[11]

I earlier went through an argument for (Holism) that was based on Stalnaker's clause (b). As noted, (RI) is a kind of generalization of (b), but the argument for Holism does not generalize. Again, what mattered to Stalnaker's argument were the particular details of the form of instrumental-rationality connection he assumed. In particular, it was set up in such a way that specific relation became vacuous if the beliefs involved were inconsistent. So long as our notion of substantive rationality allows for rankings of actions as better or worse relative to belief states that can be consistent or inconsistent, there's no presupposition of consistency baked into (RI) in the way there was into (b). I do not think that the Stalnakerian argument generalizes.

This argument is blocked so long as we have available a notion of "best rationalization" that allows that the best rationalization of an agent is still not perfectly rational, allowing for inconsistent beliefs in particular. In a previous section, I made the case that a structure of co-belief, dividing the agent's mind into a set of individually consistent but potentially mutually inconsistent fragments is part of this. Supposing our theory of rationality appeals to this structure, we should really be enriching our conception of what the space of background interpretations is like. It should not only take states and classify them by type and content; it needs also to specify the co-belief structure. Facts about co-belief can then be grounded in exactly the way that facts about belief will be: by being part of the best rationalization of the agent's actions, in light of their course of experience.

I conclude that radical interpretation, though perfectly consistent with a Stalnakerian account of belief (this being exemplifed in Lewis's version of it) can also provide principled foundations for the naive conception of belief, as well as the needed co-belief structure involved in my pseudo-Stalnakerian dissolution of the problem of commitment.

---

[11] For a discussion of demonstrative thought and modes of presentation that drives this, see Dickie (2015) and the discussion in Williams (2019).

Internal Commitments

There is one loose end to tie up. Ever since I posited co-belief as the solution to problems of commitment, I've been talking as though facts about consistency and inconsistency are given from above, exogeneously to the agent's mentality. This would be so on an external conception of commitment-to-believe, but the notion of commitment that I find interesting is the internal one—I also think the costs of maintaining that clusters of mutually co-believed propositions are consistent, which is part of the price of my pseudo-Stalnakerian proposal, is far higher on the external conception. On the internal conception of commitment, the relevant notion of consistency and inconsistency are fixed by attitudinal states of the agent—their acceptance of this or that rule. If facts about what the agents accepts are themselves internally consistent, then this may not matter. But if the agent accepts contradictory rules—or if some fragment of their beliefs and behaviour is best rationalized by a different logic to another—then we should be looking for an account of the mentality of the agent which bundles together suitable acceptance states along with beliefs to generate the maximally rational fragments. This, I think, poses no new problems of principle. It may well mean that we can no longer unambiguously judge whether clusters of co-believed propositions are mutually consistent or inconsistent, since we have no cluster-transcendent and acceptance-based notion of consistency to appeal to. But such facts play no load-bearing role in this theory. The attitudes of accepting-a-rule are intentional states for which a metaphysical foundation should be provided. But the same gambit applies: insofar as they are already caught up in our theory of rationality, (RI) already provides their metaphysical basis.

IV. Conclusion

I started with a puzzle that afflicts our ordinary naive thinking about belief and commitments to believe. Drawing inspiration from a very different conception of belief, we can dissolve the puzzle. So long as agents do not believe things that are *by their own lights* inconsistent, the extra structure of co-belief allows us to characterize their commitments. We have reason to believe that co-belief should show up in a theory of (suboptimal) rationality. And because of this, the kind of metaphysics of belief that I favour will provide the necessary foundations for it.

The theory of belief-and-commitment that I offer, and the foundations thereof, are Stalnakerian and yet not Stalnakerian. They echo and learn from Stalnaker's account of belief. They are subject to some of the same costs and follow analogous escape routes to some analogous difficulties. Those of us who defend the naive picture of belief in the way described will be motivated to join forces with the Stalnakerians to make progress on shared and tricky issues, such as: how exactly to spell out a theory of suboptimal rationality via fragmentary mental states. Ultimately, one's resistance to the full-fat Stalnakerian theory might weaken, once one appreciates how much of it one is going to have to parallel.

I think the defender of the naive theory of belief should resist the temptation to throw in the towel, however. Particularly when it comes to understanding clear-eyed logical uncertainty, I find the Stalnakerian model to give too few resources—it does not allow me to capture adequately the attitude I adopt when I am agnostic over whether Ada or Beth has the right logic (Williams 2017). A version of Stalnaker's theory with a different modal base—where content is modelled by sets of doxastically possible worlds rather than sets of metaphysical possibilities—would do the job, but as Stalnaker persuasively argues, what is a minor switch from a formal point of view would require entirely different metaphysical foundations and would require giving up Stalnaker's motivating foundational picture.

If what I've said here is on the right tracks, there is plenty more to be done. There is the theory of suboptimal rationality. There is generalizing what has been said here to the kind of framework I defended in (2017), which both involves degrees of belief and generalizes the notion of "acceptance of a rule" to a broader category of modal attitude (accepting-as-doxastically-necessary, accepting-as-doxastically-possible). And much more could and should be said about the way that co-belief and acceptance-of-rules arise out of Radical Interpretation—to say that (RI) as I have characterized it provides foundations for these attitudes is not yet to say that the predictions that ensue are extensionally adequate.

References

Berto, F. 2019. "Simple hyperintensional belief revision." *Erkenntnis* 84(3): 559–75.
Dickie, I. 2015. *Fixing Reference*. Oxford: Oxford University Press.
Jago, M. 2014. *The Impossible: An Essay on Hyperintensionality*. Oxford: Oxford University Press.
Leitgeb, H. 2017. *The Stability of Belief*. Oxford: Oxford University Press.
Lewis, D. 1974. "Radical interpretation." *Synthese* 27: 309–23.
Lewis, D. 1986. *On the Plurality of Worlds*. Oxford: Oxford University Press.
Makinson, D. C. 1965. "The paradox of the preface." *Analysis* 25: 205–7.
Rayo, A. 2013. *The Construction of Logical Space*. Oxford: Oxford University Press.
Stalnaker, R. 1984. *Inquiry*. Cambridge, MA: MIT Press.
Williams, J. R. G. 2016. "Representational scepticism: the bubble puzzle." *Philosophical Perspectives* 30(1): 419–42.
Williams, J. R. G. 2017. "Rational illogicality." *Australasian Journal of Philosophy* 96(1): 127–41.
Williams, J. R. G. 2018. "Normative reference magnets." *Philosophical Review* 127(1): 41–71.
Williams, J. R. G. 2019. *The Metaphysics of Representation*. Oxford: Oxford University Press.

Expressivism and Propositions

Robert Stalnaker

I. Introduction

Expressivism began with emotivism, a meta-ethical theory developed and defended by Charles Stevenson and A. J. Ayer.[1] The view starts with a distinction between factual (cognitive) discourse, and discourse about values. Value judgments do not make claims about what the world is like—claims that are true or false. Instead, they express attitudes and feelings, and have the role of urging others to share the attitudes expressed, and to act on them. Emotivism was sometimes described, both by its defenders and its critics, as a *subjective* theory of value, since it grounds values in the attitudes of subjects, but central to the emotivist doctrine was a distinction between judgments *about* one's attitudes and judgments that *express* one's attitudes. A subjectivist theory of value that contrasts with emotivism holds that value judgments are factual propositions about one's own values: to say that racism is wrong is to say something like, "I abhor racism." The emotivist rejects this view; "Racism is wrong" does not make a claim about the speaker's values, or about anything. Rather it *expresses* abhorrence for racism. It is more like "Boo to racism". One salient difference between the explicit subjectivist thesis and emotivism comes out when one considers value judgments about counterfactual situations. On the subjectivist analysis, "If I were a racist, racism would not be wrong" says something like "If I were a racist, I would not abhor racism," which could well be true. But the emotivist who finds a situation where he himself is a racist to be especially abhorrent can say, "racism would be wrong even if I were a racist," since this means something like "boo to racism, even in situations where I approve of it."

So there are two related distinctions that are central to the original expressivist theories, and that remain central to contemporary versions of expressivism: (1) between factual judgments that aim to describe the world, and value judgments that do not, but instead express a non-cognitive attitude, or promote or endorse a plan of action; (2) between an assertion that one has an attitude, and a speech act that expresses an attitude. The second distinction can be applied to cognitive

---

[1] See Ayer (1936) and Stevenson (1937).

attitudes such as belief and knowledge as well as to attitudes such as abhorrence or approval: An ordinary factual claim such as "Trump was the Republican nominee for president" *expresses* the speaker's belief that Trump was the Republican nominee, but does not *say* that the speaker has this belief.

Contemporary expressivism, whose most prominent developer and defender has been Allan Gibbard,[2] acknowledges its roots in emotivism and non-cognitivism, but departs from the older theories in at least three significant ways: First, it broadens the range of concepts to which expressivist analyses are applied. Expressivism began as meta-ethics, and discourse about morality remains an important application, but Gibbard takes the central normative concept to be *rationality*. Normative discourse is about what it makes sense to believe, as well as what it makes sense to feel and to do, so an expressivist about norms should be expressivist about the concepts of epistemology. Second, contemporary expressivists develop more sophisticated semantic tools for responding to the technical problems that have been thought to plague non-cognitivist meta-ethical theories. While expressivism claims that normative judgments do not state facts, the sentences used to make them have the same indicative form as factual statements, and sentences with normative content combine with each other, and with factual claims. The traditional non-cognitivist did not offer any systematic account of the compositional semantics of normative-factual discourse, but contemporary expressivists have given this problem a lot of attention. Third, Gibbard and others such as Hartry Field[3] and Paul Horwich[4] have linked expressivism with a more general theory of meaning that includes a minimalist theory of truth, and that, in effect, gives an expressivist account of factual as well as normative discourse.

I will consider the application of expressivism to epistemology in Section 4, but in the next two sections I want to consider more general questions about the form that an expressivist theory should take. First, in Section 2, I will describe Gibbard's solution to the technical problem, as developed in his early book (1990), or at least one way of understanding that solution. I took Gibbard's account of what he called "normative logic" to provide a spot-on diagnosis of the problems about compositional semantics for normative discourse, and a definitive solution to the problems, but as I read more of Gibbard's later work, I came to see that my interpretation of this solution is different from his, and that I have a different understanding of the commitments of expressivism. So after explaining and defending my understanding of Gibbard's normative logic, I will criticize, in Section 3, his expressivist account of truth, which I think blurs the line between expressivism about norms and the non-natural realism that Gibbard took, at least initially, to contrast with expressivism.

---

[2] Gibbard (1990, 2003 and 2012). See also Blackburn (1993).
[3] See the papers in Field (2001).   [4] Horwich (1990, 1998).

II. Normative Logic

Gibbard's "first rough formulation" of his expressivist analysis is this: "to call an act, belief or emotion rational is to express one's acceptance of a system of norms that permits it."[5]

This is not quite right, even as a rough formulation, since a judgment about the rationality of an action, feeling or belief involves not just the acceptance of a system of norms, but also factual beliefs. The norms are conditional: they say what it makes sense to do "in a wide range of actual and hypothetical circumstances," but a judgment, for example, that it does not make sense to vote for Donald Trump expresses the acceptance of a system of norms that require that one not vote for him *in circumstances that we take to be actual*. So a second rough formulation might say that to call an act, belief or emotion rational is to express one's acceptance of a system of norms that permits in in circumstances that one takes to be actual.

Gibbard identifies three problems that an expressivist analysis of this kind faces, and then proposes a unified solution to them all. The first problem is the most familiar: the so-called Frege-Geach problem:

> Suppose we have an adequate account of the states of mind expressed by such simple statements as 'it makes sense for Antony to give battle.' What are we to say of more complex contexts, like 'Whenever Antony does anything it doesn't make sense to do, he clings to his purpose stubbornly.' Sentences of indefinite complexity…get their meanings from the meanings of their elements in systematic ways.[6]

We know how to do truth-conditional compositional semantics for purely factual sentences, that express beliefs, but we need to show how to do this for normative sentences, and for sentences that mix normative and factual terms, in a way that is compatible with the expressivist program.

The second problem is the problem of communication. When Cleopatra says that some action or attitude is rational, she expresses her acceptance of a system of norms that permit it, but there will normally be many systems of norms that permit it, and nothing is said or expressed about what specific system Cleopatra accepts. Accepting a (partial or complete) system of norms is a holistic state, but a particular normative judgment is only a partial characterization of the state. We need an account of the normative *content* of an individual normative claim that is common to the different states that are compatible with it.

---

[5] Gibbard (1990, 83).   [6] Gibbard (1990, 90).

The third problem, closely related to the problem of communication, is labeled 'the problem of *normative naivete*'. Suppose we accept what Cleopatra says, on her authority, when she makes a normative claim. "What state of mind constitutes this acceptance?...What could it be...to accept a normative conclusion—to accept, in effect, a property of a combined normative system and set of beliefs—and yet fail to accept any specific normative system that together with our beliefs, has that property?"[7] Again, the source of the problem is that a combined system of norms and state of belief is a holistic state, while the content of a particular normative claim is just a partial constraint on such a combined system.

The common solution (as I think it should be interpreted) is to give a systematic account of factual-normative content that is independent of the various mental states that these contents can be used to describe. The strategy follows the precedent of truth-conditional semantics for purely factual sentences, so let me start with an exposition of a version of that strategy that sets up the generalization to the content of combined normative-factual systems.

When we theorize about factual belief and assertion using traditional truth-conditional semantics, we separate the question, *what are the contents of speech acts and propositional attitudes?* from the question, *what is it to assert, or to believe something with a certain content?* We do compositional semantics on the abstract objects that are provided by the answer to the first question. Without considering what it is to believe a proposition, we can consider how a complex sentence determines a proposition as a function of the semantic values of the component parts. An answer to the second question tells us what it is to be in a certain global state of belief, which determines which propositions are believed by someone in such a state, and what beliefs are expressed in a statement with a certain propositional content, but we can do the compositional semantics without addressing the second question.

It is essential to this strategy that our theory of *propositions* can be characterized independently of any assumptions about the mental states that those propositions are used to describe, or of any account of the speech acts in which propositions are expressed. Our compositional semantics will assume a domain of propositions with a certain structure, and an account of what propositions are. The structure will be a Boolean algebra that can be represented as subsets of a state space, or a set of possible worlds. Propositions can be thought of as properties that the world as a whole might have. If you think of them this way, then *true* propositions can be thought of as the properties of this kind that the world actually does have.

Gibbard does not explain what possible worlds are in a way that is independent of mental states. He asks us to "imagine a god Hera who is entirely coherent and completely opinionated....[T]here is a completely determinate way w she thinks

---

[7] Gibbard (1990, 93).

the world to be."[8] I took this at the time, and I think it should be taken, to be just a rough heuristic way of getting a handle on what a possible world is. Propositions, including maximal propositions, can stand on their own as features that reality might have.

If we can understand propositions and possible worlds as abstract objects that are intelligible independently of assumptions about intentional mental states, then we can also understand *complete systems of norms* as abstract object that are intelligible independently of any agent who accepts a system of norms, and even of any account of what it is to accept a system of norms. A system of norms is "a system of permissions and requirements...what matters about a system of norms is what it requires and permits in various conceivable circumstances."[9] Since what is permissible or required, according to such a system, are actions, feelings or attitudes of persons, we can take the 'conceivable circumstances' to be possible worlds, centered on a particular person and time in the world. Then a system of norms can be represented by a function from circumstances of this kind to a set of possible worlds that is permissible in those circumstances, according to that system of norms. Gibbard is clear and explicit that a system of norms can be understood independently of whether anyone accepts the system. "We can characterize any system N of norms by a family of basic predicates, 'N-forbidden', 'N-optional', and 'N-required'.... These predicates are descriptive rather than normative: whether a thing, say, is N-permitted will be a matter of fact. It might be N-permitted without being rational, for the system N might have little to recommend it."[10]

So we have a set W of possible worlds, and a set S of normative systems, defined in terms of those possible worlds, and so a set of all the pairs consisting of a possible world and a normative system. If factual propositions correspond to sets of possible worlds, then factual-normative propositions will correspond to sets of pairs of this kind, and these sets will be the *contents* of factual and normative judgments. We can do the compositional semantics for normative-factual sentences in exactly the same way that we do compositional semantics for purely factual sentences, using this more fine-grained representation of the possibilities that the sentences of our normative-factual language distinguish between. And we can understand what is said by one making a normative claim, and how one revises one's normative-factual beliefs on accepting a normative claim, in the same way we understand these things for factual discourse. If we model a factual discourse with the help of an evolving set of possibilities representing the common ground of the participants in the discourse, then we can represent a discourse that involves normative as well as factual claims with the help of a more

---

[8] Gibbard (1990, 95). In a footnote, Gibbard attributes this conception of a possible world to me, but the contrast he is making is between my view and David Lewis's modal realism. It is not part of my view that possible worlds should be understood as maximal belief states.

[9] Gibbard (1990, 87).   [10] Gibbard (1990, 87).

fine-grained space of possibilities representing what is commonly accepted and what is in dispute in that discourse.

In stating the Frege-Geach problem, Gibbard asked, 'Can we give a systematic account of how the state of mind a complex normative sentence expresses depends on the states of mind that would be expressed by its components alone?' This suggest that the problem should be solved in the context of a certain semantic program that is well articulated in Mark Schroeder's critique of expressivism:

> We should think of expressivism as committed to an underlying semantic program that looks something very much like assertability semantics. The central ideas of assertability semantics are (1) that the role of semantics is to assign an assertability condition to each sentence of the language, understood as the condition under which it is semantically permissible for a speaker to assert it. (2) These assertability conditions typically or always say that the speaker needs to be in a certain mental state. (3) Descriptive sentences inherit their propositional contents (truth-conditions) from the belief that it is their assertability condition to be in. And (4) the assertability conditions of complex sentences are a function of the assertability conditions of their parts, where this function is given by the meanings of the sentential connectives that are used to form the complex sentences.[11]

Schroeder attributes to expressivism a commitment to this kind of semantic program, and the book is an extended argument that it cannot succeed, but on my interpretation of Gibbard's response to this set of problems, he is rejecting this strategy for doing semantics, and instead generalizing the standard truth-conditional semantics that explains content, and the relation between the content of complex sentences and the contents of their constituent parts, independently of the attitudes that those contents are used to describe. As we will see this is not Gibbard's way of understanding what his formalism accomplishes, but it is nevertheless, I will argue, the best way to develop an expressivist semantics.

III. Expressivism about Truth

In the last part of his recent book, *Meaning and Normativity*, Gibbard sets his overall expressivist theory in a context that explicitly rejects the interpretation of normative logic sketched in Section II:

> Frege begins with content...and then invokes different attitudes one can have toward the same piece of content....I undertake to explain normative thinking

---

[11] Schroeder (2008, 31).

in the opposite direction. I begin with a state of mind and then let talk of content emerge.... I follow Horwich in treating all mental content as explained by states of mind. I'll speak broadly of "expressivists" in this essay, but mean only expressivists who develop their approach in the ways I advocate. I'll call those who begin their explanations with items of content and explain states of mind as relations a thinker can have with items of content as "Fregeans". (This regardless of whether a theorist accepts the more specific doctrines of Frege, or of Russell, or of anyone else.)[12]

The interpretation of normative logic that I gave in Section II above is manifestly Fregean in this sense. I will argue that the reversal of the order of explanation that Gibbard proposes cannot work on its own terms, but my main point will be that a defense of an expressivist theory in the spirit of the traditional non-cognitive accounts of normative judgments does not require the broader conception of expressivism that Gibbard articulates in his later work.

Let's return to the myth about Hera "who is entirely coherent and completely opinionated both normatively and factually. She suffers no factual uncertainty; there is a completely determinate way w she takes the world to be." This time let's take this not just as a heuristic for getting a handle on the idea of a maximal proposition, or a possible state of the world, but really as a representation of a state of mind. Of course it is not a state of mind of any actual person—no one is really completely opinionated. We can understand this only as an abstract object—something like the content of a possible state of mind. What explanatory advantage is provided by thinking of these abstract objects as possible states of mind, rather than as maximal propositions (or better as *centered* maximal propositions) that might be the content of a state of mind?

Gibbard is not interested in modeling only fully opinionated states of mind. His aim is to use these abstract objects to model states of mind that are only partially opinionated. The idea seems to be to represent a partially opinionated belief state with the set of all the fully opinionated states that the subject could be in if she learned more, but did not change her mind about anything. But that won't work, since our states of mind will include beliefs about our own present and future beliefs. It is one of my firmly held beliefs that I will *never* be fully opinionated, and I am sure that Gibbard, and all reasonable people who have thought about it, have analogous beliefs. But this means that my belief state cannot be represented by any set of fully opinionated belief states, since there are *no* fully opinionated states that are consistent with it. If we think of the objects used to model a belief state as possible states of the world, or maximal propositions we don't have this problem, since a fully determinate state of the world might be a

---

[12] Gibbard (2012, 273).

state according to which all agents, throughout their lives, are in only partially opinionated states of mind.

Why is Gibbard suspicious of propositions, thought of as sets of possible worlds, and what advantage does he think one gains if one talks instead about states of belief? I conjecture that the source of his suspicion is that the hypothesis that such objects are contents of belief fails to solve the problem of intentionality—it fails to provide an explanation of what it is about an agent and his or her place in the world that makes it the case that she believes the propositions that she believes. "Some philosophers," he says, maintain "that states of affairs (or 'propositions') can be believed or disbelieved as such, and not just as conceived via one thought or another."[13] I am not sure what it means to conceive of a proposition via one thought or another, or to believe something 'as such', but one should not assume that to say that someone believes that φ is to deny that there is any story to be told about *how* it is believed: about what the relation is between the believer and the proposition believed. The idea of the strategy that Gibbard calls 'Fregean' is to explain content independently of the use to which content is put to describe states of mind. What is assumed by saying that a proposition, in this sense, is the content of an intentional state of mind is only that such states of mind have truth-conditions—they are true under certain conditions, and false under others. A proposition (in the coarse-grained sense defined) is a truth-condition.

At one point, Gibbard says that a version of "the line of thought I am inveighing against treats 'propositions' as sets of possible worlds, *worlds as viewed from nowhere*."[14] But I think Thomas Nagel's oxymoronic metaphor of a view from nowhere is misleading in suggesting that there is something mysterious in the idea of conceiving of a thing as it is in itself. Possible worlds, like anything else, are viewed both by their adherents and by their critics, from the perspectives of those adherents and critics. Saul Kripke, for example, when he wrote his introduction to *Naming and Necessity*, was conceiving of possible worlds from the time and place at which he wrote that introduction, which was somewhere, and not nowhere. But that time and place (or any other distinctive time and place) are not part of what he was conceiving. To use an analogy, it would not be right to describe the moon as being viewed from nowhere because it is not part of what it is to be the moon that we view it from the earth.

However we answer the questions about how believers are related to the contents of their beliefs—of what makes it the case that their states of mind have the truth-conditions that they have—it does not seem unreasonable to assume that those states can be described as states with propositional content, and to assume that we have some grasp of the abstract objects that propositions are. I have said that propositions (and possible worlds, which are maximal propositions) are

---

[13] Gibbard (2012, 31).   [14] Gibbard (2012, 31). The phrase comes from Nagel (1986).

something like *properties* that reality as a whole might have, and this presupposes that propositions are the kind of thing that will be true or false, according to whether the world (reality as a whole) has the property, or does not. Gibbard favors a deflationary or minimalist conception of truth: to assert that a proposition is true is just to assert it, to believe that it is true is just to believe it. (He is agnostic, but skeptical, about whether there is any more demanding notion of truth.) But I think the minimalist account fails to distinguish between at least two distinct conceptions of truth, which I will label 'Aristotelian' and 'Protagorean'. This distinction matters, I will further argue, for the characterization of expressivism. Gibbard likes to cite the Aristotelian truism, "to speak truly is to say of what is that it is, and of what is not that it is not," and he takes this to be a characterization of a deflationary conception, but what is distinctive about the Aristotelian slogan is that it presupposes a distinction between *what is* and *what is said to be*. The Protagorean conception makes no such conceptual distinction. It can distinguish between what one says (or believes) and what another says (or believes) about what the one says (or believes): Jones can say that what Smith said was false, which will be true in the Protagorean sense for Jones. We, from our perspective, can in turn say that Jones spoke falsely. Of course we are not *saying* that what Jones said is false *for us*, but we are *expressing* that it is false from our perspective.

The distinction is elusive, since even on the Aristotelian conception, in saying that something is true, one is expressing one's belief, but the theory of propositions, and the derivative notion of a normative-descriptive proposition, help to clarify the distinction. There is a clear and coherent notion of relative truth that is definable within the abstract theory of propositions—truth relative to a possible world. If propositions are modeled by subsets of the space of possible worlds, then they can also be modeled by the equivalent characteristic functions— functions from worlds to any pair of objects, {1,0} or {True, False}. A proposition P is true at, or relative to, a possible world w if and only if w is a member of the set P, or if and only if the characteristic function that corresponds to P takes w to Truth. Relative truth is all we need for doing compositional semantics, for the most part, but if our abstract objects are something like properties the world might have, we also want a notion of absolute truth, or equivalently, a notion of the *actual* world. The notion of truth, as a monadic property of propositions, and the notion of a possible world that is actual are interdefinable. Since what we call 'possible worlds' are maximal propositions, the actual world can be defined as the maximal proposition that is true. Or if you want your analysis to go the other way, Aristotelian truth can be defined as relative truth, relative to the actual world (that is, a proposition, modeled by a set of possible worlds, is true iff it contains the actual world).[15]

---

[15] There is more than one notion of relative truth. The relativist notion I have defined is not really Protagorean, since it takes truth to be relative to a possible world, while the real Protagorean takes truth to be relative to a state of belief. Gibbard's general strategy of beginning with states of mind,

Socrates argued (in Plato's *Theatetus*), that the Protagorean conception of truth was incoherent, but the notion of relative truth that I have defined, in the context of a theory of propositions, is unproblematic. Would it be coherent to hold that relative truth, in this sense, was the only kind of truth we can make sense of? It may be coherent, but I don't think this kind of extreme anti-realism is plausible.[16]

According to Gibbard's normative logic, as I have interpreted it, we refine our possibility space by using norm-world pairs, rather than just possible worlds, as the points in the space on which we define our compositional semantics, and it is straightforward to extend our notion of relative truth to this more refined space. A normative-factual proposition will be a set of norm-world pairs, and such a proposition P will be true, relative to norm-world pair $\langle w,N \rangle$ if and only if $\langle w,N \rangle \in$ P. As Gibbard says, "If I oppose stealing...that commits me to thinking that it is true that stealing is bad. The sense of 'true' here is deflationary, so that 'It is true that stealing is bad' says no more than that stealing is bad." This is fine, so long as the notion of truth we are using is the relativist one. Gibbard adds, "No one, in my view, has explained satisfactorily a more demanding sense of 'true'."[17] I have tried to do this by suggesting that anyone who is a realist about the world of fact should acknowledge a distinction between monadic, or absolute truth, and a notion of truth relative to a possible state of the world. And if we acknowledge this distinction, then we can ask whether the monadic notion applies to factual-normative propositions. Our theory of factual propositions assumes there is an actual world—one maximal factual proposition that is true. But is there also an *actual* system of norms? If we separate, as I have tried to do, conceptions of content (factual, or normative-factual) from any account of what it is to be in a state of mind with content, then we can ask whether the monadic notion of truth, applied to systems of norms, should be part of our theory of factual-normative content. The expressivist should welcome this conceptual resource since it allows us to draw a clear line between expressivists about norms and normative realists. The normative realist answers 'yes' to the question (is there an *actual* set of norms?). On the non-natural realist view, normative claims describe a part of reality as it is in itself. The expressivist should answer 'no', since for the expressivist the application of a system of norms is grounded in the states of mind that systems of norms are used to express.

---

rather than states of the world, would yield a notion of relative truth that is closer to the real Protagorean's view. I should emphasize that I am not saying that the deflationary notion of truth that Gibbard defends is a notion of relative truth, in either of these senses. Rather, I am saying that the deflationary characterization of truth does not discriminate the absolute notion from the relativist notions.

[16] David Lewis's modal realism, ironically, might be understood as a version of the view that truth, relative to a possible world, is the only kind of truth there is—at least the only kind of contingent truth. Contingent truth, on Lewis's metaphysical picture, is essentially perspectival. The world that is actual (for us) is just the one we happen to be in. Beings that we are inclined to call 'counterfactual' are just beings that are somewhere else.

[17] Gibbard (2012, 20).

In the last chapter of *Meaning and Normativity*, Gibbard argues that non-naturalism and expressivism may in the end coincide in their theses, but I think his account is unable to distinguish them only because his deflationary notion of truth blurs a conceptual line that a different explanatory framework can use to distinguish the two metaphysical accounts. What Gibbard initially found mysterious in non-naturalism is the idea that "there is a normative realm distinct from the natural realm, and that we have ways to discern how things stand in that realm."[18] The idea was that (according to the non-naturalist realist) a distinction between the natural and the non-natural is a distinction between two more or less distinct and independent domains of reality, a distinction like the one that was once made between the celestial and the terrestrial, or that one might make between the natural and the supernatural. This view seems mysterious, Gibbard says, because "even if there were such a normative realm detached from all things natural, why would our methods of thinking enable us to discern how things stand in this realm?"[19]

For the expressivist, the distinction between the natural and the normative is nothing like this. "In my picture," Gibbard once said, "all strict facts will be naturalistic.... Apparently normative facts will come out, strictly, as no real facts at all. Instead there will be facts about what we are doing when we make normative judgments."[20] The notion of the "strictly factual" is not a restriction to a special domain of fact, but is used to characterize whatever there is a fact of the matter about, and I take the Aristotelian notion of truth (as contrasted with the useful notion of relative truth) to be an intelligible notion that marks this distinction.

All of the points of agreement between expressivists and non-naturalists that Gibbard notes in his ecumenical chapter are compatible with the interpretation I have given of his normative logic, and with the sharp line marked by the contrasting answer to the question whether there is there a system of norms that is actual in the way that one of the factual states of the world is actual. Gibbard takes Tim Scanlon as his example of a non-naturalist, and quotes him as saying that he finds himself "strongly drawn to a cognitivist understanding of moral and practical judgments.... They obey the principles of standard propositional and quantificational logic, and satisfy (at least most of) the other 'platitudes' about truth." After quoting these comments, Gibbard remarks, "my expressivism lets me agree with Scanlon," and his account of normative logic does explain how he can agree with Scanlon's observations.[21] But Gibbard's minimalism about truth is not a necessary part of the explanation.[22]

---

[18] Gibbard (2012, 235). [19] Gibbard (2012, 236).
[20] Gibbard (1990, 23). [21] Gibbard (2012, 230).
[22] Whether or not Gibbard is right that he and Scanlon do not really disagree in doctrine is a further question.

It may seem that it is Gibbard's minimalism about truth that allows him to say "We can speak of the 'world' and normative 'facts' in deflationary senses, so that, in the extreme case, if peas are yucky, then it's a 'fact' that peas are yucky, and this fact characterizes the 'world'."[23] But my claim was that the deflationary notion equivocates between the relativist and the Aristotelian notion of truth. You can, if you like, use the words 'fact' and 'world' (so long as you retains Gibbard's scare quotes) for notions definable in terms of the intelligible relativist notion of truth, but if you also have the Aristotelian notion, you can make sense of a use of the word 'fact' that is restricted to what there is a fact of the matter about.

Most importantly, an expressivist can make the distinction between relativist and monadic truth, and deny (as the emotivists did) that normative judgments are true or false, in the stronger sense, while still retaining the sense in which the content of normative judgments are objective. "Expressivism allows us to interpret the normative conviction that some oughts hold independently of our beliefs and motivations—that one ought not to kick dogs for fun, for example. That one ought not to kick dogs for fun holds true in a possible situation regardless of what anyone thinks or how anyone feels about it, so long as kicking a dog hurts it."[24] What this observation expresses is the acceptance of a system of norms according to which it is not permissible to kick dogs for fun, even in possible circumstances where no one accepts a system of norms that has this consequence. One could accept a system of norms of this kind while also saying that it is not a *fact* that this system is correct.

Gibbard's normative logic is just one example of a general strategy of refining a space of possibilities. A more fine-grained notion of a possibility can be defined by adding a second parameter to the possible-state-of-the-world parameter, which might, as in Gibbard's original exposition of normative logic be a system of norms, but might be some other parameter that relative truth may be defined as relative to. It is useful to have a more general notion of *proposition* that has the same structure as the basic notion of a set of ways the world might be or have been, a notion that may make distinctions between possibilities that the facts do not, in the end, settle. A refinement of this kind lets us generalize the methods that apply to the explanation of factual discourse in two different ways: first, we can extend the methods of compositional semantics to the explanation of the contents of speech acts and propositional attitudes beyond those that aim to represent the way the world in fact is. The generalization is straightforward because the compositional explanation of how the proposition expressed by a complex expression is a function of the propositions expressed by its constituents (with propositions represented as sets of possibilities) can be applied however one individuates the possibilities. Second, we can generalize our pragmatic account of

---

[23] Gibbard (2012, 232).   [24] Gibbard (2012, 233).

the dynamics of discourse, and of the changing relationships between the attitudes of different rational agents. A discourse (on the kind of model of discourse that I have promoted) takes place against an evolving body of information that represents what is presumed by the participants to be a common background of shared assumptions. These assumptions can include both shared factual information (or misinformation) and shared values or norms. The generalized notion of content helps to show how the structure of a discussion, debate, or cooperative exchange of 'information' can take the same form, at a certain level of abstraction, whether what is under discussion is a factual matter, or a question about what to do, or how to think about something. Often, there will be a meta-question in dispute—a question about whether or not there is a fact of the matter about some question. The common structure helps to represent discussions and debates, even at a point at which such meta-questions remain unresolved.

As I have noted, Gibbard argues for a reversal of the order of explanation from the Fregean approach: we should begin with states of mind, rather than with a notion of propositional content. He agrees with Mark Schroeder that the kind of expressivist program that he is advocating takes for granted a notion of *disagreement* between states of mind, and he emphasizes that this is a notion that applies more widely than to the attitude of factual belief. I agree with Gibbard that the task of explaining the broader notions of agreement and disagreement is a central *motivation* for the generalization of the notion of a proposition, but my argument is the best way to clarify this notion is to distinguish a more general notion of content, from its application to an account of attitudes and discourse. The distinction seems to me to be intelligible, and it helps to sharpen the Aristotelian notion of truth that is essential to a clear distinction between expressivism and non-naturalist realism.

IV. Expressivism about Epistemic Norms

I have focused thus far on very general issues about the distinction between expressivism and non-natural realism, and on the representation of the interaction of factual and normative content. In this final section I will look briefly at some more specific issues concerning epistemic norms with the aims, first of illustrating the way the general normative logic framework works, and second of showing how the framework might clarify some traditional problems about epistemology, and epistemic discourse.

The central general point was that one should characterize normative-factual *content* independently of an account of the attitudes. First, factual content, represented by a set of possible states of the world, is generalized by adding a second parameter, yielding a finer-grained notion of a possibility. Second, one explains the role of the finer-grained content in an account of attitudes, or of discourse.

I will first illustrate a version of this strategy in which the second parameter is not, as in Gibbard's theory, a system of norms, but an information state, following some ideas developed in Eric Swanson's constraint semantics, and Seth Yalcin's Bayesian expressivism for epistemic modals.[25] Second, I will look at some issues that arise when we apply Gibbard's specific definition of a system of norms to norms for a Bayesian representation of an epistemic state.

In the Swanson and Yalcin accounts, the extra parameter is an information state, represented by a space of possible worlds and a probability function on it. So the more fine-grained propositions are sets of pairs consisting of a factual world w and an information state of this kind, S. This refinement allows for a straightforward compositional semantics for epistemic modal expressions such as 'might' 'must' and 'probably'. 'It might be that ϕ' will be true, relative to $\langle S,w \rangle$, iff the proposition expressed by ϕ (in context) is true in some possible worlds in the information state S. 'Probably ϕ' is true relative to $\langle S,w \rangle$ iff the probability of the proposition expressed by ϕ is greater than one half in information state S. But now the second and harder question is, what is the pragmatic role of these 'propositions'? What is one doing when one 'asserts' one? The idea is that a possibility of this kind represents an information state that it is permissible to be in. A set of possibilities of this kind can represent the common ground—what is mutually agreed—about what is true, and also about what credences it is permissible to have, given the information that we have. In the original, purely factual account, an assertion with propositional content **P** is a proposal to accept **P**, which means to add this information to the common ground. With the more fine-grained propositions, the idea is generalized: an assertion of a more fine-grained proposition of this kind is a proposal to accept (in addition to the factual information entailed by the proposition) a constraint on the credences that are permissible (according to the information that we share). This simple example illustrates the way the notion of finer-grained content, allows for both a smooth generalization of the compositional semantics, and a smooth generalization of a pragmatic account of discourse. The account counts as expressivist because it takes the assertions of epistemic modal claims as *expressing* epistemic attitudes (that we, the participants in the conversation, are or are not in a position to have), but not as statements *about* our epistemic attitudes. And the account does not require that there be a fact of the matter about what we are in a position to believe, and what credenees we are in a position to have.

Now let me suggest how we might apply the Gibbardian characterization of a system of norms to norms for Bayesian epistemology. A system of norms, recall, can be represented by a function taking specific situations that an agent might be in (which may be represented by a possible world, centered on an agent and a

---

[25] See e.g. Yalcin (2012) and Swanson (2016). See also Moss (2018).

time in that world) to a 'sphere of permissibility': a set of (centered) possible worlds that are permissible (according to the system) for that agent in that situation. In this case, a world will be permissible iff the agent has a credence function that is permissible in the situation in question. But what are the relevant features of the situation that determines what credences it is permissible to have?

A general expressivist epistemology should have something to say about the norms governing claims to *knowledge*, but I am going to focus here on just one part of the problem by taking *what we know* as part of what defines the conditions relative to which credences are judged to be permissible, or not. Of the propositions not known, but compatible with your knowledge, some are judged much more probable than others. Our question will be about how a system of epistemic norms should assess what *partial* beliefs it is permissible to have in a situation that is in part defined by what one knows in that situation.

It is a general presupposition of the Gibbardian framework that what is permissible is a function of the objective facts about a particular situation, but in order for a rule saying what is permissible or required to be a reasonable rule, the facts that define the conditions for its application must be, normally at least, accessible to the agent. 'Add salt when the water boils', for example, is a reasonable part of a recipe only if one can normally tell when the water boils. Still, the recipe does not say 'add salt when you *think* the water is boiling.' You have failed to follow the recipe if the water was not in fact boiling when you added the salt, even if you thought (and even if you had good reason to think) that it was.[26] The point will apply to a norm that tells you what credences are permitted or required, conditional on what you know. If you are mistaken about what you know in a given situation, you may have credences that fail to conform to norms for credences that you accept, even if you have done your best to conform to those norms. But as with recipes, norms for credence will be reasonable only if agents are *normally* in a position to act on those norms.

So far we have assumed just the following: a system of Bayesian norms can be represented by a function from a specific situation for an agent (one salient feature of which is what the agent knows in that situation) to a set of credence functions that it is permissible for the agent to have in that situation. What more can be said about what a reasonable system of Bayesian norms should look like? We can assume that permissible credence functions will all be ones that assign probability one to all propositions that are known. Among systems meeting these conditions, we can distinguish more permissive from more restrictive norms. At the permissive extreme, a system of norms might allow any coherent credence function that assigns probability one to all the propositions known. At the restrictive extreme, a norm might imply that there is a unique credence function that is

---

[26] This is a point emphasized by Timothy Williamson, with this example, in his discussion of rules and norms. See Williamson (2000, 223).

permissible in any given situation. It is important not to confuse expressivism in general with permissivism.[27] Epistemic expressivism (as contrasted with normative realism) is the thesis that there is no fact of the matter about what system of epistemic norms is correct. Epistemic permissivism is a thesis about the kind of system of norms we should accept. The two theses are independent: one might be a permissivist and a normative realist, holding that it is a matter of fact that alternative credence functions are permissible in a given situation. On the other hand, one might accept a highly restrictive system of epistemic norms that determines a unique credence function for each situation, while holding, in one's meta-theory, that it is not a matter of fact that any particular system of norms is correct.

Let us assume, for the moment that our epistemic norms are demanding, yielding a unique credence function for each situation. So we are assuming that the system of Bayesian norms we accept determines a function taking any factual proposition (the agent's total evidence—what he knows) to a credence function defined on a space of possibilities that is compatible with that evidence. One natural version of a function of this kind could be represented by a prior probability function, with the credence functions that are admissible in a specific situation defined by conditionalization on the total evidence available to the agent in that situation. It is important to note that the assumption that a system of norms should take this form, while it is a very abstract assumption, is a further constraint on a system of Bayesian norms, one that restricts the relationships between the credence functions that are mandated for different situations. The result of accepting this constraint would be an account of epistemic probability of the kind that Timothy Williamson has given, transposed into a Gibbardian expressivist setting.[28] I want to suggest that the expressivist setting may help to explain the status of an epistemic prior probability function of the kind that Williamson posits.

According to Williamson, the epistemic prior is a measure of 'intrinsic plausibility', but he has little to say about where it comes from. It is sometimes said that the Bayesian story presupposes an ur-probability function, representing what credences it would be reasonable to have if one had no empirical evidence at all. According to Alan Hajek, David Lewis used the term "Bayesian Superbabies" for logically perfect rational agents "as they begin their Bayesian odysseys." The credence functions of these hypothetical creatures encode what one's credences should be before receiving any empirical evidence.[29] But is it reasonable to assume that the epistemic norms we in fact accept determine what we should believe in a wholly unrealistic situation in which we have had no experience, and have acquired no knowledge at all about contingent matters of fact? I think there is a better way to think about what such a prior might represent, one that derives

---

[27] See White (2005) for a characterization and critique of permissivism.
[28] See Williamson (2000, ch. 10).   [29] Hajek (2010).

the norms that an agent actually accepts from the facts about that agent's dispositions to form and endorse credences, and to assess the credences of others.

As Gibbard emphasized in his general account, it is a (natural) fact that an agent accepts a certain (perhaps partial) system of norms. To accept such a system is, in part, to be disposed to do, and to endorse, only what that system of norms permits. It is also a (natural) fact about an agent at a particular time that he has certain credences, and having those credences will be part of what determines the epistemic norms that he accepts. It won't follow that the agent's actual credence function (at a certain time) is thereby compatible with the norms that he accepts at that time for the reason mentioned above: he may be mistaken about what his evidence is. But we should assume that, at least normally, an agent's actual credences in a given situation will be credences that he is permitted to have, according to norms he accepts, in a situation where what he knows is what he takes himself to know.

The credences of agents change over time as they receive new evidence, including evidence about the credences of others. The way that agents are disposed to respond to possible new evidence, and the way their changing credences are disposed to be influenced by the information received about the credences of others are further facts that it will be relevant to determining what system of epistemic norms the agent accepts. I may ask myself, not just what my credence in some proposition is or should be right now, but what it would or should be under counterfactual circumstances in which I had different evidence than I in fact have. And I may ask what someone else with evidence different from mine should believe. Some questions of this kind will have clear answers for me, others not, but the cases for which the questions have answers (perhaps implicit in my epistemic dispositions, if not in my ability to articulate an answer) will be enough to attribute to me some norms of the appropriate kind.

Some of my beliefs and policies for revising my beliefs are more stable, and more widely shared with others who I take to be epistemic peers, but who may have different specific evidence than I have. Others of my current beliefs and policies are more local, idiosyncratic, and easily revised. (Think of Quine's metaphor of a web of belief, with a stable core, and changes at the periphery.) It may be reasonable to think of a prior probability function as representing the more stable features of my credence function, and such a representation may provide answers to the question of what Bayesian norms I accept.

The kind of prior that we might extract in this way from the credences and belief revision policies of an agent might (and in any remotely realistic case will) assign probability one to some contingent propositions. Suppose contingent proposition P has prior probability one. What do my norms say about what credences a person should have in a situation in which he or she learns that P is false? There are two kinds of cases: Some remote possibilities, while conceivable, are not taken seriously enough for me to have any policies for dealing with possible evidence that they may be actual. That is just to say that our system of epistemic norms may be partial. But it may be that sometimes my epistemic norms give me direction even in situations where propositions with prior probability one are discovered to be false. In this kind of case, one receives evidence that one's prior needs to be revised. One may have policies for doing this, and these policies need not be based on some more neutral background prior. One can be a Bayesian without assuming that *every* application of one's norms in a particular situation is based on conditionalizing on a universal prior. It might be (according to a system of norms that I accept) that the appropriate prior for me to have in a given situation is dependent on the facts about that situation.[30]

References

Ayer, A. 1936. *Language, Truth and Logic*. London: Victor Gollancz Ltd.
Blackburn, S. 1993. *Essays in Quasi-Realism*. Oxford: Oxford University Press.
Field, H. 2001. *Truth and the Absence of Fact*. Oxford: Clarendon Press.
Gibbard, A. 1990. *Wise Choices, Apt Feelings*. Cambridge, MA: Harvard University Press.
Gibbard, A. 2003. *Thinking How to Live*. Cambridge, MA: Harvard University Press.
Gibbard, A. 2012. *Meaning and Normativity*. Oxford: Oxford University Press.
Hajek, A. 2010. "Staying regular." Unpublished manuscript.
Horwich, P. 1990. *Truth*. Oxford: Oxford University Press.
Horwich, P. 1998. *Meaning*. Oxford: Clarendon Press.
Moss, S. 2018. *Probabilistic Knowledge*. Oxford: Oxford University Press.
Nagel, T. 1986. *The View from Nowhere*. New York: Oxford University Press.
Schroeder, M. 2008. *Being For: Evaluating the Semantic Program of Expressivism*. Oxford: Oxford University Press.
Stevenson, C. 1937. "The emotive theory of ethical terms." *Mind* 46: 14–31.
Swanson, E. 2016. "The application of constraint semantics to the language of subjective uncertainty." *Journal of Philosophical Logic* 45: 121–46.
White, R. 2005. "Epistemic Permissiveness," *Philosophical Perspectives* 19: 445–59.
Williamson, T. 2000. *Knowledge and Its Limits*. Oxford: Oxford University Press.
Yalcin, S. 2012. "Bayesian Expressivism," *Proceedings of the Aristotelian Society* 112: 123–60.

Robert Stalnaker, *Expressivism and Propositions* In: *Unstructured Content*. Edited by: Peter van Elswyk, Dirk Kindermann, Cameron Domenico Kirk-Giannini and Andy Egan, Oxford University Press.
© Oxford University Press 2025. DOI: 10.1093/9780191862175.003.0003

---

[30] Thanks to Seth Yalcin for discussion and correspondence, both about expressivism in general and about its application to epistemic norms.

PART 2
TRUTHMAKER-STYLE APPROACHES

A Theory of Partial Truth

Kit Fine

This chapter develops a theory of partial truth within the framework of truthmaker content expounded in two of my earlier papers (Fine 2017a, 2017b). It will be helpful, though not essential, to have these two other papers at hand, and especially the first, while reading the present paper. The paper should have interest both as an account of partial truth and as a partial vindication of the truthmaker framework within which it is developed. For without something like the present framework, it is hard to see how a reasonable alternative account of partial truth might be given.

The concept of partial truth is intimately related to the concept of partial content, since we naturally suppose that a proposition is partially true when some part of it is true. The connection between the two concepts can also be put to work in the opposite direction, since we may provide a semantics for the logic of partial content by appeal to partial truth (as in §9 of Fine 2016). There is also a close connection with the concept of verisimilitude. For a proposition will be partially true when it has 'more truth' than a proposition that is not partially true; and the investigation of the concept of partial truth may, in fact, serve as a useful prolegomenon to the investigation of the more complicated concept of verisimilitude.[1]

The present theory of partial truth is developed almost exclusively at the level of propositions. I say what it is for a proposition, conceived in abstraction from how it might be expressed, to be partially true. One advantage of this approach is that there is then no danger of making illegitimate appeal to the linguistic means by which the proposition is expressed; and a related advantage is that it makes clear in the most direct way possible what the truth-conditions for a statement of partial truth should be. All the same, it would be of interest to supplement the present approach with a more linguistic approach, in which we set up a formal language for making statements of partial truth and specify formal rules for reasoning within such a language. I do not think this would be difficult, but it is not something I have attempted to do.

---

[1] The present paper was written in the mid-2010s but, for a variety of reasons, its publication was delayed. An application of truthmaker semantics to the concept of verisimilitude may be found in Fine (2019).

I begin with an informal introduction to some of the main ideas and conclude with a formal appendix. The introduction and appendix can in principle be read in isolation from the other though they are best read together. The most extensive previous treatment of the topic that I know of is in Humberstone (2003); and a related account of partial truth is given in §1.3 of Yablo (2014). The major difference from Humberstone is that he stipulates the truth-tables for a logic of partial truth while I derive them from an underlying account of partial truth; and the major difference from Yablo is that I provide an account of partial truth directly in terms of truthmakers and not indirectly through the notion of partial content.

I. The Truth-Maker Framework

Let me begin by providing a capsule account of the framework within which we shall be working (a fuller exposition is to be found in Fine 2017a, 2017b). Under what I call the 'unilateral' conception, we may identify a proposition with the set of conditions or 'states' which, intuitively, make it true. These states can be possible, and not merely actual, and we also allow them to be impossible or 'inconsistent'. But what is more important is that we require that the state should be relevant as a whole to the proposition that it makes true—it should, in other words, be an *exact* verifier of the proposition. Exact verification is not minimal verification. The presence of rain and wind exactly verifies the proposition that there is rain or rain and wind but it does not minimally verify the proposition since the mere presence of rain would be sufficient to make the proposition true.

We take the states (or conditions) that serve as the verifiers of propositions to enter into relationships of part-whole. So, for example, the state of rain or of wind will be a part of the state of rain and wind. We also suppose that the fusion of any states will exist. Thus given any states $s_1, s_2, \ldots$, there will exist a fusion $s = s_1 \sqcup s_2 \sqcup \ldots$ of them, formed by putting them 'together'. This means in particular that there will be a 'null' state $\square$, which is the fusion of no states whatever and thereby a part of every state, and a 'full' state ■, which is the fusion of all states and thereby inclusive of every state.

It will often be convenient to subject the propositions under consideration to two mereological constraints:

Closure: The fusion of any non-empty set of verifiers of a proposition is also a verifier of the proposition.

Convexity: Any state that lies between two verifiers of a proposition is also a verifier of the proposition.

Propositions conforming to these two constraints are said to be 'regular'. In the present context, the imposition of this constraint is relatively harmless since the status of a proposition as a partial truth will usually be the same regardless of whether we are looking at a given irregular proposition or its 'regular closure' (the smallest regular proposition to contain it).

We may now define the Boolean operations on propositions. The conjunction of two propositions P and Q is taken to be the set of all states $p \sqcup q$ which are a fusion of a verifier p of P and a verifier q of Q; and the disjunction of two propositions P and Q is taken to be set of those states that verify either P or Q (or the regular closure of this set if we insist upon regularity).

When it comes to negation, we would like to take the verifiers of the negation $\neg P$ of P to be the falsifiers of P. But this raises a difficulty since the set of falsifiers of a proposition are not in general determinable from the set of its verifiers. We therefore adopt a bilateral conception of propositions, under which a proposition P is identified with the pair (P, P') of its set P of verifiers and its set P' of falsifiers.

If we wish to extend the operations of conjunction and disjunction to bilateral propositions, then we should take the conjunction **R** of the bilateral propositions **P** = (P, P') and **Q** = (Q, Q') to be the bilateral proposition (R, R'), where R is the (unilateral) conjunction of P and Q and R' the (unilateral) disjunction of P' and Q' and, similarly, the disjunction **R** of the bilateral propositions **P** = (P, P') and **Q** = (Q, Q') should be taken to be the bilateral proposition (R, R'), where R is the disjunction of P and Q and R' the conjunction of P' and Q'. In this way, we obtain a complete account of the Boolean operations of conjunction, disjunction and negation.

We shall also find it convenient to subject the bilateral propositions to two modal constraints:

Exclusivity: No verifier and falsifier of a proposition should be compatible.

Exhaustivity: Any consistent state is either compatible with a verifier or with a falsifier of any given proposition.

Propositions conforming to these two constraints are said to be 'classical', since the first corresponds to the requirement that a proposition should not be both true and false and the second to the requirement that a proposition should be either true or false.

For many purposes, we are only interested in the positive content of a proposition, i.e. with the set of its verifiers, and so we can ignore its falsifiers and work with the unilateral conception. But for other purposes, we will also be interested in the negative content of a proposition, i.e. with the set of its falsifiers; and, for this reason and for the sake of completeness, we should also work with the bilateral conception.

Two important concepts within the present framework are those of *partial content* and *subject-matter*. Suppose that P and Q are verifiable propositions (in the sense that they each have a verifier). Then the proposition P is said to be part of the content of a proposition Q if: (i) each verifier of P is included in a verifier of Q; and (ii) each verifier of Q contains a verifier of P. The definition may be extended to bilateral propositions by further requiring: (iii) every falsifier of Q' is a falsifier of P'. It is readily verified that the conjuncts P and Q of a conjunction $P \wedge Q$ are part of its content, though it is not in general true that $P \vee Q$ is part of the content of P.

The subject-matter p of a unilateral proposition $P = \{p_1, p_2, ...\}$ is the fusion $p_1 \sqcup p_2 \sqcup ...$ of all of its verifiers $p_1, p_2, ...$ It is, so to speak, the repository of truth for the proposition—the agglomeration of states from which its verifiers are drawn. When a proposition is both regular and verifiable, then its subject-matter will itself be one of the verifiers of the proposition. A bilateral proposition $P = (P, P')$ will have two subject-matters: its *positive* subject-matter p, which is the subject-matter of its set of verifiers P; and its *negative* subject-matter, which is the subject-matter p' of its set of falsifiers P'.

There are a number of interesting subject-theoretic concepts which we may define (further discussion may be found in Fine 2017a). Let me mention two. First, given some arbitrary subject-matter s and an arbitrary proposition P, we may say that P is *partially about s* if p and s overlap, i.e. have a common non-null part. Thus, for a proposition to be about some subject-matter is for the subject-matter to be at least partially relevant to the verification of the proposition. In the second place, given an arbitrary proposition $P = \{p_1, p_2, ...\}$ and some subject-matter s, we may define the *s-content* of P, or the content of P with regard to s, to be the set of states $\{p_1 \sqcap s, p_2 \sqcap s, ...\}$, where each $p_i \sqcap s$ is the common part of p_i and s. Thus, the required restriction of P to s is obtained by restricting the verifiers of P to s. The restriction of the proposition P to the subject-matter s will be part of the content of P (when P is a verifiable proposition). Moreover, the proposition P will be partially about s just in case the restriction of P to s is not completely trivial (consisting only of the null state).

We shall later see how many of the concepts within the theory of partial truth can be regarded as special cases of concepts within the general theory of subject-matter, obtained by taking the subject-matter in question to be the actual world w_0.

II. The Concept of Partial Truth

Let us examine the intuitive concept of partial truth, prior to any attempt to locate it within the truthmaker framework. One reasonable way to explain the concept (though not the only one, as we shall see) is to say that a proposition is partially true if the actual world goes some way towards making it true. But before we can proceed, some preliminary questions about this informal characterization should be cleared up.

In the first place, what if the world goes all the way to making the proposition true, i.e. what if the proposition is true? Does the proposition *thereby fail* to be partially true? Is the whole truth of a proposition a bar to its partial truth? One might, of course, employ the concept of partial truth in this way—to be partially true is to be *merely* partially true. But this exclusive concept of partial truth is perhaps more complex than a concept that allows a true proposition to be partially true; and, in what follows we shall employ the concept in the more inclusive sense.

Consider now the complementary question. Suppose the world goes all the way to making the proposition true, which is to say that the proposition is true. Does the proposition *thereby succeed* in being partially true? If we stick to our original informal characterization, then this is the question of whether the world can go *all* of the way to making the proposition true without going *some* of the way. And it might be thought to be obvious that this is impossible.

But it is not so obvious. For suppose nothing whatever is required of the world to make the proposition true. Some philosophers—especially those of the positivist tradition—have thought that nothing is required of the world to make a logical truth true or perhaps even any necessary truth true. This is not our view. For us, what makes the proposition that it is raining or not raining true is the presence or the absence of rain and what makes the proposition that $2 + 2 = 4$ true is the mathematical fact or state of affairs that $2 + 2 = 4$. So these are not especially convincing examples. But suppose that any number of propositions has a conjunction and that this holds in particular when the number is zero. Consider now the conjunction, call it T, of zero propositions. Then what makes it true? For a conjunction to be true is for all of its conjuncts to be true. And so what is required for the conjunction to be true is that each of an empty set of propositions be true. And what is required for that to be true? Absolutely nothing! There is nothing in the world that we can point to as making T true unless it is a null state, for which nothing is required for it to obtain. Thus it may well be that the world goes *all* of the way to making T true (by doing nothing, so to speak) without going some of the way to making T true (i.e. by doing something).

Before we said that to be partially true is not to be *merely* partially true. But we now appear to be willing to allow that a qualification of 'partially' is in order. For to be partially true is to be *substantially* partially true. The world must actually go some substantive way towards making the proposition true; and, on such a view, we cannot automatically assume that a true proposition will be partially true.

III. Two Puzzles

It goes against the grain to allow that some proposition might be true yet not partially true. But consider the following argument:

(1) Any proposition P is identical to the conjunction (T ∧ P) of the propositions T and P.

For the conjunction of T and P is identical to the conjunction of the conjunction of the empty set ∅ of propositions and the conjunction of the singleton set {P}, which is identical to the conjunction of the union ∅ ∪ {P} = {P} of the two sets, which, in its turn, is identical to the proposition P.

It is also plausible that:

(2) For any propositions Q and R, if the proposition Q is partially true then so is the proposition Q ∧ R.

For it the world goes some way to making Q true then surely it thereby goes some way to making Q ∧ R true.

Let us now assume:

(3) Any true proposition is partially true.

It follows that:

(4) Any proposition is partially true.

This thereby trivializes the distinction between those propositions which are partially true and those which are not. For T is true and hence partially true by (3); so T ∧ P is partially true by (2); and so P = T ∧ P is partially true by (1).

There are a number of different ways in which this puzzle might be resolved: one could deny the existence of a proposition such as T; one could take every proposition to be partially true; or one could deny that every true proposition is thereby partially true. There is something to be said for adopting the first option. But one might wish to admit such propositions as T; and then the most reasonable option is the third. One should allow that a proposition such as T can be true without being partially true.

In what follows, we shall adopt the third option, in conformity with our previous understanding of partial truth as substantial partial truth. But the exceptions to principle (3) will be strictly limited. For it is only when a proposition is *trivially* verified, i.e. verified by the null state, that its truth will not guarantee its partial truth.

There is another puzzle, which does not depend upon the assumption of exotic propositions. We assume (2) as before and also:

(5) Any proposition P is identical to the proposition P ∨ (P ∧ Q).
(6) If the proposition Q is partially true then so is the proposition P ∨ Q.

This latter assumption is very reasonable for if the world goes some way towards making the proposition P true then surely it thereby goes some way towards making the proposition P ∨ Q true.

Given these assumptions, we can now show that any proposition P is partially true, at least on the assumption that some proposition Q is partially true. For then P ∧ Q will be partially true by (2), P ∨ (P ∧ Q) will be partially true by (6), and so P = P ∨ (P ∧ Q) will be partially true by (5).

A brave soul may attempt to solve this puzzle by giving up either (2) or (6). But what the puzzle shows, I believe, is that we should give up (5) and that any satisfactory theory of partial truth must adopt a hyperintensional conception of propositions under which a proposition P is not in general identical to a proposition of the form P ∨ (P ∧ Q).

Suppose, for example, that the proposition that rain is dry is completely false (or not partially true). Then we will still want to allow the proposition that rain is dry or rain is dry and snow is white to be partially true, since snow's being white goes some way to making it true. But how can this be, one might wonder, given that the two propositions are logically equivalent? The answer is that logical equivalence—at least, of the usual sort—is not a good guide to how the world might go towards making a proposition true. For snow's being white will go some way towards making the second proposition true through making its second disjunct true, while it will not go any way towards making the first proposition true. If partial truth is to behave in the way we would like, then the usual intensional conception of propositions must be given up; and I suspect that it is largely through an adherence to an intensional conception of propositions that philosophers have previously found it so difficult to come up with a satisfactory account of partial truth or other such notions.

IV. Variant Notions

There are a number of variants of the intuitive conception of partial truth that might also be considered (and it was, in fact, through developing a more formal theory of partial truth that they came to my attention).

Consider the false proposition that Socrates is foolish. Then this is partially true according to our earlier conception of partial truth since Socrates exists and so the world goes some way, via his existence, to making it true that Socrates is foolish. But the world thereby also goes some way to making it false that Socrates is foolish. For Socrates' being wise makes it false that Socrates is foolish and Socrates existence goes some way to making it the case that Socrates is wise. Thus we here have a case in which the world's going some way to make a proposition true is, in equal measure, the world's going some way in make the proposition false. And it might be thought that, in such a case, the proposition is not properly said to be partially true.

Thus, what is required for partial truth on the current conception is that the world should go some way towards making the proposition true *rather than* false. We require an invidious conception of partial truth in which the world goes some way towards making the proposition true without thereby going some way to making it false. We might in this case talk of *part-wise* truth rather than *partial* truth.

Clearly, any part-wise truth is a partial truth for if the world goes some way to making a proposition true rather than false then it goes some way to making the proposition true. But as the previous example shows, a proposition may be partially true without being part-wise true. Part-wise truth is a more stringent requirement.

It should be noted that part-wise truth may not be well behaved with respect to composition. If a proposition P is partially true, then so are the propositions $P \wedge Q$ and $P \vee Q$. But this is not so for part-wise truth. To take an especially simple example, P may be part-wise truth but $P \wedge \neg P$ will never be part-wise true, since any tendency towards the truth of $P \wedge \neg P$ will equally be a tendency towards falsity.

Another variant notion is *partial lack of falsity*. A proposition is partially lacking in falsity if the world fails to go some way in making it false. In other words, the world would have made the proposition false if only it had not lacked something that was required to make it false. Where partial truth is partial success in being true, partial lack of falsity is partial failure in being false.

It is plausible that partial truth implies partial lack of falsity. But the converse does not hold. For consider a particular space-time point and suppose that it is in fact occupied by the particle p_0 but could have been occupied by the particles p_1, p_2,...or could have been unoccupied. Then the proposition that the point is unoccupied is presumably not partially true. However, it is partially lacking in falsehood. For there is some way, viz. the point being occupied by p_1, in which the world fails to go in making the proposition false.

Thus we have a hierarchy of notions of partial truth, with part-wise truth the most stringent, partial lack of falsity the least stringent, and partial truth in the middle.

There is another variant which might also be considered (and which is orthogonal to the others). Suppose Graham Priest asserts a proposition of the form $P \wedge \neg P$. Then does he assert a proposition that is partially true (granted, as he may not be willing to grant, that it is not true)? One reason, which we have already considered, for saying 'no' is that the world does not go some way to making the proposition true without thereby going some way to making it false. But suppose he now, more cleverly, asserts a proposition of the form $Q \wedge P \wedge \neg P$, where Q is true and independent in subject-matter from P. Is what he asserts now partially true? It is part-wise true since the world in making Q true goes some way to making the proposition $Q \wedge P \wedge \neg P$ true without going some way to making the proposition false. But it might still be thought that the proposition is not partially true since the route provided by Q to the truth is to a dead end; it cannot be realized. Thus, according to this more demanding conception of partial truth, we require that the world should go some way towards realizing a real possibility of the proposition's being true. All that is relevant to the partial truth of the proposition is the genuinely possible ways in which it might be verified.

V. Formal Characterizations

We show how the previous intuitive characterizations can be made formally precise within the truthmaker framework (mathematically rigorous definitions are given in the appendix).

We may take a proposition to be partially true if one of its verifiers overlaps with the actual world, i.e. if a non-null part of one of its verifiers is actual. This is a very natural way to define partial truth within the current truthmaker framework, since for the world to go some way to making the proposition true is for it to contribute a non-null part to some verifier of the proposition.

Recall that the (positive) subject-matter of a proposition is the fusion of its verifiers (and this too is a verifier for a regular verifiable proposition). A simpler form of the definition is then that a proposition is partially true if its positive subject-matter overlaps with the actual world.

We may take a proposition to be part-wise true if some actual part of a verifier of a proposition is not a part of any falsifier of the proposition. Under certain natural assumptions, this is equivalent to saying that the actual part of its positive subject-matter should not be a part of its negative subject-matter—that there is, in this sense, more actuality in its positive subject-matter than in its negative subject-matter.

Finally, we may say that a proposition is lacking in falsity if one of its falsifiers is not part of the actual world. Put in terms of subject-matter, this is equivalent to saying its negative subject-matter is not part of the actual world. There is also a formulation in terms of what one might call anti-actuality. Let $\overline{w}_0$ be the result ■ - w_0 of subtracting actuality from the full state; it is what remains of ■ once we remove any trace of actuality. A proposition will then be partially lacking in falsity if its negative subject-matter overlaps with anti-actuality (just as a proposition is partially true if its positive subject-matter overlaps with actuality).

Note that the last two definitions require appeal to both the verifiers and the falsifiers of the proposition and therefore call for a bilateral conception of propositions, whilst the first definition appeals only to the verifiers of the proposition and can therefore be stated within the unilateral conception.

We may also give analogous definitions on the side of falsehood. A proposition will be partially false, for example, if one of its falsifiers overlaps with the actual world; and so, given that the falsifiers of a proposition are the verifiers of its negation, a proposition will be partially false just in case its negation is partially true. We may also explicate the 'more demanding' criterion of partial truth considered above. For we can insist not merely that a verifier of the proposition overlap with actuality but that a *consistent* verifier of the proposition overlap with actuality (and similarly for the other cases).

Given these definitions, we are in a position to see how the theory of partial truth might be subsumed under the more general theory of subject-matter developed in Fine (2017a, 2017b). In the special case in which we take the subject-matter s under consideration to be actuality, i.e. the actual world w_0, then we see that a proposition P will be partially true if it is partially about that subject-matter. We also see that the restriction of P to the subject-matter s will, in this case, be its truth-content, or the *truth in P*. The truth-content of P will then be part of the content of P; and P will be partially true just in case its truth-content is not completely trivial.

VI. Compositional Principles for Partial Truth and Falsity

For a suitable range of propositions, we can readily establish the following 'compositionality' principles for partial truth and falsity:

(1) $\neg P$ is partially true (false) iff P is partially false (true).
(2) $P \wedge Q$ is partially true (false) iff either P or Q is partially true (false).
(3) $P \vee Q$ is partially true (false) iff either P or Q is partially true (false).

This means that it is possible to determine the partial truth-value status—partial truth or partial falsity—of a Boolean compound on the basis of the partial truth-value status of its components.

Partial truth and partial falsity cannot themselves be regarded as truth-values since they are not exclusive of one another; a proposition, such as Obama is a Muslim president, may be both partially true and partially false. However, we can determine four exclusive truth-values by combining the options. Let us use t and f, respectively, for partial truth and partial falsity and, $\bar{t}$ respectively $\bar{f}$, for the absence of partial truth and the absence of partial falsity. The assignment of t$\bar{f}$ to a proposition, for example, indicates that it is partially true but not partially false. We therefore have the following four combinations of values:

tf   t$\bar{f}$ $\bar{f}$t $\bar{t}\bar{f}$

For which we may use the nomenclature **b** (for both partial truth and falsity), **t** (for exclusive partial truth), **f** (for exclusive partial falsity), and **n** (for neither partial true nor falsity).

If we take the notions of partial truth and falsity to be relative to a world w_0, then the fourth case cannot arise and we simply have the three truth-values **b**, **t** and **f**; for any proposition will be true or false and hence will either have a (non-null) verifier or a (non-null) falsifier. But we may need the fourth value **n** if the notions of partial truth and falsity are taken to be relative to an arbitrary state, since an arbitrary state need not overlap with either the positive or the negative subject-matter of a given proposition.

Whether or not we have the full range of truth-values **b**, **t**, **f**, and **n**, we may, on the basis of the compositional principles (1)–(3) above, work out the truth-tables for these values. Rather than specifying the table in full detail, it may perhaps be more helpful to lay down some general principles by which they can be determined. We may set out the truth-values in the following lattice structure:

The truth-tables for the Boolean operators are then given by the following two principles:

(I) Negation flips the diagram from left to right—thus ¬**b** = **b**, ¬**n** = **n**, ¬**t** = **f** and ¬**f** = **t**.

(II) $x \wedge y$ and $x \vee y$ are each the least upper bound of x and y.

Note that no truth-value other than **n** can lead to **n** and so **n** can safely be omitted from the truth-tables.

We may consider the present 'partial' truth-values in combination with the 'complete' truth-values of 1 (for truth) and 0 (for falsity). As long as truth and partial truth are evaluated relative to a possible world w_0, then any proposition with truth-value **t** (exclusive partial truth) will be true, i.e. assume the value 1 and, likewise, any proposition with truth-value **f** will be false, i.e. assume the value 0; for the proposition will be either true or false and cannot be true without being partially true or false without being partially false.

A proposition that is both partially true and false, on the other hand, can be either true or false. This suggests that we should divide the truth-value **b** into two, depending upon whether we have truth or falsity and leave the two other values—**t** and **f**—alone. This gives us four truth-values in all (since **n** does not enter into the picture).

In computing the truth-values of Boolean compounds, it will be helpful to think of each truth-value as a combination of a partial and a complete truth-value. Thus, **t** will give way to (**t**, 1), **f** to (**f**, 0), and **b** to (**b**, 1) and (**b**, 0). (**t**, 1) corresponds to *pure* truth, i.e. truth without any admixture of falsity, (**f**, 0) to *pure* falsity, i.e. falsity without any admixture of truth, and (**b**, 1) and (**b**, 0) to *impure* truth and falsity.

The computation of truth-values then proceeds in a straightforward component-wise manner. We evaluate on the left according to the previous rules and separately on the right according to the classical truth-tables. So, for example, the conjunction of (**t**, 1) and (**f**, 0) will be (**b**, 0). It should be noted that we will never suffer the embarrassment of having to assign (**t**, 0) or (**f**, 1) to a complex proposition, given that these values are not assigned to any of the component propositions.

When we evaluate truth and partial truth relative to an arbitrary state, then things get more complicated. For the truth and falsity of a proposition, like its partial truth and falsity, will now be independent of one another. There are therefore four values on the right (both truth and falsity, exclusive truth, exclusive falsity, neither truth nor falsity) and four values on the left, both of which are independent of one another. This gives sixteen values in all; and the four values on the left are evaluated as before and the values on the right are evaluated according to the four-valued truth-tables for first-degree entailment.

VII. Partials

I have said what it is for a proposition to be partially true (or partially false), but I have not said what the proposition that a given proposition is partially true is. Given our conception of propositions as sets of verifiers—or sets of verifiers and falsifiers—this is a matter of saying what verifies or falsifies the proposition that a given proposition is partially true or partially false.

A natural response to this question naturally suggests itself within the current framework (though I do not know if it is the only reasonable response that might be given). Call the proposition that a given proposition is partially true the *partial* of that proposition. Then we may take a state to verify the partial of a proposition if it is a non-null part of one of the verifiers of the proposition, for the obtaining of such a state is exactly what is required for the proposition to be partially true. Any falsifier of a partial must 'exclude' the verifiers of the partial; and so we may take a state to falsify a partial just in case it is a non-null part of the given proposition's negative subject-matter and is incompatible with each verifier of the partial. It may be shown, given this definition and under suitable assumptions, that desirable properties of proposition will be preserved under the operation of forming a partial. In particular, the partial of a proposition will be classical when the proposition itself is classical.

The truth-tables for the Boolean operations may be extended to partials. For it may be shown that the partial of a given proposition will be partially true (or partially false) just in case the proposition itself is partially true or partially false. Thus the truth-table for the values **t, f, b** will in effect be the 'identity' table.

The determination of truth and falsity is less straightforward. It may be shown that the partial proposition $P°$ will be true just in case the given proposition P is partially true, just as one would have expected. Thus, the partial operation $°$ will take both (**b**, 1) and (**b**, 0) to (**b**, 1). We thereby lose the component-wise computation of the truth-values since 0, on the right, will sometimes go to 0 (as with (**f**, 0)) and sometimes go to 1 (as with (**b**, 0)).

Formal Appendix

A1. Preliminaries

Recall that $\sqsubseteq$ is a *partial order* (po) *on* S if it is a reflexive, transitive and anti-symmetric relation on S. Given a po $\sqsubseteq$ on S, we shall make use of the following (mostly standard) definitions (with $s, t, u \in S$ and $T \subseteq S$):

s is an *upper bound of* T if $t \sqsubseteq s$ for each $t \in T$.

s is a *least upper bound* (lub) *of* T if s is an upper bound of T and $s \sqsubseteq s'$ for any upper bound s' of T.

s is *null* if $s \sqsubseteq s'$ for each $s' \in S$ and otherwise is *non-null*.

s is *full* if $s' \sqsubseteq s$ for each $s' \in S$.

$s \sqsubset t$ (s is a *proper part of t*) if $s \sqsubseteq t$ but not $t \sqsubseteq s$.

s *overlaps* t if for some non-null u, $u \sqsubseteq s$ and $u \sqsubseteq t$.

s is *disjoint from* t if s does not overlap t.

An (*unmodalized*) *state space* S is a pair $(S, \sqsubseteq)$, where S (*states*) is a non-empty set and $\sqsubseteq$ is a binary relation on S subject to the following two conditions:

Partial Order (PO): $\sqsubseteq$ is a po on S.

Completeness: Any subset of S has a least upper bound.

The least upper bound of $T \subseteq S$ is unique (since if s and s' are least upper bounds, then $s \sqsubseteq s'$ and $s' \sqsubseteq s$ and so, by anti-symmetry, $s = s'$). We denote it by $\sqcup T$ and call it the *fusion of* T (or of the members of T). When $T = \{t_1, t_2, \ldots\}$, we shall often write $\sqcup T$ more perspicuously as $t_1 \sqcup t_2 \sqcup \ldots \sqcup \emptyset$, which we denote by □, is the bottom element of the space and $\sqcup S$, which we denote by ■, is the top element. Given that the least upper bound $\sqcup T$ always exists, it follows that the greatest lower bound $\sqcap T$ will always exist (defined by $\sqcup \{s: \text{for all } t \in T, s \sqsubseteq t\}$).

A space S is said to be *distributive* if $s \sqcap (t_1 \sqcup t_2 \sqcup \ldots) = (s \sqcap t_1) \sqcup (s \sqcap t_2) \sqcup \ldots$ for any $s, t_1, t_2, \ldots \in S$. In what follows, we shall assume that the space is distributive, although not all of our results will depend upon this assumption. In a distributive space, the following principle will hold:

Overlap: if s overlaps $t_1 \sqcup t_2 \sqcup \ldots$ then it overlaps some t_i.

For if s overlaps $t_1 \sqcup t_2 \sqcup \ldots$, then $s \sqcap (t_1 \sqcup t_2 \sqcup \ldots)$ is non-null; so $(s \sqcap t_1) \sqcup (s \sqcap t_2) \sqcup \ldots$ is non-null; so some $s \sqcap t_i$ is non-null; and so s overlaps some t_i.

Given states t and s with $s \sqsubseteq t$, we use $t - s$ for $\sqcup\{r: r \text{ is disjoint from } s \text{ and } r \sqcup s = t\}$. Note that $t - s$, as so defined, is bound to exist and also that, given Overlap, it will be disjoint from s. However, there is no guarantee that $(t - s) \sqcup s = t$. When it is, we dub $r = (t - s)$ the *remainder of t given* $s \sqsubseteq t$; and the space S itself is said to be *remaindered* if it is distributive and if for any states $s, t \in S$ with $s \sqsubseteq t$, the remainder $(t - s)$ exists. We may extend the notion of remainder to arbitrary t and s by taking $t - s = t - (t \sqcap s)$.

We state without proof the following facts about remainders within a remaindered space, to which implicit appeal will sometimes be made in what follows:

(i) $(t - u) \sqcup u = t$ for $u \sqsubseteq t$.
(ii) $t - u$ and u are disjoint.
(iii) If $s \sqsubseteq t$ and is disjoint from $u \sqsubseteq t$ then $s \sqsubseteq t - u$.
(iv) If $t \sqsubseteq t'$ and $s' \sqsubseteq s$ then $t - s \sqsubseteq t' - s'$.
(v) $(s \sqcup t) - u = (s - u) \sqcup (t - u)$.

A *modalized state space* S is an ordered triple $(S, S^\diamond, \sqsubseteq)$, where $(S, \sqsubseteq)$ is an unmodalized state space and $S^\diamond$ (possible states) is a non-empty subset of S subject to:

Downward Closure: $t \in S^\diamond$ whenever $s \in S^\diamond$ and $t \sqsubseteq s$.

We also say that a state s is *consistent* if $s \in S^\diamond$ and *inconsistent* otherwise. A subset T of states is said to be *compatible* if their fusion belongs to $S^\diamond$ and to be *incompatible* otherwise.

A subset I of states from a modalized space $S = (S, S^\diamond, \sqsubseteq)$ is said to be a *consistent ideal* if it satisfies the following three conditions:

(i) Consistency: Each state in I is consistent.
(ii) Upward Closure: Any fusion of some members of I belongs to I if it is consistent.
(iii) Downward Closure: Any part of a member of I is a member of I.

A modalized space is said to be *representative* if for every ideal I there is a state $s \in S$ for which $I = \{t \in S^\diamond: t \sqsubseteq s\}$. Many of the subsequent definitions will make most sense if they are taken to hold within a representative space. Fine (2014) contains information on the construction of representative spaces.

Of special interest are spaces that contain possible worlds. Say that the state s of a modalized space $S = (S, S^\diamond, \sqsubseteq)$ is a *world-state* if it is consistent and if any consistent state is either a part of s or incompatible with s; and say that the space S itself is a *W-space* if every consistent state of S is part of a world-state. It is often helpful to think of ourselves as working within a W-space, although most of our results will not depend upon this assumption.

We will sometimes want to pick out a distinguished world-state of a W-space as the actual world. In this case, we obtain an *actualized* W-space or what I shall also call an *A-space*. This is an ordered quadruple $(S, S^\diamond, w_0, \sqsubseteq)$, where $S = (S, S^\diamond, \sqsubseteq)$ is a W-space and w_0 is a world-state of S. w_0 is called the *actual world* of the actualized W-space and we sometimes denote $\{s: s \sqsubseteq w_0\}$ by A_0. We say that a state s of an actualized world space $(S, S^\diamond, w_0, \sqsubseteq)$ *obtains* or is *actual* if $s \sqsubseteq w_0$, i.e. if $s \in A_0$.

A particular kind of W-space may be constructed from the sentential atoms $p_1, p_2, \ldots$ of some language. Let us denote the negation ¬p of an atom p by p̄ and call the atoms p and their negations *literals*. Then the (*modalized*) *canonical* space S_c over the atoms $\{p_1, p_2, \ldots\}$ is the triple $(S, S^{\Diamond}, \sqsubseteq)$, where:

(i) $S = \{L: L \text{ is a set of literals}\}$.
(ii) $S^{\Diamond} = \{L \in S: L \text{ does not contain both a sentence letter p and its negation p̄}\}$.
(iii) $\sqsubseteq = \{(K, L): K \subseteq L \subseteq S\}$.

In this case, we shall often write p, say, in place of {p} or p̄q in place of {p̄, q}. It is readily verified that S_c is a W-space whose world-states are all sets of literals containing exactly one of p and p̄ for each atom p. We may also convert S_c into an actualized W-space $(S, S^{\Diamond}, w_0, \sqsubseteq)$ by letting $w_0 = \{p: p \text{ a sentence letter}\}$. We assume, in effect, that all the unnegated literals are true (and all the negated literals false).

We shall sometimes have need of product spaces. Given two spaces $S = (S, \sqsubseteq)$ and $S' = (S', \sqsubseteq')$, we define the *product space* $\mathbf{S} \times \mathbf{S}'$ to be $\mathbf{S} = (S \times S', \sqsubseteq^*)$, where:

$(s, t) \sqsubseteq^* (s', t')$ iff $s \sqsubseteq s'$ and $t \sqsubseteq t'$.

We readily show:

Lemma 1: If S and S' are state spaces then so is $\mathbf{S} \times \mathbf{S}'$, with $(s_1, t_1) \sqcup^* (s_2, t_2) \sqcup^* \ldots = (s_1 \sqcup s_2 \sqcup \ldots, t_1 \sqcup t_2 \sqcup \ldots)$ for $s_1, s_2, \ldots \in S$ and $t_1, t_2, \ldots \in T$.

A2. Regular Propositions

Under the 'unilateral' conception, we identify a proposition with a set of states (intuitively, those that verify it) and denote such propositions by the letters '*P*','*Q*','*R*' etc.; and, under the 'bilateral' conception, we identify a proposition with a pair (P, P') of unilateral propositions (intuitively, the set *P* of its verifiers and the set *P'* of its falsifiers) and denote such propositions by the letters '***P***','***Q***','***R***' etc.

A unilateral proposition $P \subseteq S$ is said to be:

Closed (*under fusion*) if $\sqcup Q \in P$ for any non-empty subset Q of P.
Convex if $p \in P$ whenever $p', p^+ \in P$ and $p' \sqsubseteq p \sqsubseteq p^+$.
Semi-regular if convex.
Regular if both convex and closed.

Similarly, a bilateral proposition $\mathbf{P} = (P, P')$ is said to have any of the above properties if they are possessed both by P and by P'.

Given a proposition P, we use P^* for the smallest proposition $Q \supseteq P$ to be closed, P. for the smallest proposition $Q \supseteq P$ to be convex, and $P^*_{.}$ for the smallest proposition $Q \supseteq P$ to be both closed and convex. We also use p for $\sqcup P$. Given that P is non-empty and closed under fusion, $p \in P$; and, in this case, p is the maximal verifier of P. We identify p with the subject-matter of P.

We say that a unilateral proposition P is *true at* a state s if some verifier of P is a part of s; and we say that a bilateral proposition $\mathbf{P} = (P, P')$ is *true at* a state s if P is true at s and that P is *false at* s if P' is true at s. Given an actualized W-space, a unilateral proposition P is said to be *true* simpliciter if it is true at the actual world of the space and a bilateral proposition $\mathbf{P}$ is said to be *false* simpliciter if it is false at the actual world of the space.

A3. Containment and Entailment

Given propositions P and Q from a state space, we say P *contains* Q—in symbols, $P \geq Q$—if (i) for all $p \in P$ there is a $q \in Q$ for which $p \sqsupseteq q$ and (ii) for all $q \in Q$ there is a $p \in P$ for which $q \sqsubseteq p$. We say P *entails* Q if $P \subseteq Q$. We sometimes say Q is a *conjunctive* (*disjunctive*) *part of* P if P is contained in (entails) Q.

A4. Partial Truth

We say that the unilateral proposition P is *partially true* (in an actualized space $S = (S, S^\Diamond, w_0, \sqsubseteq))$ if w_0 overlaps with p and that P is *partially lacking in truth* if $\mathbf{p} \not\sqsubseteq w_0$. The definition is, in effect, relative to the state w_0 and we might also make it relative to any state s whatever. Nearly all of our results will apply to the more general notion, though we shall only state them for the more specific case of partial truth.

We have the following straightforward equivalences (of which we shall often make implicit use):

Lemma 2: For any proposition P, the following are equivalent to one another:

   (i) P is partially true.
   (ii) Some non-null part of p is actual.
   (iii) Some verifier p of P overlaps with w_0.

And the following are also equivalent to one another:

   (iv) P is partially lacking in truth.
   (v) Some part of p is non-actual.
   (vi) $p \not\sqsubseteq w_0$ for some verifier p of P.

Proof:

   (i) ⇒ (ii). Suppose P is partially true. Then p overlaps with w_0. So p and w_0 have a common non-null part and hence some non-null part of p is actual.
   (ii) ⇒ (iii). Suppose some non-null part p of p is actual. p is the fusion $p_1 \sqcup p_2 \sqcup \ldots$ of all of the verifiers $p_1, p_2, \ldots$ of P. By Overlap, p overlaps with a p_i; and hence p is a common non-null part of p_i and w_0.
   (iii) ⇒ (i). Suppose some verifier p of P overlaps with w_0. Since $p \sqsubseteq p$, p overlaps with w_0 and hence P is partially true.
   (iv) ⇒ (v). Suppose P is partially lacking in truth. Then $\mathbf{p} \not\sqsubseteq w_0$; and so p itself is part of p that is non-actual.
   (v) ⇒ (vi). Suppose (vi) is false, i.e. $p \sqsubseteq w_0$ for each verifier p of P. Then $\mathbf{p} \sqsubseteq w_0$ and no part of p is non-actual.
   (vi) ⇒ (iv). Suppose $p \not\sqsubseteq w_0$ for some verifier p of P. Now $p \sqsubseteq \mathbf{p}$; and so $\mathbf{p} \not\sqsubseteq w_0$ and P is partially lacking in truth.

We say that a proposition P is *non-trivially true* if it has a non-null verifier which is actual, that it is *trivially true* if it has the null state as a verifier, that it is *non-trivially lacking in truth* if it is not true and yet distinct from $F_\square$ ($= \emptyset$) and that it is *trivially lacking in truth* if it is identical to $F_\square$.

Lemma 3: For any proposition P:

  (i) P is non-trivially true implies P is partially true.
  (ii) P is non-trivially lacking in truth implies P is partially lacking in truth.

Proof (i): Suppose P is non-trivially true. Then $p \sqsubseteq w_0$ for some non-null verifier $p \in P$. But p is then a common non-null part of $\mathbf{p}$ and w_0 and P is partially true.

(ii) Suppose P is non-trivially lacking in truth. Pick a $p \in P$. Then $p \not\sqsubseteq w_0$; and hence $\mathbf{p} \not\sqsubseteq w_0$ and P is partially lacking in truth.

It should be noted that the mere truth of P does not imply its partial truth and the mere non-truth of P does not imply its partial lack of truth. For suppose that $\square \in P$ but that p does not overlap with w_0. Then P is true, since $\square \sqsubseteq w_0$ but not partially true. Now suppose $P = F_\square$. Then P is lacking in truth and yet not partially lacking in truth.

Taking the regular closure of a proposition makes no difference to its partial truth or lack of truth (though it may make a difference to how they might be characterized):

Lemma 4: For any proposition P:

P is partially true (partially lacking in truth) iff $P^*_\cdot$ is partially true (partially lacking in truth).

Proof: P is partially true iff $\mathbf{p} = \sqcup P$ overlaps with w_0 and $P^*_\cdot$ is partially true iff $\sqcup(P^*_\cdot)$ overlaps with w_0. But $\sqcup P = \sqcup(P^*_\cdot)$; and so P is partially true iff $P^*_\cdot$ is partially true. The proof for partial lack of truth is similar.

The next result states how the notions of partial truth and partial lack of truth 'distribute' over conjunction and disjunction (this is a case in which the results can be derived from more general results on subject-aboutness, as in Fine 2017b).

Theorem 5: For regular verifiable propositions P and Q, the following are equivalent:

  (i) $P \wedge Q$ is partially true (lacking in truth).
  (ii) $P \vee Q$ is partially true (lacking in truth).
  (iii) P is partially true (partially lacking in truth) or Q is partially true (partially lacking in truth).

Proof: Let $R = P \wedge Q$ and $R' = P \vee Q$. Then $\mathbf{r} = \mathbf{r}' = \mathbf{p} \sqcup \mathbf{q}$; and so $P \wedge Q$ is partially true (partially lacking in truth) iff $P \vee Q$ is partially true (partially lacking in truth). This takes care of the equivalence of (i) and (ii) with respect to partial truth and partial lack of truth.

Let us deal next with the equivalence of (i) and (iii) with respect to partial truth. First suppose $R = P \wedge Q$ is partially true. Then w_0 overlaps with $\mathbf{r} = \mathbf{p} \sqcup \mathbf{q}$. By Overlap, w_0 overlaps with $\mathbf{p}$ or with $\mathbf{q}$ and so P or Q is partially true. Now suppose P is partially true (the case in which Q is partially true is similar). Then w_0 overlaps with $\mathbf{p}$ and hence overlaps with $\mathbf{r} = \mathbf{p} \sqcup \mathbf{q}$; and so $P \wedge Q$ is partially true.

Finally, let us deal with the equivalence of (i) and (iii) with respect to partial lack of truth. First suppose $R = P \wedge Q$ is partially lacking in truth. Then $\mathbf{r} = \mathbf{p} \sqcup \mathbf{q} \not\sqsubseteq w_0$. But then either $\mathbf{p} \not\sqsubseteq w_0$ or $\mathbf{q} \not\sqsubseteq w_0$; and so either P or Q is partially lacking in truth.

Now suppose P is partially lacking in truth (the case in which Q is partially lacking in truth is similar). Then $\mathbf{p} \not\sqsubseteq w_0$ and so $\mathbf{r} = \mathbf{p} \sqcup \mathbf{q} \not\sqsubseteq w_0$; and $P \wedge Q$ is partially lacking in truth.

We can readily prove an analogue of the preceding result for infinitary conjunctions and disjunctions. As an almost immediate consequence of the theorem, we have:

Corollary 6: For regular verifiable P and Q, if P is a conjunctive or disjunctive part of Q then the partial truth (partial lack of truth) of P implies the partial truth (partial lack of truth) of Q.

Proof: Suppose P is a conjunctive (disjunctive) part of Q. Then $Q = P \wedge Q$ $(P \vee Q)$ and so by the theorem, if P is partially true (lacking in truth) then so is Q.

We can also state alternative criteria for partial truth (or partial lack of truth) in terms of conjunctive (or disjunctive) part:

Theorem 7: For any regular proposition P:

(i) P is partially true iff it has a regular conjunctive part that is non-trivially true.
(ii) P is partially lacking in truth iff it has a regular disjunctive part that is non-trivially lacking in truth.

Proof: (i) Suppose that P is partially true. Then p overlaps with w_0 and $p \in P$. Let $p' = p \sqcap w_0$ and $P' = [P \cup \{p'\}]^*_\sqsubseteq$. Clearly, P' is regular and it is readily shown that $P' \leq P$. But p' is actual and non-null and so P' is non-trivially true.

Now suppose that P has a conjunctive part P' that is non-trivially true. Then some non-null verifier p' of P' is actual. Since $P' \leq P$, $p' \sqsubseteq p$ for some $p \in P$ and so P is partially true.

(ii) Suppose P is partially lacking in truth. Then $\mathbf{p} \not\sqsubseteq w_0$ with $p \in P$ and so, for some $p' \in P$, $p' \not\sqsubseteq w_0$. Let $P' = \{p'\}$. Clearly, P' is a regular disjunctive part of P and, given that $p' \not\sqsubseteq w_0$, P' is not true and so P' is non-trivially lacking in truth.

Now suppose P has a disjunctive part $P' \subseteq P$ that is non-trivially lacking in truth. Then P' has a member p' for which $p' \not\sqsubseteq w_0$. But $p' \in P$ and so P is partially lacking in truth.

We may also provide an alternative criterion for partial lack of truth in terms of anti-actuality rather than actuality. Given the actual world w_0, let the *anti-world* $\bar{w}_0$ be $\blacksquare - w_0$. We make the following assumption:

World Remainder: If w is a world-state and if $s \not\sqsubseteq w$ then there is a state $s' \sqsubseteq s$ disjoint from w.

This says that when a state s does not obtain in a world there must be some part of the state that is disjoint from the world. Even if this is not a plausible assumption for an arbitrary state t in place of a world-state, it has a great deal of plausibility when t is a world-state.

Theorem 8: Given World Remainder, a proposition P is partially lacking in truth iff p overlaps with the anti-world $\bar{w}_0$ (i.e. iff P is partially about $\bar{w}_0$).

Proof: P is partially lacking in truth
 iff $p \not\sqsubseteq w_0$;
 iff some non-null part of p is disjoint from w_0 (by World Remainder);
 iff p overlaps with $\bar{w}_0$.

We say that the unilateral proposition P is *perfectly true* if it is true but not partially lacking in truth and that P is *perfectly lacking in truth* if it is neither true nor partially true. Say that a state s is *anti-actual* if it is not actual and no non-null part of it is actual—or, equivalently, if it is non-null and no non-null part of it is actual. We then have the following criteria for perfect truth and the perfect lack of truth.

Theorem 9: For any proposition P:

(i) P is perfectly true iff it is distinct from F_0 and all of its verifiers are actual
iff it is distinct from F_0 and $\boldsymbol{p}$ is actual.
(ii) P is perfectly lacking in truth iff all of its verifiers are anti-actual
iff P is identical to F_0 or $\boldsymbol{p}$ is anti-actual and $\square \notin P$.

Proof: (i) Suppose P is perfectly true. Then it is true and hence has a verifier and is distinct from F_0. Suppose now, for reductio, that one of the verifiers p of P is non-actual. Then $p \not\sqsubseteq w_0$ and hence $\boldsymbol{p} \not\sqsubseteq w_0$ and P is partially lacking in truth.

Suppose P is distinct from F_0 and all of its verifiers $p_1, p_2, \ldots$ are actual. Then $\boldsymbol{p} = p_1 \sqcup p_2 \sqcup \ldots$ is actual (thereby establishing the second equivalent).

Finally, suppose P is distinct from F_0 and $\boldsymbol{p}$ is actual. Then P has a verifier $p \sqsubseteq \boldsymbol{p}$. But p is actual and so P is true. Also, $\boldsymbol{p} \sqsubseteq w_0$ and so P is not lacking in truth.

(ii) Suppose the second equivalent is false, i.e. some verifier p of P is not anti-actual. Then either (a) it is actual or (b) it contains a non-null actual part p'. In case (a), P is true and in case (b), $\boldsymbol{p}$ overlaps with w_0 and so P is partially true. In neither case is P perfectly lacking in truth.

Suppose now that all of the verifiers of $p_1, p_2, \ldots$ of P are anti-actual and that P is not identical to F_0 (to show $\boldsymbol{p}$ is anti-actual and $\square \notin P$). Clearly, $\square \notin P$. Also, $\boldsymbol{p} = p_1 \sqcup p_2 \sqcup \ldots$ is anti-actual. For clearly, it is non-null since the p_i are non-null and there are some p_i. Moreover, if $\boldsymbol{p}$ had an actual non-null part q then q would overlap with some p_i and so p_i would not be anti-actual after all.

Finally, suppose P is identical to F_0 or $\boldsymbol{p}$ is anti-actual and $\square \notin P$. In case P is identical to F_0, P is neither true nor partially true and hence P is perfectly lacking in truth. So suppose $\boldsymbol{p}$ is anti-actual and $\square \notin P$. Then $\boldsymbol{p}$ does not overlap with w_0 and so P is not partially true. Moreover, P is not true since otherwise it would contain a non-null actual verifier p and $\boldsymbol{p} \sqsupseteq p$ would not be anti-actual.

We should note that the most perfect truth, of which all other perfect truths are part, is *the whole truth*, i.e. the proposition $P_t = \{w_0\}$. For clearly, $\boldsymbol{p}_t = w_0$ and so P_t is a perfect truth. Moreover, if P is a perfect truth then w_0 contains each verifier p of P and each verifier p of P is contained in w_0; and so each perfect truth is a part of P_t.

We turn to the topic of the truth or truthless content of a proposition. We take the *truth-content* P^t of the unilateral proposition P to be $\{p \sqcap w_0 : p \in P\}$ and the *truthless-content* $P^{\bar{t}}$ to be $\{p \sqcap \bar{w}_0 : p \in P\}$. Within the canonical space, the truth content of $\{p\bar{q}, \bar{p}q\}$, for example, will be $\{p, q\}$ while its truthless-content will be $\{\bar{q}, \bar{p}\}$. These notions are special cases of a more general concept. Where s is a state (intuitively, some subject-matter) and P a proposition, then the restriction P^s of P to s is taken to be the proposition $\{p \sqcap s : p \in P\}$. Thus, P^t is the special case of P^s in which the subject-matter s is actuality and $P^{\bar{t}}$ is the special case of P^s in which the subject-matter s is anti-actuality. In connection with the theory of verisimilitude, we might also wish to consider the case in which s some particular part of actuality, such as physical actuality or nomic actuality.

We have the following connection between truth and truthless content, on the one hand, and the perfect truth or lack of partial truth, on the other.

Theorem 10: For P a verifiable proposition:

(i) P^t is the greatest conjunctive part of P to be perfectly true.
(ii) P^f is the greatest conjunctive part of P that fails to be partially true.

Proof: (i) $P^t = \{p \sqcap w_0 : p \in P\}$. Since P has a verifier p, P^t has a verifier $p \sqcap w_0$, which is actual, and so P^t is true. Clearly, for every member $q = p \sqcap w_0$ of P^t, $q \sqsubseteq w_0$ and so P^t is not partially lacking in truth. Thus, P^t is perfectly true.

Also, P^t is a conjunctive part of P. For take $p \in P$. Then $p \sqcap w_0 \in P^t$, with $p \sqcap w_0 \sqsubseteq p$. Now take $q \in P^t$. Then q is of the form $p \sqcap w_0$ for $p \in P$ and $q \sqsubseteq p$.

To show P^t is the greatest such part, suppose that Q is a conjunctive part of P and is perfectly true. Then for each member $q \sqsubseteq Q$, $q \sqsubseteq w_0$. Since Q is a conjunctive part of P, $q \sqsubseteq p$ for some $p \in P$. But then $q = q \sqcap w_0 \sqsubseteq p \sqcap w_0 \in P^t$. Now suppose $p \sqcap w_0 \in P^t$ for $p \in P$. Since Q is a conjunctive part of P, there is a $q \in Q$ for which $q \sqsubseteq p$. But then $q = q \sqcap w_0 \sqsubseteq p \sqcap w_0 \in P^t$. It follows that Q is a conjunctive part of P^t.

(ii) $P^f = \{p \sqcap \bar{w}_0 : p \in P\}$. Clearly, no member $p \sqcap \bar{w}_0$ overlaps with w_0 and so P is not partially true.

The rest of the proof is as for the first part but with $\bar{w}_0$ in place of w_0.

We have a characterization of partial truth and partial lack of truth in terms of truth- and truthless-content.

Theorem 11: For any proposition P:

(i) P is partially true iff P^t is distinct from $T_\square$ and $F_\square$.
(ii) P is partially lacking in truth iff P^f is distinct from $T_\square$ and $F_\square$ (given World Remainder).

Proof: (i) Suppose P is partially true. Then some $p \in P$ overlaps with w_0, i.e. $p \sqcap w_0 \in P^t$ is non-null. But then P^t is distinct from $T_\square$ and $F_\square$.

Suppose P^t is distinct from $T_\square$ and $F_\square$. Then P^t contains a non-null actual member $q = p \sqcap w_0$ with $p \in P$. But then q is a common non-null part of p and w_0 and P is partially true.

(ii) Suppose P is partially lacking in truth. Then $p \not\sqsubseteq w_0$ for some verifier p of P. By World Remainder, $p \sqcap \bar{w}_0 \in P^f$ is non-null and so P^f is distinct from $T_\square$ and $F_\square$.

Suppose P^f is distinct from $T_\square$ and $F_\square$. Then some member $q = p \sqcap \bar{w}_0$ of P^f, with $p \in P$, is non-null. But then q is a common non-null part of p and $\bar{w}_0$ and hence of p and $\bar{w}_0$ and so, by theorem 8, P is partially lacking in truth.

Let us extend the previous definitions and results to bilateral propositions. Given an arbitrary bilateral proposition $\mathbf{P} = (P, P')$, we make the following definitions:

$\mathbf{P}$ is *partially true* if P is partially true.
$\mathbf{P}$ is *partially lacking in truth* if P is partially lacking in truth.
$\mathbf{P}$ is *part-wise true* if $p \sqcap w_0 \not\sqsubseteq p'$.
$\mathbf{P}$ is *partially false* (*partially lacking in falsity*, *part-wise false*) if $\neg \mathbf{P}$ is partially true (partially lacking in truth, part-wise true).

Note that the partial truth and partial lack of truth of $\mathbf{P}$ just depends upon its positive content and the partial falsity and lack of falsity of $\mathbf{P}$ just depends upon its negative content, while the part-wise truth and falsity of $\mathbf{P}$ depends upon both its positive and its negative content, with the part-wise truth of a proposition requiring that the actual world go some way towards making the proposition true as opposed to false and with the part-wise falsity of a proposition requiring that the actual world go some way towards making the proposition false as opposed to true.

We have the following alternative characterization of part-wise truth:

Theorem 12: For any regular falsifiable bilateral proposition P, P is part-wise true just in case some actual part of a verifier of P is not a part of any falsifier of P.

Proof: Suppose P is part-wise true. Then $p \sqcap w_0 \not\sqsubseteq p'$. So $p \sqcap w_0$ and hence p is non-null. But then given that P is regular, p is a verifier of P; and so the actual part $p \sqcap w_0$ of the verifier p of P is not part of any falsifier p' of P, given that $p' \sqsubseteq p'$.

Now suppose some actual part q of a verifier p of P is not part of any falsifier of P. Given P is a regular falsifiable proposition, p' is a falsifier of P; and so $q \not\sqsubseteq p'$. But then $p \sqcap w_0 \not\sqsubseteq p'$ and, given that $p \sqsubseteq p$, $p \sqcap w_0 \not\sqsubseteq p'$.

Note that this result does not hold for the regular but unfalsifiable proposition $P = T_\square$ ($= (T_\square, F_\square)$). For $p = p' = \square$; and so $T_\square$ is not part-wise true even though some actual part $\square$ of a verifier $\square$ of $T_\square$ is not part of any falsifier of $T_\square$, given that $T_\square$ has no falsifiers.

Say that the bilateral proposition $P = (P, P')$ is *normal* if p is incompatible with any non-null part of p' and p' is incompatible with any non-null part of p. We can then show, under plausible assumptions, that the three part-theoretic notions of truth form a hierarchy (and similarly for the three part-theoretic notions of falsity):

Theorem 13: For any proposition $P = (P, P')$:

(i) If P is part-wise true then P is partially true.
(ii) If P is partially true then P is partially lacking in falsity, for normal P.

Proof (i) Suppose P is part-wise true. Then $p \sqcap w_0 \not\sqsubseteq p'$. Hence $p \sqcap w_0$ is non-null and P is partially true.

(ii) Suppose P is partially true yet not partially lacking in falsity. Then $p \sqcap w_0$ is non-null and $p' \sqsubseteq w_0$. So $p \sqcap w_0$ is a non-null part of p compatible with p', contrary to the normalcy of P.

Informal counter-examples to these implications are given in the informal introduction and are readily converted into formal counter-examples.

Clearly, the compositional results in theorem 5 can now be extended to partial truth and lack of truth and to partial falsity and lack of falsity for bilateral propositions; and it trivially follows that $\neg P$ will be partially true (lacking in truth) or partially false (lacking in falsity) just in case P is partially false (lacking in falsity) or partially true (lacking in truth). We summarize these results, in the case of partial truth and falsity, below:

Theorem 14: For regular non-vacuous propositions P and Q:

(i) $\neg P$ is partially true (false) iff P is partially false (true).
(ii) $(P \wedge Q)$ is partially true (false) iff P or Q is partially true (false).
(iii) $(P \vee Q)$ is partially true (false) iff P or Q is partially true (false).

We have analogous results for partial lack of truth or falsity, though not for part-wise truth or falsity. Thus P may be part-wise true or part-wise false while $P \wedge \neg P$ is neither.

A5. Embedding

Given a unilateral proposition P, we take P° (the *partial truth of P*) to be the proposition $\{q: q \text{ is non-null and } q \sqsubseteq p \text{ for some } p \in P\}$. We should note that, for regular P, $P^\circ = \{q: q \text{ is non-null and } q \sqsubseteq p\}$.

Say that a proposition P is *non-trivial* if it has a non-null verifier. We then have the following basic results concerning P°:

Lemma 15:

(i) P° is convex and if P is closed or regular then so is P°.
(ii) if P is not trivially true then (a) $P \leq_d P^\circ$ and (b) $P^\circ \leq_c P$.
(iii) P° is non-trivial iff P° is verifiable
 iff P is distinct from $T_\square$ and $F_\square$.
(iv) P is partially true iff P° is true
 iff P° is partially true.
(v) If P° is not true then P° is perfectly lacking in truth.
(vi) $p^\circ = p$.

Proof: (i) Take $q' \sqsubseteq q \sqsubseteq q^+$, with $q', q^+ \in P^\circ$. Then q' is non-null and so q is non-null. Moreover, $q^+ \sqsubseteq p$ for some $p \in P$; and so $q \sqsubseteq p$. But then $q \in P^\circ$.

Now suppose P is closed and take some $q_1, q_2, \ldots \in P^\circ$. Then $q_1, q_2, \ldots$ are non-null and $q_1 \sqsubseteq p_1, q_2 \sqsubseteq p_2, \ldots$ for some $p_1, p_2, \ldots \in P$. But then $q_1 \sqcup q_2 \sqcup \ldots$ is non-null and $q_1 \sqcup q_2 \sqcup \ldots \sqsubseteq p_1 \sqcup p_2 \sqcup \ldots \in P$; and so $q_1 \sqcup q_2 \sqcup \ldots \in P^\circ$.

(ii) (a) Suppose $p \in P$. Then p is non-null, given that P is non-trivial, and so $p \in P^\circ$.

(ii) (b) Suppose $q \in P^\circ$. Then $q \sqsubseteq p$ for some $p \in P$. Now suppose $p \in P$. Then p is non-null, given that P is non-trivial, and so $p \sqsupseteq p \in P^\circ$.

(iii) Clearly, if P° is non-trivial then it is verifiable and if it is verifiable then it is non-trivial, since any verifier of P° must be non-null. So we focus on the second equivalence.

Suppose P° is verifiable. Then for some non-null $q \in P^\circ$ and $p \in P$, $q \sqsubseteq p$. But then $p \in P$ is non-null; and so P is distinct from $T_\square$ and $F_\square$.

Now suppose P is distinct from $T_\square$ and $F_\square$. Then P contains a non-null member p. But then $p \in P^\circ$ and P° is verifiable.

(iv) Suppose P is partially true. Then $q = p \sqcap w_0$ is non-null for some $p \in P$; and so, given that $q \in P^\circ$, P° is true.

Suppose P° is true. Then some $q \in P^\circ$ is actual. But q is non-null; and so q overlaps with w_0 and P° is partially true.

Suppose $Q = P^\circ$ is partially true. Then $q \sqcap w_0$ is non-null. But $q = p$; and so $p \sqcap w_0$ is non-null and P is partially true.

(v) From (iv), since if P° is not true then P° is neither true nor partially true and hence is perfectly lacking in truth.

(vi) If P is identical to $T_\square$ or $F_\square$ then $p = \square$. By (iii), P° is unverifiable and so also $p^\circ = \square$. Now suppose P is distinct from $T_\square$ and $F_\square$. By (iii) again, P° is non-trivial; and so $p^\circ = p$.

A THEORY OF PARTIAL TRUTH   105

We also have the following quasi-algebraic results:

Lemma 16: For any proposition P:

  (i) $P \subseteq P^\circ$, for P not trivially true.
  (ii) $(P^\circ)^\circ = P^\circ$.
  (iii) $P \subseteq Q$ implies $P^\circ \subseteq Q^\circ$.
  (iv) $(P \wedge Q)^\circ = (P \vee Q)^\circ = (P^\circ \vee Q^\circ)$ for regular verifiable propositions P and Q.

Proof:

  (i) From lemma 15(ii)(a).
  (ii) P° is not trivially true; and so by (i), $P^\circ \subseteq P^{\circ\circ}$. Also, from the transitivity of $\sqsubseteq$, $P^{\circ\circ} \subseteq P^\circ$.
  (iii) Clear from the definition.
  (iv) The subject-matter $p \sqcup q$ of $(P \wedge Q)$ and $(P \vee Q)$ is the same and so $(P \wedge Q)^\circ = (P \vee Q)^\circ$. Now $P \subseteq (P \vee Q)$; and so $P^\circ \subseteq (P \vee Q)^\circ$ by (iii). Similarly, $Q^\circ \subseteq (P \vee Q)^\circ$. So $(P^\circ \vee Q^\circ) \subseteq (P \vee Q)^\circ$ and, consequently, $(P^\circ \vee Q^\circ) \subseteq (P \vee Q)^\circ = (P \vee Q)^\circ$ given that $(P \vee Q)^\circ$ is regular by lemma 15(i).
  For the other direction, suppose $r \in (P \vee Q)^\circ$. Then r is non-null and $r \sqsubseteq p \sqcup q$. r is of the form $r \sqcap (p \sqcup q) = (r \sqcap p) \sqcup (r \sqcap q)$. If $(r \sqcap q)$ is null, then $r \sqsubseteq p$; and so $r \in (P^\circ \vee Q^\circ)$. Similarly, $r \in (P^\circ \vee Q^\circ)$ if $(r \sqcap p)$ is null. So suppose $(r \sqcap p)$ and $(r \sqcap q)$ are both non-null. Since $(r \sqcap p) \sqsubseteq p$ and $(r \sqcap q) \sqsubseteq q$, $(r \sqcap p) \in P^\circ$ and $(r \sqcap q) \in Q^\circ$; and so $r = (r \sqcap p) \sqcup (r \sqcap q) \in (P^\circ \vee Q^\circ)$.

We turn to the bilateral case. Our aim here is to develop a theory of partial truth with satisfactory modal properties and, for simplicity, we assume that the bilateral propositions in question are regular.

Given a regular bilateral proposition $P = (P, P')$, let its *partial* be $P^\circ = (P^\circ, P)$, where P° is as before and $P = \{p' \sqsubseteq p'$: p' is non-null and incompatible with each verifier p of $P^\circ\}$. We might say that t is *through and through* incompatible with s if t is non-null and incompatible with any non-null part of s. P will then be the set of states included in p' that are through and through incompatible with p. Note that P depends on both p and p' and not just on p'. It is readily verified that P° will be regular when P is regular.

Say that a state s is *necessary* if it is compatible with every consistent state and that it is *contingent* if it is neither necessary nor inconsistent. In order to get a smooth theory, we shall take ourselves to be working within a W-space and shall adopt the following special forms of the Exclusivity condition (Exc) and the Exhaustivity condition (Exh) on the subject-matters of a regular proposition $P = (P, P')$:

Special Exclusivity (S-Exc): If p (or p') contains a necessary non-null part then p' (resp. p) is inconsistent.

Strong Exhaustivity (S-Exh): If the world-state w is incompatible with some consistent part s of p (or p') then it contains some part of p' (resp. p) that is incompatible with s.

Note that (S-Exh) and (S-Exh) are essentially condition S on the positive and negative subject-matters p and p' of the proposition P (rather than on the respective sets P and P' of its verifiers and its falsifiers). It is easy to show, for any regular proposition $P = (P, P')$, that p' is inconsistent iff some falsifier $p' \in P'$ of P is inconsistent and that p contains a necessary non-null part iff some verifier $p \in P$ of P contains a necessary non-null part (and similarly with P and P' reversed). Thus in this case S-Exc (on the positive side) takes the form:

If some verifier of P contains a necessary non-null part then some falsifier of P is inconsistent;

and what perhaps justifies the condition is that if some verifier p from P contains a necessary non-null part s then there should be a falsifier from P' that is incompatible with p by way of containing a part that is incompatible with s.

Likewise, it may be shown, in the case of regular propositions, that S-Exh (on the positive side) is equivalent to:

If the world-state w is incompatible with some consistent part s of a verifier of P then it contains some part of a falsifier of P that is incompatible with s;

and what perhaps justifies the condition in this case is that if some verifier does not obtain in a world through containing a consistent part that does not obtain in the world then there should be a falsifier which obtains in the world and whose presence accounts for the absence of the part in the world.

We have the following simple result on the positive and negative subject-matter of $P°$:

Theorem 17: Suppose that the regular bilateral proposition $P = (P, P')$ conforms to S-Exc and S-Exh and let $P° = (P°, P)$. Then $p° = p$ and $p = p'$.

Proof: It follows from lemma 12(vi) that $p° = p$. It follows from the definition of P that $p'_o \sqsubseteq p'$. So it remains to show $p' \sqsubseteq p'_o$. We distinguish three cases. (a) p' is null. Then clearly $p' \sqsubseteq p'_o$. (b) p' is non-null and p contains a necessary non-null part. By S-Exc, p' is inconsistent. But then p' is thereby incompatible with every member of $P°$ and so, given that p' is non-null, $p' \in P'_o$ and hence $p' \sqsubseteq p'_o$ (c) p' is non-null and p does not contain a necessary non-null part. Then the consistent members $p_1, p_2, \ldots$ of $P°$ are all contingent, i.e. non-necessary. So for each p_i there is a consistent state q_i, and hence a world-state w_i, incompatible with p_i. By S-Exh, p' contains, for each p_i, a state r_i incompatible with p_i. But then $r = r_1 \sqcup r_2 \sqcup \ldots$ is non-null and incompatible with each member of $P°$. Hence $r \in P'_o$; and, since $r \sqsubseteq p', p' \in P'_o$ and so $p' \sqsubseteq p'_o$.

Note that it follows from the above proof that if p' is non-null then $p' \in P'_o$ (and otherwise, of course, $p' \notin P'_o$). We immediately obtain an extension of lemma 15(iv) to bilateral propositions:

Corollary 19: For any regular bilateral proposition $P = (P, P')$:

(i) $P°$ is true iff P is partially true.
(ii) $P°$ is partially true iff P is partially true.
(iii) $P°$ is partially false iff P is partially false (given S-Exc and S-Exh).

Proof: (i) and (ii) follow immediately from lemma 15(iv). From the previous theorem, p and p' are the same. But $P°$ is partially false iff p overlaps with w_0 and P is partially false iff p' overlaps with w_0.

This result in conjunction with theorem 14 enables us to determine, in compositional manner, the partial truth, the partial falsity and the truth of a proposition constructed with the help of the Boolean operations and the partial operation °. However, the result does not apply when we evaluate truth and falsity relative to an arbitrary state, for we can then no longer say that $P°$ is false when it is not true and no other rule for the evaluation of the falsity of $P°$ suggests itself.

It will be helpful to show that the current conditions will be preserved under the formation of Boolean compounds and partials:

Lemma 20: For regular P and Q:

(i) If P satisfies S-Exc or S-Exh then so does $\neg P$.
(ii) If P and Q satisfy S-Exc or S-Exh then so does $P \wedge Q$ (for verifiable P and Q) and so does $P \vee Q$ (for falsifiable P and Q).
(iii) P° satisfies Exclusivity, if P satisfies S-Exc or S-Exh then so does P°, and if P satisfies S-Exh then P° satisfies Exhaustivity.

Proof:

(i) Suppose P satisfies S-Exc or S-Exh. Then it is evident from the symmetry of the conditions that the same is true of $\neg P$.

(ii) We focus on the case of $R = P \wedge Q$, since the case of $P \vee Q$ is similar (as is the infinitary case). We then have $r = p \sqcup q$ and $r' = p' \sqcup q'$.

Suppose first that P and Q satisfy S-Exc and that $r = p \sqcup q$ contains a necessary non-null part s (the case in which $r' = p' \sqcup q'$ contains a necessary non-null part is similar). Then $s = s \sqcap (p \sqcup q) = (s \sqcap p) \sqcup (s \sqcap q)$. Since s is non-null, $(s \sqcap p)$ or $(s \sqcap q)$ is non-null. Say it is $(s \sqcap p)$. Then $(s \sqcap p) \sqsubseteq s$ and so $(s \sqcap p)$ is also necessary. By S-Exc, p' is inconsistent and hence $r' = p' \sqcup q'$ is inconsistent.

Now suppose that P and Q satisfy S-Exh and that the world-state w is incompatible with some consistent part s of $r = p \sqcup q$. Now $s = s \sqcap (p \sqcup q) = (s \sqcap p) \sqcup (s \sqcap q)$ and so either $(s \sqcap p) \not\sqsubseteq w$ or $(s \sqcap q) \not\sqsubseteq w$ since otherwise $s = (s \sqcap p) \sqcup (s \sqcap q) \sqsubseteq w$ and s is not incompatible with w. Say $s' = (s \sqcap p) \not\sqsubseteq w$. Then s' is incompatible with w. By S-Exh, w contains a part of p' that is incompatible with s'. But then w contains a part of $r' = p' \sqcup q'$ that is incompatible with s.

(iii) It follows from the definition of P° that P° satisfies Exclusivity. It also follows from theorem 17 that if P satisfies S-Exc or S-Exh then so does P°. This leaves the Exhaustivity case. Suppose P satisfies S-Exh and consider a world-state w that is incompatible with each verifier from P°. Let $p_1, p_2, \ldots$ be all of the consistent verifiers from P°. It follows from S-Exh that, for each i, w contains a part q_i of p' that is incompatible with p_i. Let $q = q_1 \sqcup q_2 \sqcup \ldots$. Then q is incompatible with each verifier from P°, $q \sqsubseteq p'$ and is non-null, and hence $q \in P$. Moreover, $q \sqsubseteq w$ and hence is compatible with w.

Summing up:

Theorem 21: The class of regular non-vacuous propositions satisfying Exc, Exh, S-Exc and S-Exh is closed under negation, conjunction, disjunction and partials.

References

Fine K. 2014. "Truthmaker semantics for intuitionistic logic." *Journal of Philosophical Logic* 43(2): 549–77; repr. in *Philosophers' Annual* for 2014.
Fine K. 2016. "Angellic content." *Journal of Philosophical Logic* 45(2): 199–226.
Fine K., 2017a. "A theory of truthmaker content I: conjunction, disjunction and negation." *Journal of Philosophical Logic* 46(6): 625–74, doi: 10.1007/s10992-016-9413-y.
Fine K. 2017b. "A theory of truthmaker content II: subject-matter, common content, remainder and ground." *Journal of Philosophical Logic* 46(6): 675–702, doi: 10.1007/s10992-016-9419-5.

Fine K. 2019. "Verisimilitude and truth-making." *Erkenntnis* 86(5): 1239–76.
Humberstone L. 2003. "False though partly true: an experiment in logic." *Journal of Philosophical Logic* 32: 613–65.
Yablo S. 2014. *Aboutness*. Princeton: Princeton University Press.

Relevance without Minimality

Stephen Yablo

I. Introduction

A notion that comes up everywhere in philosophy is that of a circumstance "contributing" to a result or outcome—or being a "factor" in, or "helpful" or "relevant" to, the result or outcome.[1] One is looking in most cases for a Q that is *wholly* helpful: free of irrelevant accretions making no real difference.

Causes should bear positively on their effects. Material to which an effect is not beholden should be kept as far as possible out of the cause. An argument's premises, or the assumptions employed in a proof, should help to make the case for its conclusion. If a premise can be dropped without invalidating the argument, it probably shouldn't have been there in the first place.

Grounds should contribute to what they ground, both in toto and throughout. That it would redress an injustice is a reason for φ-ing only if its redressing the injustice counts in favor of φ-ing. Insofar as other properties of φ-ing (it is normally done at night) do not count in its favor, these other properties do not form part of the reason for φ-ing. An observation does not confirm a hypothesis if it is irrelevant to whether the hypothesis is true. One would not expect an irrelevant observation to figure in the evidence for that hypothesis.[2]

This last example, of confirming P or figuring in the evidence for it, helps to clarify the kind of relevance at issue. Hempel distinguishes three notions of confirmation—absolute, comparative, and quantitative—to focus attention on the first (Hempel 1945). Quantitative confirmation theory tries to develop measures of the extent to which Q confirms P. Comparative confirmation theory tries to make sense of Q confirming P *more* than Q' confirms P. Absolute confirmation

---

[1] Versions of this material were presented at Harvard (as the 2016 Whitehead Lectures), Rutgers (at the 2017 Unstructured Conference), Sydney, Monash, ANU, Otago, Toronto, Amsterdam, UNAM and elsewhere. I owe thanks to Lloyd Humberstone, Tim Williamson, Nathaniel Baron-Schmitt, Daniel Muñoz, Brad Skow, Sally Haslanger, Kit Fine, Andy Egan, Dirk Kindermann, Sam Carter, Cian Dorr, Daniel Hoek, Friederike Moltmann, Agustín Rayo, Melisa Vivanco, Axel Barceló, Katrin Shulz, Robert van Rooy, Francesco Berto, Ivano Ciardelli, Floris Roelofsen, Kenny Easwaran, Roxanne Kurtz, Ned Hall, Christine Korsgaard, Laura Schroeter, Greg Restall, Frank Jackson and David Chalmers.

[2] I am hedging a bit because Q need not be "intrinsically" relevant to be relevant in the circumstances.

is a binary affair, both in involving two elements—Q and P—and allowing only two verdicts: Q confirms P, or else it fails to confirm P. Hempel mentions comparative and quantitative confirmation only to set them aside for a later stage of the investigation.

Relevance in the sense of this chapter is a binary affair too. Z contributes to Y, or it does not, period.[3] Not a lot will be said about comparative helpfulness, or degrees of helpfulness. Various other subtleties will be set aside as well. Our focus will be on actual, rather than generic, or potential helpfulness. This means, first, that Z is helpful to Y only if both obtain.[4] Also that a factor that normally works against Y—Y holds, if it does, *despite* this factor—may yet be helpful to it on a particular occasion, and vice versa. Likewise a normally neutral Z may join forces with Y's friends on some occasions, and its enemies on others.

Plan of the chapter: Relevance is usually explained in terms of notions like *minimality, difference-making, essentiality,* and *non-redundancy*. This sort of explanation is reviewed in the next two sections, first from an analytic, then a quasi-historical perspective. We will see that it does not get to the heart of things. Z can still contribute to Y even if Z does not figure indispensably in the conditions for Y, and even where minimality considerations do not apply. The problem is seen to have hyperintensional aspects. A diagnosis is attempted and a solution sketched in terms of "focused" minimality, or minimality where a certain subject matter is concerned.

II. Dependence

One imagines to begin with that Z contributes to Y just if Y counterfactually depends on Z, that is, Y would not have obtained if not for Z. Writing $\gg$ for the counterfactual conditional and using an upper bar for negation:

[C1] Z contributes to Y just if: $\bar{Z} \gg \bar{Y}$.

This will not long satisfy us, for a couple of reasons. One is that Z and Y will in some applications (grounding, entailment,....) be necessary truths. $\bar{Z} \gg \bar{Y}$ is in that case a counterpossible conditional. These are at least as theoretically elusive as positive relevance, and raise a lot of the same problems, for example to do with hyperintensionality.

The second reason not to rest too much on counterfactuals comes from the theory of causation. Z can contribute causally to Y even if Y would still have

---

[3] Helpfulness may be contingent on other facts, but they are not among its relata.
[4] Just as both need to obtain for Y to hold despite Z. Helpfulness in our sense is something like the opposite of despiteness.

obtained (on some alternative basis) in Z's absence. The mismatch is often explained as follows.[5] Y depends on Z if an X obtains with four properties:

(i) X contains Z.
(ii) X suffices for Y ($X \Rightarrow Y$).
(iii) X\Z does not suffice for Y ($X\backslash Z \not\Rightarrow Y$).
(iv) Y is not overdetermined—there is no backup condition B (actual or counterfactual) that would do the job if X didn't.

But, granted that Y does not *depend* on Z if Y is overdetermined, why should this undermine Z's claim to be making a contribution? Whether there are, or would be, other contributors about, even ones sufficient for Y, seems just irrelevant to the issue of whether Z itself contributes to Y. This suggests our focus should not have been on dependence, but a deeper fact (defined by (i)–(iii)) that sometimes *makes for* dependence:

[C2] Z contributes to Y just if:
Z is part of an actual X such that $X \Rightarrow Y$, but $X\backslash Z \not\Rightarrow Y$.

Merely counterfactual backups drop out of the picture on this approach. Alternative *actual* backups are taken in stride and seen as posing no threat. X need not be in any sense unique, on [C2], for Z to qualify as helpful to Y by figuring essentially in X. Z achieves relevance by pulling an "almost" sufficient condition A (aka X\Z) over the finish line: A does not itself suffice for Y, but A+Z suffices.

A problem remains. Z could pull A over the finish line even if it was partly irrelevant to Y, provided it was also partly relevant. Did Socrates die because he drank hemlock in a toga? Of course not. But drinking-hemlock-in-a-toga is by [C2]'s lights just as helpful to his death as drinking hemlock. If adding hemlock-drinking to the right sort of insufficient condition A yields a sufficient condition for death, then adding hemlock-drinking-in-a-toga does too.

Here we can just double down on the idea behind [C2]. Rather than requiring only of Z that it be essential to X qua basis for Y, we should ask *everything* in X to be essential to it qua basis for Y.

[C3] Z contributes to Y just if:
an X obtains such that $Z \leq X$, $X \Rightarrow Y$, and $\forall U < X (U \not\Rightarrow Y)$.

The new requirement reaches down to Z's parts, since these will also be part of X by transitivity of part/whole. Given that an X including the toga can be cut down to a no less sufficient U leaving the toga out, drinking hemlock in a toga

---

[5] Kment (2014), Strevens (2007).

does not count by the new rule as a factor in Socrates' death. [C3] says in effect that Z contributes if it is contained in a *minimal* sufficient condition for Y, a sufficient condition X whose proper subconditions are always insufficient. This, the minimal sufficiency model of relevance, is what we are going to make trouble for in this chapter. It admits, like any philosophical model, of various refinements.[6] But we will not bother too much about these, since they do not affect the problem we're coming to. That problem runs deep and is not easily tweaked away.

The problem formally speaking is that not everything *has* a minimal basis. We do not want to conclude from the fact that sufficient conditions for Y always contain smaller such conditions that none of these are wholly, pervasively helpful to Y. Especially if nothing counts as helpful at all except by participating in a sufficient X that is helpful through and through.

The problem intuitively is that X, to be wholly helpful, need only be wholly *welcome* from Y's perspective. So far is this from requiring X's parts to be one and all essential to X, qua sufficient condition for Y, they can be one and all *inessential*. X can be composed of elements that would none of them be missed, though of course large enough combinations of them would be missed.

Consider the (utterly banal) idea of "extra help." Extra help is a contradiction in terms on the minimal sufficiency model. For suppose Z was extra, or not strictly needed; $X\backslash Z$ would have been enough. Then the result X of adding Z to $X\backslash Z$ was not minimally sufficient. So Z did not contribute? This runs completely counter to intuition. When the winning team in a tug of war is larger than necessary, we don't feel that some strange magic occurred, in which a team achieved victory with no help from its members. Yet we should feel this, if particular rope-tuggers, to be helpful, must pull an otherwise losing team over the line.

III. The Humean Package

Let's re-approach the question "historically" (note the scare quotes). When did minimality pressures begin to make themselves felt? When do we first encounter the point just noted—that Z, to be welcome from Y's perspective, need not be a sine qua non of Y, even in the relaxed sense of being a that-without-which-X-would-not-suffice?

Sufficiency had a long run in philosophy before anyone thought to worry about irrelevant add-ons. There was the Principle of Sufficient Reason. Causes were events given which the effect was sure to follow. Validity was a matter of premise-truth sufficing for the truth of the conclusion. Grounds for a higher-level fact were, and sometimes still are, items or conditions prior to that fact and sufficient for it.

---

[6] For instance one might want to add, for certain applications, a "contiguous chain" requirement along the lines of Kim (1973).

These proposals put a lower bound on, say, the cause, but not an upper bound, since $X \Rightarrow Y$ is monotonic in X (X^+ suffices if X does). The analysanda are more discerning. Socrates died not because he drank the hemlock in a toga, but because he drank the hemlock. The existence of even primes is grounded in 2 being an even prime, not that together with 9 being an odd non-prime.

If sufficiency allows causes to get too big, we might think of asking X also to be *necessary* for Y. Hume considers this in the *Treatise* but rejects it on the basis that effects need not have been caused at all, let alone by their actual causes:

> If we define a 'cause' to be *An object precedent and contiguous to another, and where all the objects resembling the former are similarly precedent and contiguous to objects that resemble the latter*, we can easily grasp that there is no absolute or metaphysical necessity that every beginning of existence should be preceded by such an object. (Hume 1740/2003, Bk I, §14, "Of the Idea of Necessary Connexion")

The issue for us is *natural* necessity, not metaphysical, and Y's specific cause rather than its being caused at all. But specific causes are not naturally necessary either, for Hume. From *Objects resembling X are always succeeded by objects resembling Y*, it does not follow that *Objects resembling Y are always preceded by objects resembling X*.[7]

Hume does appreciate, even in the *Treatise*, that causes as he officially defines them are liable to be overloaded with extraneous detail. We find him in the very next section (I, 15, "Rules by which to judge of causes and effects") looking for ways to block this:

> where several different objects produce the same effect, it must be by means of some quality, which we discover to be common amongst them...in order to arrive at the decisive point, we must carefully separate whatever is superfluous, and enquire by new experiments, if every particular circumstance of the first experiment was essential to it.

He suggests here a different way of keeping X within bounds. Rather than requiring causes to be necessary—so that Y no longer *holds* given just part of X—we ask them only to be non-redundant—Y is not *ensured* by just part of X. This becomes in the *Enquiry* (Hume 1740/2006) a full-blown proportionality requirement:

> we must proportion the [cause] to the [effect] and can never be allowed to ascribe to the cause any qualities, but what are exactly sufficient to produce the effect.[8]

---

[7] Similarly a truth does not have only one possible truthmaker, and there is more than one possible reason for doing a thing.
[8] "A body of ten ounces raised in any scale may serve as a proof, that the counterbalancing weight exceeds ten ounces; but can never afford a reason that it exceeds a hundred" (Hume 1740/2003).

A proportional cause is an X such that X suffices for Y *and nothing less suffices*:[9]

[P] X is proportional to Y ($X \propto Y$) iff:

(i) X suffices for Y ($X \Rightarrow Y$).
(ii) For all $X' \leq X$, if $X' \Rightarrow Y$, then $X' = X$.

Of course we are often interested in "contributory" causes that are not sufficient, and hence not proportional. But Hume has an easy way to bring these on board. Z contributes to Y if it is *contained* in a proportional cause X of Y:

[H] Z contributes to Y ($Z \rightarrow Y$) iff an X obtains such that $Z \leq X$ and $X \propto Y$.

By the *Humean Package* (*HP*), we'll mean these two ideas together. The first idea: X is proportional to Y just if it is minimally sufficient for Y. The second: Z contributes to, or is relevant or helpful to, Y just if Z is contained in a proportional X. What the two together offer is an account of relevance in terms of the prima facie much clearer notions of sufficiency and minimality.

The Humean Package has a lot going for it. It is powerful and illuminating and deals correctly with a great many cases. And it's adaptable. [P] and [H], since they do not contain the word "cause," offer a general template that is potentially of very wide application. Indeed it is hard to think of an area of philosophical inquiry that hasn't employed the template. The Hypothetico-Deductive model of confirmation is Humean in spirit; E confirms H just if H figures essentially in some suitable E-entailing body of information. An action's right-making features, on one account, are those included in a condition that is minimally sufficient for its rightness. Theories of presupposition have been trading in recent years on the "relevance," explained in difference-maker terms, of an embedded sentence's truth-value to the truth-value of the whole.[10] "Q is a difference-making ground for P" is defined by Krämer and Roski like this:

for some scenario S which contains a full ground of P, S minus the fact that Q does not contain a full ground of P. (Krämer and Roski 2017, with inessential relettering)

How can the fact Q that 5 is prime be relevant to the fact P that there are primes, when that fact cannot fail to obtain? A scenario S consisting precisely of 5 and its indivisibility by 2, 3 and 4 contains a full ground of P. No lesser scenario contains a full ground, and in particular S minus the fact Q of 5's indivisibility by

---

[9] "Proportionality" in this chapter is only roughly analogous to the notion in Yablo (1992b) and (1992a).
[10] Schlenker (2008). A close cousin of the minimality problem is raised in Schlenker (2009, 52–3). (Thanks here to Danny Fox.)

2 does not fully ground P. 5's oddness contributes to the existence of primes because it makes the difference between a minimal ground for primes' existence and a near-ground.

IV. Extra Help

And yet a *non*-minimal condition X—one with elements that it doesn't need, to suffice for Y—can still be wholly, entirely helpful. Extra help is still help, and sometimes it is the only kind of help around. This goes back in a way to Zeno. A solid sphere takes up space. It has measure 1, say. The sphere's component points are helpful, surely? They are clearly helpful en masse—en masse they just *are* the sphere. And it is hard to see how they could be helpful together, if they were irrelevant individually. Still, since each point has measure 0, they would none of them be missed. None of the sphere's component points lies in a minimal subregion of measure 1, because there *are* no minimal subregions of measure 1.[11]

Hume might have known, when he wrote the *Enquiry*, of Zeno's paradox of measure. He would not have known of the next example, as it grows out of events taking place that same year (1748). God is pleased, let's imagine, if he is praised infinitely many days. Being praised *every* day should be pleasing, surely.[12] But no, not if we go by the Humean Package. The reason was noted in effect by John Newton in *Amazing Grace*:[13]

> When we've been here ten thousand years
> Bright shining like the sun.
> We've no less days to sing His praise
> Than when we'd just begun.

---

[11] Skyrms (1983) is an interesting discussion. "Zeno's paradox of measure rests on the following premises:
  (I) Partition: [the sphere] can be partitioned into an infinite number of parts such that
  (II) Measurability: the concept of magnitude applies to the parts.
  (III) Invariance: the parts all have equal positive magnitude, or zero magnitude.
  (IV) Archimedean Axiom: there are no infinitesimal magnitudes.
  (V) Ultra-Additivity: the magnitude of the whole is the sum of the magnitudes of the parts.
Ancient responses focused largely on (I) and (II). Doctrines of finite indivisible magnitudes (certainly Epicurus and probably Democritus and Leucippus) rejected (I). Aristotle rejected (I) and (II). It is possible that a doctrine of infinitesimal indivisible magnitudes was also current (possibly held by Xenocrates, possibly by Democritus) which rejected (IV). (III) could have also been challenged by a holder of a doctrine of infinitesimal magnitudes. (V), Ultra-Additivity, appears to have been accepted without question by every party to the dispute. It is ironic that it is just here that the standard modern theory of measure finds the fallacy" (235).

[12] Assume the future is infinite.

[13] Newton's religious phase began in 1748, when his ship nearly went down in a storm off the coast of Ireland. He was returning from Africa, where he had been first a slave trader, then himself enslaved to a colleague's African wife. The ship miraculously righted itself and Newton promised to change his ways. He was ordained as an Anglican priest in 1764. *Amazing Grace* was written a few years later.

Singing *every* day is out of proportion with the effect, on Hume's definition, since God would still be pleased if we waited 10,000 years before beginning. And of course the same is true for any other set of days one might choose. There *is* no least infinite set of days. Every praise-day is helpful to the cause, but not because it figures in a minimal sufficer.

Minimality had better not be required for relevance, because you can't always get it. It is not always required, in fact, even when you *can* get it. The pope's crown was once supposedly made of three smaller crowns. Suleiman the Magnificent, not to be outdone, had *four* crowns in his crown. Suleiman's crown was wholly relevant to *There are crowns*. But you could lop the upper sub-crowns off and still have a sufficient condition for the sentence's truth. Here we *can* point to a minimal sufficient basis for *There are crowns*. But there is no reason to do so. Suleiman's total crown is no less helpful for being four times larger than necessary.

The US Senate cannot conduct certain kinds of business unless fifty-one members are present (a quorum); it is not "in order" without a quorum. Suppose that fifty-two senators are present on a given occasion. They all arrived at the same time and the situation is in other ways symmetrical. The presence of these senators—the Gang of 52, call them—seems wholly helpful to order obtaining. True, there is a Gang of 51 present as well which also suffices, in fact there are fifty-two such gangs. Somehow though this does not detract from our initial judgment. The Gang of 52 is wholly relevant despite the fact that not all its members had to be there.

V. Previous Proposals

That *X* can still be wholly relevant to *Y*, even if not all of it is needed, has not gone unnoticed. Fine makes the point in connection with truthmaking (proportional truthmakers in his system are *exact* rather than *inexact*) (Fine 2017c).[14] Humeans in effect take the exact verifiers to be the minimal inexact verifiers, those that inexactly verify without properly containing an inexact verifier.

But while piling on random extras ruins an exact verifier,[15] piling on additional exact verifiers does not:

> Given the facts $f, g, h, \ldots$, we take there to be a *composite* fact or *fusion* $f \bullet g \bullet h \bullet \ldots$ that is the 'factual conjunction' of the component facts $f, g, h, \ldots$,

---

[14] "With inexact verification, the state should be at least partially relevant to the statement; and with exact verification, it should be wholly relevant. Thus the presence of rain will be an exact verifier for the statement 'it is rainy'; the presence of wind and rain will be an inexact verifier for the statement 'it is rainy', though not an exact verifier" (Fine 2017c).

[15] "On our understanding of verification as relevant verification, it should *not* be supposed that if f verifies a truth A then *any* 'larger' fact $f \bullet g$ must also verify A" (Fine 2012b, 7, emphasis added; see also Fine 2012a).

obtaining just in case all of the component facts obtain; and we shall suppose that whenever the facts $f, g, h, \ldots$ verify the truth A, their fusion $f{\bullet}g{\bullet}h{\bullet}\ldots$ also verifies A ....(Fine 2012b, 7)

The presence $r{\bullet}w$ of rain and wind exactly verifies *It is rainy or windy* without minimally verifying it. Rain and wind are more than $R \vee W$ needs, but there is nothing in $r{\bullet}w$ that is irrelevant to the statement's truth.

Kratzer's theory of exemplification strikes a similar note. The fact of two teapots exemplifies *There are teapots*, she says, despite its non-minimality. The fact of a teapot and a dog does not. Why is the extra dog more of a problem than the extra teapot? The parts of a P-exemplifying situation s must "earn their keep" by figuring crucially, not perhaps in s itself, but in a minimal P-verifying part of s.

s exemplifies P iff for all s' such that $s' \leq s$ and P is not true in s', there is an s'' such that $s' \leq s'' \leq s$, and s' is a minimal situation in which P is true. (A minimal situation in which P is true is a situation that has no proper parts in which P is true.) (Kratzer 2002: 660)

The fact of two teapots exemplifies *There are teapots* (P) despite its non-minimality because everything in it is part of some minimal P-verifier or other. Here s and P are like our X and Y and exemplification is like being-sufficient-for-and-wholly-helpful-to.

Kratzer's theory does loosen the bonds between relevance and minimality. But minimality is still playing its same old role one level down; a non-minimal verifier needs to contain minimal verifiers. It is a problem, then, if "a statement may have inexact verifiers without having any minimal verifiers" (Fine 2017c).[16]

Similarly a cause might still be wholly helpful to an effect, even if all its sufficient parts contain smaller such parts all the way down. Imagine a detector that buzzes

---

[16] Kratzer is aware of this. Her example is *There are infinitely many stars* ((7) in her paper):

If the proposition expressed by (7) is the proposition P that is true in any possible situation in which there are infinitely many stars, we are in trouble. [The] definition would predict that there couldn't be a fact that makes P true .... Situations with five or six stars, for example, ... are not part of any minimal situation in which P is true (Kratzer 2002, 662)

She notes that that (7) has a reading "that the German sentence (8) brings out more clearly":

(8) Sterne gibt es unendlich viele.
Stars are there infinitely many.
As for stars, there are infinitely many of them.

In (8), the common noun "Stern" has been topicalized. The proposition expressed by (8) might now be taken to be the proposition Q that is true in a situation s iff (i) s contains all the stars in the world of s, and (ii) there are infinitely many stars in s. Consequently, if Q is true in a world at all, there is always a minimal situation in which it is true, hence there is always a fact that exemplifies it (Kratzer 2002, 662).

But, although (7) *can* be understood so that it comes out with minimal verifiers, this is not the only way of understanding it. And there might be other examples where topicalization is not an option.

when presented with infinitely many point particles, or with a single particle of any positive mass.[17]

Infinitary relevance can *sometimes* be dealt with as follows.[18] Take again Zeno's Paradox of Measure. How do the individual points in a sphere contribute to its volume, when each point is of measure zero? Well, the points are *collectively* relevant, and none is more relevant than any other. Perhaps Y is wholly helpful to X if:

(1) Y subdivides into the Y_i's.
(2) X fails if *all* the Y_i's fail.
(3) one Y_i is as relevant to X as another.

Or, looking back at Amazing Grace, we might reason like this. The *number* of praise-days does not shrink if we add one more day, but the *set* does shrink. And cardinality considered as a measure on sets is a coarsening of membership; size in the how-many sense is monotonically grounded in size in the membership sense. Perhaps Y is wholly helpful to X if:

(1) X is to the effect that Y is at least so big by a certain measure.
(2) That measure is monotonically grounded in another, finer measure.
(3) Each Y_i bears on Y's size by this finer measure.

Both ideas are worth pursuing. I don't want to pursue them here, for a couple of reasons. The first is that they seem insufficiently general. (Why should X be to the effect that Y is "at least so big by a certain measure"?) The second is that relevance presents, as we are about to see, logical challenges that they're ill equipped to meet.

VI. Hyperintensionality

One problem for the Humean package ([H] and [P]) is that minimality is not always available. Another is that minimality is not always even desirable. Now we turn to a third, importantly different, problem.

Humean proportionality is prima facie intensional: if X and Y are necessarily equivalent to X^* and Y^*, then Y is proportional to X only if Y^* is proportional to X^*.

---

[17] Yablo (2017a).
[18] These ideas were prompted by an observation of Williamson's about content-parts in propositional logic. B is analytically contained in A, I had proposed, if $\forall \alpha \, \exists \beta \, \beta \subseteq \alpha$ and $\forall \beta \, \exists \alpha \, \beta \subseteq \alpha$; the Greek letters range over minimal models of A and B. Williamson pointed out (p.c., 2006) that containment continues to make sense in infinitary settings where A's models are all non-minimal. *Infinitely many atomic truths exist* appears, for instance, to contain *Atomic truths exist*. (For analytic containment see Angell 1989, Correia 2004, Yablo 2014, 59 and Fine 2015).

For proportionality is defined by [P] in terms of sufficiency and minimality, which are themselves intensional.[19]

Is the relation of "being entirely relevant to" intensional? It is not. An example on the X side: *His praise is sung infinitely many days* (X) is true in the same worlds as *His praise is sung infinitely many days after 12019* (X*). Singing every day starting now (Y) is wholly helpful to X, but overkill when it comes to X*. Singing today is absolutely beside the point when it comes to singing infinitely often in the distant future.

An example on the Y side:[20] In Alternative Eden, there are infinitely many apples on the Tree of Life, but only one, BadApple, on the Tree of Knowledge of Good and Evil. Eve can't recall God's precise instructions, and decides to check it out with the serpent:

EVE. What did God allow me to do again?
SERPENT. Hmmmm, I'm not sure, but I remember it was equivalent to this: *You eat infinitely many apples.*
[Eve eats all the apples and is expelled from Eden.]
EVE, FURIOUS. Why did you say God had allowed me to eat infinitely many apples?!?
SERPENT. Wait, I said it was *equivalent* to that. And it was. *You eat infinitely many apples v such that v ≠ BadApple* (Y) holds in the same worlds as *You eat infinitely many apples, period* (Y*). One apple cannot make the difference between an infinite set and a finite one.

Let X be *Eve did as she was told*. Y's truth is wholly helpful to X, given that God had allowed Eve to eat infinitely many apples other than BadApple. There is no disobedient way of doing that (see below for "ways"). Whereas Y*'s truth is not wholly helpful to X, since there are ways for Y* to hold that have Eve disobeying God.

VII. Mereology

What is it for X' to be $\leq X$ in [P]? You might think that $X' \leq X$ iff X implies, or necessitates, X'. But although this is how content-parts have sometimes been understood, the view quickly runs into trouble.[21] For one thing it allows X to be knocked out of proportion with Y by $X \vee S$, provided that S too is sufficient for Y. Which is the wrong result.

---

[19] "Prima facie" because the part-relation < plays a role as well. It could turn out that necessary equivalents are not freely substitutable on the right-hand side of $U < Y$. Best to ignore this as it's not the issue here. (See Section VII.)
[20] Fine (2017).   [21] Gemes (1994, 1997), Fine (2013), Yablo (2014), Fine (2015).

Socrates' drinking the hemlock on an empty stomach (*X*) suffices, let's assume, for his death (*Y*). *X* is proportional to the death only if nothing less suffices. Yet something less is bound to suffice, if ≤ is just the converse of implication. For let *S* be any other sufficient basis for death, say, falling off a high cliff. Then *X*∨*S* is a weaker sufficient condition for *Y* than *X* is. *X*∨*S* knocks *X* out of proportion with *Y*, if ≤ means is-implied-by. So it had better mean more than that. The answer we'd like to give is that *X*∨*S*, although *weaker* than *X*, is not *contained* in *X*. To be proportional to *Y*, *X* should have no proper *parts* sufficient for *Y*.

This notion of content-part is not available to the Humean, as it is hyperintensional, e.g. *P*∨*Q* is part of *P*∨*PQ* but not of *P*. Hyperintensionality, looking ahead a bit, is going to be explained with *ways*. The difference between *X* and *X**—*His praise is sung infinitely many days starting now* and *His praise is sung infinitely many days after 12019*—is that while they hold in the same worlds, they don't hold in the same ways in those worlds. Not a single way of singing infinitely many days after 12019 involves singing tomorrow. Singing tomorrow may well have a role to play, however, in how God's praise is sung infinitely many days starting now. Ways are the key as well to content-parts:

X′ ≤ *X* iff:

(i) Every way for *X* to hold implies a way for *X*′ to hold.
(ii) Every way for *X*′ to hold is implied by a way for *X* to hold.[22]

They bear too, finally, on the problem we are mainly concerned with in this chapter, the problem of minimality. Details will have to wait; suffice it for now to say that although the Humean Package faces a number of challenges, they all push in the same theoretical direction.

VIII. Bottomless Kinds

A fractal is a geometrical figure containing isomorphic copies of itself; these will then contain isomorphic copies of *them*selves, and so on all the way down. An example is tree *t* below.

Fractals are counterexamples par excellence to the minimality requirement. The fact that *t* exists ([*t exists*], for short) is as helpful as it could be to *There are fractals*. You are not going to find a better candidate for a proportional, discerning, basis for the truth of *There are fractals* than the existence of *t*.

---

[22] Gemes (1994, 1997), Yablo (2014), Fine (2015), Yablo (2016), Fine (2017). (Where I have "implies," others say "contains." This is not the place.)

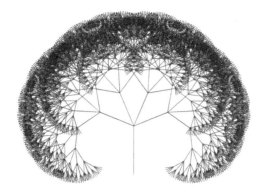

A fact that is clearly out of proportion with *There are fractals* is [*t exists and Sparky is a dog*]. What is the difference exactly? You can throw the Sparky conjunct out, of course, and still be left with a fact sufficient for the existence of fractals. But one can also throw out part of the fact that *t* exists. For the immediate right subtree *u* of *t* is also a fractal, and *t*'s existence consists in the joint existence of *u* and *v* (*v* is the rest of *t*). It is not clear as yet why [*u exists and v exists*] would be more proportional to *There are fractals* than [*t exists and Sparky is a dog*], or for that matter [*u exists and Sparky is a dog*], given that the second conjunct is in each case dispensable.

Call a kind *K* bottomless if to be a *K* is to contain smaller *K*s. If *K* is bottomless, then clearly, a minimal *K* is not to be expected. Are there other bottomless kinds, besides *fractal*?

A set is infinite iff all of its members can be paired off 1-1 with its members other than *x*, for some *x* in the set. Suppose that *S* is equipotent in that sense with $S_1 = S\setminus\{x\}$. Then if $y \in S_1$, it follows on standard assumptions that S_1 is equipotent with $S_2 = S_1\setminus\{y\}$, and so on without limit. *Infinite set* is thus a bottomless kind.

A property is *dissective* if a thing cannot instantiate it unless all its parts do.[23] This does not ensure bottomlessness all by itself, but it does if we add that proper parts always exist. Sellars uses the notion to illustrate his distinction between the "scientific" and "manifest" images of reality:

Color expanses in the manifest world consist of regions which are themselves color expanses.[24]

The manifestly colored expanses form a bottomless kind for Sellars. (Of an especially pure sort. Fractals can contain non-fractals, but the parts of a blue expanse are all blue.) Aristotelian water is supposed to be dissective, and a stretch

---

[23] Goodman (1951).   [24] Sellars (1963), 35.

of continuous motion always subdivides into smaller stretches of continuous motion. A minimal verifier of *The particle was moving continuously at noon* is not to be hoped for.

Why do people think that X cannot be wholly relevant to Y, if less than X suffices, when these problems are so obvious? A condition may retain its hold on us, it is true, even after we see that it cannot always be met. A set of everything is impossible, too, but that doesn't make it any less "what we wanted." Logicians *regret* the unavailability of a universal set; they look for ways of approximating or simulating it.[25] There is nothing to regret in the fact that we can't lay our hands on a minimal fractal.

IX. Schematization

The Humean Package is more of a schema than a claim. Z is *causally* relevant to Y iff it's part an X that *causally* suffices for Y, where nothing less causally suffices. Z is *ground*-relevant to Y (it is a difference-making ground; see Section III) iff it is part of a full ground X of Y such that nothing less than X fully grounds Y. Z helps to justify Y iff it is part of an X that fully justifies Y, but ceases to do so when anything is deleted. The "generic" notions of sufficiency ($\Rightarrow$), proportionality ($\propto$) and helpfulness ($\leadsto$) in [H] and [P] should be read as shorthands for particular flavors $\Rightarrow^k$, $\propto^k$ and $\leadsto^k$ of these notions:

[H] $Z \leadsto^k Y$ iff $Z \leq X$ for some (actual) X such that $X \propto^k Y$.
[P] $X \propto^k Y$ iff (i) $X \Rightarrow^k Y$, (ii) for all $X' \leq X$, if $X' \Rightarrow^k Y$, then $X' = X$.

The superscripted arrows $\Rightarrow^k$, $\propto^k$ and $\leadsto^k$ stand ambiguously for the various sorts of sufficiency and relevance with which philosophers have concerned themselves: causal, logical, modal, nomological, explanatory, evidential and so on.

Dividing things up in this way doesn't *help* with minimality, but it does bring out the problem's breadth, and the kind(s) of trouble we're in if we can't figure it out. *He is praised infinitely many days* has an unending chain of progressively weaker sufficers: he is praised every day from today on (X_0), every day from tomorrow on (X_1),..., every day from day n on (X_n), and so on. The sufficiency in this case is ground-flavored. Writing $\Rightarrow^g$ for "is sufficient in the manner characteristic of a full ground for," we have:

$X_0 \Rightarrow^g Y$
$X_1 \Rightarrow^g Y$
$X_2 \Rightarrow^g Y$

---

[25] This is part of the attraction of plural quantification.

$X_3 \Rightarrow^g Y$

....

$X_n \Rightarrow^g Y$

....

But it holds of no X_i on the list that $X_i \propto^g Y$, for each X_i has a proper part X_{i+1} such that $X_{i+1} \Rightarrow^g Y$. If indeed proportional grounds in the sense of [$\mathbb{P}$] don't exist, then (to go by [$\mathbb{H}$]) it is never true that $Z \rightsquigarrow^g Y$. (Difference-making grounds have to be parts of proportional grounds.) It somehow contributes nothing to *He is praised on infinitely many days* that he is praised today, or throughout 12019.

That was the ground-theoretic variation on our descending chain theme. For the causal variation, let Y be *God is pleased*. It holds of no X_i on the list that $X_i \Rightarrow^c Y$, since each X_i has a proper part X_{i+1} such that $X_{i+1} \Rightarrow^c Y$. And so it is never true, by the same reasoning as before, that $Z \rightsquigarrow^c Y$. God does to be sure wind up pleased if praised every day. It's just that this is not due even in part to the praise received on any specific day(s).[26] Examples of the same sort can be given for any variety of relevance: moral, evidential, nomological, etc.

The Humean Package—a theory $\mathbb{H}$ of relevance built on the back of a theory $\mathbb{P}$ of proportionality—evidently needs work. That work begins, in Section XI, with a particular *kind* of non-Humean proportionality, the kind $\propto^t$ appropriate to ways of being true. The hope is that other sorts of proportionality can be recovered from it, and other sorts of relevance ($\rightsquigarrow^c$, etc.) from them.

X. Ways and Worlds

Parthood and proportionality are hyperintensional notions; so is indifference which we'll be getting to soon. To do them justice, we will have to expand our toolkit ("The possible worlds apparatus can only draw intensional, not hyperintensional, distinctions."[27]) Lucky for us, the role traditionally played by worlds is better played in any case by *ways*.[28] And ways are hyperintensional right out of the box. P is true in the same worlds as $(P \equiv Q) \vee (P \equiv \neg Q)$, but the latter has different ways of being true.[29] Events that necessarily co-occur may have different ways of occurring, e.g., this ball bouncing off that one, and that one bouncing off this.[30] A solid figure occupies almost all of the open sphere $\{<x, y, z> \mid x^2 + y^2 + z^2 < 1\}$ in

---

[26] A case with fewer distractions: A buzzer sounds at the weigh station when a truck enters weighing over 70,000 pounds. The buzzer goes off "for no particular reason," judging by [$\mathbb{P}$] and [$\mathbb{H}$]. Reasons have to be drawn from conditions minimally causally sufficient for the effect. And numbers don't exist that are minimally larger than 70,000.
[27] Berto (2017). [28] Yablo (2014, 2017b).
[29] The second can be true by way of *P*'s truth and *Q*'s falsity.
[30] For this ball to bounce elastically off that one, retaining all its velocity, is a way for the first event to occur but not the second.

a world w just if it occupies almost all of the closed sphere $\{<x, y, z> \mid x^2 + y^2 + z^2 \leq 1\}$. But these outcomes obtain in different ways. Occupying all of the closed sphere is a way of occupying almost all of it, but not of occupying almost all of the *open* sphere.[31]

What is meant by a "way ω for P to hold"? I don't know how to define the notion and won't even try. There is nothing scandalous about this. Does Lewis put possible worlds semantics on hold until he can define "P-world w"? Not at all. Two issues have to be distinguished in his view:

(1) What is a "world in which proposition P is true"?
(2) What is the "proposition P expressed by *P*"?

(1) is trivial, if propositions are sets of worlds. P is true in w iff w is a member of P. (2), the problem of associating propositions with sentences, is nothing special to do with worlds, nor does the worldly view of propositions make it more difficult. One approach lets the intensions of atomic expressions be given outright; semantics comes in to derive the intensions of complex expressions. Or, atomic intensions could be assigned on some kind of covariational basis. Lewis himself works backwards from sentence intensions, using reference magnetism as a tie-breaker.[32]

None of this need change if propositions are made up of non-worldly circumstances c. S is true at c just if c belongs to S = the proposition that S. There will be time enough later to explain how a sentence comes to express this proposition rather than that. This is par for the course in semantics. Propositions for Kratzer are sets of situations. Propositions for Humberstone are sets of possibilities. Propositions for new-style expressivists like Yalcin and Moss are sets of probability-measures.[33] Propositions in truthmaker semantics are sets of ways.

XI. The *Only In Part By* Test

Suppose I am right that way-for-it-to-be-that-*P* is on a par methodologically with world-in-which-*P*. Neither requires for semantic purposes an analysis. There is still the question of *which* unanalyzed notion is intended. Here my job is in one respect easier than Lewis's: "way for P to be the case" is a familiar, commonsensical notion. But it's in another respect harder. Ways are a miscellaneous lot, and

---

[31] Continuous motion occurs in the same worlds as continuous motion*s*. But for this particle to move continuously from noon to one, and then that one from three to four, is a way for continuous motion*s* to occur. Distinct particles moving at different times is overkill when it comes to continuous motion. (Kit Fine's example.)
[32] Lewis (1974, 1983).   [33] Yalcin (2012), Moss (2018).

I need to direct your attention to an elusive sub-genre. Our target in the end is ways for it to be that *P*, but it helps to look more generally at ways for a thing *x* to φ. (Ways for it to be that *P* fall out as the case where *x* is a world and to φ is to be the kind of world that verifies *P*.)

So, let's try it. Here to get us going are some paradigms of ways for *x* to do a certain thing, or instantiate a certain property:

Disjuncts: For *x* to sing is a way for *x* to sing or dance.
Instances: For *x* to sing is a way for something to sing.
Determinates: For *x* to yodel is a way for *x* to sing.

And here are some foils, that is, paradigms of failure to be a way:

Conjunctions: To sing and dance is NOT a way of singing.
Generalizations: For everyone to sing is NOT a way for *x* to sing.
Manners: To yodel badly is NOT a way of singing.
Prequels: Practicing is NOT a way of getting to Carnegie Hall.[34]
Prerequisites: To dance is NOT a way of persisting over time.[35]

Some principles will help us to sort these cases out. There will be no epiphanies. But we should get some amount of insight into why the line is drawn where it is.

A first condition on ψ, if it is to count as a way of φ-ing, involves the notion of *only* φ-ing. Why is singing and dancing not a way of singing? A way of singing is not a *further* thing one does, in addition to singing. Singing of its nature has to be done in some way or other (by yodeling, say), just as eating involves there being something or other that one eats. This is why to eat carrots, or yodel, is not to do a further thing besides eating, or singing. To sing and dance *is* in part to do a further thing, namely dance.[36] That one also dances means that one isn't only singing. Our first test, then, is:

---

[34] Dancing is not in our sense a way of failing the course, even if the instructor disapproves of dancing, or dancing cuts into your study time.
[35] An instantaneous entity cannot dance.
[36] The idea is from Kratzer (1989): "One evening in 1905, Paula painted a still life with apples and bananas. She spent most of the evening painting and left the easel only to make herself a cup of tea, eat a piece of bread, discard a banana or look for an apple displaying a particular shade of red. Against the background of this situation, consider the following two dialogues that might have taken place the following day."

Dialogue with a Pedant
PEDANT: What did you do yesterday evening?
PAULA: The only thing I did yesterday evening was paint this still life over there.
PEDANT: This cannot be true. You must have done something else like eat, drink, look out of the window.
PAULA: Yes, strictly speaking, I did other things besides paint this still life. I made myself a cup of tea, etc.

126 UNSTRUCTURED CONTENT

Only-Way: To ψ is a way of φ-ing only if: *x ψ-d* is compatible with *x only φ-d*.

Al yodeled is compatible with *Al only sang*. But *Al sang* is likewise compatible with *Al only yodeled*, and singing is not a way of yodeling. One thing we could say here is that ψ-ing should necessitate φ-ing (as singing does not necessitate yodeling). But singing-while-persisting-over-time, which does necessitate singing, also passes the ONLY test. And we don't want to say that singing-while-persisting is a way of singing.

The difference is that one doesn't persist *by* singing, or for that matter sing by singing and dancing. Whereas one does sing by yodeling, and sing or dance by singing. And one arranges for someone to sing, by arranging for Bert to do so. This gives us a second condition:

By-Way: To ψ is a way of φ-ing only if: *x* φ-s *by* ψ-ing.

This still lets too much in. One can fail the course by dancing—when one ought to be studying—and to dance is not in the relevant sense a way of failing the course. If the answer to "How do I get to Carnegie Hall?" is "Practice!," still practicing is not a way of getting to Carnegie Hall. The dancing is more like a cause, or facilitator, of—let us say, *prequel* to—failing the course, and the practicing is a prequel to Carnegie Hall. Here is a third principle aimed at prequels:

Way-In: To ψ is a way of φ-ing only if: *x* φ-s *in* ψ-ing.

One may fail a course by dancing, but not (certain courses aside) in the act of dancing. No one gets in the act of practicing to Carnegie Hall. Singing and yodeling are different in this respect. Hank Williams sang not only by yodeling, but in the act of yodeling.

Only one of the foils remains to be dealt with. Yodeling badly is not supposed to be a way of singing. But can't a Hank Williams impersonator sing both by, and in, yodeling badly? Intuitions may differ on this, but let's allow it is possible. A different explanation will then be needed of why yodeling badly does not count as a way of singing. I know what I *want* to say: as long as Bert is yodeling, how well or badly he does it is irrelevant to whether he sings. This does not get us very far, however. For have no account as yet of (ir)relevance; the whole point of this

Dialogue with a Lunatic
LUNATIC: What did you do yesterday evening?
PAULA: The only thing I did yesterday evening was paint this still life over there.
LUNATIC: This is not true. You also painted these apples and you also painted these bananas. Hence painting this still life was not the only thing you did yesterday evening. (608)

The pedant is technically correct, if a bore. But Kratzer rightly objects to the lunatic that Paula "didn't paint apples and bananas *apart* from painting a still life. Painting apples and painting bananas was part of her painting a still life" (608).

chapter is that (ir)relevance begins to elude our grasp once we see that it cannot be captured Hume-style in terms of minimality.

Ah, but what if the particular *type* of irrelevance now at issue was independently identifiable, without getting into grander issues about relevance as such? Ways in the relevant sense are intimately related to *parts*; and relevance has a counterpart virtue on the side of parts that is easier to get a grip on. (1)–(6) show that to be G is part of being F, in many cases, just if to be $\bar{G}$ is a way of being $\bar{F}$:[37]

(1) To be $\begin{pmatrix} R \\ \bar{R} \end{pmatrix}$ is $\begin{pmatrix} \text{part} \\ \text{a way} \end{pmatrix}$ of being $\begin{pmatrix} R \wedge S \\ \bar{R} \vee \bar{S} \end{pmatrix}$.

(2) To be $\begin{pmatrix} R \vee S \\ \bar{R} \wedge \bar{S} \end{pmatrix}$ is NOT $\begin{pmatrix} \text{part} \\ \text{a way} \end{pmatrix}$ of being $\begin{pmatrix} S \\ \bar{S} \end{pmatrix}$.

(3) To be $\begin{pmatrix} R \vee S \\ \bar{R} \wedge \bar{S} \end{pmatrix}$ is $\begin{pmatrix} \text{part} \\ \text{a way} \end{pmatrix}$ of being $\begin{pmatrix} R \veebar S \\ R \equiv S \end{pmatrix}$.

(4) To be $\begin{pmatrix} R \supset S \\ R \wedge \bar{S} \end{pmatrix}$ is NOT $\begin{pmatrix} \text{part} \\ \text{a way} \end{pmatrix}$ of being $\begin{pmatrix} R \wedge S \\ \bar{R} \vee \bar{S} \end{pmatrix}$.

(5) To be $\begin{pmatrix} R \supset S \\ R \wedge \bar{S} \end{pmatrix}$ is $\begin{pmatrix} \text{part} \\ \text{a way} \end{pmatrix}$ of being $\begin{pmatrix} R \equiv S \\ R \not\equiv S \end{pmatrix}$.

(6) To be $\begin{pmatrix} R \equiv S \\ R \not\equiv S \end{pmatrix}$ is NOT $\begin{pmatrix} \text{part} \\ \text{a way} \end{pmatrix}$ of being $\begin{pmatrix} R \wedge S \\ \bar{R} \vee \bar{S} \end{pmatrix}$.

So, (1) to be red is part of being red and square, and its negation non-red is a way of being the negation of red and square, viz. non-red or non-square. (2) To be red or square is no part of being square, and to be neither red nor square is not a way of being non-square. (3) To be red inclusive-or square is part of being red exclusive-or square, and to be neither red nor square is a way of being red iff square. (4) To be non-red or square is not part of being red and square, while to be red and non-square is not a way of being non-red or non-square. (5) To be square if red is part of being square iff red, and to be red and non-square is a way of failing to be square iff red. (6) To be square iff red is NOT part of being square and red, and failing to be square iff red is not a way of being non-red or non-square.

Parts and ways are shaping up to be *duals* (like ∀/∃, or □/◇). That ψ is necessary for φ iff φ suffices for ψ has as its hyperintensional counterpart that ψ-ing is part of φ-ing just if $\bar{\psi}$-ing is a way of $\bar{\varphi}$-ing. Rearranging and swapping positives for negatives, we get the following as our final necessary condition on ways:

Part-Way: To ψ is a way of φ-ing only if: to $\bar{\psi}$ is part of what is involved in $\bar{\varphi}$-ing.

---

[37] ⊻ is exclusive disjunction.

This catches irrelevant or non-contributing manners that the other conditions are apt to miss. Bad manners give rise under negation to sore-thumb disjuncts that prevent $\bar{\psi}$ from being part of $\bar{\varphi}$. Take yodeling badly. It is a way of singing only if part of what is involved in *not* singing is *not* yodeling badly: either not yodeling at all, or else yodeling well. Not yodeling may indeed be part of what it takes not to sing. But to yodel well, one must sing! This makes it hard to see yodeling-well as caught up (even disjunctively) in not-singing. The latter to contain not-yodeling-or-yodeling-well should intuitively contain yodeling-well. But it's *inconsistent* with yodeling-well.

Yodeling badly is by our fourth condition not a way of singing. This is good since yodeling-badly was a foil, not a paradigm. Part-Way looks favorably on our paradigms. To sing remains a way of singing or dancing, since to do neither is in part not to sing. Yodeling remains a way of singing, since not to sing is in part not to yodel. For Bert to sing remains a way for someone to sing, since part of what is involved in no one's singing is for Bert in particular not to sing.

Four necessary conditions have been laid down: Only-Way, By-Way, Way-In and Part-Way. They constitute together the *Only-In-Part-By* test for way-hood. I say "test" because the conditions do not pretend to get at what ways really are. They aim only to sort the cases out properly, and they seem so far to succeed at this. Questions can be raised about all of them, and there are other conditions that might be considered as well. But not here. Our topic is relevance and it is time to get back to it.

XII. Indifference

God is pleased has an unending chain of progressively weaker sufficers: He is praised every day from today on, every day from tomorrow on,..., every day after 12019, and so on. The weaker ones are no better, if all God wants is to be praised infinitely many days. The chain's endlessness would be unfortunate, if knocking off initial segments brought a feeling of progress, of getting closer to God's real reason for being pleased. But we never do get closer and progress is never made.

Cantor was disappointed in what we now call the infinite numbers. No $\aleph_\alpha$ could satisfy him, because there was always a bigger one down the road; and bigger, in the infinity department, is better. A *truly* infinite number would be as large as possible. This is why he called the $\aleph$as "transfinite," reserving "infinite" for a (putative) number too big for his system.[38] Cantor preferred larger numbers because they had more of what he wanted: size. If we perceive no advantage in X' (singing every day after 12019) as the cause of God's pleasure, over X (singing

---

[38] Hallett (1986). To continue with the coincidences, Cantor was hospitalized for depression in 1899. *That Obscure Object of Desire*, or the novel it is based on, appeared the year before.

every day henceforth), it stands to reason that X' does not have more of what we wanted. It does no better proportionality-wise than X did, which means that X did no worse.

The idea that smaller is not necessarily better—that X and X' are "the same to Y," in symbols, $X' \equiv_Y X$—seems worth looking into.[39] Trouble is, we don't know what "same to Y" means as yet. If we did, we would take our existing account of proportionality:

[P1] $X \propto^k Y$ iff (i) $X \Rightarrow^k Y$, (ii) for all $X' \leq X$, if $X' \Rightarrow^k Y$, then $X' = X$.

and replace the final identity with $X' \equiv^k_Y X$ to obtain:

[P2] $X \propto^k Y$ iff (i) $X \Rightarrow^k Y$, (ii) for all $X' \leq X$, if $X' \Rightarrow^k Y$, then $X' \equiv^k_Y X$.

For a sense of how this might work, let Y be *There are infinitely many whatnots*. Y is about size in the *how-many* sense, not the *inclusion* sense. That is why there is nothing to be gained proportionality-wise by deleting one of the whatnots. Y doesn't *care* about, it is not *concerned* with, the kind of size where subsets are smaller. When we fix our attention on the *how-many* notion of size, we find that X' offers no advantages over X.

XIII. Aboutness

Time to take stock. Z contributes[k] to Y just if it is part of an X that is proportional[k] to Y. X is proportional[k] to Y if Y does not care about any differences that might obtain between X and those of its proper parts X' that also suffice[k] for Y. (Not caring is expressed by $X' \equiv^k_Y X$.) X does not have to be minimal in all respects to be proportional to Y, the thought is, just the respects that matter, the ones Y is concerned about.

The "concern" is metaphorical, you'll be glad to hear. But the "about" and the "mattering" are not; they will be cashed out in terms of ways of being true. How is it that $P \lor \neg P$ is about a different matter than $Q \lor \neg Q$, when they are true in the same worlds? Well, they are true in different ways in those worlds. Why does the subject matter of $P \& Q$ include the subject matter of P, but not that of $(P\&Q) \lor R$, when $|P\&Q|$ (writing $|S|$ for the set of S-worlds) is a subset both of $|P|$ and $|(P\&Q) \lor R|$? Well, $(P\&Q) \lor R$ holds, sometimes, in ways not implied by any way for $P\&Q$ to hold; the same cannot be said of P in relation to $P\&Q$.

---

[39] A better notation, since they could conceivably be the same to Y as *causes*, but different as *grounds*, or *reasons*, would be $X' \equiv^k_Y X$.

This section attempts to make the notion of subject matter a bit precise—as precise as it needs to be for the proposed application to "minimality in the respects that matter." We start by asking, what are subject matters considered as entities in their own right? This sets up a second question: what is *the* subject matter of a particular sentence S?

A subject matter **m**—**the number of stars**, is Lewis's example—is given by specifying all the ways things can be where **m** is concerned. The ways they can be number-of-stars-wise are for there to be no stars, or one star, or two stars, or etc. Formally we can think of **m** as a collection of set-of-worlds propositions P. **m** = {A, B, C,....} just if A, B, C,...constitute between them all the ways that things are liable to play out **m**-wise.

Subject matters can be more or less fine-grained. **The number of stars** is coarser-grained than **which stars exist** (henceforth **the stars**). It is finer-grained, though, than **whether the number of stars is prime**. **m** is as fine-grained as **n** when each n-cell subdivides into m-cells, and finer-grained when this holds in one direction only. The reader can check that this definition "delivers the right results" if:

The stars =
{|*Nothing is a star*|, |*The only star is Sol*|,..., |*The stars are Sol, Polaris, Vega,...*|,...}.
The number of stars =
{|$\exists_0 x\ star(x)$|, |$\exists_1 x\ star(x)$|,..., |$\exists_k x\ star(x)$|,...}.
Whether the number of stars is prime =
{$\cup_{prime(k)}$ |$\exists_k x\ star(x)$|, $\cup_{\sim prime(k)}$ |$\exists_k x\ star(x)$|}.

Next the subject matter of particular sentences. S's subject matter **s** is made up of S's various ways of being true; it is the set of all set-of-worlds propositions P such that S is true in way P in some world w. If *Stars exist* has a way of being true for each possible non-empty roster of stars, its subject matter will be what above we called **the stars**, except that the first, star-less, cell must be dropped since *Stars exist* is false in that cell.

XIV. Every Bit as Sufficient

The idea behind ℙ2: Z is relevant^k to Y just if Z is part of an X that is proportional^k to Y—an X no proper part of which undercuts X by sufficing^k for Y on a more economical basis. But, when *does* a still-sufficient proper part of X undercut X in this way? How indeed can X *not* be undercut by X', if X' is every bit as sufficient for Y? Ways were supposed to shed light on this.

For X' to be "every bit as sufficient" as X for Y seems at first to mean that Y holds in as high a proportion of X'-worlds as X-worlds, viz. all of them.

But another, more discerning reading is possible when statements holding in the same worlds can hold in a greater or lesser variety of ways.

Alice has three children and Bert has two. Is Alice any more of a parent than Bert? Certainly it is no more *true* of Alice that she is a parent. But she has some sort of advantage parental-status-wise; for the truth of *Alice is a parent* is more thoroughly witnessed than that of *Bert is a parent*. The advantage is clearest if the witnesses to the one truth form a proper subset of the witnesses to the other. Alice has two children with Bert, let's say, and one not with Bert. Now she becomes, in addition to being more often a parent, more *richly* or *comprehensively* a parent than Bert is. Her status as parent is witnessed by all the children witnessing Bert's parental status, and other children as well.

This is how X can avoid being undercut by X', though Y is no less definitely true in X'-worlds than X-worlds: Y is not as richly provided for in X'-worlds as in X-worlds. *God is praised every day from now on* is better proportioned to *God is pleased* than *God is praised and dogs bark every day from now on*, since the effect is just as richly guaranteed whether dogs bark or not. Can we maintain on a similar basis that *God is praised every day from tomorrow on* is better proportioned to *God is pleased* than *God is praised every day from now on*? We cannot, for the effect is *more* richly guaranteed in worlds where the praise starts today. Where it's truth that is more richly guaranteed, we'll speak of relative truthiness.

Suppose P and Q are both true in w. P is as truthy there as Q if every way Q holds in w is also a way that P holds in w ($\|Q\|^w \subseteq \|P\|^w$); it is truthier if Q holds in additional ways besides. So, for instance, A is as truthy as $A \vee B$ in worlds where B is false. But the disjunction is truthier in worlds where A and B are both true; A is true in w in a proper subset of the ways in which $A \vee B$ is true. Let's now add a transworld version. Writing $\|P\|^u$ for P's ways of being true in u, P is as truthy in u as Q is in v just if $\|Q\|^v$ is a subset of $\|P\|^u$. And P is truthier in u if $\|Q\|^v$ is a proper subset of $\|P\|^u$. Imagine that goats eat cans in both worlds but abstain from bottles in v. Then *Goats eat cans* is exactly as truthy in u as *Goats eats cans or bottles* is in v. If on the other hand goats eat bottles in v as well as cans, the disjunction is truthier in v than *Goats eat cans* is in u.

Now we are ready to say why a still-sufficient part X' of X sometimes, but not always, knocks X out of proportion with Y. X' undercuts X if it guarantees Y, not only as *surely* as X does, but also as *fully* as X does. X' does not undercut X if X compensates for its extra strength by guaranteeing Y more fully. Guaranteeing more fully is a matter of $\exists W (W \Rightarrow^k Y)$ being truthier on the whole in X-worlds than X'-worlds; there is for each X-world an X'-world where it's less truthy, but not vice versa. The official definition is as follows ($\Uparrow^k Y$ is short for $\exists W (W \Rightarrow^k Y)$, that is, Y is guaranteed^k):

[S] X guarantees^k Y more fully than X' does iff:
  (i) $X \Rightarrow^k Y$ and $X' \Rightarrow^k Y$
  (ii) $(\forall X\text{-worlds } u)(\exists X'\text{-world } v)$ [$\Uparrow^k Y$ is truthier in u than in v], but
  (iii) $\neg(\forall X'\text{-worlds } v)(\exists X\text{-world } u)$ [$\Uparrow^k Y$ is truthier in v than in u].

Return with [S] in mind to *God is praised every day from today on* (X) and *God is praised every day from tomorrow on* (X'). They both causally guarantee *God is pleased* (Y). But X provides a fuller guarantee, since *God's pleasure is guaranteed* is truthier in X-worlds where God's praises are sung every day than X'-worlds where the praise begins tomorrow.[40] X guaranteeing Y more fully, X' is in no position to knock it out of proportion with Y.

XV. Super-Humeanism

Hume conceived of proportionality as minimal sufficiency. Perhaps there is something right about this after all, *if* we are careful about what is being minimized, subject to which constraints. A proportional X is one that is minimal among conditions guaranteeing Y as fully as X does:

[P3] X is proportional^k to Y ($X \propto^k Y$) iff:
  1. X guarantees^k Y ($X \Rightarrow^k Y$).
  2. $(\forall X' \leq X)$ [if X' guarantees^k Y as fully as X, then $X'=X$].[41]

The super-Humean package is [P3] plus:

[H] Z is helpful^k to Y ($Z \rightsquigarrow^k Y$) iff an X obtains such that $Z \leq X$ and $X \propto^k Y$.

Helpfulness is a simple, deep, and elusive idea. Hume thought he had explained it with minimality. But the explanation didn't work, because some Xs are helpful all the way down. A variant using *focused* minimality—minimality where a certain subject matter is concerned—seems to do better.

---

[40] Objection: Let X'' be *God is cursed today and praised from tomorrow on*. X'' suffices^c for *His pleasure is guaranteed*. If [$X'' \Rightarrow^c Y$] and the like are allowed as truthmakers for $\Uparrow^k Y$, then $\Uparrow^k Y$ isn't truthier in u than v after all; it is made true in v, but not u, by [$X'' \Rightarrow^c Y$]. Reply: Why think [$X'' \Rightarrow^c Y$] is a way for $\Uparrow^k Y$ to be true? The Only- In- Part- By test suggests otherwise. *I saw to it that God was cursed and then praised* undercuts *I ONLY saw to it that God's pleasure was guaranteed*. And I don't arrange for that guarantee BY arranging that God be cursed today and praised thereafter; God was pleased despite the cursing.

[41] This is a version of [P2] if "$X' \equiv^k_Y X$" is suitably unpacked. X' and X are the same to Y if X', although weaker than X, also provides less of a guarantee.

References

Angell, R. B. 1989. "Deducibility, entailment and analytic containment." In *Directions in Relevant Logic*, eds Norman J. and R. Sylvan. Dordrecht: Kluwer Academic Publishers.

Baron-Schmitt, N. 2021. "Contingent grounding." *Synthese* 199(1): 4561–80.

Berto, F. 2017. "Impossible worlds and the logic of imagination." *Erkenntnis* 82(6): 1277–97.

Correia, F. 2004. "Semantics for analytic containment." *Studia Logica* 77(1): 87–104.

Fine, K. 2012a. "Guide to ground." In *Metaphysical Grounding: Understanding the Structure of Reality*, eds F. Correia and B. Schnieder. Cambridge: Cambridge University Press, 37–80.

Fine, K. 2012b. "The pure logic of ground." *Review of Symbolic Logic* 5(1): 1–25.

Fine, K. 2013. "A note on partial content." *Analysis* 73(3): 413–19.

Fine, K. 2016. "Angellic content." *Journal of Philosophical Logic* 45(2): 199–226.

Fine, K. 2017a. "A theory of truth-conditional content (I): Conjunction, disjunction and negation." *Journal of Philosophical Logic* 46(6): 625–74.

Fine, K. 2017b. "A theory of truth-conditional content (II): Subject-matter, common content, remainder, and ground." *Journal of Philosophical Logic* 46(6): 675–702.

Fine, K. 2017c. "Truthmaker semantics." In *A Companion to the Philosophy of Language*, eds B. Hale, A. Miller, and C. Wright. Oxford: Wiley, 556–77.

Gemes, K. 1994. "A new theory of content I: Basic content." *Journal of Philosophical Logic* 23(6): 595–620.

Gemes, K. 1997. "A new theory of content II: Model theory and some alternatives." *Journal of Philosophical Logic* 26(4): 449–76.

Goodman, N. 1951. *The Structure of Appearance*. Cambridge, MA: Harvard University Press.

Hallett, M. 1986. *Cantorian Set Theory and Limitation of Size*. Oxford: Oxford University Press.

Hempel, C. G. 1945. "Studies in the logic of confirmation (I)." *Mind* 54(213): 1–26.

Hume, D. 1740/2003. *A Treatise of Human Nature*. Oxford: Oxford University Press.

Hume, D. 1740/2006. *An Enquiry Concerning Human Understanding*. Oxford: Clarendon Press.

Kim, J. 1973. "Causation, nomic subsumption, and the concept of event." *Journal of Philosophy* 70(8): 217–36.

Kment, B. 2014. *Modality and Explanatory Reasoning*. Oxford: Oxford University Press.

Krämer, S. and S. Roski. 2017. "Difference-making grounds." *Philosophical Studies* 174(5): 1191–1215.

Kratzer, A. 2002. "Facts: particulars or information units?" *Linguistics and Philosophy* 25(5–6): 655–70.

Kratzer, A. 1989. "An investigation of the lumps of thought." *Linguistics and Philosophy* 12: 607–53.

Lewis, D. 1974. "Radical interpretation." *Synthese* 27(3–4): 331–44.

Lewis, D. 1983. "New work for a theory of universals." *Australasian Journal of Philosophy* 61(4): 343–77.

Moss, S. 2018. *Probabilistic Knowledge*. Oxford: Oxford University Press.

Muñoz, D. 2019. "Defeaters and disqualifiers." *MIND* 128(511): 887–906.

Schlenker, P. 2008. "Be articulate: a pragmatic theory of presupposition projection." *Theoretical Linguistics* 34(3): 157–212.

Schlenker, P. 2009. "Local contexts." *Semantics & Pragmatics* 2(3): 1–78.

Sellars, W. 1963. "Philosophy and the scientific image of man." In *Science, Perception and Reality*, ed. W. Sellars. New York: Humanities Press: 1–40.

Skyrms, B. 1983. "Zeno's paradox of measure." In *Physics, Philosophy, and Psychoanalysis: Essays in Honor of Adolf Grunbaum*, ed. R. Cohen and L. Laudan, 223–54. Dordrecht: D. Reidel.
Strevens, M. 2007. "Mackie remixed." In *Causation and Explanation*, ed. J. K. Campbell, M. O'Rourke and H. S. Silverstein, 4–93. Cambridge, MA: MIT Press.
Yablo, S. 1992a. "Cause and essence." *Synthese* 93(3): 403–49.
Yablo, S. 1992b. "Mental causation." *Philosophical Review* 101(2): 245–80.
Yablo, S. 2014. *Aboutness*. Princeton: Princeton University Press.
Yablo, S. 2016. "Parts and differences." *Philosophical Studies* 173(1): 141–57.
Yablo, S. 2017a. "Kment on counterfactuals." *Analysis* 77(1): 148–55.
Yablo, S. 2017b. "Precis of *Aboutness*." *Philosophical Studies* 174(3): 771–77.
Yalcin, S. 2012. "Bayesian expressivism." *Proceedings of the Aristotelian Society* 112: 123–60. Oxford: Oxford University Press.

Outline of an Object-Based Truthmaker Semantics for Modals and Propositional Attitudes

Friederike Moltmann

I. Introduction

Possible-worlds semantics certainly is the most common approach to the semantics of modals, and it is also a dominant approach to the semantics of attitude reports, at least in linguistic semantics. While philosophers have discussed problems with possible-worlds semantics for quite some time, possible-worlds semantics continues to have a range of attractive features that have made it persevere as a central tool of analysis in formal semantics. First of all, possible-worlds semantics appears to have the very general advantage of allowing for a unified compositional semantics of intensional and extensional expressions of various sorts, in the tradition of Montague grammar. In addition, possible-worlds semantics appears to have more specific advantages, such as being a suitable basis for accounting for various sorts of connections between modals and attitude reports, for the way presuppositions are satisfied in attitude reports and in modal sentences, and for how utterances of sentences of different sorts contribute to the discourse context or common ground, which is standardly construed in terms of possible worlds (as a set of worlds, a context set).

The main shortcomings of possible-worlds semantics are well known, foremost the identification of the meanings of logically equivalent sentences and more generally the problem of sets of possible worlds giving a too coarse-grained notion of content. The need for a more fine-grained notion of content, especially for attitude reports, was the motivation for an alternative, structured conception of content, replacing sets of worlds by structured propositions, n-tuples of objects or concepts. The structured-propositions view comes with its own problems, however. For one thing, it raises serious conceptual problems (the unity of propositions problem, the arbitrariness of the order of propositional constituents). Moreover, it is tailored for attitude reports of a certain sort but not modals, and is hard to make use of for general semantic purposes, such as compositionality.

A third approach to the semantics of attitude reports makes use of situations rather than entire worlds, an approach that also gives a more fine-grained notion of content, though of a different sort. One recent version of such an approach is truthmaker semantics (Fine 2017, 2018a, 2018b). Truthmaker semantics is based on the relation of exact truthmaking or satisfaction between a situation or action and a sentence, as well as a corresponding relation of exact falsemaking or violation. Truthmaker semantics has been applied to a range of semantic and logical topics, including conditionals and deontic modals, but not attitude verbs and modals in general.

This chapter gives an outline of an approach to the semantics of attitude verbs and modals that I call *object-based truthmaker semantics*. Object-based truthmaker semantics carries the various advantages of truthmaker semantics, making use of situations or actions in the role of exact truthmaker or satisfiers, though not just of sentences but also of a range of objects which I call *modal and attitudinal objects*, entities of the sort of obligations, permissions, claims, requests, and judgments. Object-based truthmaker avoids the problems of possible-worlds semantics, yet it aims to retain similar advantages, in particular in providing a unified semantics of modals and attitude reports and a way of dealing with the connections between modals and attitude reports and the contribution of sentences to a discourse context. In addition to avoiding a too coarse-grained notion of context, it also has specific advantages, for example by providing a better account of modals in embedded contexts (harmonic modals).

Object-based truthmaker semantics is based on an ontology of modal and attitudinal objects, entities like obligations, permissions, claims, requests, and judgments. These objects are considered the primary content bearers (bearers of truth or satisfaction conditions), not propositions. Unlike in Fine's sentence-based truthmaker semantics, object-based truthmaker semantics assigns truthmakers (situations or actions) not just to sentences, but also to modal and attitudinal objects. More precisely, each modal or attitudinal object is assigned a set of truthmakers or satisfiers and a set of falsemakers or violators.

Object-based truthmaker semantics assigns very different logical forms to attitude reports and modal sentences than the standard view does. The standard view is that clauses when they are embedded under an attitude verb act as singular terms standing for propositions. The present view is that such clauses act semantically as predicates of the attitudinal object associated with the attitude verb. The standard view is that modal predicates act as quantifiers over possible worlds and that what I will call the *sentential unit* associated with the modal predicate (complement clause, subject clause, or prejacent) acts as the scope of such a quantifier. The present view is that the sentential unit associated with a modal acts as a predicate of the relevant modal object. Clauses act as predicates of modal or attitudinal objects by giving their truthmaking or satisfaction conditions, which, I will argue, are best cast in terms of truthmaker semantics.

This chapter will first give a general outline of object-based truthmaker semantics against the background of the standard semantic view of attitude reports and modals and then apply object-based truthmaker semantics to different sorts of attitude and modal predicates. The applications will concern besides attitude reports and modal sentences in general, the semantics of different types of attitude verbs, performative and descriptive uses of modals, modals embedded under attitude verbs, and dynamic aspects of meaning. The chapter will not give a thorough discussion of the syntactic basis of the semantic analyses that are presented and does not aim for a fully developed compositional semantics.

II. Standard Views of Propositional Attitudes and Modals

The Relational Analysis of Attitude Reports and the Standard Analysis of Modals

The standard analysis of clausal complements of attitude verbs as in (1a) takes them to be terms standing for propositions, which in turn will be arguments of the embedding attitude verb. This is what I call the *relational analysis* (Moltmann 2003, 2013), given for (1a) in (1b):

(1) a. John believes that Mary is happy.
  b. believe (John, [*that Mary is happy*])

Propositions are entities that are generally taken to play three roles: to be (the primary) bearers of truth values, to be the meanings of sentences (or referents of embedded clauses), and to be the contents or 'objects' of propositional attitudes.

There are two standard views about the content of propositional attitudes: the possible-worlds view, on which the content of propositional attitudes consists in a set of worlds, and the structured propositions view, according to which that content is a structured proposition, such as, in a very simple case, a pair consisting of a property and an object. While there are various difficulties for both views, the second view has gained more popularity among philosophers, whereas the first view is generally adopted by linguists. One reason for the attraction of the possible-worlds view to linguists is a range of connections between attitude reports and modals that can, it appears, be easily formulated within the possible-worlds view.

The standard view of modals consists in the *quantificational analysis*, according to which a modal of necessity as in (2a) has the meaning given in (2b), and a modal of possibility as in (3a) the meaning given in (3b):

(2) a. John needs to leave.
  b. $\forall w(w \in f(w_o) \rightarrow [\textit{John leave}]^w = \text{true})$

(3) a. John is allowed to leave.
    b. $\exists w(w \in f(w_o)$ & $[John\ leave]^w = true)$

The contextually given function f maps the world of evaluation w_o to the relevant set of worlds. The quantificational analysis of modals was extended to verbs expressing belief and knowledge by Hintikka, and the Hintikka-style analysis has since become a common approach to the semantics of attitude verbs in natural language semantics. Thus, (4a), on that view, has the truth conditions in (4b), where $bel_{w,j}$ represents the set of worlds compatible with what John believes in w:

(4) a. John believes that S.
    b. $\forall w'(w' \in bel_{w,j} \to [S]^{w'} = true)$.

(4b) can be reformulated straightforwardly in terms of the relational analysis, making use of a proposition p (the set of worlds in which the sentence S is true) as an argument of the attitude verb:

(5) $believe(J, p)$ iff $\forall w'(w' \in bel_{w,j} \to w' \in p)$.

Such a modal analysis of attitude verbs has generally has been applied only to attitude verbs that are taken to involve universal quantification over worlds, such as belief and knowledge.[1] It is not obvious in fact that there are verbs expressing mental attitudes that are correlates of modals of possibility and thus would involve not universal but existential quantification over worlds. Perhaps there are uses of *think* that functions that was ('thinking' in the sense of taking a possibility into consideration), and there are verbs like *hypothesize*. Clearly, though, there are speech act verbs that correspond to modals of possibility, acts of giving permission as well as acts of inviting or offering: permissions, invitations, and offers are associated with possibility, not necessity.

III. The Attraction of Possible-Worlds Semantic Account of Modals and Propositional Attitudes

The possible-worlds account of content is most plausible for implicit beliefs, including those of animals and small children, where not a particular structure of thought matters but rather the agent's dispositions regarding particular circumstances (Stalnaker 1984). However, the view is much less plausible for various other attitudes, involving mental or illocutionary acts.

---

[1] Some attitude verbs have been considered imposing an ordering of preference along worlds such as *want, wish, be happy* (Heim 1992).

Possible-worlds semantics, though, has been attractive to formal semanticists for other reasons. First, possible-worlds semantics, it appears, allows for a unified compositional semantics of the sentential units (clausal complements or subjects or prejacents) associated with both attitudinal and modal predicates. Sentential units, on that view, always stand for sets of possible worlds, which are obtained compositionally from possible-world-based meanings of subsentential expressions.

Possible worlds have also played an important role for representing the common ground. The common ground is generally conceived as an unstructured content of what the interlocutors take for granted, as a set of worlds or context set. The common ground plays a central role in theories of presuppositions, in the so-called the satisfaction theory of presupposition projection (Heim 1983). On the satisfaction theory, the presuppositions of a sentence S need to be true in the worlds of the common ground C (a set of worlds) in order for C to be updated with the proposition p expressed by S (a set of worlds) with C (which means intersecting p with C). Complex sentences such as conjunctions and conditionals involve complex conditions on updating. Updating a context set C with the utterance of a conjunction S & S' consist in first intersecting C with the proposition expressed by S and then intersecting the result with the proposition expressed by S'.

In addition to the primary context set representing what is shared by the interlocutors, various *secondary context sets* need to be distinguished, representing what the interlocutors take the content of a particular type of attitude of a particular agent to be.

Further additions to the context set (or the context sets) are needed in order to account for updating with questions as well as with imperatives and performatively used deontic modals, that is, modals that put a requirement in place rather than describing it, as possibly below:[2]

(6) You must leave.

Thus, Portner (2004) proposes to augment the common ground with a sets of issues (a set of propositions) for updating with questions, as well as a *to do*-list (a set of properties or action types) for updating with imperatives and performatively used deontic modals (or several such lists; cf. Portner 2007).

There are also particular connections among propositional attitudes and modals. I will focus on just two. One of them consists in that attitude or illocutionary act reports may permit particular inferences to modal sentences such as, under suitable circumstances, the inferences below:

[2] For more on the notion of a performative use of a modal see Portner (2007).

(7) John asked Mary to leave.
Mary must leave.

(8) John offered Mary to use the house.
Mary may use the house.

Another connection between attitude reports and modals is so-called *harmonic modals* (Kratzer 2016). Harmonic modals are occurrences of modals in the complement clause of an attitude verb that appear to resume the modal force associated with the reported attitude rather than contributing to a modal content of that attitude:

(9) John insisted that Mary should leave.

Again, possible-worlds semantics appears to be suited to capture this sort of connection between modals and propositional attitudes (Section 4).

Other sorts of connections between attitude reports and modals include the interpretation of epistemic modals in complement clauses of attitude reports (Pranav and Hacquard 2013).

The Structured-Propositions View

Structured propositions have been proposed as an alternative to propositions as sets of worlds since they give a more fine-grained notion of content. A structured proposition is generally conceived as an n-tuple consisting of meanings of elementary constituents. Thus, a simple type of structured proposition, as the meaning of the subject-predicate sentence *Mary is happy*, would be a pair consisting of a property (the property of being happy) and an object (Mary). With structured propositions as their meanings, two sentences that are logically equivalent but involve significantly different syntactic structures are distinguished, as are sentences that about different objects or involve different properties. Though structured proposition appear more suited than sets of worlds for the content of propositional attitudes, structured propositions come with conceptual problems of their own, especially the problem of the unity of propositions: truth conditions for structured propositions need to be stipulated and are not inherent in the nature of structured propositions as such (Jubien 2001, Moltmann 2003b, 2014, Soames 2010, Hanks 2011). Moreover, the structured-propositions view imposes a fineness of grain that is not generally needed for the semantics of modals, and perhaps the semantics of various sorts of implicit attitudes, and sometimes even for explicit attitudes. Thus, the distinction between an active and a passive sentence often does not matter even for explicit attitudes.

Furthermore, construing the objects of at least some attitudes as structured propositions could not permit accounting for the connections between propositional attitudes and modals that were mentioned in the last section.

Yet, it appears that for certain sorts of attitude reports a highly fine-grained, structured notion of content is unavoidable, especially for reports with verbs of saying (including (occurrent) *think*, Moltmann 2017b). The sensitivity of reports of acts of saying to syntactic structure and perhaps even the choice of words can be enforced by the use of *literally* as below:

(10) John literally said that S.

However, if for verbs of saying, the particular choice of words as well as the syntactic structure of the complement clause may matter, this should not so much motivate a particular conception of sentence meaning as such (structure propositions as opposed to sets of worlds). Rather it motivates a view according to which the complement of verbs of saying contributes differently to the characterization of the reported attitude than the complement of other attitude verbs, namely by specifying the structure of the product of a locutionary act, rather than just providing a propositional content (or the truth or satisfaction conditions of the reported attitudinal object) (Moltmann 2017b). In what follows, therefore I will set aside verbs of saying, as they arguably involve a rather different overall semantics than other attitude verbs.

IV. Truthmaker Semantics

Truthmaker semantics, as recently developed by Fine (2017a, 2018a, 2018b), gives a notion of content that is more fine-grained than that of possible-worlds semantics, but yet not as fine-grained as that of the structured-propositions view. In particular, content is not taken to reflect syntactic structure in the way structured propositions do. The following is a very brief outline of Fine's truthmaker semantics, which should suffice for the present purposes.

Truthmaker semantics is based on situations and actions (rather than entire worlds), as well as the relation of exact truthmaking or satisfaction holding between situations or actions and sentences. More precisely, truthmaker semantics involves a domain of situations or actions containing actual, possible as well as impossible situations and actions. This domain is ordered by a part relation and is closed under sum formation. A situation or action s stands in the relation $\Vdash$ of exact truthmaking (or exact satisfaction) to a sentence S just in case s makes S true and is wholly relevant for the truth of S. $\Vdash$ applies to both declarative and imperative sentences: declarative sentences are made true by situations that are their exact truthmakers, imperatives are complied with by actions that are their exact satisfiers. The following standard conditions on the truthmaking of sentences with conjunctions, disjunctions, and existential quantification then hold:[3]

(11) a. s ⊪ S *and* S' iff for some s' and s", s = sum(s', s") and s' ⊪ S and s" ⊪ S'.
   b. s ⊪ S *or* S' iff s ⊪ S or s ⊪ S'.
(12) For a one-place property P, s ⊪ ∃x S iff s ⊪ S[x/d] for some individual d.

Truthmaker semantics assigns sentences not only truthmakers or satisfiers but also falsifiers or violators. Making use of the relation of (exact) falsification or violation allows a straightforward formulation of the truthmaking conditions of negative sentences: a truthmaker for ¬ S is a falsifier for S. With ⊫ as the relation of (exact) falsification or violation, the truthmaking condition for negation is given below:

(13) s ⊪ *not* S iff s ⊫ S.

Also complex sentences are assigned both verification and falsification conditions. For conjunctions and disjunctions the falsification conditions are those below:

(14) a. s ⊫ S *and* S' iff s ⊫ S or s ⊫ S'.
   b. s ⊫ S *or* S' iff for some s' and s", s = sum(s', s") and s' ⊫ S and s" ⊫ S'.

A sentence S then has as its meaning a pair <pos(S), neg(S)> consisting of a *positive denotation*, the set pos(S) of verifiers of S, and a *negative denotation*, the set neg(S) of falsifiers of S. In truthmaker semantics, logically equivalent sentences have different semantic values as long as they have different subject matters (i.e., are about different entities or more generally describe different situations).

Truthmaker semantics as developed by Fine assigns content only to sentences and has not been developed so as to allow for an application to attitude reports and modals in general.[4] An obvious way in which one might try to apply truthmaker semantics to attitude reports would be to take the truth-maker-based meanings of sentences to be the arguments of attitudinal relations. This means that (15a) would be analysed in (15b):

(15) a. John believes that S.
   b. believe(John, <pos(S), neg(S)>)

---

[3] The truthmaking condition for sentences with universal quantification and conditionals are less obvious and would require a lot more exposition.
[4] Fine (2018a, 2018b) applies truthmaker semantics to deontic modality, focusing on logical, rather than linguistic aspects.

However, there are a range of reasons why such an analysis would be unsatisfactory. One reason is that it could hardly be used to account for the connections between modals and attitude reports. Another reason is that (15b) would fall under the relational analysis of attitude reports, which is associated with a range of philosophical and linguistic difficulties, as will be discussed in the next section.

V. Problems for the Relational Analysis of Attitude Reports and the Importance of Modal and Attitudinal Objects

The relational analysis on which attitude verbs take propositions as arguments allow for more or less fine-grained notions of content: a proposition may be construed as a set of worlds or as a structured proposition of some sort. There are a range of philosophical and linguistic difficulties, however, for the relational analysis.[5] I will just mention them briefly, since they are elaborated elsewhere in the literature and my own previous work.

[1] The relational analysis fails to make a distinction between the content and the object of an attitude, treating propositions as things agents have attitudes to, rather than as the contents of attitudes that agents engage in.
[2] Abstract propositions raise a number of conceptual problems, which are a major topic of discussion in contemporary philosophy of language. Those problems include the problem of the graspability of propositions and the problem of how propositions as abstract objects can be true or false.
[3] The relational analysis has difficulty accounting for the Substitution Problem, the problem of the unacceptability of (16b) as an inference from (16a), and the Objectivization Effect, the difference in the understanding between (17a) and (17b):

(16) a. John assumed that S.
   b. ?? John assumed the proposition that S.

(17) a. John fears that S.
   b. John fears the proposition that S.

[4] The relational analysis has difficulties accounting for the semantics of nominal constructions. Clausal complements of nouns as in (18) do not behave like arguments, since they are not obligatory even if the verb requires a complement:

(18) John's request that S.

---

[5] See Moltmann (2003b, 2013 ch. 4, 2014) and reference therein.

Semantically, the *that*-clause in (18) seems to stand for what the entire NP stands for (a request), rather than providing an object entering a thematic relation to the noun *request*. Yet, the clausal complement would stand for a proposition and a proposition is not the same thing as a request. For example, a request can be fulfilled or ignored, but a proposition cannot (at least not in the same sense) (See Section 4).[6]

> [5] Another general problem for the relational analysis comes from the semantic behavior of what I call *special quantifiers* (Moltmann 2003a, 2003b, 2013). Special quantifiers (and pronouns), which include *something*, *everything*, *that*, and *what*, have the ability of taking the position of clauses (as well as predicative and other nonreferential complements). In the complement position of attitude verbs, they are generally taken to range over propositions, the shared content of attitudes of different agents, as below:

(19) John assumed the same thing as Mary.

However, predicates acting as restrictors of special quantifiers that are complement of attitude verbs are not generally understood as predicates of propositions, but rather as predicates of attitudinal objects:

(20) a. John asserted something shocking.
 b. John demanded something impossible to comply with.

Shocking and *impossible to comply with* express properties that can be attributed to attitudinal objects (assertions, demands) but not abstract propositions (which cannot be 'shocking' or 'impossible to comply with').

The same point can be made for the special relative pronoun *what* in reports of sharing as below:

(21) John asserted what Mary asserted.

There are particular constraints on reports on sharing that are not compatible with the relational analysis (Moltmann 2003a, 2003b, 2013). Roughly, the two attitude verbs in such a report need to involve the same force and flavor, but may differ in certain other respects such as strength:

---

[6] The syntactic status of clausal complements of nouns, though, is far from obvious and there is a significant syntactic controversy surrounding it. Some researchers assimilate them to relative clauses (Arsenijević 2009, Moulton 2009, Kayne 2010). Others have argued against such assimilation (de Cuba 2017). The present view that clauses semantically act as predicates would go along well with the view that clausal complements of nouns, and even verbs, are relative clauses, but it is compatible with a different syntactic analysis of complement clauses, as long as the analysis permits them to be in some way interpreted as properties Note that even some relative clauses, unrestrictive relative clauses, have been analysed not as semantic predicates, but as (E-type) pronouns. See Cinque (2008) for discussion and further references.

(22) a. ??? John promised what Mary asserted, that he will come back.
   b. ??? John asserted what Mary demanded, that he will be back in an hour.
(23) a. John suggested what Mary asserted.
   b. John requested what Mary demanded.

The constraints on quantifier restrictions and on reports of sharing support the view that special quantifiers are *nominalizing quantifiers*, ranging not over force-neutral propositions but entities like assertions, demands, and promises, suggestions and requests, that is, attitudinal objects (or kinds of them) (Moltmann 2003a, 2003b, 2013).

VI. The Ontology of Modal and Attitudinal Objects

Object-based truthmaker semantics pursues an alternative to the propositions-based relational analysis of attitude reports as well as to the quantificational analysis of modal sentences. It is an alternative that is based on a novel ontology of attitudinal and modal objects, which is what this section will briefly expand on.

Attitudinal and modal objects are part of the ontology implicit in natural language: they act as semantic values of nouns (especially deverbal nominalizations) and of special quantifiers, as referents associated with *that*-clauses in certain contexts, and as implicit arguments of predicates. The characteristic properties of attitudinal and modal objects are reflected in the semantics of those constructions, though there are also various language-independent intuitions that give support to that ontology.

Modal and attitudinal objects generally have a limited life span and may display other features of concreteness. But they also share three content-related properties, which distinguish them from related entities, in particular from acts and propositions:

[1] Attitudinal and modal objects are bearers of truth or satisfaction condition.
[2] Attitudinal and modal objects enter exact or close similarity relations just on the basis of being the same in content.
[3] The part structure of attitudinal and modal is based on partial content only.

These properties sharply distinguish attitudinal and modal objects from actions and, at least in part, from propositions.

Ad [1]: Attitudinal and modal objects generally have truth conditions, or rather, more generally, satisfaction conditions. This is reflected in the great range of predicates of satisfaction to that can apply to them (*was satisfied, was fulfilled, was executed, was followed, was broken, was complied with*). The applicability of such predicates sharply distinguishes attitudinal and modal objects both from sentences, propositions and 'mental representations', and from actions. Thus, neither sentences, propositions, mental representations or acts can be 'fulfilled', 'satisfied' or 'broken' (Ulrich 1979, Moltmann 2017a, 2021).[7]

Ad [2]: For two attitudinal or modal objects of the same type to be exactly similar or 'the same', it suffices that they be the same in content. This is how *John's thought is the same as Mary's, John's promise is the same as Bill's, John's obligation is the same as Joe's* are understood (Moltmann 2013, ch. 4, 2014, 2017a). Obviously this condition fails to obtain for actions.

Ad [3]: Unlike actions, attitudinal and modal objects have a part structure that is strictly based on partial content (Moltmann 2017a, 2017c). Thus, the expression *part of* when applied to attitudinal and modal objects (as in *part of the claim/thought/promise/request/obligation/need*) can pick out only a partial content, not a temporal part.

Some attitudinal objects are products of acts in the sense of Twardowski's (1911) distinction between actions and products. Thus, a claim is the (illocutionary) product of an act of claiming, a promise the (illocutionary) product of an act of promising, and a decision the (cognitive) product of an act of deciding.[8] Cognitive and illocutionary products generally do not last longer than the acts that produce them, and like the corresponding acts, they come with a 'force', not just a content. However, products have fundamentally different sorts of properties from acts (only some of which were noted by Twardowski). Most importantly, they have the properties [1]–[3]. Modal products (not recognized as such by Twardowski) are modal objects produced by actions, the same actions that may have produced illocutionary products. Thus the same act (of demanding) may produce a demand and an obligation. Modal products share the properties [1]–[3] with cognitive and illocutionary products, but they may endure past the act that establishes them (Moltmann 2017a, 2018).

Representational properties (including satisfaction conditions) are characteristic of all attitudinal and modal objects, including those that do not result from acts, such as state-like attitudinal objects (intentions, beliefs, desires, fears) and weak permissions and obligations. This means that the representational ability of modal and attitudinal objects should not be viewed as resulting from intentional acts, but is better to be attributed to primitive intentionality, as the hallmark of the mental.

There is also language-independent support for attitudinal and modal objects. Thus, attitudinal objects such as beliefs, intentions, judgments and decisions carry a content and play causal roles, which propositions can't (we are made to

---

[7] Predicates of satisfaction clearly show that nominalizations of attitude verbs like *decision, promise* and *request* cannot be viewed as ambiguous between standing for propositions and standing for acts, as the standard view would have it (e.g. Pustejovsky 1995). Rather they unambiguously stand for entities of a third kind, attitudinal objects.

[8] Products in Twardowski's sense are best understood as artifacts that lack a material realization or, in the case of decisions, a physical realization, 'abstract' artifacts in Thomasson's (1999) sense (Moltmann 2014, 2017a).

act by a decision, an intention, a fear, not by a proposition). Moreover, attitudinal and modal objects, rather than propositions, appear to act as the content-bearing objects of memory (decisions, intentions, fears, thoughts and obligations are what we remember, not propositions).

Kinds of attitudinal objects also play an important role in the semantics of attitude reports and modal sentences, and they are well reflected in natural language: explicitly with terms of the sort *the thought that* S, *the claim that* S etc. and implicitly in the semantics of special quantifiers and pronouns. Two particular attitudinal objects (of the same sort) belong to the same kind just in case they are exactly or closely similar ('are the same'), which means they are the same in content. Thus, if John's thought is the same as Mary's thought, John and Mary share a thought and if John's claim is the same as Mary's, they made the same claim.

VII. Motivations for Object-Based Truthmaker Semantics

Intentionality and Truthmaking as a Matter of the Mental

On the present view, sentences embedded under attitude verbs act as predicates of attitudinal objects specifying their satisfaction conditions. Propositions as entities that are both the meanings of sentences (in a context) and the objects of attitudes then play no longer a role. Problems for propositions such as how propositions have truth conditions and can be grasped therefore no longer arise.

In object-based truthmaker semantics, truthmaking applies to both sentences and attitudinal objects, which allows linking truthmaker semantics to the intentionality of the mind. Attitudinal objects such as intentions and decisions come with inherent satisfaction or realization conditions, and are satisfied or realized not by worlds or world states, but rather by actions.[9] Object-based truthmaker semantics accounts for the fact that it may depend on the particular attitudinal or modal object what the satisfiers in question are, say, actions or situations. Moreover, as Searle (1983) points out, intentions and requests do not take just actions as satisfiers, but rather actions 'by way of' realizing or fulfilling the intention or request, that is, actions with a particular gloss that makes reference to the intention or request itself. Thus, to use Searle's example, doing something that accidentally kills my neighbor is not an action that fulfills my intention to kill my neighbor, rather only an action with the intention of doing so is. Other attitudinal or modal objects (hopes, beliefs, epistemic modal objects, for example) do not require their satisfiers or truthmakers to be of that sort.

---

[9] In fact, a rudimentary truthmaker semantics for mental states and products has been put forward by Searle (1983), for whom intentions and decisions (which come with a world-to-word/mind direction of fit) have actions as satisfiers, and beliefs, judgments, desires etc. have states of affairs as truthmakers or satisfiers.

Weak and Strong Permissions

Another important case that shows well how truthmakers depend on the type of modal or attitudinal object is the distinction between weak and strong permissions (von Wright 1963). Weak and strong permissions are two different types of objects, at least on the present view. Strong permissions generally are the products of particular acts of permitting, whereas weak permissions are states of what is explicitly or implicitly permitted. Strong permissions have different satisfaction conditions from weak permissions. Strong permissions have as satisfiers only actions meeting what is explicitly permitted, whereas weak permissions have as satisfiers also actions that are just not in violation of what is obligatory and in that sense are implicitly permitted. It thus depends on the type of modal object in question what actions count as satisfiers.

The distinction between the two sorts of permissions is well reflected English, in the contrast between simple predicates (*be* + impersonal adjectival passive) as in (24a), which display the weak reading (as well as a strong one), and complex predicates (light verb + nominal), as in (24b, 24c), which display the strong reading (only):

(24) a. Mary *is permitted to* take a walk.
    b. Mary *has permission* to take a walk.
    c. John *gave permission* for Mary to take a walk.

The possible-worlds-based account would give the same semantics to the two sorts of permission sentences: for a permission sentence such as (24b) to be true, the clausal complement would have to be true in *some* world compatible with the agent's obligations. But having a permission means more than that: it means that there was an act whose content is, at least in part, given by the complement clause and whose product, the permission, can be taken up by performing the act described by the complement clause. Moreover, giving or receiving a permission does involve a change, but not in the set of worlds compatible what the agent is obliged to do. Rather it involves a change in a set of options to act that are at the agent's disposal. The complex predicates in (24b, 24c) involve explicit reference to a permission, the product of an act of permitting, and the complement clause serves to give the content of that product. By contrast, (24a) contains a stative predicate *is permitted* describing a deontic state, rather than the product of an act, and it is that state that the complement relates to. The strong reading thus will go along with the compositional semantics of complex predicates as in (24b, 24c), and the weak reading with that of a simple stative predicate, as in (24a).

Also propositional attitudes display such contrasts:

(25) a. John *thought* that S.
   b. John *had the thought* that S.
(26) a. John *assumed* that S.
   b. John *made the assumption* that S.

Whereas (25a) and (26a) may just describe dispositional states of John, (25b) and (26b) describe cognitive products resulting from acts.

Underspecification of Content

Another important advantage of object-based truthmaker semantics concerns the possibility of underspecification of the content of certain types of attitudinal or modal objects by the complement clause or associated sentential unit. One relevant case that has been discussed in the literature is the underspecification of a desire as in the desire report below (Graff Fara 2013):

(27) a. Fiona wants to catch a fish.

Fiona's desire, according to (27a) is not satisfied if she catches any fish whatsoever, but, most likely, only a fish she can eat. Note that the speaker uttering (27a) need not know what the exact constraints are that Fiona's desire may impose on what satisfies it.

Also certain types of modals allow for this sort of underspecification, in particular teleological and deontic modals as below:

(27) b. Fiona needs to catch a fish (in order to have something for dinner).
   c. John needs to write a letter (and therefore cannot be disturbed).

The need reported in (27b) may exhibit the very same underspecification as the desire reported in (27a). The speaker need not know about the particular conditions imposed on the satisfaction of the need, the kind of fish Mary needs to catch in (27b) and the sort of letter John has to write in (27c).

The underspecification of desire reports constitutes a serious problem for the standard view according to which the clausal complement of an attitude verb gives the full truth or satisfaction conditions of the reported attitude (Graff Fara 2013). By contrast, it is unproblematic for the present analysis of attitude reports within object-based truthmaker semantics. The underspecification exhibited in (27a) as well as in (27b, 27c) simply means that what the satisfiers in question are depends on the particular attitudinal or modal object in question, not the sentence used to characterize it (which may give only necessary, not sufficient conditions for its satisfaction). That is, the reported desire or need itself may come with constraints as to what will satisfy it, constraints that may be given only partially by the complement clause (or sentential unit).

Not all attitude verbs and modals permit such underspecification, though. Thus, with *claim* and *believe*, as below, the clausal complement must give the full truth conditions of the reported belief or claim (possibly together with particular 'unarticulated constituents', which have to be part of the speaker's intended meaning):

(28) a. John believes that Fiona caught a fish.
     b. John claimed Fiona caught a fish.

The intuition about (28a, 28b) is that John's belief or claim is true just in case Fiona catches any fish whatsoever (at the relevant time); the belief or claim could not be false, say, because Fiona caught a dead fish. With *claim* and *believe*, the complement clause does not give a partial content of the reported attitudinal object, but rather (together with its unarticulated constituents) its complete content.

The relevant sort of underspecification is also unavailable for epistemic modals, as below:

(28) c. Fiona must have caught a fish.

The epistemic state reported in (28c) is correct just in case Fiona caught some fish or another, not just in case she catches a suitable one.

What distinguishes attitude verbs and modals that allow the complement clause (or sentential unit) to give only partial truth or satisfaction conditions of the reported attitudinal or modal object from those that requires it to give full truth or satisfaction conditions? It appears that the difference resides in whether an attitudinal or modal object has satisfaction conditions as opposed to truth conditions. A desire and a need can only 'be satisfied' and not 'be true'. By contrast, a claim and a belief can only 'be true', not 'be satisfied', and so for an epistemic state associated with an epistemic modal. Satisfaction conditions and truth conditions go along with different directions of fit, to use Searle's (1969, 1983) term.[10] Desires (and deontic or teleological modal objects) have a world-to-word/mind direction of fit, whereas claims and beliefs (and epistemic modal objects) have a word/mind-to-world direction of fit. That is, the aim of a desire or need is to have the world

---

[10] This is discussed in greater detail in Moltmann (2021).

match the representation, whereas the aim of a belief, claim, or epistemic state is to have the representation match the world.[11]

Of course, the challenge then is to explain why a particular direction of fit goes along with the possibility of the relevant sort of underspecification. This is something to be left for future research. In the present context, we will have to settle on simply positing two distinct meanings of clauses, depending on the direction of fit of the attitudinal or modal object associated with the embedding predicate.

VIII. Sentences as Predicates of Modal and Attitudinal Objects

We can now turn to the formal semantics of clauses as predicates of content bearers (attitudinal or modal objects), specifying their truth or satisfaction conditions. For the semantics of attitude reports, I will make use of Davidsonian event semantics (Davidson 1967). Davidsonian event arguments of an attitude verb will be the events, acts or states described by the attitude verb. I will assume, certainly simplifying, that there is a unique attitudinal object $att\text{-}obj(e)$ associated with a Davidsonian event argument e of an attitude verb.[12] The clausal complement of the attitude verb will then be predicated of the attitudinal object associate with the event argument as below:

(29) a. John claimed that S.
   b. $\exists e(\text{claim}(e, \text{John}) \& [that\ S](att\text{-}obj(e)))$.

The semantics of attitude reports in (29b) is (almost) overtly reflected in the corresponding complex-predicate construction in (30), which involves explicit reference to an attitudinal object (or a kind of attitudinal object):[13]

(30) John made the claim that S.

---

[11] One might think that the difference consists in the nature of the satisfiers: desires and need, as in (27a, 27b) have actions as satisfiers, whereas truth-directed attitudinal objects have situations as verifiers. However, the relevant sort of underspecification appears not only with desires whose satisfaction is obtained by actions of the relevant agent. It also appears with desires whose satisfaction is obtained by situations, as in *John wants to receive enough milk, John wants Milllie to drink milk, John would like there to be enough milk for everyone on earth* etc. Moreover, the underspecification appears with hope, where fulfilment conditions may not involve any action on the part of the agent (*John hopes that there is milk in the fridge, John hope that there was milk in the fridge, when Millie got home yesterday, John hopes that Bill caught a fish* etc.).
[12] See Moltmann (2017a, 2019a) for more on the relation of the Davidsonian event argument of the verb and the relevant attitudinal object.
[13] In fact, languages tend to show an alternation between the simple and the complex-predicate construction, which further motivates the semantics in (29b) (Moltmann 2017a, 2018).

Clausal modifiers of nominalizations of attitude verbs will act as predicates of the attitudinal object described by the nominalization, as in (31b) for (31a):

(31) a. John's claim that S.
   b. ιd[claim(d, John) & [S](d)].

What is the property that sentences as predicates of modal or attitudinal object express? In the case of modal and attitudinal objects with a world-to-word/mind direction of fit, the clause will give a partial specification of satisfaction conditions. This means that it will express the property below, where $\Vdash$ is the relation of exact truthmaking or satisfaction now holding between situations or actions s and modal or attitudinal objects d (as well as sentences):

(32) $[S] = \lambda d[\forall s(s \Vdash d \rightarrow \exists s'(s' \Vdash S \ \& \ s < s') \ \& \ \forall s'(s' \Vdash S \rightarrow \exists s(s \Vdash d \ \& \ s < s'))]$.

According to (32), a sentence S expresses the property that holds of a modal or attitudinal object d just in case every satisfier of d is part of a satisfiers of S and every satisfier of S contains a satisfier of d as part—which just means that the content of S is a partial content of the content of d (Yablo 2015, Fine 2017).

(32) cannot yet be adequate, though, since it would not allow distinguishing necessity and possibility semantically. Given (32), a permission (for Mary to enter the house) could be a modal object with the very same satisfaction conditions as an obligation (for Mary to enter the house). But the permission for Mary to enter the house is not an obligation for Mary to enter the house.

What distinguishes a permission from an obligation? Permissions allow for certain actions, those they permit. Obligations allow for certain actions, those that comply with them, but unlike permissions they also exclude certain actions, those that violate them. The permission for Mary to enter the house allows for actions of Mary entering the house, but it does not exclude any other actions. By contrast, the obligation for Mary to enter the house allows for actions of Mary entering the house and excludes actions of Mary's not doing so. This means that permissions have only satisfiers, whereas obligations have both satisfiers and violators.

Also illocutionary products are distinguished in that way. An offer or an invitation has only satisfiers, but no violators. By contrast, a request or an order has both satisfiers and violators.

To account for that difference between modal forces requires modifying (32) by adding a condition on the falsification or violation of the modal or attitudinal object, namely that every falsifier of the sentence also be a falsifier or violator of the modal or attitudinal object. The modified meaning of a sentence S then is as follows, where the relation of falsification or violation $\dashv\!|$ now also obtains between actions or situations and modal or attitudinal objects:

(33) [S] = λd[∀s(s ⊩ d → ∃s'(s' ⊩ S & s < s') & ∀s'(s' ⊩ S → ∃s(s ⊩ d & s < s')) & (neg(d) ≠ ∅) → ∀s(s ⫤ S → s ⫤ d))].

That is, a sentence S expresses the property that holds of a modal or attitudinal object d just in case the content of S is a partial content of d and every falsifier of S is a violator of d, should there be a violator of d.

On this account, sentences conveying necessity and sentences conveying possibility will have exactly the same logical form; but they involve different sorts of modal or attitudinal objects with different satisfaction and violation conditions.[14] This is given for (34a) and (34b) in (35a) and (35b) respectively, based on the same meaning of the complement clause in (36):

(34) a. John asked Mary to leave the house.
   b. John allowed Mary to leave the house.
(35) a. ∃e(ask(e, j, m) & [Mary leave the house](att-obj(e))).
   b. ∃e(allow(e, j, m) & [Mary leave the house](att-obj(e))).
(36) [Mary to leave the house] = λd[∀s(s ⊩ d → ∃s'(s' ⊩ Mary leave the house & s < s') & ∀s'(s' ⊩ Mary to leave the house → ∃s(s ⊩ d & s < s')) & (neg(d) ≠ ∅) → ∀s(s ⫤ Mary to leave the house → s ⫤ d)]

Similarly, modal sentences involve predication of the sentential unit associated with the modal predicate of the modal object (which may be taken to be the event argument itself). (37a) and (38a) will then have the logical forms in (37b) and (38b) respectively:

(37) a. John needs to leave.
   b. ∃d(need(d) & [John to leave](d)).
(38) a. John is permitted to leave.
   b. ∃d(is permitted(d) & [John to leave](d)).

Unlike possible-worlds semantics, this gives an adequate account of strong permissions (and obligations). If the object d is a permission, the sentential unit will specify which sorts of actions will be exact satisfiers of d, it will not just say what is true in some world in which the permission is satisfied.

If the modal or attitudinal object has a word/mind-to-world direction of fit, the sentential unit will give its full truth or satisfaction conditions. In this case, the meaning of the sentential unit will be as below:[15]

---

[14] This is one advantage of a truthmaker-based account of the content of content bearers over a possible-worlds-based account; see Moltmann (2019a).
[15] The sentence S may be truth-conditionally incomplete by containing unarticulated constituents that are part of the speaker's intention when uttering the sentence and need to be understood as such

(39) [S] = λd[∀s(s ⊩ d ↔ s ⊩ S) & ∀s(s ⊣ d → s ⊣ S)].

Of course, making the meaning of an embedded clause dependent on the embedding predicate (the direction of fitted of the associated modal or attitudinal object) is unsatisfactory and goes against compositionality. There must be a reason why the role of a sentential unit specifying either the partial or the complete content depends on the direction of fit of the attitudinal or modal object, and thus ultimately the polysemy reflected in (33) and (39) will have to give way to a different account.

IX. The Semantics of Different Types of Attitude Verbs

Not all attitude verbs involve a semantics on which their clausal complement is just predicated of the attitudinal object associated with the event argument of the verb. Some attitude verbs involve a semantics on which the clausal complement in addition serves as a predicate of a contextually given attitudinal object, for example a claim, suggestion, or guess relevant in the discourse context. This is the case with what Cattell (1978) called *response-stance verbs*, verbs such as *repeat, confirm, agree,* and *remind,* as in the sentences below:

(40) a. John repeated that it will rain.
  b. John confirmed that it was raining.
  c. John agreed to surrender.
  d. John reminded Mary to return the keys.

In general, response-stance verbs have a clausal complement that serves to characterize both the reported attitudinal object and a contextually given attitudinal object. Thus, in (40a) the complement clause gives the content of two attitudinal objects: John's assertion (or perhaps just act of saying) and a contextually given claim, which may be John's or another person's previous claim. In (40b), the clausal complement gives the satisfaction condition of John's assertion as well as a previous assertive utterance with a much weaker illocutionary force. In (40c), the infinitival complement specifies actions as satisfiers of John's statement of intent as well as, say, a previous request. In (40d), the complement clause gives the satisfaction conditions of Mary's intention (as target of John's locutionary act) as well as those of a previous thought or intention of Mary's. The lexical meaning of the verb constrains the nature of the contextually given attitudinal object and its relation to the attitudinal object of the reported agent.

---

by the addressee. This means that S should in fact be relativized to a context of utterance specifying implicit elements meant to be part of the content of the utterance of the sentence.

The logical form of a sentence with a response-stance verb cannot simply be as in (41b) for (41a), where *d* is the relevant contextually given content bearer:

(41) a. John agreed that S.
b. ∃e(agree(e, John) & [*that* S](att-obj(e)) & [*that* S](d))

That is because the act reported in (41a) would not be an act of agreeing without the contextually given speech act. Rather the predication of the complement clause of two different attitudinal objects would involve lexical decomposition of the verb's content, as schematically below:

(41) c. ∃e'(C_1(e) & [*that* S](att-obj(e)) & C_2(d) & R(att-obj(e), d))

In (41c), the lexical content of the attitude verbs is decomposed into two conditions C_1 and C_2 (for the two attitudinal objects) as well as a relation R (holding between the two attitudinal objects). Alternatively, the logical form of (41a) could be that in (41d), where *agree* is now a three-place predicate taking the contextually given attitudinal object as a third argument:

(41) d. ∃e(agree(e, John, d) & [*that* S](att-obj(e)) & [*that* S](d))

There is specific support for (41d), and that is the general substitutability of the clausal complement of a response stance verb by an NP explicitly referring to the contextually given attitudinal object (plus sometimes a preposition):

(42) a. John agreed with the request to leave.
b. John repeated the claim that it is raining.
c. John confirmed the speculation that it was raining.
d. John reminded Mary of the requirement / request to return the key.

Further support for (41d) comes from the observation that response-stance verbs permit a reading of adverbs like *partly* quantifying over parts of the content of the contextually given attitudinal object:

(43) John partly confirmed that Mary is incompetent.

The same sort of reading of *partly* is generally available with transitive verbs, as below:

(44) a. John partly ate the cake.
b. John partly liked the concert.

Such a reading, however, is unavailable with what Cattell (1978) calls *volunteered-stance verbs*, verbs such as *claim* and *think* (Moltmann 2017c):

(45) a. ??? John partly claims that Mary is incompetent.
   b. ??? John partly thinks that that the students are talented.

(45a) has a conceivable reading on which it means that John claims that Mary is partly incompetent, and (45b) on which it means that John thinks that only some of the students are talented. Those readings should be available if *claim* and *think* were to take propositions (the putative referents of their clausal complements) as arguments. The unavailability of such a reading makes again clear that clausal complements of attitude verbs (of the volunteered-stance sort) do not provide arguments of the attitude verb.

Response-stance verbs pattern together with factive verbs with respect to their syntactic behavior (for example adjunct extraction) (Cattell 1978). However, the analyses in (40c, 40d) are inapplicable to factive verbs. With factive verbs such as *know, recognize, note* the clausal complement more plausibly characterizes a fact (however that may be conceived), in addition to characterizing the content of a mental state or act. Some factive verbs allow for substitution of the clausal complement by an explicit fact description (*notice that* S → *notice the fact that* S, *recognize that* S → *recognize the fact that* S). Others do not (*see that* S does not imply *see the fact that* S, *realize that* S does not imply *realize the fact that* S). The analogy of response-stance verbs and factive verbs requires a greater discussion of their syntax and semantics; the present purposes was simply to outline the sort of semantics that factive verbs may have within object-based truthmaker semantics.

There are two options for a semantic analysis of factive verbs. One option is that *that*-clauses, at least with factive verbs not allowing substitution by an explicit fact description, act as predicates of the epistemic attitudinal object and impose a condition on the truth of the complement. For that purpose, I will make use of a world of evaluation for the entire sentence. The condition on the truth of the clausal complement then consists in the requirement that the set of situations that are part of the world of evaluation and the positive extension of the complement clause be non-empty:

(46) a. John realizes that S.
   b. $\exists e(\text{realizes}(e, \text{John}) \ \& \ [\text{that S}](\text{att-object}(e)) \ \& \ \text{pos}(\textit{that S}) \cap \{s | s < w\} \neq \emptyset)$.

Here the clausal complement does not have a predicative function but figures only in the condition (or presupposition) on the truth of the clausal complement.

Another option would be to allow non-worldly facts to be modal objects of a sort, namely modal objects whose satisfiers are situations that are part of the actual world. If we take F to be a world-relative sortal for such factive modal objects, then the logical form of (46c):

(46) c. $\exists d \exists e(\text{realize}(e, \text{John}) \ \& \ [\text{that S}](\text{att-obj}(e)) \ \& \ [\text{that S}](d) \ \& \ F_w(d)))$.

Alternatively, more suited for factive verbs allowing for substitution of their complement, it could be as below, where *f* is a world-relative operator mapping the semantic value of a sentence onto the factive modal object:

(46) ∃e(realize(e, John, f$_w$([S])).

There are also good reasons to assume that clausal subjects with a predicate like *is true* or *is correct* give the content of a contextually given content-bearer (a claim, rumor or suggestion) (Moltmann 2021). Thus, a sentence like (47a) is generally understood in such a way that *that* S serves to give the truth conditions of a contextually given attitudinal object, a claim or speculation (note that *correct* does not apply to a proposition, referred to as such):

(47) a. That S is correct.

This means that (47a) has the logical form in (47b), for the relevant contextually given attitudinal object d:

(47) b. true([that S](d)).

Other clausal subjects may instead be predicated of an object that is an implicit argument of the verb or closely related to it. Thus, the clausal subjects of *is possible* is best viewed as acting as a predicate of the modal object, itself here considered the Davidsonian event argument. This gives the logical of (48a) as in (48b):

(48) a. That John will be late is possible.
b. ∃e(possible(e) & [that John will be late](e)).

Of course, a particular semantic role of a clausal subject would have to be based on particular semantically identifiable features. In the present context of an outline of object-based truthmaker semantics, the aim was simply to show the plausibility of clausal subjects serving particular semantic roles which are not that of standing for a proposition.

X. Object-Based Truthmaker Semantics and the Connections between Modality and Propositional Attitudes

Inferential Connections between Modals and Attitude Reports

The present approach accounts straightforwardly for inferential connections between attitude reports and modal sentences. That is because attitudinal objects may entail the existence of a modal object and attitudinal and modal object and they may share their satisfaction conditions. Thus, (8) and (9) repeated below are valid on the relevant reading because the command and the obligation share the same satisfiers:

(49) John asked Mary to leave.
Mary must leave.

(50) John offered Mary to use the house.
Mary may use the house.

Similarly, imperatives and performatively used modal sentences stand in inferential relations under suitable conditions. Thus, in suitable contexts, both (51) and (52) are valid, in the sense that any act that fulfills the antecedent also satisfies the consequent:

(51) Leave the room!
You must leave the room.

(52) Take an apple!
You may take an apple.

This follows from the fact that the request or permission produced by the utterance with an imperative entails, under suitable normative conditions, the existence of a modal object of obligation or permission with the very same satisfaction conditions.

Harmonic Modals

Object-based truthmaker semantics has a particular application to what Kratzer (2016) calls *harmonic modals*. Harmonic modals occur in clauses embedded under speech act verbs, where they do not contribute to the content of the reported speech but rather appear to just reflect the inherent modality associated with the embedding predicate:

(53) John insisted that Mary *should* leave.

There are also harmonic uses of modals of possibility, with suitable embedding verbs:

(54) a. John suggested that Bill *might* be at home.
b. The document indicates that Bill *might* be guilty.

For Kratzer, harmonic modals spell out the inherent modality of the content-bearing object of which the clause is to be predicated (an insistence, suggestion, indication in (53, 54)). Her account of harmonic modals is based on a possible-worlds-based property of the meaning of clauses. Focusing on modals of necessity as in (53), she proposes that the 'harmonic' modal in the embedded clause spells out universal quantification over the possible worlds that make up the content *f(d)* of the content-bearing object *d*, as below:

(55) λd[∀w(w ∈ f(d) → [S]^w = true)].

The problem for such a possible worlds-based account, though, and that is that it is inapplicable to modals of possibility, as in (54a, 54b) (Moltmann 2019b). Thus, (56) does not make sense as the meaning of the clauses in (54a–c), with the existential quantifier spelling out the contribution of *could* or *might*:

(56) λd[∃w(w ∈ f(d) & [S]^w = true)].

In (54a), the *that*-clause does not just specify what is the case in some world in which John's offer is taken up; it specifies (at least) what is the case in all the worlds in which the offer is taken up. Similarly in (54b), the *that*-clause does not just say what is the case in some world compatible with what document says, but what is the case in all such worlds.

Object-based truthmaker semantics allows for a straightforward account of harmonic modals of both necessity and possibility (Moltmann 2019b). On this account, harmonic modals are considered performative uses of modals in embedded contexts. In object-based truthmaker semantics, sentences with a performative use of a modal such as (57a, 57b) will express properties of modal products meant to be produced by uttering the sentence, as in (58a, 58b) (Moltmann 2017a):

(57) a. You must leave!
 b. You may leave!

(58) a. λd[must(d) & [(addressee) *leave*](d)].
 b. λd[may(d) & [(addressee) *leave*](d)].

With a harmonic modal acting as a performative modal in an embedded context, (53) will simply have logical form in (59b) based on the meaning of the embedded clause in (59a), and (54b) the one in (60b), based on (60a):

(59) a. [*that Mary should leave*] = λd[should(d) & [*Mary leave*](d)].
 b. ∃e(insist(e, John) & [*that Mary should leave*](modal-product(e))).

(60) a. [*that Bill might be guilty*] = λd[might(d) & [*Bill be guilty*](d)].
 b. ∃e(indicate(e, the document) & [*that Bill might be guilty*](modal-product(e))).

A modal product can be produced by the very same illocutionary act as an illocutionary product, and it will have the very same satisfaction conditions as the illocutionary product (Moltmann 2017a). An act of demanding produces a demand as well as possibly an obligation, and an act of permitting a permission as an illocutionary product and a permission as a modal product.

Thus, harmonic modals are a phenomenon where object-based truthmaker semantics appears to have a significant advantage over possible-worlds semantics with its quantificational analysis of modals.

XI. Object-Based Truthmaker Semantics and the Dynamic Semantic Perspective

Possible worlds are generally used to represent the common ground, the target of updating with the utterance of sentences, given a dynamic semantic perspective. That is, possible worlds are generally used to represent the context set, the target of updating with declarative sentences, as well as a to-do list, the target of updating with the utterance of imperative or deontic modal sentences on a performative use.[16] Such a dynamic perspective can be recast within the terms of object-based truthmaker semantics roughly along the following lines.

Rather than making use of a context set as a set of worlds, the common ground will contain an attitudinal object of acceptance as the target for updating by declarative sentences, or perhaps rather a modal object, as has recently been argued (Geurts 2018). Such an attitudinal or modal object will of course have a collective agent (the interlocutors) (or perhaps the speaker identifying himself with everyone in the discourse, in the way of generic 'one'). A *to do*-list is naturally considered a (deontic) modal object that has future possible actions or situations involving the relevant agent as satisfiers. Of course, as there may be various to do-lists as part of the common ground (Portner 2007), there can be various modal objects as targets of utterances of imperatives or modal sentences of different strengths and forces. Also, of course, a set of issues (the target for updating with questions) may be construed as an attitudinal or modal object, one whose satisfiers are, say, attitudinal objects of assertion. The common ground will thus consist of various attitudinal and modal objects (with collective, generic or particular agents) that will be the target for updating with the utterance of sentences of different types.

Updating itself then means the following. With the utterance of an independent sentence S a speaker produces an attitudinal or modal object d whose truth or satisfaction conditions are given by S. Updating the common ground C with d will consist, roughly, in the fusion of d with the relevant modal or attitudinal object in C.[17] The operation of fusion $\odot$ on modal or attitudinal objects is given

---

[16] Possible worlds are also used in dynamic semantics (of the non-representational sort), that is, theories according to which the meaning of sentences is a function from contexts to contexts. I will set dynamic semantic theories aside for present purposes.

[17] See Moltmann (2018a) for the operation of fusion applied to attitudinal or modal objects.

below, based on the operation of sum formation of situations or actions (somewhat simplifying the definition given in Moltmann 2018a):

(61) For modal or attitudinal objects d_1 and d_2 of the same type, the fusion d_1 and d_2, $d_1 \odot d_2$ = the modal or attitudinal object d that has d_1 and d_2 as parts and that is such that pos(d) = {sum(s_1, s_2)| $s_1 \in$ pos(d_1) & $s_2 \in$ pos(d_2)} and neg(d) = {s |s $\in$ neg(d_1) v s $\in$ neg(d_2)}.

Updating the common ground, actually, may not just consist in the fusion of d with the relevant attitudinal or modal object from the common ground, but may require mapping d onto a closely related object d' with same satisfaction conditions as d, but that matches the modal or attitudinal force of d'. This is needed in particular for objects that are assertions, which can undergo fusion only with an attitudinal object of the same force, say acceptance. If S carries presuppositions, then before applying fusion with an object o from the common ground, it needs to be verified that the presuppositions of S are entailed by o. How is entailment here to be understood? Attitudinal and modal objects (and sentences) enter entailment relations in virtue of standing in relations of partial content.

Note that the common ground may contain attitudinal objects of explicit and of implicit acceptance, for different sorts of presuppositions (anaphoric and non-anaphoric ones).

Also the updating conditions of complex sentences can be recast in terms of object-based truthmaker semantics. For example, updating of a common ground C with an attitudinal or modal object a with conjunctive content S and S' will involve fusion of the relevant object o in C with first d and then fusion of the result with d', where d' is that part of a whose content is given by S and d' is that part of a whose content is given by S'.[18]

While a more detailed and formal development of this way of updating and a comparison with the standard account will have to await another occasion, one overall advantage of it obviously is that the common ground will now consist in modal and attitudinal objects whose content is more fine-grained than the possible-worlds-based notion of a context set.

XII. Summary

Possible-worlds semantics has been a dominant approach in formal semantics, despite its obvious shortcomings, since it appears particularly suited for a compositional analysis of natural language sentences in a context of discourse.

---

[18] See Moltmann (2018) for more on content-based parts of attitudinal or modal objects.

This chapter has given a broad outline of an alternative approach, object-based truthmaker semantics. This approach provides a more fine-grained notion of content while being able, it appears, to capture various connections between modal and attitude verbs and to recast insights of the dynamic perspective meaning. Of course, this general outline awaits numerous elaborations of empirical and formal detail, as well as more thorough comparisons with standard approaches for particular applications.

References

Arsenijevic, Boban 2009. "Clausal complementization as relativization." *Lingua* 119(1): 39–50.

Cattell, Ray 1978. 'On the Source of Interrogative Adverbs'. *Language* 54, 61–77.

Cinque, Guglielmo 2008. "Two types of non-restrictive relative clauses." In *Empirical Issues in Syntax and Semantics* 7, ed. Oliver Bonami and Patricia Cabredo Hofherr, 99–137. Paris: CSSP.

Davidson, Donald 1967. "The logical form of action sentences." In *The Logic of Decision and Action*, ed. Nicholas Rescher, 81–95. Pittsburgh University Press, Pittsburgh.

De Cuba, Carlos 2017. "Noun complement clauses as referential modifiers." *Glossa* 2(1): 1–46.

Fine, K. 2017. "Truthmaker semantics." In *A Companion to the Philosophy of Language*, ed. Bob Hale, Crispin Wright and Alan Miller. Chichester: John Wiley & Sons, Ltd, 556–577.

Fine, K. 2018a. 'Compliance and Command I'. *Review of Symbolic Logic* 11, 609–633.

Fine, K. 2018b. 'Compliance and Command II'. *Review of Symbolic Logic* 11, 634–664.

Geurts, B. 2018. "Convention and common ground." *Mind and Language* 33: 115–29.

Graff Fara, Delia 2013. "Specifying desire." *Noûs* 47(2): 250–72.

Hanks, Peter W. 2011. "Propositions as types." *Mind* 120: 11–52.

Heim, Irene 1983. "On the projection problem for presuppositions." In *Proceedings of WCCFL 2 (Second West Coast Conference Formal Semantics)*, ed. Daniel P. Flickinger,. 114–25. Stanford: Stanford University.

Heim, Irene 1992. "Presupposition projection and the semantics of attitude verbs." *Journal of Semantics* 9: 183–221.

Jubien, Michael 2001. "Propositions and the objects of thought." *Philosophical Studies* 104: 47–62.

Kayne, Richard 2010. "Why isn't *this* a complementizer?" In *Comparisons and Contrasts*, ed. R. Kayne, 190–227, Oxford University Press, Oxford.

Kratzer, Angelika 2016. "Evidential moods in attitude and speech reports (slides)." Available at https://works.bepress.com/angelika_kratzer/.

Moltmann, Friederike 2003a. "Nominalizing quantifiers." *Journal of Philosophical Logic* 35(5): 445–81.

Moltmann, Friederike 2003b. "Propositional attitudes without propositions." *Synthese* 135: 70–118.

Moltmann, F. 2013. *Abstract Objects and the Semantics of Natural Language*. Oxford: Oxford University Press.

Moltmann, F. 2014. "Propositions, attitudinal objects, and the distinction between actions and products." *Canadian Journal of Philosophy* 43(5–6): 679–701.

Moltmann, Friederike 2017a. "Cognitive products and the semantics of attitude reports and deontic modals." In *Act-Based Conceptions of Propositions: Contemporary and*

Historical Contributions, ed. Friederike Moltmann and Mark Textor, 254–90. Oxford: Oxford University Press.

Moltmann, Friederike 2017b. "Levels of linguistic acts and the semantics of saying and quoting." In *Interpreting Austin: Critical Essays*, ed. Savas L. Tsohatzidis. Cambridge: Cambridge University Press, 34–59.

Moltmann, F. 2017c. "Partial content and expressions of part and whole: discussion of Stephen Yablo: *Aboutness*." *Philosophical Studies* 174(3): 797–808.

Moltmann, F. 2018. "An object-based truthmaker semantics for modals." *Philosophical Issues* 28(1): 255–88.

Moltmann, F. 2021. "Truth predicates, truth bearers, and their variants." *Synthese* 198: 689–716.

Moltmann, Friederike 2019a. "Attitudinal objects. their ontology and importance for philosophy and natural language semantics." In *Judgment: Act and Object*, ed. Brian Ball and Chistoph Schuringa, 180–201, Routledge Studies in Contemporary Philosophy. London: Routledge.

Moltmann, Friederike 2019b. "Clauses as semantic predicates: difficulties for possible-worlds semantics." In *Making Worlds Accessible. Festschrift for Angelika Kratzer*, ed. Rajesh Bhatt, Ilaria Frana and Paola Menendez-Benito. Amherst: University of Massachusetts at Amherst, online.

Moulton, Keir 2009. "Natural selection and the syntax of clausal complementation." PhD dissertation. Amherst: University of Massachusetts.

Portner, Paul 2004. "The semantics of imperatives within a theory of clause types." In *Proceedings of SALT 14*, ed. K. Watanabe and R. Young, 235–52. Fort Washington, PA: CLC Publications.

Portner, Paul 2007. "Imperatives and modals." *Natural Language Semantics* 15(1): 351–83.

Pranav, Anand and Valentine Hacquard. 2013. "Epistemics and attitudes." *Semantics and Pragmatics* 6: 1–59.

Pustejovsky, James 1995. *The Generative Lexicon*. Cambridge, MA: MIT Press.

Searle, John 1969. *Speech Acts*. Cambridge: Cambridge University Press.

Searle, John 1983. *Intentionality*. Cambridge: Cambridge University Press.

Soames, Scott 2010. *What Is Meaning?* Princeton: Princeton University Press.

Stalnaker, Robert 1984. *Inquiry*. Cambridge, MA: MIT Press.

Thomasson, Amie 1999. *Fiction and Metaphysics*. Cambridge: Cambridge University Press.

Twardowski, Kasmierz 1911. "Actions and products: some remarks on the borderline of psychology, grammar, and logic." In *Kazimierz Twardowski. On Actions, Products, and Other Topics in the Philosophy*, ed. J. Brandl and J. Wolenski, 103–32. Amsterdam and Atlanta: Rodopi.

von Wright, G. H. 1963. *Norm and Action. A Logical Inquiry*. London: Routledge and Kegan Paul.

Yablo, Steven 2015. *Aboutness*. Cambridge, MA: MIT Press.

PART 3
ASSESSING UNSTRUCTURED APPROACHES

Unstructured Content

Jeffrey C. King

I am a structured content guy.[1] I became convinced of the superiority of the structured approach to content in the late 1980s and there is a sense in which I haven't looked back much. Instead, I have devoted my time to trying to figure out exactly how to understand what structured content is. Back in the late '80s and early '90s, it was common for structured proposition theorists to represent structured propositions as n-tuples. For example, in Soames (1987) we find the following:

> The proposition expressed by an atomic formula $[Pt_1, \ldots, t_n]$ relative to a context C and assignment f is $<<o_1, \ldots, o_n>, P^*>$, where P^* is the property expressed by P, and o_i is the content of t_i relative to C and f.

It seemed to me that representing structured propositions as n-tuples of their constituents raised a dilemma for structured proposition theorists.[2] Either such theorists were claiming that structured propositions *just are* n-tuples of their constituents or they were simply using n-tuples to *represent* or *stand in for* structured propositions. The former claim struck me as quite implausible for reasons I won't rehearse here.[3] Hence, it seemed to me structured proposition theorists were stuck with the claim that they were simply using n-tuples to represent structured propositions. But this meant that they hadn't yet said what structured propositions really are. Starting in the mid-'90s I set out to do that.

Since I spent my time thinking about those issues, I didn't take much time to think carefully about the reasons I abandoned the unstructured conception of content to begin with. Being asked to speak at a conference on unstructured content seemed to me to provide a perfect opportunity to examine what many have thought to be central difficulties with unstructured content and what can be said in response to them. I am also eager to hear what folks here might have to say about these issues that is new. Because of limitations of time, though I will

---

[1] Thanks to Thony Gillies, Jeff Speaks and Una Stojnic for very helpful comments on an earlier version of this paper. Thanks also to the audience at the Unstructured Conference at Rutgers University April 22–3, 2016, and especially to Robert Stalnaker, for an excellent discussion of an earlier version of this paper.
[2] As I made clear in King (2007, 7–9).   [3] See King (2007, 7–9).

mention what I take to be four main problems with unstructured content and gesture at what has been said in response, I will only consider one such problem in detail.

Though there are different conceptions of unstructured content, the view I am going to consider is the view that unstructured sentential contents are functions from the domain of possible worlds to {0,1}. I'll call this conception of content *P(ossible) W(orld) C(ontent)*. I think it is fair to say that PWC has been the most influential theory of unstructured content in recent philosophy of language. So far as I can see, the problems I will discuss arise for views on which unstructured contents are functions from more complex indices—indices that include more features than just a possible world—to {0,1}. Because Robert Stalnaker has done more than anyone to address the problems I'm going to discuss, as we'll see, a good subtitle for this paper would be *All About Bob*.

The first problem for PWC is that it has trouble saying intuitive things regarding what propositions are about. Since propositions don't have constituents according to PWC, its advocates can't adopt the intuitive claim that propositions are about their constituents. Stalnaker (1984) suggests that using functions from individuals to propositions—propositional functions—one could say that proposition P is about individual a iff P is the value of some propositional function f when it takes the argument a. But he hastens to add that this can't work, since for any individual a and any proposition P, there is a function mapping a to P. He suggests that perhaps we could get better results by somehow limiting our attention to a certain privileged subclass of propositional functions but he admits doesn't know how to do that. Stalnaker (1999) suggests that according to PWC, a *singular proposition* is "a proposition whose truth in any given possible world depends on the properties of some particular individual."[4] This might be thought to give at least a limited notion of aboutness for such singular propositions. But there are two problems. First it gives no account of the fact that the following are about George W. and George H. W. Bush, 2 and arithmetic, respectively:

> The proposition that if George W. Bush exists, he is the son of George H. W. Bush.
> The proposition that 2 is the even prime.
> The proposition that arithmetic is incomplete if consistent.

This seems to me at least very counterintuitive. Second, if the proposition that Orcutt is a spy is a singular proposition about Orcutt because its truth in a given possible world depends on Orcutt's properties there, then consider the proposition that Vicky is whistling. The truth of this proposition in a given possible world depends on the properties of Vicky's lips there. But then this proposition is

---

[4] Stalnaker (1999, 160).

a singular proposition about Vicky's lips on the proposed account of singular propositions and aboutness.[5] Examples could easily be multiplied. So it looks like the account yields very counterintuitive, indeed I would say *incorrect*, results in many, many cases.

The second problem with PWC is a problem for many theories of propositions. It is the problem of explaining how/why propositions have truth conditions and so represent the world as being a certain way.[6] That a thing has truth conditions, that it represents things as being a certain way, seems to be precisely the sort of thing that is not metaphysically basic and requires further explanation. There are certain properties the possession of which seem to call out for further explanation and whose possession seems as though they should be grounded in the possession of "more basic" properties. It may be hard to give a criterion for being such a property, but properties like *being alive, believing that snow is white*, and *being morally good* seem to be examples of such properties. *Having truth conditions* seems to be an example as well. When we consider other things that represent, we have the same inclination to explain what possession of that property consists in and how/why the thing in question manages to possess the property. Sentences, minds, maps, and perceptual experiences all represent. And in each case we feel compelled to explain how/why such things manage to do this. Surely it would seem utterly mysterious to adopt the view that, for example, there is no explanation of how/why perceptual experiences represent things as being a certain why because that they do so is metaphysically basic. The feeling one gets when one hears such a view is "how could something like *that* have no further explanation?". I think we should think that same thing about the claim that propositions have truth conditions. It just isn't the kind of thing that could have no further explanation.

Now according to PWC, propositions are functions from worlds to exactly two arbitrary elements, say 0 and 1. Stalnaker (1984) makes this point concisely:

> A proposition is a function from possible worlds into truth-values.... There are just two truth-values—true and false. What are they: mysterious Fregean objects, properties, relations of correspondence and noncorrespondence? The answer is that it does not matter what they are; there is nothing essential to them except that there are exactly two of them.[7]

But why/how would such functions have truth conditions or represent the world as being a certain way? Certainly, there are lots of functions from a set of elements to {0,1} or some other pair of arbitrary elements that don't have truth conditions. But then why do functions from a set of *worlds* to {1, 0} have truth conditions?

---

[5] Thanks to Jeff Speaks for this point.
[6] See King (2013, 82–3).   [7] Stalnaker (1984, 2).

170   UNSTRUCTURED CONTENT

There just isn't anything in the functions themselves, taken independently of minds and languages, that determines that they have truth conditions.

Further, it does not seem like the functions taken independently of minds and languages determine *specific* truth conditions either. If a function maps w to 1, is it true or false at w? Recall that Stalnaker thinks that it doesn't matter what T and F are so long as there are exactly two of them. Okay, let's use Los Angeles and New York instead. If a function maps w to Los Angeles, is it true or false at w? Surely, it is hard to take this question seriously—as a question that has some determinate answer in the absence of stipulation.

So the second problem for PWC is that it can't explain why propositions have truth conditions generally, nor why a given proposition has the specific truth conditions it does.

Robert Stalnaker (2012) has objected to this way of putting the second problem for PWC as follows:

> One central problem for any theory of propositions, King argues, is to explain their capacity to "represent how the world is," to explain "how propositions have truth conditions." But on the account of propositions I will defend, propositions *are* truth conditions.[8]

Stalnaker suggests here that since propositions don't *have* truth conditions but rather *are* truth conditions, there is no need to explain their having truth conditions. They don't have them. I have to say I'm not sure I understand what Stalnaker means here. Further later in the same work he says that propositions *have* truth conditions:

> ... however propositions are individuated, all who are willing to talk of propositions at all should agree that propositions, as they understand them, *have* truth conditions....[9]

And in earlier work Stalnaker was happy to say that propositions represent the world as being a certain way:

> ... an act of assertion is, among other things, the expression of a proposition—something that represents the world as being a certain way.[10]

and have truth conditions:

---

[8] Stalnaker (2012, 11), emphasis in original.
[9] Stalnaker (2012, 26), emphasis in original. A similar remark occurs on p. 101.
[10] Stalnaker (1999, 78).

Furthermore, I will assume that the objects of belief—the propositions—are relatively simple unstructured things: that they are, just as truth-conditional semantics would like to assume, entities that are individuated by their truth conditions.[11]

In any case, when I say propositions have truth conditions, all I mean is that they impose conditions a world must meet for the proposition to be true at that world, and so are true and false at worlds. But then we can reformulate the second problem for PWC in slightly different terms. Propositions are true or false at possible worlds. Many other things, including people, stars, numbers and sets, are not. Having truth-values at worlds is a rather remarkable thing. There should be some explanation as to how propositions manage to do this. After all, we explain how sentences and beliefs manage to have truth-values at worlds by saying they express or have as their objects propositions. To now say that there is no explanation of how propositions themselves manage to have truth-values at worlds seems mysterious. It also makes the explanation of how sentences and beliefs manage to have truth-values at worlds quite shallow. For the "explanation" is that beliefs and sentences have truth-values at worlds by being associated with entities that primitively take truth-values at worlds. That doesn't seem like much progress.

Now according to PWC, propositions are functions from worlds to exactly two arbitrary elements, say 1 and 0. But why/how would such a function have truth-values relative to worlds? There are lots of functions from a set of elements to {0,1} that don't have truth-values relative to those elements. So we need to be told why functions from a set of worlds to {0,1} have truth-values at worlds. There just isn't anything in the functions themselves, taken independently of minds and languages, that determines that they have truth-values relative to worlds. Further, it does not seem like the functions taken independently of minds and languages determine *specific* truth-values at worlds either. If a function maps w to 1, is it true or false at w? As before, since it isn't supposed to matter what T or F are as long as there are two of them, let's use Los Angeles and New York instead. If a function maps w to Los Angeles, is it true or false at w? Again, it is hard to believe that this question has some determinate answer in the absence of stipulation.

So the point here is that construing propositions as functions from worlds to two arbitrary elements doesn't allow us to explain why propositions have truth-values at worlds generally nor why a given such function has the specific truth-values at worlds it is alleged to have.

The third problem for PWC comprises a cluster of difficulties that Stalnaker (1984) has dubbed *the problem of deduction*. PWC seems to require belief and

---

[11] Stalnaker (1999, 150). More recently, in responding to Scott Soames in Thomson and Byrne (2006), Stalnaker writes: 'The main presupposition [of Stalnaker's model of discourse] is that discourse involves the expression of propositions, and that propositions have truth conditions.'

knowledge to be closed under logical consequence; and it seems to require trivial belief in the necessary proposition and trivial non-belief in the impossible proposition. But knowledge and belief don't seem to be closed under logical consequence; and it seems possible to non-trivially believe a necessary truth, to doubt a necessary truth, to believe an impossibility and to non-trivially fail to believe an impossibility. The best attempt known to me for dealing with these problems is due to Stalnaker himself. When we seem to truly attribute to someone non-trivial belief in a necessary proposition, Stalnaker claims that we are really attributing belief in a contingent proposition about the semantic relation between the sentence expressing the necessary proposition and the proposition itself. When we seem to truly attribute belief in the impossible proposition, we are doing something similar: we are attributing belief in a contingently false proposition about the relation between a sentence and the necessary truth.[12] Failure to have one's beliefs closed under logical consequence is explained by having *compartmentalized* or *fragmented* belief states. I'll touch on some of these issues below. As we'll see, I am skeptical about the prospects of these strategies to successfully resolve the problem of deduction.

Now for the final problem and the one I'll discuss in some detail. Notoriously, according to PWC, propositions that are necessarily equivalent are identical: propositions that map the same worlds to 0 and 1 are the same. If we assume that sentences have as their semantic (assertoric) contents relative to contexts propositions, and something like the following:

(RA) An individual i satisfies [x believes/asserts that S] relative to context c and world w iff i in w stands in the believing/asserting relation to the semantic/assertoric content of S in c.

we get the result that belief/assertion ascriptions whose that-clauses contain sentences that express the same proposition relative to c and don't differ otherwise can't diverge in truth-value relative to any w. As virtually everyone in the universe has noted, for PWC this means that belief ascriptions whose that-clauses express necessary truths and don't differ otherwise can't diverge in truth-value. But, assuming truths of mathematics and the truth that Hesperus is Phosphorus are necessarily true, examples such as the following make this appear false:

1a. Keelin believes that $2 + 2 = 4$.
1b. Keelin believes that there are an infinite number of primes.
2a. Keelin believes that Hesperus is Hesperus.
2b. Keelin believes that Hesperus is Phosphorus.

---

[12] Stalnaker (1984, 75).

It is easy to imagine situations in which the first member of each pair seems true and the second seems false. Following Robert Stalnaker (1984), call this the *problem of equivalence*. Again here, the most sophisticated strategy for dealing with the problem known to me is Stalnaker's (1984, 1987) own. Hence I propose to examine it.

First, some preliminaries. Stalnaker holds that in conversations there is a body of information—*the common ground*—that conversational participants presume to be mutually available. The common ground is a set of propositions and a proposition ϕ is in the common ground just in case conversational participants accept ϕ (for the purposes of the conversation), accept that they all accept it, accept that they all accept that they all accept it and so on.[13] A conversational participant *presupposes* that ϕ iff she accepts that it is common ground that ϕ. Throughout I'll assume that conversational participants presuppose the same things (i.e. that the contexts are *non-defective*). Stalnaker represents the common ground by a set of worlds: the set of worlds in which all the propositions in the common ground are true. Stalnaker calls this the *context set*. Here are two principles that Stalnaker (1978) claims govern assertion and the context set:

1. A proposition asserted is true in some but not all worlds in the context set.
2. The same proposition is expressed by an assertively uttered sentence in each world in the context set.

The first principle is an injunction against asserting propositions that are presupposed or presupposed false. The second principle requires making clear what proposition one intends to assert in uttering a sentence.

Stalnaker endorses the orthodox Kripkean semantics for names.[14] Hence, he holds that 'Hesperus is Phosphorus' semantically expresses the necessary truth. This is a proposition that everyone believes: since it is true in all possible worlds, for any person it is true in every world compatible with what she believes. But then it doesn't appear that this sentence could be informatively uttered. However, utterances of it *can* be true and informative. In order to explain this it appears that PWC must somehow associate with an utterance of 'Hesperus is Phosphorus' a contingently true proposition. Stalnaker famously has an ingenious way of accomplishing that. In a situation in which speakers felicitously and informatively utter 'Hesperus is Phosphorus', what would the context set be like? Well, suppose O'Leary and Daniels are our speakers. Assuming they are not presupposing that Venus is not seen in the morning or the evening the way it is seen in the actual world, the actual world i will be in the context set. But there will also be worlds in which the skies appear more or less as they do in the actual world, but in which

---

[13] Stalnaker (2014, 25).   [14] Stalnaker (1999, 13).

some other heavenly body, say Mars, appears in the evening exactly where Venus actually appears. Let j be one such world and suppose for simplicity that the context set is {i, j}. Now imagine Daniels utters 'Hesperus is Phosphorus'. Intuitively, in making this utterance Daniels is conveying a proposition that is true in i and false in j. Since it will be presupposed that he has made this utterance, Daniels makes this utterance in every world in the context set. So we can sensibly ask what proposition Daniels thereby asserts in each world in the context set. Now in j, ancient astronomers will have called Mars by a name from which our name 'Hesperus' derives. So in such a world, utterances of 'Hesperus' refer to Mars and those of 'Phosphorus' refers to Venus. But then, again assuming the orthodox semantics for sentences like 'Hesperus is Phosphorus', the utterance of it express a necessary truth in i and an impossibility in j. We can represent this with the following *propositional concept*:

	i	j
i	T	T
j	F	F

The first row represents the fact that 'Hesperus is Phosphorus' expresses a necessary truth in the actual world; and the second row represents the fact that utterances of that sentence in j express an impossibility. But it should be clear that we have now violated Stalnaker's second principle above governing assertions and presuppositions. In such a case, Stalnaker thinks that in order to bring us back in conformity with that principle while avoiding the assertion of something trivial or trivially false, we *reinterpret* the sentence 'Hesperus is Phosphorus' as expressing the proposition true in i and false in j. This proposition is represented by the diagonal in the above propositional concept and so is called the *diagonal proposition* (of that propositional concept); we can also talk, as Stalnaker does, of conversational participants reinterpreting 'Hesperus is Phosphorus' by *diagonalizing*. So Stalnaker's claim is that what is said/asserted by uttering 'Hesperus is Phosphorus' in a case of this sort is the diagonal proposition. He notes that this seems to capture the information a speaker is intuitively trying to convey in such a case, since as we said she intends to rule out j. Let me re-emphasize a crucial point that I'll return to below: reinterpreting the utterance by diagonalizing is triggered by the violation of the second pragmatic principle above.

Finally, it was implicit in what I just said that there are two separable parts to Stalnaker's diagonalization account of how utterances of 'Hesperus is Phosphorus' manage to be informative, as he himself makes admirably clear.[15]

---

[15] Stalnaker (1987, 119).

First, such informative utterances of 'Hesperus is Phosphorus' must somehow be conveying a contingent proposition. Hence, we must first identify this proposition. Second, we must give a systematic account of how/why the sentence in the contexts in question conveys that proposition. The diagonalization-as-repair-strategy story addresses this second question.

Stalnaker wants to generalize this diagonalization account to explain how and why utterances of 2a and 2b can assert different propositions and so diverge in truth-value. Specifically, in such cases the that-clause in 2b will turn out *not to designate* the necessary proposition, just as informative unembedded utterances of 'Hesperus is Phosphorus' *don't assert* the necessary proposition. Suppose that Daniels and O'Leary are again talking. They both know Keelin and are discussing her. For each world in the context set of their conversation, Keelin is in a belief state that determines the set of worlds not excluded by it. The union of these sets for each world in the context set determines the set of worlds that for all O'Leary and Daniels presuppose are compatible with Keelin's beliefs. This set is the *derived context set* for the conversation about Keelin's beliefs.[16] Suppose the derived context set contains the actual world i, where of course Venus occurs in certain places in the morning and the evening, and worlds in which Venus appears exactly where it actually does in the morning and Mars appears exactly where Venus actually appears in the evening. Let j be such a world. For simplicity, then, say for all O'Leary and Daniels presuppose to this point in the conversation, the set of worlds compatible with Keelin's beliefs—the derived context set—is {i,j}. O'Leary then utters 2b. Suppose now we want to define the propositional concept associated with the that-clause in the utterance of 2b on the derived context set. Assume that a that-clause designates the same proposition that the sentence it contains expresses. Notice we cannot ask what proposition the that-clause in O'Leary's utterance designates in j. For if Keelin isn't present and isn't aware of O'Leary's utterance, it (or perhaps a counterpart of it) won't exist in j. However, we can suppose that O'Leary were to utter in j as he is actually uttering and ask in that case what the that-clause in his utterance *would* designate. Since in that case, his utterance of 'Hesperus' would refer to Mars, the that-clause would designate the impossible proposition in j. Of course in i, it designates the necessary proposition. So we get the following propositional concept associated with the sentence in O'Leary's that-clause:

	i	j
i	T	T
j	F	F

---

[16] Stalnaker (1988, 157). Stalnaker (2014, 92–93).

Stalnaker claims that O'Leary's utterance of 2b asserts that Keelin believes the diagonal proposition of this propositional concept: the proposition true in i and false in j. Note that this does seem to intuitively capture what Keelin is being said to believe: she is being said to believe something that rules out j. Hence, 2b expresses a different proposition than 2a in such a case. If O'Leary's assertion is accepted, any world will be dropped from the context set in which Keelin's belief state doesn't exclude j (and since j is in the derived context set, there must be such a world). Note that if O'Leary and Daniels are mistaken about Keelin's beliefs, 2b could well be false in this case, though of course 2a will be true in this situation.

One would think that as in the previous case, diagonalizing has to be triggered by something here. After all, the standard semantics for the that-clause in 2b has it designating the necessary proposition. Something has to override that. That is, as before we need to give a systematic account of how the that-clauses in such cases designate the diagonal proposition. So far as I can see, Stalnaker doesn't say what the trigger for diagonalization is in this case. But here is a thought. 2b semantically expresses a proposition that asserts that Keelin stands in the belief relation to the necessary proposition. But, one might think, since conversational participants presuppose that everyone believes the necessary proposition, they presuppose that Keelin does. Hence, the semantic content of 2b is presupposed and so true in all worlds in the context set. But then asserting it violates principle 1 above. Further, the above propositional concept shows that in i the complement of 2b expresses a necessary truth and in j an impossibility. The conversational participants can't be sure which of these 2b is ascribing belief in and ascribing belief in either would be infelicitous (since Keelin trivially believes the necessary proposition and trivially fails to believes the impossible one). However, if we reinterpret 2b so that its that-clause designates the diagonal proposition of the above propositional concept, we get something that is true in some but not all worlds in the context set, conformity with principle 1 is reinstated and we avoid ascribing belief in something trivially believed or trivially disbelieved. So once again here, diagonalization is triggered by the violation of pragmatic principles and reinterpreting the that-clause is a repair strategy.

In discussing his diagonalization account, Stalnaker is explicit that the explanation for when reinterpretation by diagonalizing occurs exploits a Gricean strategy. For Grice, real or apparent violations of conversational maxims result in sentences conveying information that is no part of their semantic contents. Similarly, as I've already suggested, according to Stalnaker's diagonalization account, the utterance of a sentence results in a violation of pragmatic principles that then triggers a reinterpretation of the sentence uttered. Indeed, Stalnaker appears to compare what triggers diagonalizing to the flouting of a Gricean maxim. After introducing the idea of reinterpreting by diagonalizing, he writes:

> To make the hypothesis precise, we need only spell out the conditions under which the operation is performed. I have tried to go some way toward doing this in Chapter 4 ['Assertion']. The strategy is a Gricean one. There are various independently motivated pragmatic maxims governing discourse. When a speaker seems to be violating one of these in a blatant way, a cooperative conversational strategy may require that the addressee reinterpret what is said in a way that makes it conform to the maxim. One way to reinterpret—a way appropriate to the violation of a particular pragmatic maxim—is to diagonalize: to take the assertion to express the diagonal of the propositional concept determined by the utterance and its context.[17]

Note that here Stalnaker talks of a speaker seeming to violate a pragmatic maxim *in a blatant way*. That sounds a lot like the flouting of a Gricean maxim.

What is important for present concerns is that according to Stalnaker diagonalization, with the result that 'Hesperus is Phosphorus' expresses, and 'that Hesperus is Phosphorus' designates, a contingent truth, is a *repair strategy*. It is triggered by a violation of a pragmatic principle and its operation restores conformity with that principle. I said above that Stalnaker's diagonalization account is ingenious. It is, but I think the account has difficulties. A central difficulty is traceable to the point just made: that diagonalization is a repair strategy. It seems to me that this is implausible. There are several reasons for thinking so.

First, consider a context in which 'Hesperus is Phosphorus' is felicitously uttered. As we saw, this means that not only does the sentence express different propositions in different worlds in the context set but in addition in each world of the context set the sentence expresses either the non-informative necessary truth or the impossible proposition. In order for this to trigger a reinterpretation by conversational participants of the sentence uttered, conversational participants must in some sense be aware of these violations of pragmatic principles. But in such cases, conversational participants are certainly not consciously aware of the utterance being anomalous. It isn't as though in such cases conversational participants aren't sure which of two propositions the speaker intends to assert and recognize that the speaker is either asserting something trivial or impossible. Nor are speakers aware of reinterpreting the sentence in question. This means that the awareness of the violation of a pragmatic principle and the resulting reinterpretation must be unconscious and highly tacit. I'll note that this already looks quite different from what happens when Gricean maxims are flouted.

But even if awareness of the violation and resulting reinterpretation is unconscious and tacit, one would expect that conversational participants could be made aware of the fact that they were tacitly sensing an anomaly and reinterpreting.

[17] Stalnaker (1987, 124–5). See similar remarks in Stalnaker (2004, 304–5).

Compare the case of conversational implicatures generated by flouting a maxim. Consider a case like an utterance of 'War is war' in which Grice claims that the first maxim of Quantity is flouted. In such a case, Grice claims that hearers recognize that the uttered sentence is uninformative in any context and hence must violate the first maxim of Quantity. They can see that the speaker knows this and is thus blatantly violating the maxim. Assuming the speaker is nonetheless being cooperative, they identify what the speaker intended by reflecting on why the speaker choose that "particular patent tautology".[18] When ordinary speakers who have not previously heard of conversational implicatures hear this story, it strikes them as plausible that they go through something like the process described: they sense the uninformativeness of the utterance and then try to figure out what the speaker intends to convey by the utterance by reflecting on the situation they are in and why the speaker chose the tautology she did. For one thing, when ordinary speakers are given this explanation, they *are* able to recognize that the sentence uttered *was* tautologous and that they were likely at least tacitly aware of this upon hearing the utterance if not explicitly aware of it.

Even in cases in which a conversational implicature is not generated by the flouting of a maxim but by a more subtle means, hearers can be made aware of the fact that they interpreted speakers as conveying additional information not semantically expressed by the sentence uttered in order to preserve the supposition that speakers are conforming to the maxims or at least the Cooperative Principle. Take Grice's (1975) famous example:

A: I am out of petrol.
B: There is a garage round the corner.[19]

I have taught Grice (1975) many times and I have found that when students confront this example, are told that B implicates/conveys/suggests that the garage is open, sells petrol and so on and does so because only taking B in this way can we see her remarks as a relevant response to A's, they find it very plausible both that they did so interpret B and that the story about why they did is correct. That is, they find it plausible that they tacitly interpreted B in the way described by the means described.

In the case of Stalnaker's diagonalization account and 'Hesperus is Phosphorus' the matter couldn't be more different. I have found that when speakers hear this story, they *don't* recognize that they were at least tacitly aware of the alleged fact that they weren't sure which of the necessary and impossible propositions the speaker intended to convey by uttering the sentence she did nor do they recognize that they performed the act of reinterpreting the speaker's utterance. This seems

---

[18] Grice (1975, 33).   [19] Grice (1975, 32).

to me to cast tremendous doubt on the plausibility of Stalnaker's diagonalization account. For it means that the alleged process we go through in arriving at the diagonal interpretation is something we are not in any way consciously aware of nor can we be made to see that we were tacitly aware of it. This is unlike the case of conversational implicatures and just doesn't sound like a pragmatic process at all, but rather sounds like something that is hardwired.

Exactly similar considerations apply to reinterpreting the that-clause in cases like 2b above. Here too we have no awareness of sensing something anomalous about the utterance and reinterpreting the that-clause by means of a propositional concept defined on the derived context set. Here too even once we are told the story, we do not see that perhaps we really did tacitly go through such a process. And so here too, I think serious doubt is cast on the account.

A second difficulty is that Stalnaker's diagonalization account requires conversational participants to at least tacitly be aware of the fact that 'Hesperus is Phosphorus' expresses either a necessary or an impossible proposition. For only then could conversational participants be tacitly aware of the propositional concept discussed above leading to the alleged diagonal reinterpretation of the sentence. But I don't think that in general ordinary speakers can be tacitly aware of the fact that 'Hesperus is Phosphorus' expresses a necessary or impossible proposition.[20] It is important here to remember that Kripke (1980) gave *extensive arguments* in for the claim that 'Hesperus is Phosphorus' expresses a necessary truth.[21] He clearly thought the view that it expresses a contingent truth was more intuitive at the time. My hunch is that large numbers of ordinary people would find that view more intuitive as well. At any rate, certainly some will. Others will likely have no opinion on the matter, find the issue confusing or never have thought about it. Consider the group of people comprising those who think that 'Hesperus is Phosphorus' expresses a contingent truth, those who have no opinion on the matter, those who find the question of whether it expresses a necessary or contingent truth confusing and those who have never thought about it. Certainly an informative utterance of the sentence 'Hesperus is Phosphorus' will seem neither trivially true nor trivially false to such people. Stalnaker must explain that by claiming they are tacitly aware of the propositional concept above and reinterpret the sentence as expressing the diagonal. That requires them to be tacitly aware that 'Hesperus is Phosphorus' expresses a necessary truth or an impossibility. It is hard to see how people who when probed about the matter are disposed to think that 'Hesperus is Phosphorus' could have been false or are unsure what to think or have never thought about it are nonetheless tacitly aware that it expresses either a necessary or impossible proposition. So I think that the fact that such

---

[20] The entry on modal illusions in the Internet Encyclopedia of Philosophy says that 'Hesperus is Phosphorus' strikes many people as contingent on first consideration.
[21] Kripke (1980, 97–103 and 107–10).

people could find 'Hesperus is Phosphorus' informative is a real problem for the diagonalization account.

Above I argued that the claim that both in the case of 'Hesperus is Phosphorus' and 'that Hesperus is Phosphorus' speakers reinterpreting by means of the diagonal is a repair strategy is implausible. What about getting around these worries by claiming instead that it isn't a repair strategy but is obligatory? That is, whenever the diagonal is different from the horizontal(s), the sentence or that-clause gets obligatorily reinterpreted by means of the diagonal. Call this the *obligatory diagonal approach*. On this view, nothing—e.g. no violation of any pragmatic rule—is needed to trigger diagonalization. I think this view has problems too.

A first worry is that though the rule that we obligatorily reinterpret seems as though it has to be some sort of *pragmatic* rule, it has features that appear inconsistent with that status. Why think it is a pragmatic and not a semantic rule? Well, it is a rule about reinterpreting a sentence as expressing something other than the proposition it semantically expresses as a result of it expressing different propositions in different worlds in the context set. That a sentence expresses different propositions in different worlds in the context set is a matter of conversational participants being ignorant about the semantic values of certain expressions in the sentence.[22] But then the rule to obligatorily reinterpret via the diagonal is a rule to the effect that when conversational participants are ignorant about the semantic value of some constituent of a sentence that has been uttered, the sentence is to be reinterpreted as expressing a proposition other than the one it semantically expresses. Surely this has to be some sort of pragmatic rule, talking as it does about reinterpreting a sentence in terms of something that isn't its semantic value when conversational participants are ignorant in certain ways. A second reason for thinking the rule to obligatorily reinterpret via the diagonal is a pragmatic rule is that it is a rule that governs propositional concepts. Stalnaker is very clear that propositional concepts are not semantic values of any sort.[23] They are only associated with utterances of sentences in context and are used to model the epistemic situation of conversational participants. But then a rule that operates on such non-semantic objects must be a pragmatic rule.

However, the rule appears to have features that strongly suggest it *can't* be a pragmatic rule. First, as I indicated above, speakers are unaware of applying the rule. Further, again as previously discussed, even after the operation of the rule is explained to speakers they cannot come to see that they are in fact applying it. This is very unlike commonly accepted pragmatic rules. Take the Gricean maxim of Quantity, for example. When students first encounter it, they recognize that

---

[22] This need not be a matter of conversational participants being semantically incompetent with an expression in the sentence. For example, it could be a matter of participants not being sure who/what a speaker intends to refer to with a use of a pronoun.

[23] Stalnaker (1999, 9–10).

they by and large follow something like this rule. By contrast, when they are told that they are obligatorily reinterpreting by means of the diagonal in cases of the informative use of 'Hesperus is Phosphorus', they do not at all recognize that they have been reinterpreting. Second, that the obligatory diagonalization rule applies obligatorily and cannot be suspended, ignored or cancelled makes it unlike commonly accepted pragmatic rules. Again, we can choose not to follow the maxim of Quantity and we see that we sometimes do so. Third, for any pragmatic rule, one would expect there to be a neo-Gricean story about why rational beings like us who are interested in cooperative, efficient communication would follow the rule. Again, it is pretty easy to tell such a story about why speakers obey the maxim of Quantity. Of course, the diagonalize-as-repair-strategy account was just such a story about why cooperative speakers diagonalize under certain conditions. But the obligatory diagonal approach currently under consideration is supposed to be an alternative to that story that avoids its downsides. However, we now lack any suitable explanation as to why rational communicators would follow such an allegedly pragmatic rule. Fourth, the obligatory diagonal approach is subject to the last problem discussed with the diagonalization-as-repair-strategy approach. Even if diagonalization is obligatory, it has to be performed on the propositional concept mentioned above. For conversational participants to do that, they must be at least tacitly aware that 'Hesperus is Phosphorus' expresses a necessary or impossible proposition. But, as I argued above, in many conversations in which the latter is informative or 2b is, there is good reason to think speakers will not be even tacitly aware of this.

A number of different kinds of examples provide a final argument against the obligatory diagonal approach. Consider the following exchange:

3. A: Hesperus is Phosphorus.
   B: Really, Hesperus is Phosphorus? Huh!
   A: Yes, and in fact that is necessarily true.

Surely A's final utterance can be read as true. But that requires her use of 'that' to designate a necessary truth. It seems hard to deny that it designates the proposition expressed by A's first utterance and B's utterance. But that has to be the contingent diagonal if the obligatory diagonal approach is correct and A's first utterance is informative. Similarly, one would think that the obligatory diagonal approach would have the consequence that the following is false when uttered informatively:

4. It is true and even necessary that Hesperus is Phosphorus.

That seems wrong. Further, consider the following:

5a. That Hesperus is Phosphorus is necessary and believed by Keelin.
5b. Keelin believes the necessary truth that Hesperus is Phosphorus.

If the that-clause in 5a designates the contingent proposition the obligatory diagonal approach says it does, the sentence should be false. However it seems it could easily be true. 5b could be true and informative and surely seems to say that Keelin believes a necessary truth. But that requires 'the necessary truth that Hesperus is Phosphorus' to designate a necessary truth contrary to what the obligatory diagonal approach says.

It is worth noting that 3–5 are also a problem for Stalnaker's original proposal on which diagonalizing is a repair strategy. It is easy to imagine 3–5 occurring in situations in which Stalnaker would want to say that conversational participants repair by diagonalizing. For example, 3 could occur in a situation in which A's first utterance is informative (indeed, it is naturally read that way). Similarly for 4. Finally, 5a and 5b are naturally heard as attributing a non-trivial belief to Keelin.

In summary, I think the considerations adduced here show that Stalnaker's diagonal strategy, both for unembedded occurrences of 'Hesperus is Phosphorus' and for the that-clause in 2b, has significant problems.

Let's now turn to Stalnaker's strategy for explaining how 1a and 1b could diverge in truth-value. Imagine a case in which 1a seems true and 1b seems false. But how could 1b seem false when the that-clause in it designates the necessary truth, which everyone, including Keelin, believes? According to Stalnaker, 1b in the imagined situation will not convey the claim that she so believes. When sentence structure is complicated, as Stalnaker thinks is the case with the complement of 1b, there is room for doubt as to what proposition the sentence expresses. Stalnaker thinks that in the case at hand, what Keelin doubts is that the complement of 1b expresses the necessary proposition. He claims that 1b conveys the false information that Keelin *believes* that the complement of 1b expresses the necessary proposition (or a truth) and this is why it seems false to us. So far so good, though I think we need more of a pragmatic story about how/why 1b conveys the false information it does and I'll return to this below. According to Stalnaker's strategy here, when belief ascriptions that appear to falsely ascribe belief in a necessary mathematical truth to a subject, they are really falsely ascribing belief in a contingent proposition to the effect that the complement of the ascription designates a necessary truth. Though Stalnaker has given reasons for thinking this isn't a good label, I'll call this the *metalinguistic strategy*.

Field (1978, 2001b) points out that this strategy won't work in some cases.[24] Field considers the conditional whose antecedent is the conjunction of the axioms

---

[24] Field (1978, 34–5 and 2001b, 100–3). Stalnaker (1984) credits a similar point to Larry Powers and Saul Kripke as well. See Stalnaker (1984, 76 n. 17).

of set theory (including the axiom of choice) and whose consequent is the Banach-Tarski theorem. Call this the *Banach-Tarski conditional* (*BTC*). This conditional is a logical truth and so the proposition it expresses is the necessary one. Field considers a person, say O'Leary, who dissents from BTC because he believes set theory but, as we would put it, believes the Banach-Tarski theorem to be false. Then the following will seem false when S is BTC:

6. O'Leary believes that S.

According to the metalinguistic strategy, such a person does not really doubt the proposition expressed by BTC (the necessary proposition), but rather doubts the proposition expressed by the following:

7. The semantic rules for the language of set theory relate BTC to the necessary truth.

Further, Stalnaker claims that 6 in the relevant context conveys the claim that O'Leary believes 7 and that is why it seems false.[25] Now, Field says, suppose O'Leary knows what the semantic rules of the language of set theory are. Let their statement be R. The only way O'Leary could doubt what is expressed by 7 is if he doubts what is expressed by:

8. The semantic rules R relate BTC to the necessary truth.

But 8 expresses a necessary truth and so cannot by what O'Leary doubts. So Stalnaker's attempt to explain why 1a and 1b can seem to diverge in truth-value when their complements are logically equivalent by claiming that sometimes sentences like 1b convey not that Keelin believes the propositions expressed by their complements, but rather that she believes that the complements express truths appears to fail in at least some cases. Specifically, Stalnaker's account can't explain how 6 could seem false and the following could seem true:

9. O'Leary believes that 2 + 2 = 4.

The problem Field notes here with explaining how 6 could seem false by means of the metalinguistic strategy is that it ends up once again requiring us to say that O'Leary doubts the necessary truth 8 repeated here:

8. The semantic rules R relate BTC to the necessary truth.

---

[25] Stalnaker (1984, 73–4).

184 UNSTRUCTURED CONTENT

And so, as Field says, nothing has been gained by the metalinguistic ascent to explain why 6 seems false. But perhaps Stalnaker could appeal to a different strategy to explain why it seems true to say O'Leary doubts 8. For Stalnaker, the notion of believing a proposition is to be understood in terms of the more basic notion of a *belief state*. This is represented as the set of worlds compatible with the belief state: the set of worlds that are ways things might be. To believe that P is for P to be true in all the possible worlds in one's belief states. Now Stalnaker thinks that a given agent can be in multiple belief states that aren't integrated with each other. In such a case beliefs are *fragmented* or *compartmentalized*:

> It is compatible with the pragmatic account that the rational dispositions that a person has at one time should arise from several different belief states. A person may be disposed in one kind of context, or with respect to one kind of action, to behave in ways that are explained by one belief state, and at the same time be disposed in another kind of context or with respect to another kind of action to behave in ways that would be explained by a different belief state.[26]

For the most part, Stalnaker uses these non-integrated belief states to explain the fact that one's beliefs are not closed under logical consequence and that one can have inconsistent beliefs. A given belief state *will* be closed under logical consequence. Consider a belief state B of agent A and suppose A believes that P relative to B. Then P is true in all the worlds in B. If P entails Q, then Q is true in all the worlds in B. So A believes Q relative to B. However, if an agent A is in belief state B_1 and believes R relative to it, and A is also in belief state B_2 and believes S relative to it and B_1 and B_2 are not integrated, there may be no belief state such that A believes R&S relative to it. In such a case, A believes R and A believes S, but A does not believe R&S.[27] Similarly, A may believe P relative to B_1 and ~P relative to B_2, where B_1 and B_2 are not integrated. In such a case there is a sense in which A has inconsistent beliefs but we avoid the disastrous conclusion that A believes P&~P relative to any one belief state and so believes everything.[28]

However, at one point Stalnaker appears to use compartmentalized belief in a somewhat different way to explain apparent ignorance of mathematical truth:[29]

> To take a simple case of calculation, a person may display his belief that four plus three equals seven by performing certain operations on numerals that

---

[26] Stalnaker (1984, 83).   [27] Stalnaker (1984, 83).   [28] Stalnaker (1984, 83).

[29] Mathematical truths will be true relative to any belief state. Hence, you could not explain S's apparent ignorance of mathematical truth M by saying that though S believes P and Q and these jointly entail M, P is believed relative to belief state B_1 and Q is believed relative to belief state B_2 and S has not integrated B_1 and B_2. The problem, of course, is that S trivially believes M relative to both B_1 and B_2, and so is in no sense ignorant of M. Thus my talk of *apparent* ignorance of M and compartmentalized belief being used here in a *different way*.

contain three and four as digits—for example by writing down "7" as the first step in adding sixty-four and twenty-three. A person who is competent at doing sums but not particularly quick or intuitive could manifest *his separate beliefs that four plus three equals seven* and *that six plus two equals eight* in calculating the sum of sixty-four and twenty-three, but *he would show that before doing the calculation he did not have the belief that sixty-four plus twenty-three is eighty-seven. That last belief results only after the two simpler arithmetic beliefs were put together against a background of more general beliefs and presuppositions about arithmetic operations.*[30]

The passage is puzzling because in the italicized passages Stalnaker mentions three beliefs using that-clauses that by standard semantic rules designate necessary truths: the belief that four plus three equals seven, that six plus two equals eight and that sixty-four plus twenty-three equals eighty-seven. The first two beliefs are said to be "separate", which I take it means they are initially believed relative to different, non-integrated belief states. Since necessary truths are believed relative to every belief state, I take it that the that-clauses 'that four plus three equals seven' and 'that six plus two equals eight' must not designate the necessary truth in the quotation. Perhaps Stalnaker thinks that they designate contingently true propositions about the relation between a sentence and the necessary truth. That is, perhaps Stalnaker is assuming the metalinguistic strategy here in talking about these beliefs not being integrated. But what of the claim that the person in question didn't believe that sixty-four plus twenty-three equals eighty-seven prior to performing the calculation? This can't be a denial that the person believed the necessary truth prior to performing the calculation. I also don't think it can be a denial that the person believed a proposition about the relation between the sentence 'sixty-four plus twenty-three equals eighty-seven' and the necessary truth. For earlier Stalnaker appears to deny that the metalinguistic strategy yields a plausible account of the ignorance of the result of a calculation:

> The suggestion [the metalinguistic strategy] implies that whenever a person fails to know some mathematical truth, there is a nonfactual possible world compatible with his knowledge in which the mathematical statement says something different than it says in this world.... But this does not seem to locate the source of mathematical ignorance in the right place.
> Take a simple case of calculation: I did not know before I performed some calculations that $689 \times 43 = 29{,}627$. But it is surely not plausible to explain my ignorance with an epistemically possible world in which '689' or '43' denotes a different number or in which the multiplication sign represents a different operation.[31]

---

[30] Stalnaker (1984, 86–7), my emphasis.   [31] Stalnaker (1984, 76).

186 UNSTRUCTURED CONTENT

It looks like what Stalnaker is claiming in the previous quotation is that the person's ignorance *that sixty-four plus twenty-three equals eighty-seven* is ignorance of a contingent proposition that is entailed by the separate metalinguistic beliefs that four plus three equals seven and that two plus six equals eight, together with "general beliefs and presuppositions about arithmetic operations". I am not sure exactly which proposition that is, but Stalnaker must think that the that-clause 'that sixty-four plus twenty-three equals eighty-seven' designates it here.

The question is: in saying that O'Leary doubts and hence is ignorant of 8 above, can we apply a similar strategy? That is, when we say that O'Leary doubts that the semantic rules R relate BTC to the necessary truth, can we say that the that-clause here designates some contingent proposition that is entailed by some non-integrated beliefs, perhaps together with other background beliefs and presuppositions and that this is what O'Leary is said to be ignorant of? The only candidates I can think of for being the relevant non-integrated beliefs are things like the beliefs that R are the semantic rules governing the language of set theory, that C is the conjunction of the axioms of set theory, that the BTC has C as its antecedent and such-and-such mathematical statement, which is in fact the Banach-Tarski theorem, as its consequent and so on. The problem is that it appears that we can tell our story about O'Leary in such a way that these candidate beliefs seem to be integrated and yet it still seems true to say that O'Leary doubts 8.[32] Just imagine that he is attending to the semantic rules R, the conjunction C and BTC, while applying the rules R to BTC. We can even imagine that he is performing inferences that require all the relevant beliefs: perhaps he is applying the rules R to BTC and inferring that the antecedent of BTC is true iff each conjunct is true, and so on. But then surely all the relevant beliefs must be integrated. Since it could still seem true to say that O'Leary doubts 8, it can't be that we are using that claim to convey the claim that O'Leary is ignorant of some contingent proposition P, where the ignorance is due to the fact that the relevant beliefs entailing P are believed relative to different, non-integrated belief states. So in the end, it seems to me that Field's objection here to the metalinguistic strategy stands.

I'll add as an aside that considerations of the general sort we just adduced in the case of O'Leary make me skeptical of the claim that the fragmented belief approach will be capable of accounting for all cases in which belief and knowledge aren't closed under logical consequence and all cases of coherent inconsistent belief. For it seems that we will be able to describe cases in which a subject has integrated the relevant beliefs and still fails to believe some of their consequences. And we'll be able to describe cases in which a subject coherently believes integrated inconsistent beliefs.[33]

A second worry with the metalinguistic strategy concerns how 6 above manages to convey not the claim that O'Leary believes the necessary truth, but rather the

---

[32] Closely related points are made in Field (2001b).
[33] Field (2001a, 102) makes this latter point.

claim that O'Leary believes that the complement of 6 designates the necessary truth. Stalnaker is a bit cagey about this, but I think he thinks it is just a matter of diagonalizing again.[34] I *think* the idea is this. In a context in which someone would utter 6, for all the conversational participants are presupposing, in some of O'Leary's belief worlds the complement of 6—BTC—designates a necessary falsehood and in some of O'Leary's belief worlds the complement designates a necessary truth. Call a representative world of the former sort i and a representative world of the latter sort j. Then we can take {i,j} to be the derived context set for the conversation about O'Leary's beliefs. This means that the propositional concept associated with the that-clause in 6 looks as follows:

	i	j
i	F	F
j	T	T

Now we reason just as we did in the case of Keelin and 2b above. 6 semantically expresses a proposition that asserts that O'Leary stands in the belief relation to the necessary proposition. But one might think, since conversational participants presuppose that everyone believes the necessary proposition, they presuppose that O'Leary does. That means that the semantic content of 6 is presupposed and so true in all worlds in the context set. But then asserting that violates principle 1 above. Further, the above propositional concept shows that in j the complement of 6 expresses a necessary truth and in i an impossibility. We can't be sure which of these 6 is ascribing belief in and ascribing belief in either would be infelicitous (since O'Leary trivially believes the necessary proposition and trivially fails to believe the impossible one). However, if we reinterpret 6 so that its that-clause designates the diagonal proposition of the above propositional concept, we get something that is true in some but not all worlds in the context set, conformity with principle 1 is reinstated and we avoid ascribing belief in something trivially believed or trivially disbelieved. Further, the diagonal proposition does seem to be about the relation between the that-clause/embedded sentence in 6 and the necessary truth. For it is the proposition that is true in the world where the that-clause designates the necessary truth and false in the world where it designates the impossible proposition.

Unfortunately, however, this is just the diagonalization-as-repair-strategy approach all over again. But then the arguments we gave against it above in the cases of 'Hesperus is Phosphorus' and 'Keelin believes that Hesperus is Phosphorus' apply here as well. Specifically, once again in the case of both informative utterances of 'There are an infinite number of primes' and 'Keelin believes there are an infinite

---

[34] This is suggested by remarks in Stalnaker (1986, 120–1) and in Stalnaker (1984, 73–4) and n. 16.

number of primes' speakers are not consciously aware of sensing an anomaly and reinterpreting to avoid it. That means these processes must be highly tacit. But again here, even after speakers are told that they are going through these allegedly highly tacit processes, they are unable to recognize they have done so. Just as before, this does not look like a pragmatic process at all.

Finally, there is a further problem with the diagonalization/metalinguistic strategy applied to 1b that is an analog of another problem I raised with the account of Keelin and 2b above. As we saw, to arrive at the above propositional concept for the complement of 6 we assumed that for all the conversational participants presuppose, the complement of 6 expresses the necessary proposition in some of O'Leary's belief worlds and the impossible proposition in the others. However, why do the conversational participants presuppose that in each of O'Leary's belief worlds the complement of 6 designates either the necessary or impossible proposition? It must be because they presuppose that O'Leary knows that mathematical sentences express necessary truths or necessary falsehoods. But why would they presuppose that? O'Leary is just an ordinary guy who like most ordinary guys has thought almost not at all about metaphysical possibility and necessity. Or maybe O'Leary has thought about it and sides with Descartes' view that God could have made the truths of mathematics false or thinks such truths could have been false for other reasons. When you Google 'Could the truths of mathematics have been false?' or 'Could God have made the truths of mathematics false?' you find such gems as the following:

QA "It is therefore more correct to say that God says what shall be true for his creation, and mathematical truth is part of this truth."

QB "The basic idea is: if we ever had empirical evidence that some truth of arithmetic was false we would have to admit that it was false. But if so then mathematics is empirically justified. To make the case consider the following scenario. Suppose that you had two pens of sheep; one with 6 and one with 7 sheep. Now suppose that you counted the sheep individually in each pen (and got 6 and 7) and then you counted all of the sheep and got 14. Suppose you did it again. 1. 2. 3. 4. 5. 6. Yep six sheep in that pen. 1. 2. 3. 4. 5. 6. 7. Yep seven sheep in that pen. Then all the sheep. 1. 2. 3. 4. 5. 6. 7. 8. 9. 10. 11. 12. 13. 14. Suppose that this was repeated by all of your friends with the same results. Suppose that it was on the news and tested scientifically and confirmed. Suppose that this phenomenon was wide spread, observable, and repeatable. If this were the case we would be forced to admit that $7 + 6 = 14$ is true therefore mathematics is empirically justified."

QC "Mathematics is an invention of the human mind and exists only when human minds do."

QD "Hence, mathematical definitions were chosen by humans to model physical reality so that we could make useful predictions, not to encapsulate metaphysical truth, so really, why should we expect math to be true?"

QA shows that some people take God to decide what the mathematical truths are. The author makes clear that God could have settled on different "truths for his creation". QB shows that some people take arithmetic to be something like true generalizations from experience and the author makes clear that if our experience were different, we would truly generalize differently. The author of QC makes clear that he thinks that mathematics would not exist if human minds didn't and presumably in such a case mathematical truths wouldn't be true. QD is representative of a surprising number of people who think that at least much of mathematics isn't *actually* true but most such people seem to think that it could have been (e.g. had the universe been more "ideal"). So lots of people think that mathematical sentences express claims that are contingent. Many more have never considered the question of the modal status of the propositions expressed by mathematical sentences or have no opinion on the matter.[35] But that means that in very many ordinary conversations people will not presuppose that mathematical sentences express necessary or impossible propositions either because they think that is false, or because they have no view on the matter or because they have never given it any thought. When such people are talking about O'Leary and presuppose he is like them in this regard, it will simply not be true that they presuppose that in each of O'Leary's belief worlds the complement of 6 expresses the necessary or the impossible proposition. But then in such a context, the propositional concept above will not be associated with the complement of 6 and so it won't designate the diagonal of that propositional concept. This means that the metalinguistic strategy cannot explain why 6 could well seem false in such contexts. For such cases we would need some other as yet unknown explanation of this.

Finally, though I won't rehearse them again, all the arguments against the obligatory diagonal account that I gave above in the case of 'Hesperus is Phosphorus' and 'Keelin believes that Hesperus is Phosphorus' apply equally here.

Conclusion

I began by enumerating four outstanding problems for PWC:

1. It can't give an intuitively correct account of what propositions are about.
2. It can't explain why propositions are the kinds of things that have truth conditions or are true and false relative to worlds, nor why a given proposition has the specific truth conditions it does or the truth-values it does relative to worlds.

---

[35] I discovered this by asking people on chair lifts whether it could have been false that 2 + 2 = 4 when I was on sabbatical and skiing at Mammoth Mountain in the 2015–16 ski season. Of the many people I asked, only one ventured the opinion that she didn't see how that could be.

3. It faces the problem of explaining why beliefs don't seem to be closed under logical consequence, why it seems one can fail to believe or non-trivially believe necessary truths and why it seems one can believe or non-trivially fail to believe the impossible (the problem of deduction).
4. It must explain how/why two belief ascriptions that differ only in having different that-clauses that both designate the necessary truth can appear to express different propositions and so diverge in truth-value (the problem of equivalence).

In the case of 1, I suggested some strategies for addressing the problem and found them wanting. In the case of 3, I mentioned the best strategy for addressing the problem known to me and argued that at least in cases of the sort brought out by Field the strategy seems to fail.

4 was the problem I spent most of my time on. I first argued that there were problems with the explanation of how/why the following sentences could express different propositions and so diverge in truth-value:

2a. Keelin believes that Hesperus is Hesperus.
2b. Keelin believes that Hesperus is Phosphorus.

First, I argued that the idea that 2b can express a different proposition from 2a because the that-clause in it gets reinterpreted as designating a contingent proposition by means of a repair strategy is implausible. Second, I argued that the explanation required that conversational participants be at least tacitly aware that 'Hesperus is Phosphorus' expresses a necessary or impossible proposition and that in general this was implausible. Finally, I considered the idea that diagonalization was obligatory instead of a repair strategy. I noted that obligatory diagonalization appeared to be a pragmatic and not a semantic rule. I then argued that it had features that strongly suggested it couldn't be a pragmatic rule.

Finally, I turned to the explanation PWC gives for how the following could express different propositions and so diverge in truth-value:

1a. Keelin believes that $2 + 2 = 4$.
1b. Keelin believes that there are an infinite number of primes.

Here I argued, first, that the strategy cannot work in cases of the sort raised by Hartry Field (1978, 2001b). Second, I claimed that again here Stalnaker relies on the diagonalization-as-repair-strategy approach and hence that the arguments I gave earlier against that approach apply here as well. Finally, I argued that the explanation assumed that conversational participants presuppose that sentences of mathematics express necessary or impossible propositions (and presuppose that subjects of their ascriptions presuppose this) and that in the general case this is implausible. If these arguments are correct, 4 appears still to be a significant problem for PWC despite heroic attempts by its adherents to address it.

References

Field, H. 1978. "Mental Representation." *Erkenntnis* 13: 9–61. Reprinted in Field (2001a). I use the pagination of the latter.

Field, H. 2001a. *Truth and the Absence of Fact*. Oxford: Clarendon Press.

Field, H. 2001b. "Stalnaker on Intentionality." In Field (2001a). First appeared in slightly different form as "Critical Notice: Robert Stalnaker's *Inquiry*." *Philosophy of Science* 53 (1986): 425–48.

Grice, P. 1975. "Logic and Conversation." In *Syntax and Semantics*, vol. 3, ed. P. Cole and J. Morgan. New York: Academic Press. Reprinted in Grice (1989). I use the pagination of the latter.

Grice, P. 1989. *Studies in the Way of Words*. Cambridge, MA: Harvard University Press.

King, J. C. 2007. *The Nature and Structure of Content*. New York: Oxford University Press.

King, J. C. 2013. "Propositional unity: what's the problem, who has it and who solves it?" *Philosophical Studies* 165(1): 71–93.

Kripke, S. 1980. *Naming and Necessity*. Cambridge, MA: Harvard University Press.

Soames, S. 1987. "Direct reference, propositional attitudes and semantic content." *Philosophical Topics* 15: 47–87.

Stalnaker, R. 1978. "Assertion." *Syntax and Semantics* 9. New York: Academic Press. Reprinted in Stalnaker (1999). I use the pagination of the latter.

Stalnaker, R. 1984. *Inquiry*. Cambridge, MA: MIT Press.

Stalnaker, R. 1986. "Replies to Schiffer and Field." *Pacific Philosophical Quarterly* 67: 113–23.

Stalnaker, R. 1987. "Semantics for belief." *Philosophical Topics* 15. Reprinted in Stalnaker (1999). I use the pagination of the latter.

Stalnaker, R. 1988. "Belief attribution and context." In *Contents of Thought*, ed. Grimm R.H. and D. D. Merrill. Tucson: University of Arizona Press. Reprinted in Stalnaker (1999). I use the pagination of the latter.

Stalnaker, R. 1999. *Context and Content: Essays on Intentionality in Speech and Thought*. Oxford: Oxford University Press.

Stalnaker, R. 2004. "Assertion revisited: on the interpretation of two-dimensional modal semantics." *Philosophical Studies* 118: 299–322.

Stalnaker, R. 2012. *Mere Possibilities: Metaphysical Foundations of Modal Semantics*. Princeton: Princeton University Press.

Stalnaker, R. 2014. *Context*. New York: Oxford University Press.

Thomson, J. and A. Byrne, eds. 2006. *Content and Modality: Themes from the Philosophy of Robert Stalnaker*. New York: Oxford University Press.

Attitudes and Propositions

John Perry

In "On Sense and Reference" (Frege 1892/1960), Frege maintains that sentences refer to truth-values. This clearly doesn't work for attitude reports. "Berkeley is west of Santa Cruz" and "Mogadishu is the capital of Somalia" are both true, but Elwood may well believe that Mogadishu is the capital of Somalia, but not that Berkeley is west of Santa Cruz. Frege's solution is that in the context of attitude reports sentences do not have their customary references; they refer to the *Gedanken* or *Thoughts* that they customarily express, and their parts refer to their customary senses. Thoughts are abstract objects, denizens of a "Third Realm". Thoughts are essentially unchanging; events may make them true or false, and persons may come to believe them or disbelieve them, but the essential nature of the Thoughts is not changed. I capitalize the word when I use it in this sense.

This suggests a certain picture of the attitudes: they are relations to propositions. We now think of propositions as sets of possible worlds—very little structure—or sequences of properties and objects—a lot more structure. The latter conception is closer to Frege's ideas than the first. On my view, Frege's thoughts are essentially higher-order circumstances. In his *Begriffsschrift* Frege (1879) assigned circumstances (*Umstände*) to sentences.[1] Circumstances are basically abstract objects composed of properties (by which I will mean properties and relations) and the entities that fall under them. In the case of what I call "first-level" circumstances, the entities are objects, like Venus or the number 5. "Hesperus is a planet" and "Phosphorus is a planet" stand for the same circumstance, since both names

---

[1] Frege uses the term pretty consistently in the *Begriffsschrift*, but doesn't say much about it. I accord more importance to the concept of a circumstance than Frege did. I think he found it an intuitive concept that fit well with his idea of falling under. I think it is important to distinguish being true from being factual, which Frege did not do. As I see it, truth is a property of beliefs, statements, and other representations. Representations have truth-conditions in virtue of their structure, their components, and the relation those components have to properties and objects. It is wrong to say that Elwood's utterance of "Mogadishu is the capital of Somalia" is true if and only if Mogadishu is the capital of Somalia. That is a necessary condition, but not a sufficient one, because Mogadishu being the capital of Somalia is not sufficient for Elwood to have said anything.

Being a fact is a property of circumstances. The circumstance that Mogadishu is the capital of Somalia is a fact if and only if Mogadishu is the capital of Somalia. A "disappearance theory" of being factual works fine. Circumstances are abstract objects we use to keep track of events, in terms of the relations they establish between the objects and properties we use to think about what goes on in the world. Propositions are abstract objects we use to keep track of the truth-conditions of representations.

denote Venus. In the case of higher-level circumstances, we have properties falling under higher-level properties, an idea that connects with Frege's brilliant treatment of quantification. "A Roman conquered Gaul" denotes the circumstance that the properties of being a Roman and conquering Gaul stand in the higher-order relation, that there is something that instantiates both.

The movement from the *Begriffsschrift* theory to the theory of sense and denotation was, on my interpretation, a matter of disregarding first-level circumstances; thoughts are higher-level circumstances. While contemporary philosophers do not typically think of propositions as denizens of a Fregean Third Realm, the structured propositions approach seems closer to what he had in mind with Thoughts than the possible worlds approach. In particular, I'm pretty sure that Frege would not want to have only one proposition, the set of all possible worlds, to work with in analyzing logic and mathematics. So, if I were to cast a vote based on what I think Frege would have preferred, I'd go with structured propositions.

But it is not any particular view of propositions, but the whole idea that the attitudes should be viewed as relations to propositions, that is the target of this essay. This is the direction we are pointed in "On Sense and Reference". I think it was the wrong direction. We've been on a detour.[2] We searched for the Holy Grail of the philosophy of language and mind, a treatment of propositions that would handle all of the problems we find in the semantics of attitude reports. Are they transparent or opaque, or sometimes one and sometimes the other? Does quantification into attitude reports make sense? Is there a concept of a proposition that makes the pragmatics/semantics distinction clear? The search for this Holy Grail is a mistake.

I. Two Pictures

Elwood believes that Mogidishu is the capital of Somalia. On what I'll call the "propositional picture," this involves Elwood, the relation of belief, and the proposition that Mogidishu is the capital of Somalia. I think this picture is wrong.

When Elwood believes that Mogidishu is the capital of Somalia, he has a certain belief. A belief, as I shall use the term, is a structured brain state, involving ideas. I doubt that ideas are basic elements of the brains. They are what Locke would call "modes," structures that involve different more basic elements as time passes. A ripple in a pond is a mode; according to Locke, as far as it is in the ability of philosophers to tell, persons are modes (see Uzgalis 2007). Locke didn't think of ideas as modes, but on my physicalist view, they are. Like files or programs or macros on our computer, ideas are phenomena grounded in more basic

---

[2] I argue at length for this in my forthcoming book, *Frege's Detour*.

events going inside of something, that we use to control and predict and explain what the things they are inside of do. Ideas are structured into thoughts of various sorts: beliefs, desires, intentions and so on. For this chapter, I'll leave it at that.

Beliefs have truth-conditions, in virtue of what the ideas involved in them signify and how they are structured. Elwood has an idea of the relation of being the capital of, and notions—my term for notions of objects—of Mogadishu and Somalia. The structure of the belief, and the significations of the ideas, give Elwood's belief truth-conditions. Elwood's belief is true if Mogadishu is the capital of Somalia. These truth-conditions of Elwood's belief are determined by his ideas, and what they are ideas of, and the structure of the cognitive state. Propositions are not involved.

The truth-conditions of Elwood's belief are an important property of it, and we can use propositions to keep track of truth-conditions. So belief *induces* a relation between beliefs and propositions. I'll call this relation "Bel". At a first pass, Bel is a relation between an agent at a time, which obtains if Elwood has a belief at that time with truth-conditions that the proposition encodes.

Unlike Frege's Thoughts, most modern conceptions of propositions do not have truth-conditions intrinsically. We think of a proposition consisting of a set of worlds as true if the actual world belongs to the set. But that is not a set theoretical property of such sets. It is a property some sets have because philosophers have used such sets to characterize true beliefs and statements. It is a natural choice, but not one dictated by set theoretical properties. The same goes for propositions consisting of ordered n-tuples of properties and objects.

I call the view that belief is a relation of an agent at a time to a proposition a "picture" rather than a theory, because it is seldom spelled out or defended. I'm sure that many who have this picture would not deny that there are structures of ideas involved in belief, much less deny that structures of words are involved in assertion.[3] The implicit assumption is that it is the propositions believed or expressed that are crucial, at least in semantics.

II. On Truth-Conditions

Behind this implicit assumption is what Jon Barwise and I called "the fallacy of misplaced information". This is the view that when we believe or assert, there is a unique proposition or Thought that incorporates all of the truth-conditions of the belief or assertion. But this is wrong.

J. M. Mackie gave us the important concept of an INUS condition. What we call "the cause" of an event is not, at least typically, a complete sufficient condition for

---

[3] I use "assertion" and "assertions" rather than "saying" and "sayings" simply because it sounds better, not because I am limiting what I say to assertions.

the event. It is usually something that *completes* a set of sufficient conditions. If my wife says, "The milk soured because you didn't put it back in the refrigerator" I'd count what she says as true. I wouldn't reply: "Well it wouldn't have soured if you didn't insist on heating the house above forty degrees" or "It's not my fault that milk sours at normal temperatures". She has identified an INUS condition, that is a necessary (or at least non-redundant) part of a set of sufficient conditions, which are not themselves necessary—the milk could have soured because of some stray bacteria or because, although I put it back in the refrigerator, there was a power outage. She has identified a necessary part of the actual sufficient conditions of the milk souring. The other parts of the set, such that the temperature in our house is above forty degrees or that milk sours at such temperatures, we both take for granted. That I am not responsible for those factors is beside the point.

I think we need to apply the concept of INUS conditions not only to "the cause" but also to "the truth-conditions". There is nothing wrong with saying that the truth-conditions of Elwood's assertion are that Mogidishu is the capital of Somalia. But that's not *all* that was involved in the truth of his assertion. It's *what else* was required *given* that he was speaking English, using words that stood for Mogadishu, Somalia, and the relation of being the capital of, in a certain grammatical structure. Given all of that, his assertion is true if and only if Mogadishu is the capital of Somalia. It is an INUS truth-condition.

The truth-condition of a belief or assertion is basically what the world has to be like for the belief or assertion to be true. But the answer to that question depends on what we are taking as given. What I will call the *referential* truth conditions is what else is required for truth if, in addition to the components and structure of a belief or assertion, we take as given what the components refer to. What I call the *reflexive* truth conditions is what else is required for truth, if we don't take these facts as given.

The word "reflexive" derives simply from the fact that these truth-conditions will be conditions on the components of the belief or assertion *itself*. I do not mean to imply these components refer to themselves. It suffices that they are themselves.

Consider Elwood utterance of "Mogadishu is the capital of Somalia." Call it u. Here are the reflexive truth-conditions for a u;

Given that u is an utterance by Elwood in English of "Mogadishu is the capital of Somalia", u is true iff:

(i) There are R, x, y such that:
"is the capital of" refers to R in English;
"Magadishu" refers to x in English;
"Somalia" refers to y in English;

(ii) R(x,y).

This is what else needs to be the case, in addition to what is given, for Elwood's utterance to be true.

If we add to what is given that "Mogadishu" refers to Mogadishu, "Somalia" refers to Somalia, and "is the capital of" refers to the relation of being the capital of, then what else is needed for truth is simply that Mogadishu is the capital of Somalia; what I call the *referential* truth-conditions.

In addition, there are "hybrid" truth-conditions, when we take some referential facts as given, but not all. Take it as given that "Mogadishu" refers to Mogadishu and "Somalia" refers to Somalia. Then what else has to be the case for u to be true is that "is capital of" has to refer to a relation Mogadishu has to Somalia.

Suppose that Elwood is teaching English to emigrants from Somalia. A student asks, "what does 'is the capital of' mean?" Elwood replies with u. He knows that the student knows the names "Mogadishu" and "Somalia" and knows a lot about the city and nation to which they refer. So he will learn from what Elwood says that "capital of" signifies a relation that holds between the city and the nation. The most obvious relation between them is that the city is the capital of the nation. Elwood relies on the student's basic knowledge of the way English works, his knowledge of Somalia, and common sense to teach him the meaning "is the capital of".

Another example. I put a plate of kale before my grandchildren. I say (lying) "You will like this kale". They learn that the vegetable they have been served has the name "kale" (and, a bit later, that their grandfather is a liar).

These cases illustrate that speakers are quite aware of the fact that the referential truth-conditions do not exhaust the truth-conditions of utterances.

III. Attitudes as Evidence and as Explanation

Why then do attitude reports and indirect discourse focus on referential truth-conditions? Because referential truth-conditions are what language is basically concerned with. We use language to communicate information. If Elwood—no longer a teacher—tells me "Mogadishu is the capital of Somalia," he most likely intends to give me information about a city and a country, not about the meanings of English words. If I tell you "Elwood said that Mogadishu is the capital of Somalia" or "Elwood believes that Mogadishu is the capital of Somalia," I am most likely using Elwood's utterance and the belief it expressed as evidence for the fact that Mogadishu is the capital of Somalia. When we use and report language to share information about the world, it is the referential truth-conditions on which we focus.

But we also use such reports as explanations, and when we do, referential content don't do the job. Suppose that Fred doesn't know that Mark Twain is Samuel Clemens. When he comes to the question "True or False: Samuel Clemens wrote *Huckelberry Finn*" on the exam he marks it False. I can't very well explain this by saying, "Fred didn't believe that Mark Twain wrote *Huckelberry Finn*." I've got the referential content right, but I've left out important things, and said something misleading. Perhaps he marked the question "True or False: Mark Twain wrote *Huckelberry Finn*" True.

In this case, the key fact is that Fred didn't know that "Samuel Clemens" was a name of Mark Twain, and hence a name of the author of *Huckelberry Finn*. He was ignorant of a referential fact, involving a name and an author; we can't get at the fact simply by naming the author. When we describe assertions and beliefs simply in terms of their referential content, we leave something out. For information, it usually doesn't matter; for explanation, it often does.

When we are using the attitudes as explanations, we are reluctant to substitute co-referring expression, the phenomenon called "opacity". In the above example, if I say "Fred didn't know that Samuel Clemens wrote Huckelberry Finn", I've given a good explanation of why he missed the question. If I substitute the co-referential "Mark Twain" I no longer have a good explanation.

My original explanation was good, because of the assumption that I was using more or less the same words to report Fred's beliefs that he would use to express them. The assumption is correct with the original explanation, but not with the result of substitution.

The fact is that in ordinary language we leave a lot out. We take a lot as given, and focus on: *what else*. We leave a lot *unarticulated* that has to be taken account of in a theorist's explanation of what is going on. My son calls me at 1 p.m. California time and says, "It's ten o'clock, so I'm going to bed." There is no such thing as being ten o'clock. He has left out an important parameter of circumstance; it's ten o'clock *Paris time*. Even if I don't know that he is in Paris, it all makes sense. I know that for his remark to be true, and provide a reasonable explanation for his going to bed, he has to be in a place relative to which it is ten o'clock, and be reporting the time at that place.

Reports of action typically leave a lot out. You say, "I went to the store." Grammatically, that's perfectly complete. But I know that you either walked or drove or jogged or took the bus. Action reports focus on the accomplishment of interest, usually the intended goal of the activity. But we don't regard *going to* as a relation between an agent and a set of worlds in which they are at some place or another. Everyone knows that when one accomplishes something, they do so in virtue of movements of body or mind, which in virtue of circumstances lead to the desired result; they do it in some way or another. If we want to know how, we just ask: "Did you walk or drive? What route did you take?" We are all aware that going to the store involves a lot more than an agent at a time and a proposition that encodes what he accomplishes.

Well, actually some philosophers do seem to regard action as a relation to propositions. Where we might ordinarily say, "I can go to the store," Peter van Inwagen says "I could have rendered it true that I went to the store." That allows him to formulate the key step in his argument for incompatibilism as "If I can render P true, and Q is a true statement about the past, then I can render P&Q true." If I can go to the store, then I can render it true that I go to the store and Caesar conquered Gaul." I leave discussion of whether this is illuminating or fogs the relevant issues for another occasion.[4]

With attitude reports and indirect discourse, we also leave a lot out. "Fred didn't know that Samuel Clemens wrote *Huckleberry Finn*." I don't explicitly tell you that he doesn't know this *via* his "Samuel Clemens" notion, but you assume that if it weren't, I wouldn't have used that name. When referential truth-conditions and common-sense pragmatics don't do the job, we just ask.

The truth-conditions that are relevant to explanation are reflexive or hybrid. Why does Kripke's Pierre say that London is ugly but Londres is pretty, when London and Londres are the same city? Why do I learn something from "Hesperus is Phosphorus" that I don't learn from "Hesperus is Hesperus"? Because the reflexive truth-conditions are different. On Kripke's scenario, Pierre has two notions of London, one acquired as a youth in France, and associated with the name, or vocable, "Londres", the other acquired when he moved to London and associated with that vocable. So he has two beliefs, with inconsistent referential truth-conditions but consistent reflexive truth-conditions. When you tell me "Hesperus is Phosphorus" my beliefs about "Hesperus" and "Phosphorus" change so as to accommodate the fact that the two names co-refer; in virtue of those changes, I believe something new about the planet(s) Hesperus and Phosphorus, that they are identical.

When we use attitude reports as explanations, and the possibility of having two notions of the same thing is relevant, it's easy to handle in ordinary life, however problematic in semantics. If I simply say, "Pierre believes that London is ugly when he's thinking of it as *London*, but believes it is pretty when he thinks of it as *Londres*," people will understand what I'm saying. In a more theoretical mood, I might say, "Pierre believes London is pretty via one notion he has of it that he associates with the vocable 'Londres', but ugly via another notion he has of it, associated with the vocable 'London'".

A lot of twentieth-century philosophy of language and mind consisted in trying to find a concept of a proposition that handles both uses of attitude reports—a search for a Holy Grail that would never be found.

IV. Refined Concepts of Belief

Still, propositions are very useful things for keeping track of truth-conditions. They connect us with the wonderful resources of logic; on any reasonable

---

[4] See my forthexisting book, *Wretched Subterfuge*.

construction of propositions, logical connections among them will be tractable. We don't simply use attitudes for evidence and explanation, we use them for assessment, to see if our beliefs and those of others are consistent and our inferences are sound.

We can have access to the riches of propositions by developing a more refined substitute for believing, the relation between agents at time and propositions I called Bel. I said that, at a first pass, Bel is a relation between an agent at a time, which obtains if the agent has a belief at that time with truth-conditions that the proposition encodes.

But the first pass isn't very satisfactory. To have an adequate Bel predicate that deals with both information and explanation without appeal to pragmatics, we need to explicitly articulate the things that we handle in ordinary language in a more haphazard manner. This is the idea that Mark Crimmins and I put forward in "The prince and the phone booth" (1989) and he developed in *Talk about Beliefs* (1992).

Bel should be conceived as a relation with a varying number of arguments. A person believes that via ideas and notions he has of the objects and properties involved. Where n and n' are Pierre's first and second notions of London, "Pierre believes via n that London is pretty" and "Pierre believes via n' that London is pretty" have different truth-values, for the perfectly straightforward reason that what a person Bels is relative to the notions employed in the belief being reported.

Thus in Pierre's case we have:

Pierre Bel, via his "Londres"-notion, that London is pretty.
Pierre Bel, via his "London"-notion, that London is ugly.

So constructed, our Bel predicate supplies both the referential truth-conditions and the hybrid truth-conditions, that is, the condition that his notions must fulfill for his belief to be true, given what "is pretty" and "is ugly" mean. So, in a way, he provides what we were searching for, a predicate for believing that supplies what is needed for both information and explanation. But it doesn't do so by finding a single proposition that encodes both.[5]

Conclusion

I have argued that belief is not a matter of having a relation to a proposition, or a property, but a matter of having an inner states composed of ideas in a certain structure, which determines the reflexive truth-conditions of the belief, which,

---

[5] In "Roles, Rigidity, and Quantification in Epistemic Logic" Wesley Holliday and I (2014) develop a similar treatment in the framework of epistemic logic for a belief operator.

together with the facts of reference, determine their referential truth-conditions. In ordinary language, if reflexive or hybrid truth-conditions are relevant, we have plenty of devices for focusing on them. Since beliefs have truth-conditions, they can be usefully classified with propositions. But when we develop conceptions of belief that systematize this, we need to bring in explicitly parameters for ideas which are left implicit in ordinary language, where we focus on referential content.

References

Baldwin, J. M., ed. 1905. *Dictionary of Philosophy and Psychology*. New York: Macmillan.
Crimmins, M. 1992. *Talk about Beliefs*. Cambridge, MA: MIT Press.
Crimmins, M. and J. Perry. 1989. "The prince and the phone booth: reporting puzzling beliefs." *Journal of Philosophy* 86: 685–711.
Frege, G. 1879. *Begriffsschrift, eine der arithmetischen nachgebildete Formelsprache des reinen Denkens*. Halle an der Saale: Verlag von Louis Nebert .
Frege, G. 1892. "Über Sinn und Bedeutung." *Zeitschrift für Philosophische Kritik*, 100: 25–50. Trans. M. Black. 1960. "On Sense and Reference." In *Translations from the Philosophical Writings of Gottlob Frege*, ed. P. Geach and M. Black. Oxford: Basil Blackwell.
Holliday, W. H. and J. Perry. 2014. "Roles, rigidity, and quantification in epistemic logic." In *Trends in Logic, Outstanding Contributions: Johan F. A. K. van Benthem on Logical and Informational Dynamics*, ed. A. Baltag and S. Smets, 591–629. New York: Springer.
Perry, J. 2019. Frege's Detour. An Essay on Meaning, Reference, and Truth. Oxford: Oxford University Press. https://global.oup.com/academic/product/freges-detour-9780198812821.
Russell, B. 1903. *The Principles of Mathematics*. Cambridge: Cambridge University Press.
Uzgalis, W. 2007. *Locke's Essay Concerning Human Understanding—A Reader's Guide*. London: Continuum.

Fregean Particularism

Susanna Schellenberg

It is Monday morning and I am riding the train through the post-industrial wasteland of northern New Jersey. I gaze out of the window and, suddenly, I see a deer. Let's call it Frederik. The next morning, I am again on the train, riding through northern New Jersey. And, again, I see a deer. Let's call it Ferdinand. It is the same time of day. Everything looks exactly the same on Tuesday as it did on Monday—including the deer. However, unbeknownst to me, the deer I see on Tuesday is not the same as the one I saw on Monday. So I am seeing different particulars.[1]

How does the fact that I am seeing Frederik on Monday and Ferdinand on Tuesday affect my perceptual state? One possible answer is to argue that the content of my perceptual state on Monday is constituted by Frederik, while the content of my perceptual state on Tuesday is constituted by Ferdinand. If this is right, what is the nature of this singular perceptual content? When we suffer a non-veridical hallucination as of an object, then it seems to us that there is a particular object present, where in fact there is no such object. If veridical perceptual states have singular content, what is the content of a hallucination? Since in hallucination, we are not perceptually related to the particulars we seem to see, a hallucination cannot have singular content. What content, then, does a hallucination have? Finally, what accounts for the phenomenal character of hallucination, whereby it seems to us that a particular is present when no such particular is actually before us?

These questions can be put into focus by articulating two desiderata for any account of perception. One desideratum is to explain perceptual particularity, that is, to explain in virtue of what a perceptual state is constituted by the perceived particular. Let's call this the *particularity desideratum*. The other desideratum is to explain what accounts for the possibility that perceptions of qualitatively identical yet numerically distinct particulars could have the same phenomenal character. Let's call this the *phenomenal sameness desideratum*. More generally, the phenomenal sameness desideratum is to explain what accounts for the possibility that perceptions, hallucinations, illusions of distinct environments could have the same phenomenal character.[2]

---

[1] This paper is a reprint of Chapter 4 of Schellenberg (2018).
[2] One might argue that the only case in which two consecutive perceptions genuinely have the same phenomenal character are ones in which one consecutively perceives qualitatively identical, yet numerically distinct particulars. If one holds this, one would hold that the phenomenal sameness desideratum does not apply to cases in which a hallucination seemingly has the same phenomenal

In Section I, I will discuss these two desiderata in turn. In Section II, I will consider several ways one might attempt to satisfy both desiderata and will show why they do not succeed. In Section III, I will develop a particular way of understanding singular content that satisfies both desiderata. I will call this view *Fregean particularism*. In Section IV, I will compare Fregean particularism to competitor views. In developing this account of singular content, I will consider many views along the way. I will argue against them only to the extent that it helps motivate Fregean particularism and situate it within a broader philosophical context.

I. Two Desiderata for an Account of Perception

We can understand the claim that two experiential states have the same phenomenal character as follows:

Phenomenal Sameness: If two experiential states e_1 and e_2 of the experiencing subject S have the same phenomenal character, then S would be unable to discern any difference between e_1 and e_2, even if her perceptual and introspective abilities were ideal.

An experiential state, as understood here, is the state one is in when one is either perceiving, hallucinating or suffering an illusion. It is important to distinguish the case in which two experiences have the same phenomenal character from the case in which they are merely subjectively indistinguishable. We can all agree that we might have two consecutive experiences e_3 and e_4 that are so similar that they are subjectively indistinguishable. We may be unable to tell them apart because we fail to properly attend to the details presented to us. Or, we might attend to all the details presented to us, but nonetheless be unable to tell the two experiences apart because we lack the requisite perceptual capacities. Neither is a case in which e_3 and e_4 have the same phenomenal character. After all, in the first kind of case, we could notice the difference between e_3 and e_4 if we paid better attention; in the second kind of case, we could notice the difference between e_3 and e_4 if our perceptual capacities were better.

The classic case of two perceptions that have the same phenomenal character is the case of consecutively perceiving qualitatively identical yet numerically distinct objects, ceteris paribus. More generally, if in two consecutive perceptions there is no qualitative difference in the environment (despite there being a difference in

character as a perception. I will here assume that a hallucination could have the same phenomenal character as a perception and so will take the phenomenal sameness desideratum to apply more generally. However, the argument of this chapter would need to be adjusted only slightly to apply to the more restrictive view on which a perception and a hallucination could never have the same phenomenal character.

numerical identity of the perceived objects) and if the subject is perceptually related to the environment in the very same way, then, ceteris paribus, there is no difference in phenomenal character between the two perceptual states. In short, phenomenal character can be exactly the same even if the environment varies.

Moving on to the particularity desideratum: we can all agree that when a subject perceives a particular, she is causally related to the particular she perceives. It is uncontroversial and compatible with almost any view of perception that there is such a causal relation between a subject and a perceived particular—though views differ dramatically with regard to how much explanatory weight the causal relation can carry. Consider the case of two experiences, one of which is a perception of an object, the other of which is a hallucination with the same phenomenal character. It is uncontroversial and compatible with almost any view of perception that there is a difference in causal relation between the two experiences. When a subject perceives an object, she is causally related to the mind-independent object she is perceiving. When a subject suffers a hallucination with the same phenomenal character, she is not causally related to a mind-independent object that it seems to her she is perceiving. Acknowledging that there is a difference in causal relation between the two experiences is not sufficient to satisfy the particularity desideratum. To satisfy the particularity desideratum, we need to explain in virtue of what a subject's perceptual state M brought about by being perceptually related to the particular α is constituted by α.

We can all agree moreover that when a subject consciously perceives her environment, she is perceptually conscious of a particular. Now, our experience can be as of a particular, even if we are not in fact perceptually related to a particular. After all, when we suffer a non-veridical hallucination as of, say, a yellow rubber duck, it sensorily seems to us that there is a yellow rubber duck where in fact there is no such duck. So our phenomenal character can be as of a particular even if we are not perceptually related to that particular. In this sense, perceptual experiences are (as) of particulars. We can call this aspect of phenomenal character *phenomenological particularity*.

Phenomenological particularity: A mental state manifests phenomenological particularity if and only if it phenomenally seems to the subject that there is a particular present.

So a mental state manifests phenomenological particularity if and only if the particularity is in the scope of how things seem to the subject: phenomenological particularity does not require that there be a particular that seems to the subject to be present, but just that it seems to the subject that there is a particular present.

Every perceptual experience (as) of a particular manifests phenomenological particularity. Indeed it is unclear what it would be to have a perceptual experience that seems to be of a material, mind-independent particular without its sensorily seeming to the subject that such a particular is present. If a subject has an experience that is intentionally directed at a particular and subjectively indistinguishable from perceiving a particular, it will seem to her as if she is experiencing a particular—regardless of whether she is in fact perceptually related to a particular, or is suffering an illusion or hallucination as of a particular. So phenomenological particularity is a feature of any perceptual experience—be it a perception, a hallucination or an illusion.

We can distinguish the relatively uncontroversial idea that perceptual experience manifests phenomenological particularity from the controversial idea that perception is characterized by *relational particularity*. A mental state is characterized by relational particularity if and only if the mental state is constituted by the particular perceived. More precisely:

Relational particularity: A subject's perceptual state M brought about by being perceptually related to the particular α is characterized by relational particularity if and only if M is constituted by α.

To satisfy the particularity desideratum, we need to show how it is that a perceptual state is constituted by the particular perceived, and thus characterized by relational particularity (rather than mere phenomenological particularity).

Often relational particularity and phenomenological particularity are implicitly equated. This is problematic. One should allow for the possibility that a subject can be intentionally directed at what seems to her to be a material, mind-independent particular even if there is no such particular present and so acknowledge that a perceptual state could manifest phenomenological particularity without manifesting relational particularity. Moreover, one should allow for the possibility that perceptions of numerically distinct yet qualitatively identical particulars yield perceptual states that are constituted by different particulars, yet manifest the same phenomenological particularity. As I will show, only if we recognize the distinction between phenomenological and relational particularity can we account for the difference between perceptions of distinct yet qualitatively identical objects.[3]

The distinction between phenomenological and relational particularity allows us to reformulate the opening questions more specifically. Why think that when we perceive a particular our perceptual state is constituted by the particular perceived and thus is characterized by relational particularity in

---

[3] There is moreover a powerful tradition of sidelining relational particularity in favor of phenomenological particularity. For example, Crane—focusing on singular thought—puts all the weight on the cognitive or phenomenological role of a thought, that is, what I call phenomenological particularity: "what matters is not that the [singular] thought happens to refer to just one thing, but that it has a specific cognitive role. Singularity is a matter of the cognitive—that is, the psychological or phenomenological—role of the thought" (Crane 2011: 25). Crane's focus is not on what makes it the case that a thought is about this particular rather than that one, but rather in virtue of what thoughts have a singular character, that is, what makes them manifest phenomenological particularity.

addition to phenomenological particularity? How should we account for the fact that when we suffer a hallucination our mental state manifests phenomenological particularity, despite lacking relational particularity? In answering these questions, we can show how it is that in the case of an accurate perception, we are sensorily aware of particulars, and how it is that even when we are suffering a hallucination our experience can be as of environmental particulars despite the fact that we are not perceptually related to at least one of the particulars to which it seems to us we are related.

Relationalism and Representationalism

There are two radically different conceptions of perception. According to *relationalism*, a perceptual state is constitutively a matter of standing in an awareness or an acquaintance relation to the environment. According to *representationalism*, a perceptual state is constitutively a matter of representing the environment. So while representationalists analyze perceptual states in terms of their representational content, relationalists analyze perceptual states in terms of awareness or acquaintance relations to mind-independent particulars.

Relationalism and representationalism are widely considered to be in conflict.[4] But the debate between relationalists and representationalists sets up a false dichotomy. The source of this false dichotomy is that the standard views in the debate are either austerely relationalist or austerely representationalist. To a first approximation, *austere relationalism* has it that perception is constitutively relational and lacks any representational component. To a first approximation, *austere representationalism* has it that perception is constitutively representational and lacks any relational component that has repercussions for the experiential state.[5] Against both, I will argue that perceptual relations to the environment and the content of experience are mutually dependent. I will argue that by employing perceptual capacities we are related to our environment—at least in the case of perception. Perceptual capacities function to discriminate and

---

[4] For a recent articulation of this view, see Campbell (2002). Though see Schellenberg (2010) for a representationalist view that does not fit this dichotomy; see Beck (forthcoming) for a relationalist view that does not fit this dichotomy.

[5] For austere representationalist views, see McGinn 1982, Davies 1992, Tye 1995, Lycan 1996, Byrne 2001 and Hill 2009 among many others. For austere relationalist views, see Campbell 2002, Johnston 2004, 2014, Travis 2004, Brewer 2006, Fish 2009, Genone 2014, Logue 2014, Gomes and French 2016 and Raleigh 2014, 2015 among others. Martin (2002, 2004) leaves open the possibility that experience could have content, but his positive view of perception is structurally similar to that of austere relationalists. Campbell (2002) calls his view the "relational view," Martin (2002, 2004) calls his "naïve realism," while Brewer (2006) calls his the "object view." I will refer to the view with the label "austere relationalism," since the most distinctive features of the view are arguably the central role of relations between perceiving subjects and the world as well as its austerity.

single out particulars.[6] Thus, perception is constitutively relational. I argue moreover that the perceptual capacities employed constitute the representational content of our perceptual state. Thus, perception is constitutively representational. In this way, I will show that there is no tension between perception being constitutively both relational and representational. But first let's take a closer look at what it means for perception to be relational and what it means for perception to be representational.

Perceiving subjects have been argued to be perceptually related to many different kinds of entities. These entities fall into two groups: abstract or mind-dependent entities, such as qualia, sense-data, propositions or intentional objects, on the one hand; and, on the other hand, concrete, mind-independent objects, property-instances or events, such as a white coffee cup resting on a desk. In the current discussion, the thesis that perception is relational means always that perception is constitutively a matter of a subject being perceptually related to concrete, mind-independent objects, property-instances, events or a combination thereof.

When I speak of perception as being representational without qualification, I mean no more than the idea that perception is a matter of a subject representing her environment such that her perceptual state is characterized by representational content. There are many different ways of understanding the nature of content given this constraint. For present purposes, it will suffice to say that the content can be conceived of as a Russellian proposition, a Fregean sense, an indexical content, a map of the environment, an image-like representation or in any number of other ways. Moreover, the content can be understood to be either conceptual or non-conceptual, propositional or non-propositional, and as constituted by the particulars perceived or as independent of the particulars perceived. Finally, there are many different ways of understanding the relationship between phenomenal character and content. Indeed, accepting the thesis that perceptual experience is representational is compatible with thinking that the content and phenomenal character of mental states are entirely independent. So the thesis that perceptual experience is representational is agnostic on all possible ways of understanding the relationship between content and phenomenal character. I am using the term "representationalism" for any view that endorses the thesis that perceptual experience is constitutively a matter of representing. Representationalism, so understood, is neutral on the relationship between perceptual content and perceptual consciousness.

It will be helpful to contrast the distinction between relationalism and representationalism with an orthogonal distinction between two ways of individuating experiential states. On a *phenomenalist view*, experiential states are individuated solely by their phenomenal character. Versions of this view have been defended

---

[6] See, Schellenberg (2018), Chapter 2, for the development of this view.

by Price (1950), Moore (1953), Tye (1995), Lycan (1996), Byrne (2001) and Block (2003) among others. On an *externalist view*, experiential states are individuated not only by their phenomenal character but also by whatever external, mind-independent particulars (if any) to which the perceiver is perceptually related. Needless to say views differ wildly on just how perceived particulars make a difference to perceptual states. Versions of externalism have been defended by Searle (1983), McDowell (1984), Peacocke (1983, 2009), Byrne (2001, 2009), Campbell (2002), Martin (2002), Johnston (2004), Soteriou (2005), Brewer (2006), Hill (2009), Fish (2009), Burge (2010), Schellenberg (2010), Genone (2014) and Logue (2014) among others.

The motivations for thinking that perception is constitutively representational typically go hand in hand with the motivations for embracing the phenomenalist view. Similarly, the motivations for thinking that perception is constitutively relational typically go hand in hand with the motivations for embracing the externalist view. However, the fault line between relationalism and representationalism does not coincide with the fault line between phenomenalist and externalist views. Sense-data theory, as defended by Price (1950) and Moore (1953), is a phenomenalist view that rejects representationalism. Moreover, one can argue for an externalist view that endorses representationalism (Peacocke 1983, Searle 1983, McDowell 1984, Byrne 2009, Hill 2009, Burge 2010 and Schellenberg 2010).

In what follows, I will consider the austere versions of both representationalism and relationalism in more detail and will assess how they fare in satisfying the particularity and phenomenal sameness desiderata. As I will argue, austere representationalists can easily satisfy the phenomenal sameness desideratum, but not the particularity desideratum. By contrast, austere relationalists can easily satisfy the particularity desideratum, but not the phenomenal sameness desideratum. I will offer a synthesis of these approaches that satisfies both desiderata.

Austere Representationalism

The key idea of austere representationalism is that to have a perception, illusion or hallucination is to be in an experiential state with representational content that corresponds one to one with the phenomenal character of the experiencing subject: any changes in content go hand in hand with changes in phenomenal character and vice versa. Insofar as the representational content corresponds one to one with phenomenal character, it is phenomenal content.

If representational content is phenomenal content, then two experiential states with the same phenomenal character cannot differ in content—irrespective of what particular, if any, the subject is related to. So a perceptual state can have the same phenomenal content as a mental state brought about by suffering a hallucination or illusion. According to austere representationalism, if I see Frederik on

Monday and Ferdinand on Tuesday, my perceptual states will have the very same content. More generally, there can be an exact duplicate of an experiential state and its content, brought about by being perceptually related to particular α, in an environment in which the experiencing subject is perceptually related to the numerically distinct particular β. Furthermore, there can be an exact duplicate of an experiential state and its content in an environment in which the experiencing subject is not perceptually related to any relevant mind-independent particular. So if experiential content is phenomenal content, then it is general content. There are many different ways of understanding general contents. They can be thought of as de dicto modes of presentation, Russellian propositions, or existentially quantified content to name just a few options.

Stated more precisely, austere representationalism is committed to the following three theses:

1. Experiential states have content.
2. A perception, an illusion and a hallucination can have the same phenomenal character.
3. The content of an experiential state corresponds one to one with its phenomenal character in that any changes in content go hand in hand with changes in phenomenal character and vice versa.[7]

It follows from these three theses that:

4. Perceptual content is not constituted by the mind-independent particulars perceived.

So austere representationalists are committed to denying that perceptual content is singular content, and thus cannot satisfy the particularity desideratum by appeal to the singular content of perception. I will embrace the first two theses of austere representationalism but will reject the third. By rejecting the third thesis, the commitment to the fourth thesis can be avoided.

First, however, let's take a closer look at austere representationalism. One way of understanding experiential content under the constraint of the austere representationalist thesis is that it is existentially quantified content of the form that there is an object x that instantiates a property F:

$$(a_{p,i,h}) \quad (\exists x)Fx$$

---

[7] McGinn (1982), Davies (1992), Tye (1995), Lycan (1996), Byrne (2001) and Pautz (2009) among others have defended views that are committed to these three theses.

Most objects instantiate a multitude of properties. For example, most visually perceivable objects instantiate spatial, color and location properties. Most auditorily perceivable objects instantiate pitch, loudness, duration and timbre properties. I will work with the simplifying assumption that there can be an experience (as) of an object that instantiates only one property. My argument, however, easily generalizes to the more realistic case in which one experiences an object instantiating a multitude of properties.

The thesis that experiential content is existentially quantified content posits that an experiential state represents only that there is an object that instantiates the relevant properties in the external world. No element of the content depends on whether such an object is in fact present. So it is possible to be in a mental state with the relevant content regardless of what object is present or even whether there is an object present. The perceived object does not fall out of the picture altogether: although no reference to the particular object perceived is necessary to specify the content, the austere representationalist can say that a subject perceives an object o at a particular location only if o satisfies the existential content of the subject's experiential state. So the content is accurate only if there is an object at the relevant location that instantiates the properties specified by the content. The crucial point is that whether an object of the right kind is present bears only on the accuracy of the content. It has no repercussions for what is represented.

The main advantage of austere representationalism is that it easily and elegantly explains how a perception, hallucination and illusion could have the same phenomenal character. Indeed, accounting for this possibility is one of the main motivations for analyzing experiential content as phenomenal content. As Davies puts it: "the perceptual content of experience is a phenomenal notion: perceptual content is a matter of how the world seems to the experiencer.... If perceptual content is, in this sense, 'phenomenological content'…then, where there is no phenomenological difference for a subject, then there is no difference in content" (1992: 26). By equating experiential content with phenomenal content, austere representationalists can easily satisfy the phenomenal sameness desideratum.

The main problem with austere representationalism is that it does not satisfy the particularity desideratum. The view cannot account for the difference between the perceptual content brought about by a subject perceiving cup_1 at time t_1 and her perceptual state brought about by being perceptually related to the qualitatively identical cup_2 at time t_2. Davies explicitly embraces this view: "if two objects are genuinely indistinguishable for a subject, then a perceptual experience of one has the same content as a perceptual experience of the other" (1992: 26).[8]

---

[8] McGinn (1982) and Millar (1991) argue for a similar thesis. This view is subject to well-known counterexamples, which I will not rehearse here. They have been discussed in detail by Soteriou (2000) and Tye (2007) by expanding on Grice's (1961) discussion of so-called "veridical hallucinations."

According to austere representationalism, sameness of phenomenal character entails sameness of content. A view according to which two experiential states with the same phenomenal character cannot differ in content—irrespective of what particular, if any, the subject is related to—cannot satisfy the particularity desideratum in terms of perceptual content. Therefore, if perceptual content should reflect relational particularity, then perceptual content cannot be equated with phenomenal content.

Now an austere representationalist could say that the perceptual relation between the perceiving subject and the perceived object does play a role. After all, the austere representationalist could argue that the form of a veridical perception is a conjunction of two elements, namely, the content and the relation to the perceived particular:

(b_p) $HS<(\exists x)Fx>$ and $RS\alpha$

Subject S stands in a representation relation H to the existentially quantified content that there is an object x that instantiates the property F and S stands in a perceptual relation R to particular α. By contrast, the form of a hallucination is:

(b_h) $HS<(\exists x)Fx>$

We can call this view *conjunctivism*. Conjunctivism has it that two elements are in place in a successful perceptual experience. In the case of a hallucination, the subject stands in relation only to the proposition that there is an object that has a certain property. Conjunctivism is a representational view that individuates perceptual experiences not just by the relevant mental states, but also by the perceptual relation between the experiencing subject and the environment. The problem with conjunctivism is that the experiential state is in no way affected by the particular perceived (if any). Therefore, the particularity desideratum is not satisfied. Although conjunctivism builds perceptual relations between subjects and particulars into the form of perception, this relational element has no effect on any aspect of the perceptual state, for example, its content or phenomenal character. So conjunctivism is simply a version of austere representationalism that makes explicit that in the case of an accurate perception a perceptual relation holds between the subject and the perceived particulars.

With austere representationalists, I will argue that phenomenal character does not track relational particularity. Yet against austere representationalists, I will

---

Searle (1983) aims to account for particularity within the framework of existentially quantified contents by building causal conditions into the existential contents. In short, the idea is that a descriptive condition picks out an object as the cause of the experience. By doing so, Searle builds causal relations to particular objects into perceptual content. Given Searle's view about the relationship between content and phenomenal character, this approach is at odds with the phenomenal character of experience.

argue that perceptual content is singular content. First, however, let's assess how austere relationalism fares with regard to the particularity and phenomenal sameness desiderata.

Austere Relationalism

Austere relationalists argue that no appeal to representational content is necessary in a philosophical account of perception and that perception constitutively involves at least three components: a subject, her environment and a perceptual relation between the subject and particulars in her environment. This perceptual relation is understood as, for example, an acquaintance or a sensory awareness relation. So austere relationalists have it that perception is constitutively a matter of a subject S standing in an acquaintance or an awareness relation R to a mind-independent particular α:

(c_p) $RS\alpha$

In this way, austere relationalism conceives of the form of perception in a way that a hallucination could not possibly fit. As Brewer formulates the idea:

> The course of perceptual experience...provide[s] the subject with the grounds for her actual beliefs about the world, and also for the various other beliefs which she might equally have acquired had she noticed different things, or had her attention instead been guided by some other project or purpose. It does so, though, not by serving up any fully formed content, somehow, both in advance of, but also in light of, these attentional considerations, but, rather, by presenting her directly with the actual constituents of the physical world themselves. (2006: 178)

Austere relationalism is a radical version of disjunctivism, that is, in short, the view according to which perceptions and hallucinations share no common element or do not belong to the same fundamental kind.[9] Traditionally disjunctivists argued that while hallucinations are not representational perceptions do represent mind-independent particulars.[10] Austere relationalism is a radical version of disjunctivism insofar as it denies not only that hallucinations are representational, but that perceptions are as well.

---

[9] The metaphysical thesis that perception and hallucination share no common element was first articulated by McDowell (1982). Among others, Martin (2002) formulates the key idea of disjunctivism as being that perceptions and hallucinations do not belong to the same fundamental kind.

[10] See, for instance, Hinton (1973), Snowdon (1981) and McDowell (1982).

Austere relationalism is structurally similar to sense-data theory and is motivated in part by its insights. So it will help to contrast the two views. Both views understand phenomenal character as constituted by the particulars perceived. However, while sense-data theorists argue that the particulars perceived are sense-data, austere relationalists argue that the particulars in question are material, mind-independent objects, property-instances or events. This difference has many repercussions. One repercussion is that sense-data theorists take the structure of a perception to be the very same as that of a hallucination. In both cases a subject's experience consists in being acquainted with sense-data. Since hallucinations and perceptions have the very same structure, sense-data theorists can easily satisfy the phenomenal sameness desideratum. A second repercussion is that since sense-data theorists have it that a subject can be in the very same experiential state regardless of whether she is perceptually related to a mind-independent particular, the view is committed to denying that perceptual states are constituted by the particulars perceived. Therefore, sense-data theorists cannot satisfy the particularity desideratum.

In contrast to sense-data theorists, austere relationalists conceive of the fundamental structure of a perception in a way that precludes hallucinations from having that structure. After all, since a hallucinating subject is not perceptually related to the material, mind-independent particular she seems to be seeing, a hallucination cannot be modeled on the $RS\alpha$-form of perception. This way of thinking about perceptual experience has many virtues. The most salient for the present discussion is that austere relationalists can easily satisfy the particularity desideratum. Insofar as the subject is perceptually related to particular α, her perceptual state is constituted by α.

However, austere relationalism comes at a price. Austere relationalists account for relational particularity in terms of phenomenal character. As a consequence, the phenomenal character brought about by being perceptually related to α necessarily differs from the phenomenal character brought about by being perceptually related to β. This is the case even if α and β are qualitatively identical. Moreover, the phenomenal character of a perception will necessarily differ from the phenomenal character of a hallucination. So austere relationalists cannot satisfy the phenomenal sameness desideratum.

The natural solution to the problem is to argue that it is not the phenomenal character of a perceptual state, but rather its content, that grounds relational particularity. Since the austere relationalist holds that perceptual states do not have representational content, this solution is not open to her. In the rest of this chapter, I will present a way of satisfying the particularity desideratum while respecting the intuition that perceptions of numerically distinct, yet qualitatively identical particulars do not differ phenomenally. I will argue that although perceptions of numerically distinct particulars necessarily differ with regard to their content, this difference is not revealed in phenomenal character.

II. Varieties of Singular Content

If the content of perception is singular content, then what is the content of a hallucination? A hard-line response to this question is to argue that hallucinations have no representational content. Such a view is motivated by a particular understanding of what it means to represent an object: singular content is radically object-dependent, such that an experiential state has representational content only if the experiencing subject is perceptually related to a particular in her environment. So only if a subject is related to an object, can she represent the object. Drawing on this understanding of the conditions for representing an object, the conclusion is drawn that a hallucinating subject is not in a mental state with content: it only seems to her that she is representing. So there is only the illusion of content.[11]

A view on which perceptual content is radically object-dependent amounts to a disjunctivist view of experiential content. Content disjunctivists accept the austere relationalist thesis that perception and hallucination share no common element or do not belong to the same fundamental kind. In contrast to austere relationalists, however, they hold that a perceiving subject represents the particulars to which she is perceptually related.

Content disjunctivists face the same problems as any other disjunctivists. One problem is that the cognitive significance and the action-guiding role of experiential content is downplayed. When a subject hallucinates, the way things seem to her plays a certain cognitive role. If it seems to her that she is perceptually related to a white cup, she may, for example, reach out and try to pick it up. If one denies that hallucinations have representational content, this cannot be explained. It is not clear how the mere illusion of content could motivate the subject to act. Consider Harman's example of Ponce de Leon who was searching Florida for the fountain of youth (Harman 1990). The fountain of youth does not exist, yet Ponce de Leon was looking for something particular. As Harman argues convincingly, he was not looking for a mental object. He was looking for a mind-independent object that, as it so happened, unbeknownst to him, did not exist. A second problem—and the problem most salient for present purposes—is that, insofar as content disjunctivists hold that hallucinations do not represent, they leave unclear what explains the phenomenal character of hallucinations. So it is not clear how content disjunctivists satisfy the phenomenal sameness desideratum. While content disjunctivists acknowledge that a hallucination could seemingly have the same phenomenal character as a perception, they do little if anything to explain this phenomenon.

---

[11] Versions of this view have been defended by Hinton (1973), Snowdon (1981), Evans (1982) and McDowell (1982, 1984).

The problems of disjunctivism are avoided if perceptual content is not understood as radically object-dependent. That would allow that hallucinations can have at least some kind of content. One way to develop such a view is to argue that the content of a hallucination involves a gap that in the case of a perception is filled by a particular. Traditionally, gappy contents are thought of in terms of Russellian propositions.[12] On the gappy Russellian view, the content of hallucination expresses that the object that seems to be present seems to instantiate property F. The content of a hallucination will be an ordered pair of a gap and a property:

(d_h) <__, F>

In the case of an accurate perception of an object o, the gap is filled by that object:

(d_p) <o, F>

There are several problems with the Russellian gappy content view. One problem is that the content of hallucination has too little structure to account for hallucinations as of multiple objects. If I hallucinate a green dragon playing a red piano, the content of my experience will contain multiple gaps and nothing that marks their difference other than these gaps being bound with distinct properties. Putting aside the problem of how a gap could be bound by properties, it is unclear how such a view could account for the difference in phenomenal character between hallucinating a green dragon playing a red piano and hallucinating a green elephant riding a red bicycle.

A second problem is that to account for a hallucination as of an object that seems to be instantiating a property that is in fact an uninstantiated property, such as supersaturated red or Hume's missing shade of blue, the Russellian must conceive of the content of hallucination as potentially constituted by uninstantiated properties. By doing so, she commits herself not just to a controversial metaphysics of properties but also to a controversial view of phenomenal character. The view is metaphysically controversial since accepting the existence of uninstantiated properties requires some kind of Platonic "two realms"-view on which there is more to reality than the concrete physical world. The view is phenomenologically controversial since it is not clear what it would be to be sensorily aware of a property.[13] After all, properties are not spatio-temporally located and not causally efficacious. The Russellian could respond to the phenomenological problem by distinguishing between being sensorily and cognitively aware of

---

[12] See Braun (1993). Such a Russellian way of thinking about gappy contents has been defended also by Bach (2007) and Tye (2007). For a Fregean gappy content view, see Schellenberg 2006. This paper develops ideas from that project.
[13] For a classical elaboration of this worry, see Williams (1953).

something. This would allow her to accept that we cannot be sensorily aware of properties but argue that hallucinating subjects are cognitively aware of properties. However, now the problem arises as to how a perception and a hallucination could have the same phenomenal character. After all, being cognitively aware of something is phenomenally distinct from being sensorily aware of something (see e.g. Kriegel 2011). If this is right, then it is unclear how the Russellian could satisfy the phenomenal sameness desideratum.[14]

These problems are avoided, if perceptual content is understood as constituted by Fregean modes of presentation of mind-independent particulars rather than bare properties and objects. In the rest of this chapter, I will develop and defend Fregean particularism, which will include a Fregean account of gappy contents. By doing so, I will present a way of satisfying both the particularity and the phenomenal sameness desiderata.

III. Fregean Particularism

The austere versions of relationalism and representationalism are not the only options. An alternative is to argue that perceptual experience is constitutively both relational and representational. On such a view, a perception, a hallucination and an illusion with the same phenomenal character share a metaphysically substantial common element. However, there are also substantial differences with regard to their content: while the token content of perception is singular content, the form of illusion and hallucination is derivative of the form of perception. Perception plays multiple roles: it yields conscious mental states, it justifies beliefs and it provides us with knowledge of our environment. To account for these multiple roles, perceptual content needs to serve multiple explanatory purposes. At the very least, perceptual content must have both a component that grounds perceptual consciousness and a component that, in the case of an accurate perception, grounds perceptual particularity. By grounding perceptual particularity the content can account for the epistemic role that perception plays in our lives.

I will develop Fregean particularism by exploiting the idea that perceiving a particular is constitutively a matter of employing perceptual capacities by means of which that particular is discriminated and singled out. If one possesses a perceptual capacity, one can employ it even if no particular of the kind that the capacity functions to single out is present. Therefore, the very same perceptual capacities that are employed in perception (good case) can also be employed in illusion and hallucination (bad case).

---

[14] For a more detailed discussion of these two problems and for a discussion of alternative ways that the Russellian might respond to these two problems, see Schellenberg (2010).

Now, the employment of such perceptual capacities generates a perceptual state that is characterized by representational content for the following two reasons: the employment of perceptual capacities generates a perceptual state that is *repeatable* and has *accuracy conditions*. Being repeatable and having accuracy conditions are jointly key signatures of representational content. I will give support to each claim in turn. The very same perceptual capacity C_α can be employed to single out particular α_1 or to single out particular α_2. Moreover, the same perceptual capacity can be employed to single out α_1 at time t_1 and at time t_2 and thus yield the same perceptual state at t_1 and t_2.[15] If this is right, then there is a repeatable element that is constitutive of perceptual states, namely, the perceptual capacities employed and, moreover, employing perceptual capacities generates a perceptual state that has a repeatable element. Now, when one discriminates and singles out a particular from its surround, one may do so more or less accurately, and the perceptual state generated thereby will be more or less accurate.[16] After all, a perceiver can single out an object and correctly single out only very few of its properties; or she can single out the same object and correctly single out many of its properties. The first perceptual state will be less accurate with regard to the environment than the second.[17] So employing perceptual capacities yields perceptual states that exhibit key signatures of representational content: it yields something that is at least in part repeatable and that can be accurate or inaccurate. With a few plausible further assumptions, these considerations establish that employing perceptual capacities yields perceptual states with content. The thesis that content is constituted by employing perceptual capacities that function to single out particulars implies that perceptual content is singular. After all, if the fact that perceptual capacities single out particulars in some situations but not others has any semantic significance, then the token content yielded by employing perceptual capacities in perception will be constituted by the particulars singled out.[18]

---

[15] One could argue that different time-slices bring about a difference in perceptual states. If one holds this, then the relevant perceptual state would be different, but it would be different only in this respect.

[16] One might object here that not all discriminatory capacities yield things that have accuracy conditions. For example, thermometers discriminate temperatures, but we do not say that the state thereby produced has accuracy conditions. In response, it is apt to say that the temperature indicated by the thermometer either matches the temperature in the environment or fails to match the temperature in the environment. In this sense, the state of the thermometer in which it indicates a particular temperature has accuracy conditions.

[17] For a discussion of the relationship between singling out objects and singling out the properties this object instantiates, see Pylyshyn and Storm (1988), Pylyshyn (2007) and Fodor (2008).

[18] Here and throughout "*A* is constituted by *B*" is understood in the sense that *A* is at least partially constituted by *B*—leaving open that there may be other things that jointly with *B* constitute *A*. Moreover here and throughout "*A* is constituted by *B*" is understood such that it does not imply that *A* is materially constituted by *B*. So "*A* is constituted by *B*" does not imply that *B* is a component of *A*. There are a number of ways to understand constitution given these constraints. For the sake of specificity, I will work with the following notion of constitution: *A* is constituted by *B*, if and only if *A*

By contrast, an austere representationalist view (or any other view on which perceptual content is general) holds that the content is the very same regardless of what particular (if any) the experiencing subject is related to. A general content lays down a condition that something must satisfy to be the object determined by the content. The condition to be satisfied does not depend on the mind-independent particular that satisfies it. So the relation between content and object is simply the semantic relation of satisfaction.

Perceptual Capacities and Modes of Presentation

The idea that content is constituted by employing perceptual capacities by means of which we (purport to) single out particulars is analogous to the Fregean idea that modes of presentation are a way of grasping or referring to particulars. Indeed, it is analogous to the Fregean idea that modes of presentation both have a cognitive significance and are a means of referring to particulars. A mode of presentation is the specific way in which a subject refers to a particular. While Frege introduces the distinction between sense and reference with a perceptual case, he does not develop the notion for perceptual content. His focus was never on lowly mental faculties like perception. Nonetheless, we can apply his view of modes of presentation to the case of perception. Applied to that case, the idea is that a mode of presentation is the specific way in which a subject singles out a perceived particular. We can think of perceptual capacities as the mental counterpart of modes of presentation. While a mode of presentation is a component of a thought or a proposition, a perceptual capacity is a mental tool. According to Frege (1879), concepts are mappings from objects onto truth-values. Similarly, perceptual capacities are mappings from particulars onto accuracy conditions.

One key motivation for introducing modes of presentation is to capture a fineness of grain in content that reference to mind-independent particulars alone could not achieve. On a Russellian understanding, alternative possible modes of presentation can be expressed only insofar as one may have different cognitive attitudes to the same content. The way in which one perceives or thinks of the object is not expressed in the content proper.

Paralleling the distinction between singular and general content, there are two standard ways of thinking about Fregean modes of presentation. If one focuses on the role of modes of presentation as accounting for cognitive significance,

is grounded in *B*, where grounding is understood as a relation that can hold between entities such as mental states and material, mind-independent particulars (and not just between propositions). So when I say that A is constituted by B, I mean that A is at least partially grounded in B without B being a component of A. "A grounds B" does not entail that "A is a component of B". For example, it is generally accepted that truthmakers ground the truth of the propositions they make true, and it is generally accepted that truthmakers are not components of the propositions they make true.

then it is natural to think of them as de dicto. A de dicto mode of presentation is general in that it can be the very same regardless of what (if anything) the experiencing subject is perceptually related to. If, by contrast, one focuses on the role of modes of presentation as a way of referring to a particular, then it is natural to think of them as de re. A de re mode of presentation is singular in that what particular (if any) the subject is perceptually related to has repercussions for the token content.

A de dicto mode of presentation lays down a condition that something must satisfy to be the particular determined by the content. Chalmers, among others, understands Fregean senses in this way: "Fregean content is supposed to be a sort of phenomenal content, such that, necessarily, an experience with the same phenomenal character has the same Fregean content" (2006a: 99, see also Thompson 2009). A de dicto mode of presentation constitutes a way of representing mind-independent particulars irrespective of whether the relevant particulars are present. If the content of experiential states were constituted by de dicto modes of presentation, then the content of a perception, a hallucination or an illusion with the same phenomenal character would be:

$$(e_{p,h,i}) <MOP_d^o, MOP_d^F>$$

where MOP_d^o is a de dicto mode of presentation of an object and MOP_d^F is a de dicto mode of presentation of a property. Such an account of perceptual content implies a two-stage view of determining reference: first, we represent a general content, and in a second step, we refer to mind-independent particulars based on this content.[19] Representing a de dicto mode of presentation is, on this view, independent of the second step, in which a particular may be determined. Such a two-stage view faces the problem of how the content grounds the ability to refer to external particulars. Insofar as a de dicto mode of presentation can be the very same regardless of what (if anything) the experiencing subject is perceptually related to, this way of thinking about content amounts to a version of austere representationalism and faces all the difficulties of that view. Any view on which perceptual content is constituted by de dicto modes of presentation fails to satisfy the particularity desideratum for the same reasons that austere representationalism does.

This problem is avoided if perceptual content is analyzed as constituted by de re rather than de dicto modes of presentation. Understanding modes of presentation as de re (rather than as de dicto) is motivated by recognizing that modes of

---

[19] For an argument against such a two-stage view of determining reference, see Johnston (2004: 150–1). Johnston does not distinguish between de dicto and de re modes of presentation, and as a consequence sees the problem articulated in the main text as a problem for any Fregean view tout court. As I will show, it is only a problem for a view on which Fregean senses are de dicto rather than de re.

presentation play a dual role: they have a cognitive significance, and they single out or refer to mind-independent particulars. Understanding perceptual content as constituted by de re modes of presentation recognizes that representing a particular is not independent of singling out the particular that is the referent of the sense. By contrast to de dicto modes of presentation, de re modes of presentation are singular in the good case.

Now, on one way of understanding de re modes of presentation, a subject can have a contentful experience only if she is (perceptually) related to the very particular that she purports to single out. This view is a version of content disjunctivism, which we critically discussed in the previous section.[20] What we need is an understanding of de re modes of presentation on which modes of presentation grounds the relational particularity of accurate perceptions and the phenomenological particularity of perceptions, hallucinations and illusions.

Content Types and Token Contents

I argued that regardless of whether we are perceiving, hallucinating or suffering an illusion, we employ perceptual capacities by means of which we purport to single out mind-independent particulars. Since in the bad case, we fail to single out the particulars that we purport to single out, our perceptual capacities are employed baselessly. They are employed baselessly insofar as they do not fulfill their function to operate on environmental particulars. This failure is not at the level of employing the relevant capacity, but rather at the level of singling out a particular. Employing perceptual capacities accounts for the fact that we are intentionally directed at a seeming particular, a process that invests the hallucinatory and illusory state with structure. Moreover, the argument that employing perceptual capacities yields a perceptual state with representational content in virtue of the capacities being repeatable and constituting a phenomenal state that is either accurate or inaccurate generalizes from perception to hallucination and illusion. So given that even in the bad case the subject is employing perceptual capacities, there is good reason to think that her mental state has content.

We have distinguished between employing perceptual capacities tout court (regardless of what if anything is singled out) and employing perceptual capacities while either successfully singling out a particular or failing to do so. We can apply this distinction to content and thereby distinguish between *content types* that are constituted by the perceptual capacities employed and *token contents* that are constituted both by the perceptual capacities employed and the particulars (if any) thereby singled out.

---

[20] For a defense of such a view, see Evans (1982) and McDowell (1984).

220 UNSTRUCTURED CONTENT

A perception, a hallucination and an illusion with the same phenomenal character will all be characterized by the same content type. After all, they all result from employing the same perceptual capacities. Thus, the phenomenal sameness desideratum is satisfied. However, their content token will differ at least in part. After all, in the case of perception, the perceiver successfully singles out the particulars she purports to single out, while, in the case of hallucination and illusion, the experiencing subject fails to single out at least one particular she purports to single out. Thus, the particularity desideratum is satisfied.

Token Contents: Singular Modes of Presentation and Gappy Modes of Presentation

How should we understand the token content of a perceptual state? According to Fregean particularism, the token content of an accurate perception e_1 of a cup α_1 and the property-instance π_1 will be:

(content$_{e1}$) <MOP$_{ra}(\alpha_1)$, MOP$_{rt}(\pi_1)$>

where $MOPr_{ra}(\alpha_1)$ is a singular mode of presentation of the cup α_1 that is the product of employing a perceptual capacity that functions to single out the kind of object under which α_1 falls. So "α_1" is functioning as the name of an object. "$MOPr_{ra}$" is a functional expression that expresses a function from objects to singular modes of presentation. $MOP_{rt}(\pi_1)$ is a singular mode of presentation of the property-instance π_1 that is the product of employing a perceptual capacity that functions to single out instances of the property under which π_1 falls. So while $MOP_{ra}(\alpha_1)$ is a de re mode of presentation of the object α_1, $MOP_{rt}(\pi_1)$ is a de re mode of presentation of the property-instance π_1. I am assuming that the res of a de re mode of presentation can be any mind-independent particular perceived, be it an object, a property-instance or an event. To avoid any confusion, I will speak of singular modes of presentation rather than de re modes of presentation. For any given particular there will be many possible modes of presentation. For the content specified by $MOP_{ra}(\alpha_1)$ to be determinate, it is important that it is conceived of as one particular mode of presentation of the relevant object. Similarly, for the content specified by $MOP_{rt}(\pi_1)$ to be determinate, it is important that it is conceived of as one particular mode of presentation of the relevant property-instance.

A perception e_2 that has the same phenomenal character as e_1 and is of a qualitatively identical yet numerically distinct cup α_2 and property-instance π_2 will have the distinct content:

(content$_{e2}$) <MOP$_{ra}(\alpha_2)$, MOP$_{rt}(\pi_2)$>

Given injectivity, $MOP_{ra}(\alpha_1) \neq MOP_{ra}(\alpha_2)$ and $MOP_{rt}(\pi_1) \neq MOP_{rt}(\pi_2)$. So token contents differ depending on the particular to which the subject is perceptually related. This is the case even if the particulars are qualitatively identical.

In the case of a hallucination that has the same phenomenal character as e_1, the same perceptual capacities are employed as in e_1. But the environmental requirements for successfully singling out the particulars are not met. So no particulars are singled out. As a consequence, the capacities are employed baselessly and so the ensuing token content is defective.

One way of understanding the idea that the content is defective is to say that it is gappy. There is nothing metaphysically spooky about gaps. The gap simply marks the failure to single out a particular. So the content of a hallucination in which we purport to single out an object that instantiates a property is:

$$(\text{content}_h) <MOP_{ra}(\_\_), MOP_{rt}(\_\_)>$$

where $MOP_{ra}(\_\_)$ specifies the kind of object that would have to be present for the experience to be accurate and $MOP_{rt}(\_\_)$ specifies the properties that this object would instantiate were the experience a perception rather than a hallucination. More specifically, $MOP_{ra}(\_\_)$ is a gappy mode of presentation that is the product of employing a perceptual capacity that functions to single out objects of the kind that the hallucinating subject purports to single out while failing to single out any such object. It accounts for the intentional directedness of the experience at a (seeming) particular object. $MOP_{rt}(\_\_)$ is a gappy mode of presentation that is the product of employing a perceptual capacity that functions to single out property-instances of the kind that the hallucinating subject purports to single out while failing to single out any such property-instance. It accounts for the intentional directedness of the experience at a property-instance. In short, $MOP_{ra}(\_\_)$ is a gappy, object-related mode of presentation and $MOP_{rt}(\_\_)$ is a gappy, property-related mode of presentation. So for a perceptual capacity to be employed baselessly amounts to the ensuing token content being gappy.[21]

---

[21] Burge has been read as defending a gappy content view. However, as Burge writes of his view, "I have heard interpretations...according to which there is a 'hole' in the representational aspects of the proposition, where the hole corresponds to the object (which completes the proposition). I regard these interpretations as rather silly" (1977/2007: 75). Burge argues that there are demonstrative elements in the content of a mental state that are in place regardless of whether they refer to the object of experience. As he puts it, "I do not think that a physical *re* in the empirical world...is itself 'part of' the belief.... In my view, the Intentional side of a belief is its only side. In many cases, in my view, a belief that is in fact *de re* might not have been successfully referential (could have failed to be *de re*) and still would have remained the same belief. Moreover, the belief itself can always be individuated, or completely characterized, in terms of the Intentional content" (1991: 209). The way I am using the terms, what Burge refers to as de re would be more aptly labelled de dicto. More importantly, insofar as on Burge's view the intentional content of two experiences can be the very same regardless of the environment, the content does not reflect relational particularity.

An example will help clarify the idea. Consider Hallie who suffers a hallucination as of a white coffee cup. The content of her hallucination specifies both the kind of object that would have to be present for her experience to be accurate and the properties that this object would have to instantiate. The content is indeterminate insofar as it does not specify any particulars. The content would be accurate if the subject were related to a particular white cup. It is important that the content would be accurate regardless of whether the subject is perceptually related to this or that qualitatively identical white cup. This is just to say that the content of a hallucination does not reflect relational particularity.

Depending on how one understands the nature of properties that subjects experience, one might argue that the content of hallucination is gappy only in the object-place, but not in the property-place. On such a view, the content of hallucination would be: $(\text{content}_h)'\ <\text{MOP}_{ra}(\_\_), \text{MOP}_{r\pi}(\pi_1)>$. By contrast, I am arguing that a hallucinating subject who seems to be perceiving a property instantiated by an object is not related to a property-instance. After all, she is not related to any relevant object that could be instantiating the property. Due to this, the content of a hallucination is not just gappy in the object-place, but also in the property-place. Of course, it is possible that while hallucinating, one accurately perceives many mind-independent particulars. In this case, only some of the modes of presentation constituting the content will be gappy.

I will discuss the nature of gappy contents in more detail shortly, but for now let's turn to illusions. In the case of an illusion that has the same phenomenal character as e_1, the same perceptual capacities are employed as in e_1, but, as in the case of hallucination, the environmental requirements for successfully singling out at least one of the particulars that the subject purports to single out are not met. Since the subject fails to single out a property-instance, the token content that ensues from employing the relevant perceptual capacity is gappy:

$(\text{content}_i)\ <\text{MOP}_{ra}(\alpha_1), \text{MOP}_{r\pi}(\_\_)>$

So the token content of an illusion is gappy only in the property-place.

In sum, we can distinguish four different kinds of token contents of perceptual experience with same phenomenal character:

$(\text{content}_{e1})\ <\text{MOP}_{ra}(\alpha_1), \text{MOP}_{r\pi}(\pi_1)>$
$(\text{content}_{e2})\ <\text{MOP}_{ra}(\alpha_2), \text{MOP}_{r\pi}(\pi_2)>$
$(\text{content}_h)\ <\text{MOP}_{ra}(\_\_), \text{MOP}_{r\pi}(\_\_)>$
$(\text{content}_i)\ <\text{MOP}_{ra}(\alpha_1), \text{MOP}_{r\pi}(\_\_)>$

Each of these four experiences instantiates the following content type:

$(\text{content}_{Type})\ <\text{MOP}_{ra}[\_\_], \text{MOP}_{r\pi}[\_\_]>$

where $MOP_{ra}[\_\_]$ can be tokened by $MOP_{ra}(\alpha_1)$, $MOP_{ra}(\alpha_2)$, $MOP_{ra}(\alpha_3)$, $MOP_{ra}(\_\_)$ or any other singular mode of presentation of a particular.

So Fregean particularism is characterized by the following three conditions:

(1) The content of any two perceptions e_1 and e_1 that have the same phenomenal character and in which the subject is perceptually related to the same particular α_1 in the same way will include the token singular mode of presentation $MOP_{ra}(\alpha_1)$, where $MOP_{ra}(\alpha_1)$ is constituted by employing the perceptual capacity C_α that functions to single out particulars of the type under which α_1 falls. More specifically, $MOP_{ra}(\alpha_1)$ is the output of employing perceptual capacity C_α that takes particulars of the kind under which α_1 falls as inputs. So $MOP_{ra}(\alpha_1)$ is constituted by the perceptual capacity employed and the particular α_1 thereby singled out.

(2) A perception e_2 that has the same phenomenal character as e_1, but in which the subject is perceptually related to the numerically distinct particular α_2 will be constituted by employing the same perceptual capacity C_α. However, since the input in e_2 is a different particular than in e_1, the ensuing token content $MOP_{ra}(\alpha_2)$ is different. This is the case, even if α_1 and α_2 are qualitatively identical. So singular modes of presentation are injective: if $\alpha_1 \neq \alpha_2$, then $MOP_{ra}(\alpha_1) \neq MOP_{ra}(\alpha_2)$.

(3) A hallucination or an illusion that has the same phenomenal character as e_1 is constituted by employing the same perceptual capacity C_α but, since there is no relevant particular present, the perceptual capacity is employed baselessly. As a consequence, the token content $MOP_{ra}(\_\_)$ is gappy.

One objection waiting in the wings is that (content$_h$) is not an adequate way of characterizing the content of a hallucination since it cannot account for the fact that the content of a hallucination is inaccurate: given the presence of a gap, the content cannot determine an accuracy condition. In response, it is necessary to distinguish two ways in which a content can be inaccurate. One way is for the content to make a claim about the environment that is not accurate. A second way is for it to fail to make an accurate claim about the environment. To illustrate this second sense of inaccuracy, suppose that I claim that Pegasus lives in my apartment. This claim is inaccurate. Given that "Pegasus" does not refer, the inaccuracy in question is that I have failed to make an accurate claim about who lives in my apartment. If inaccuracy is understood in this second way, then a hallucination can have a gappy content and nonetheless be inaccurate. On this understanding of gappy contents, the fact that a content is gappy implies that the content is necessarily inaccurate insofar as a gappy content could never make an accurate claim about the world.[22]

---

[22] For a dissenting view of the truth-value of gappy propositions, see Everett (2003).

On this view, there is nothing veridical about so-called "veridical hallucinations." In such a case, a subject is hallucinating, say, an apple, and there happens to be an apple where she hallucinates one to be. But she is not perceptually related to the apple because there is a wall between her and the apple. As a consequence, the content of her experience is gappy. Indeed, the content of hallucinations with the same phenomenal character will have the same content—even if one hallucination is non-veridical and the other is a so-called "veridical hallucination."

Content Types: Potentially Singular Modes of Presentation

So far I have specified the token contents. How should we understand the content types? According to Fregean particularism, a perception, a hallucination and an illusion with the same phenomenal character share a metaphysically substantial common element: the perceptual capacities employed. Employing perceptual capacities yields a content type that experiential states with the same phenomenal character have in common. So, Fregean particularism avoids any disjunctivist commitments. There is a stock of distinct content types $MOP_{r\alpha}[\_\_\_]$, $MOP_{r\beta}[\_\_\_]$, $MOP_{r\chi}[\_\_\_]$, $MOP_{r\delta}[\_\_\_]$,… which combine with particulars to form singular modes of presentation of objects, property-instances and events.

Now, why are these content types not just general contents? In response, content types are potentially particularized contents. To motivate this, consider again Hallie who hallucinates a cup. On the basis of her hallucination, she thinks, "That is a white cup." Since there is no white cup present, she fails to refer and the content of her thought is not singular. However, it is not general either. After all, she purports to refer to a mind-independent particular. Failing to be a singular content does not imply that the content is general. There are other options. One alternative is to say that the content has the form of a singular content while failing to be a token singular content. It is a potentially singular content. As in the case of a failed singular thought, the content of hallucination is neither a general content nor a singular content. It is structured by two levels: the content type and the token content; more specifically, a potentially particularized content type and a gappy token content. In virtue of its singular form, the experience manifests phenomenological particularity. The potentially particularized content type can be analyzed as a schema that gives the conditions of satisfaction of any perceptual state with that content.

Although in the case of an accurate perception the token content is at least in part constituted by the particulars perceived, the very same content type can be tokened if no relevant particular is present. The token content of a hallucination is naturally not constituted by any mind-independent particulars perceived. While the content type is not dependent on particulars (if any) perceived it is nonetheless relational. It is relational since it is constituted by employing perceptual capacities that function to discriminate and single out particulars. As a consequence, relations to particulars are implicated in the very nature of content, even at the level of the content type.

One might object that the content of a hallucination and the content of a perception could never be tokens of the same type. After all, the former is gappy and the latter is not. In response, particulars can be tokens of the same type even if the particulars differ significantly. For them to be tokens of the same type they need only to exhibit the feature relevant to classification under that type. There are many ways to type contents. One is with regard to whether or not they are gappy. On this way, gappy contents and non-gappy contents would be tokens of different types. However, another way to type contents is with regard to the perceptual capacities employed that constitute the content. This is the kind of content types in play here.

Advantages of Fregean Particularism

The thesis that perceptual content is constituted by employing perceptual capacities allows for a substantive way of analyzing perceptual content as non-conceptual. After all, perceptual capacities can be understood as non-conceptual analogs to concepts.

A second advantage of Fregean particularism is that the thesis that perceptual content is constituted by employing perceptual capacities allows for a way to analyze the difference between perception and cognition as a difference in representational vehicle, where that difference in representational vehicle is explained in terms of a difference in the capacities employed. The representational vehicle of perceptual representation is the employment of perceptual capacities. The representational vehicle of cognition is the employment of cognitive capacities.

A third advantage is that the view neither implies that the experiencing subject stands in a propositional attitude to the content of her experience nor does it rely on there being such a relation between the subject and the content of an experience. So there is no need to say that the experiencing subject 'exes' that p,—to use Byrne's (2009) phrase.

A fourth advantage is that Fregean particularism can easily account for hallucinations as of multiple objects. We rejected the Russellian gappy content view on grounds that it cannot account for hallucinations as of multiple objects. How can Fregean particularism account for such hallucinations? In response, hallucinations as of multiple objects are unproblematic for Fregean particularism, since it is the mode of presentation that is gappy and so the content of a hallucination is not altogether gappy in the object-place. As a consequence, there is sufficient structure to account for hallucinations as of multiple objects.

Fregean Particularism, the Particularity Desideratum and the Phenomenal Sameness Desideratum

I have argued that the content of experiential states is constituted both by the perceptual capacities employed and the particulars (if any) thereby singled out. In this way, perceptual experience is constitutively both relational and representational. In this section, I will compare Fregean particularism to austere relationalism and austere representationalism. In doing so, I will show how it satisfies both the particularity and the phenomenal sameness desiderata.

Fregean particularism accepts the central relationalist insight that relations to particulars are constitutive of perceptual states. If perceptual content is constituted by perceptual capacities that function to discriminate and single out mind-independent particulars, then relations to particulars are implicated in the very nature of perceptual content. Moreover, if the fact that perceptual capacities single out mind-independent particulars in some environments but not others has any semantic significance, then the content ensuing from employing perceptual capacities will be constituted at least in part by the perceived particulars.[23]

Since perceptual content is constituted by the particulars perceived, Fregean particularism allows for a straightforward way of accounting for the particularity desideratum. The particular to which the subject is perceptually related secures the relational particularity of her perceptual state. There is a difference between the token contents of perceptions of numerically distinct but qualitatively identical objects. To explain this, consider Percy who sees a white cup at time t_1. Without Percy noticing, the cup is replaced by a qualitatively identical cup, so that at time t_2, Percy sees a cup that is numerically distinct from the one he saw at t_1. The content of his perceptual state at t_1 and at t_2 is distinct despite the fact that the difference in content is not reflected in the phenomenal character of his perceptual states. The content of Percy's perceptual states is distinct since it is constituted by a singular mode of presentation of a different object before and after the switch. So what Fregean particularism shares with relationalism (that austere representationalism lacks) is the ability to satisfy the particularity desideratum.

However, in contrast to austere relationalism, Fregean particularism can easily account for the phenomenal sameness desideratum. Fregean particularism accepts the minimal representationalist commitment that perception is constitutively a matter of representing one's environment such that one's perceptual state is characterized by representational content. Employing perceptual capacities in a sensory mode constitutes both the representational content and the phenomenal character of experiential states. In experiential states with the same phenomenal

---

[23] For a defense, see Schellenberg (2016).

character, the same perceptual capacities are employed in the same sensory mode. So in contrast to disjunctivists and austere relationalists, I am arguing that a hallucination, an illusion and a perception with the same phenomenal character share a common element that explains their sameness in phenomenal character.

How does Fregean particularism make room for content that manifests phenomenological particularity while lacking relational particularity? In response, even if one happens to be hallucinating or suffering an illusion, the capacities employed do not cease to function to do what they do in the case of perception, namely, discriminate and single out particulars in the environment. Employing them is the basis for the intentional directedness at particulars in perception and accounts for the intentional directedness at a seeming particular in illusion and hallucination. Thus, employing perceptual capacities accounts for the fact that when we suffer an illusion or a hallucination, it seems to us as if a particular is present. In this way, employing perceptual capacities grounds phenomenological particularity. So while the gap in the token content of a hallucination marks the lack of relational particularity, the intentional directedness at an object is accounted for by the (gappy) mode of presentation. Even though in the case of illusion or hallucination, the experiencing subject fails to single out at least one of the particulars that she purports to single out, the gappy token content is inherently related to external and mind-independent particulars of the type that the subject's perceptual capacities function to single out in the good case. Whether a perceptual capacity is employed baselessly will not affect the phenomenal character of the experience. Only if this is the case can the view satisfy the phenomenal sameness desideratum. For only if it is not revealed in phenomenal character whether a perceptual capacity is employed baselessly could a perception, an illusion and a hallucination have the same phenomenal character.

So, with representationalists but against austere relationalists, I am arguing that the phenomenal character of a hallucination manifests phenomenological particularity without being characterized by relational particularity. However, with relationalists and against austere representationalists, I am arguing that the content of perception grounds relational particularity. Fregean particularism satisfies the particularity desideratum since it does not equate perceptual content with phenomenal content. Although content types remain the same across experiential states with the same phenomenal character, token contents are constituted by the particulars (if any) perceived. As a consequence, there can be differences in content that are not reflected in phenomenal character. While Fregean particularism rejects the austere representationalist thesis that perceptual content is phenomenal content, and consequently is not compatible with so-called strong representationalism, it is compatible with weak representationalism. That said, if the content type is the same between two experiences, the phenomenal character will be the same. So Fregean particularism holds that there is a kind of content that covaries with phenomenal character.

IV. Fregean Particularism and Alternative Views

It has been argued that a content that purports to be of a particular object but fails to refer is best thought of as a general content (Burge 2010). It has, moreover, been argued that a singular content is object-dependent such that we cannot be in a mental state with a token content that purports to be of a particular, but fails to refer (Evans 1982, McDowell 1984).

Fregean particularism avoids the pitfalls of both approaches in that it makes room for a notion content that manifests phenomenological particularity but lacks relational particularity. According to Fregean particularism, the content of hallucination is structured by a content type and a token content, neither of which is a general content. The content type is a potentially particularized content schema. The token content is gappy. In contrast to a view on which de re modes of presentation are radically object-dependent such that there cannot be a token content if there is no object to be represented, Fregean particularism shows that de re modes of presentation are only partly constituted by the particulars perceived. Singular modes of presentation are constituted by the perceptual capacities employed and the particulars perceived. While the perceptual capacities employed provide the general element of perceptual content, the objects, events and property-instances singled out provide the particular element. If no particulars are perceived, as in the case of a total hallucination, the token content is constituted only by the perceptual capacities employed. While the token content of hallucination is defective in virtue of the perceptual capacities being employed baselessly, the mere fact that perceptual capacities are employed gives the token content enough structure to ground the phenomenal character and thus the phenomenological particularity of hallucinatory states. So Fregean particularism makes room for hallucinations to have a token content, even though no mind-independent particular is perceived.

In contrast to the gappy Russellian view discussed earlier, Fregean particularism does not posit that the object-place is gappy in the case of a hallucination. It is rather the mode of presentation in the object-place that is gappy. So even if one hallucinates multiple objects, there is enough structure in the content to distinguish the various objects that one seems to be perceiving. The structure is provided by the gappy modes of presentation.

Now, one might argue that there is no reason to appeal to gaps to account for the content of hallucinations. An alternative solution is to say that the gaps are filled by intentional objects. On such a view, experience is a matter of representing properties that are attributed to intentional objects (see Lycan 1996 and Crane 1998). These intentional objects can be thought of as existing abstracta or as non-existing concreta. Such a view is less attractive than Fregean particularism for at least two reasons. One reason is that if hallucinations are construed as relations between subjects and intentional objects, then one is pressed to construe perceptions as relations between subjects and intentional objects as well. However, doing so leads to well-known problems.[24] A second reason is that positing intentional objects does not secure any explanatory advantage over Fregean particularism with regard to the phenomenal character of experience, and is furthermore less powerful in explaining both the relational particularity of perceptions and the absence of relational particularity in hallucinations. Finally, a difference in token contents between perceptions and hallucinations with the same phenomenal character can explain the epistemic difference between them.[25] An intentional object view does not have this benefit.

I have argued that perceptual content should be understood as serving multiple explanatory roles insofar as it grounds both phenomenal character and perceptual particularity. An alternative way of satisfying these two explanatory roles is to argue that experience has multiple layers of content. On such a multiple contents view, different layers of content satisfy the two explanatory roles. There are many reasons to introduce multiple layers of content. My argument, if right, undermines at least one motivation for the multiple contents view, namely, the motivation that one layer grounds phenomenal character while another layer accounts for the reference-fixing role of perception. Chalmers (2006b) argues, for example, that one layer is a Fregean content that is associated with a primary intension that is a function from centered worlds to extensions (where the Fregean content is understood as de dicto), while the other layer is a Russellian content that is associated with a secondary intension, which is a function from uncentered worlds to extensions. What these views have in common is that one layer of content grounds phenomenal character, while the other determines the reference of the mental state.

Fregean particularism is motivated by many of the same concerns as the multiple contents view, but it does not entail the multiple contents view, and it is not a particular version of that view. The multiple contents view entails that experience has different sets of accuracy conditions associated with the different layers of content. The thesis that experience has multiple explanatory purposes involves no such entailment. While on Fregean particularism, any perception, hallucination and illusion is characterized by a content type and a token content, the content type and token content do not constitute two distinct layers of content. After all, they do not determine two different sets of accuracy conditions. Only the token content determines accuracy conditions. The content type is no more than a

---

[24] For a discussion of the skeptical problems that ensue if the content of mental states is understood as constituted by intentional objects or relations to intentional objects, see Brewer (1999). Loar (2003) argues that a view on which perception is construed as a relation to an intentional object is phenomenally implausible.
[25] [Reference omitted for blind-refereeing.]

content schema. So according to Fregean particularism, the content of a perceptual experience has only one set of accuracy conditions. Thus the view provides a way of satisfying the different explanatory roles of perceptual content without introducing a second layer of content. As the second difference between the two views will show, there are powerful reasons to resist introducing multiple layers of content to account for the different explanatory roles of perceptual content.

In contrast to the multiple contents view, Fregean particularism is a view of both the constituents of perceptual content and of what holds these constituents together. It takes seriously Frege's insight that modes of presentation play a dual role: they have a cognitive significance and they determine a reference—at least in the successful case. On the multiple contents view, the cognitive significance and the reference-determining roles of content are accounted for on different levels of content. Experiences with the same phenomenal character will have the same content on one level, but, depending on their environment, they may have a different content on the other level. The relation between the phenomenal content and the perceived object is simply the semantic relation of satisfaction.

Insofar as the multiple contents view analyzes perception as the co-instantiation of two independent elements it is a version of what I called conjunctivism. It is a version of conjunctivism on which the relational element is not simply a perceptual relation between a subject and an object, but rather constitutes an object-dependent layer of content. In contrast to the simple version of conjunctivism that I considered in Section I, the multiple contents view can satisfy the particularity desideratum, since one level of content is constituted by the particulars perceived. However, since the layer of content that accounts for relational particularity is independent of the layer of content that grounds phenomenal character, the question arises as to how phenomenal contents are connected to what they are about. Consider Chalmers's epistemic two-dimensional semantics. As Chalmers notes, "primary intensions do not determine extensions in a strong sense (although they may still determine extension relative to context)" (2006b: 596). The layer of content that grounds the phenomenal character of the experience does not itself determine an extension. Chalmers considers the possibility of accounting for the reference-determining role of modes of presentation by stipulating that the content of an expression-token is an ordered pair of its primary intension and its extension (2006b: 596). Although such an ordered pair plays the role of determining reference, it does so trivially, given that the extension is part of the ordered pair. The question remains as to how the primary intensions, that is, the phenomenal contents, are connected to what they are about.

The notion of a singular mode of presentation that I have developed cannot be identified with an ordered pair of a de dicto mode of presentation and a referent. To deny that the content can be identified with such an ordered pair is not to deny that the content can be analyzed into two layers, one of which is constituted by the perceived particular (if any), the other of which is independent of the perceived particular (if any). However, the ability to analyze A in terms of B does not imply that A is identified with B.[26] Being in a perceptual state is not just a matter of being intentionally directed at a (seeming) mind-independent particular and, in the successful case, being causally related to that mind-independent particular. Content needs to be connected to its referent by some non-attributional means. On Fregean particularism, perceptual capacities fulfill the role of connecting mental states with the particulars perceived. Perceptual capacities play both a reference-fixing role and constitute content that grounds phenomenal character. Thus, employing perceptual capacities constitutes singular modes of presentations, namely modes of presentation that are constituted by the perceptual capacities employed and the particulars thereby singled out. In this way, employing perceptual capacities constitute representational content that account for the Fregean idea that modes of presentation both have a cognitive significance and are a means of referring to particulars.

V. Coda

If a distinction is drawn between what an experience is of and what one takes one's experience to be of, then we can drive a wedge between the content and the phenomenal character of an experience, without thinking of them as entirely independent. By driving a wedge between phenomenal character and content, one can account for the possibility that a perception, a hallucination and an illusion can have the same phenomenal character while accounting for differences that are due to the experiencing subject being perceptually related to different particulars (or not being perceptually related to any particulars). Content plays the dual role of grounding relational particularity in the case of an accurate perception and grounding phenomenological particularity regardless of whether the subject is perceiving, hallucinating or suffering an illusion. Moreover, insofar as employing perceptual capacities constitutes phenomenal character and secures the reference of the perceptual state, Fregean particularism rejects all ways of factorizing perceptual content into internal and external components. In this way, the suggested view combines the virtues of relationalism and representationalism, while avoiding the difficulties of the austere versions of these views. According to Fregean particularism, perceptual content is constituted by general elements, namely the perceptual capacities employed, and particular elements, namely the external, mind-independent particulars perceived.

---

[26] For a critical discussion of two-dimensional semantics, see also Speaks (2009).

References

Bach, K. 2007. "Searle against the world: how can experiences find their objects." In *John Searle's Philosophy of Language: Force, Meaning, and Mind*, ed. S. L. Tsohatzidis, 000–00. Cambridge: Cambridge University Press.
Beck, O. Forthcoming. "Rethinking naïve realism."
Block, N. 2003. "Mental paint." In *Reflections and Replies: Essays on the Philosophy of Tyler Burge*, ed. M. Hahn and B. Ramberg, 000–00. Cambridge, MA: MIT Press.
Braun, D. 1993. "Empty names." *Noûs* 27: 449–69.
Brewer, B. 2006. "Perception and content." *European Journal of Philosophy* 14: 165–81.
Burge, T. 1977/2007. "Belief *de re*" with postscript. In *Foundations of Mind*. Oxford: Oxford University Press.
Burge, T. 1991. "Vision and intentional content." In *John Searle and His Critics*, ed. E. LePore and R. van Gulick, 000–00. Oxford: Blackwell.
Burge, T. 2010. *Origins of Objectivity*. Oxford: Oxford University Press.
Byrne, A. 2001. "Intentionalism defended." *Philosophical Review* 110: 199–240.
Byrne, A. 2009. "Experience and content." *Philosophical Quarterly* 59: 429–51.
Campbell, J. 2002. *Reference and Consciousness*. Oxford: Oxford University Press.
Chalmers, D. 2006a. "Perception and the fall from Eden." In *Perceptual Experience*, ed. T. Gendler and J. Hawthorne, 000–00. Oxford: Clarendon Press.
Chalmers, D. 2006b. "Two-dimensional semantics." In *Oxford Handbook of the Philosophy of Language*, ed. E. LePore and B. Smith, 000–00. Oxford: Oxford University Press.
Crane, T. 1998. "Intentionality as the mark of the mental." In *Contemporary Issues in the Philosophy of Mind*, ed. A. O'Hear, 000–00. Cambridge: Cambridge University Press.
Crane, T. 2011. "The singularity of singular thought." Aristotelian Society Supplementary Volume 85: 21–43.
Davies, M. 1992. "Perceptual content and local supervenience." *Proceedings of the Aristotelian Society* 92: 21–45.
Evans, G. 1982. *The Varieties of Reference*, ed. J. McDowell. Oxford: Oxford University Press.
Fish, W. 2009. *Perception, Hallucination, and Illusion*. Oxford: Oxford University Press.
Fodor, J. 2008. *LOT2: The Language of Thought Revisited*. Oxford: Oxford University Press.
Frege, G. 1879. *Begriffsschrift: Eine der Arithmetischen nachgebildete Formelsprache des reinen Denkens*. Halle: L. Nebert.
Genone, J. 2014. "Appearance and illusion." *Mind* 123: 339–76.
Gomes, A. and C. French. 2016. "On the particularity of experience." *Philosophical Studies* 173: 451–60.
Grice, H. P. 1961. "The causal theory of perception." *Proceedings of the Aristotelian Society* 35: 121–68.
Hill, C. 2009. *Consciousness*. Cambridge: Cambridge University Press.
Hill, C. forthcoming. "Existentialism sustained."
Hinton, J. M. 1973. *Experiences*. Oxford: Oxford University Press.
Johnston, M. 2004. "The obscure object of hallucination." *Philosophical Studies* 120: 113–83.
Johnston, M. 2014. "The problem with the content view." In *Does Perception Have Content?*, ed. B. Brogaard, 000–00. Oxford: Oxford University Press.
Kriegel, U. 2011. "The veil of abstracta." *Philosophical Issues* 21: 245–67.
Logue, H. 2014. "Experiential content and naïve realism: a reconciliation." In *Does Perception Have Content?*, ed. B. Brogaard, 000–00. Oxford: Oxford University Press.
Lycan, W. G. 1996. *Consciousness and Experience*. Cambridge, MA: MIT Press.
Martin, M. G. F. 2002. "Particular thoughts and singular thoughts." In *Logic, Thought and Language*, ed. A. O'Hear, 000–00. Cambridge: Cambridge University Press.
Martin, M. G. F. 2004. "The limits of self-awareness." *Philosophical Studies* 103: 37–89.
Millar, A. 1991. *Reasons and Experiences*. Oxford: Clarendon Press.

McDowell, J. 1984. "*De re* senses." *Philosophical Quarterly* 34: 283–94.
McDowell, J. 1982. "Criteria, defeasibility, and knowledge." *Proceedings of the British Academy* 68: 455–79.
McGinn, C. 1982. *The Character of Mind*. Oxford: Oxford University Press.
Moore, G. E. 1925. "A defence of common sense." In *Contemporary British Philosophy*, ed. J. H. Muirhead, 000–00. London: George Allen and Unwin. (Reprinted in G. E. Moore. 1959. *Philosophical Papers*. New York: Macmillan.)
Moore, G. E. 1953. *Some Main Problems of Philosophy*. London: George Allen and Unwin.
Pautz, A. 2009. "What are the contents of experiences?" *Philosophical Quarterly* 59: 483–507.
Peacocke, C. 1981. "Demonstrative thought and psychological explanation." *Synthese* 49: 187–217.
Peacocke, C. 1983. *Sense and Content: Experience, Thought, and Their Relations*. Oxford: Oxford University Press.
Peacocke, C. 2009. "Objectivity." *Mind* 118: 739–69.
Price, H. H. 1950. *Perception*. London: Methuen.
Pylyshyn, Z. W. 2007. *Things and Places: How the Mind Connects with the World*. Cambridge, MA: MIT Press.
Pylyshyn, Z. W. and Storm, R. W. 1988. "Tracking multiple independent targets: evidence for a parallel tracking mechanism." *Spatial Vision* 3: 179–97.
Raleigh, T. 2014. "A new approach to 'perfect' hallucinations." *Journal of Consciousness Studies* 21: 81–110.
Raleigh, T. 2015. "Phenomenology without representation." *European Journal of Philosophy* 23: 1209–37.
Schellenberg, S. 2006. Perception in Perspective. Doctoral Dissertation. University of Pittsburgh.
Schellenberg, S. 2010. "The particularity and phenomenology of perceptual experience." *Philosophical Studies* 149: 19–48.
Schellenberg, S. 2011. "Perceptual content defended." *Noûs* 45: 714–50.
Schellenberg, S. 2016. "Perceptual Particularity." *Philosophy and Phenomenological Research* 93: 25–54.
Schellenberg, S. 2018. *The Unity of Perception: Content, Consciousness, Evidence*. Oxford: Oxford University Press.
Searle, J. 1983. *Intentionality: An Essay in the Philosophy of Mind*. Cambridge: Cambridge University Press.
Snowdon, P. 1981. "Perception, vision and causation." *Proceedings of the Aristotelian Society* 81: 175–92.
Soteriou, M. 2000. "The particularity of visual perception." *European Journal of Philosophy* 8: 173–89.
Soteriou, M. 2005. "The subjective view of experience and its objective commitments." *Proceedings of the Aristotelian Society* 105: 177–90.
Speaks, J. 2009. "Transparency, intentionalism, and the nature of perceptual content." *Philosophy and Phenomenological Research* 79: 539–73.
Travis, C. 2004. "Silence of the senses." *Mind* 113: 57–94.
Tye, M. 1995. *Ten Problems of Consciousness: A Representational Theory of the Phenomenal Mind*. Cambridge, MA: MIT Press.
Tye, M. 2007. "Intentionalism and the argument from no common content." In *Philosophical Perspectives* 21, ed. J. Hawthorne, 000–00. Northridge: Ridgeview Publishing Company.
Williams, D. C. 1953. "The elements of being." *Review of Metaphysics* 7: 3–18 and 171–92.

In Defence of Fregean That-Clause Semantics

Katharina Felka and Alex Steinberg

Gottlob Frege famously held the view that expressions within natural language that-clauses that occur as parts of propositional attitude ascriptions and speech act reports do not have their ordinary denotations (what Frege called their *gewöhnliche Bedeutung*). Instead, Frege thought, they denote what is in other contexts the concept (*Sinn*) they express (Frege called this an expression's *ungerade Bedeutung*).[1] Call this view the *(Fregean) reference shift thesis*. Frege took the reference shift thesis to account for substitution failures of expressions that in ordinary contexts co-denote, while holding on to the view that the denotation of a complex expression is a function of the denotations of its constituents and its structure (call this the *compositionality thesis*). For instance, the astronomically challenged Ben might not realize that Hesperus is Phosphorus, while being under no illusion regarding the identity of Hesperus with itself. In such a case, it seems, the following sentences are true and false respectively:

(1) Ben believes that Hesperus is Hesperus.
(2) Ben believes that Hesperus is Phosphorus.

But (2) results from (1) by substitution of expressions that have the same *gewöhnliche Bedeutung*: 'Hesperus' and 'Phosphorus'. Plausibly, the sentence's structure and the denotations of the other expressions remain constant. Therefore, the denotation of the relevant occurrences of 'Hesperus' and 'Phosphorous' cannot be their *gewöhnliche Bedeutung*, given compositionality. Instead, Frege conjectures, expressions in this context denote the concepts they usually express. And indeed, substitution of expressions that in ordinary contexts express the same concept does not obviously give rise to similar substitution problems.[2]

---

[1] Cf. Frege (1892/1994: 28). A terminological note: we translate Fregean '*Bedeutung*' as 'denotation', and take this to be a stylistic variant of 'semantic value'. All types of expressions have denotations: singular terms, predicates, connectives etc. In the case of singular terms, their denotation is typically called their *reference*.

[2] Whether they indeed do so shall not concern us here, since this is not the focus of the argument we want to discuss. See e.g. Williamson (2007: ch. 3) for further discussion.

Stephen Schiffer (2003) and—in more detail—Adam Pautz (2008) raise an argument against the reference shift thesis. In a nutshell, they claim that a proponent of reference shift is either committed to the validity of an intuitively unacceptable inference or else she has to deny the universal validity of an otherwise completely unproblematic form of inference. Since both horns of the dilemma are unappealing, we should reject the reference shift thesis. In fact, Schiffer uses the argument as part of a more general case against structured propositions. He argues as follows: The only plausible candidate accounts for structured propositions are either the Fregean or the Russellian view. Both are committed to their own form of reference shift. But reference shift is false. Thus, he concludes, no view that takes propositions to be structured is true. Hence, if correct, Pautz's and Schiffer's argument against reference shift do not only cast doubt on Fregeanism, but on structured propositions in general.

In this paper we will defend the Fregean reference shift thesis against Pautz's and Schiffer's objection, and, thereby, the viability of an account of propositions as structured. We will argue that a Fregean should accept that the inference in question is invalid but deny that it is an instance of an otherwise completely unproblematic form of inference. However, we will concede that the Fregean should have something to say about *why* the inference is invalid and why certain related ones are valid. This is why we will go on to fill in a lacuna Frege left in his semantics for that-clauses. The resulting semantics systematically yields the correct answers to relevant validity questions. The plan for the paper is as follows: in Section I we present the argument against reference shift. In Section II we explain the Fregean's cause for objecting to the argument. In Section III we identify the lacuna Frege left in his semantics for that-clauses and present a straightforward but patently un-Fregean way of filling it. In Section IV we suggest a Fregean alternative on whose basis we develop our preferred Fregean semantics for that-clauses.

I. The Argument against Reference Shift

According to the Fregean reference shift thesis, the expressions in the that-clause of a propositional attitude ascription such as:

(3) Ralph believes that Atlantis is an underwater city

do not denote their ordinary denotations but the concepts they ordinarily express. Thus, for instance, while occurrences of 'is an underwater city' denote (let's assume) the property of being an underwater city in ordinary contexts, the phrase's occurrence in (3) denotes the concept [is an underwater city] instead.[3]

---

[3] Here and in what follows we use square bracket expressions in order to denote the concepts or Fregean senses the enclosed expressions ordinarily express.

Likewise, while 'Atlantis' presumably does not denote anything in ordinary contexts, it denotes its sense, [Atlantis], in (3).[4]

The argument now appeals to a plausible principle about existential quantification. It elaborates the observation that, in the standard case, positions of singular terms are open to existential quantification, and the resulting inference is valid. The following is (nearly) a quotation from Pautz (2008: 338):

> Exportation: If t in $S(t)$ is a singular tem that refers to o and makes no other contribution to the truth conditions[5] of $S(t)$, then $S(t)$ entails *There is something such that S(it)*, where o is a witness to that quantification.[6]

Now, the argument proceeds, 'Atlantis' in (3) appears to be a singular term which, according to reference shift, denotes something, to wit: [Atlantis]. Further, the sole contribution 'Atlantis' appears to make to the truth conditions of (3) is its denotation. Thus, by Exportation, the following inference should be valid:

(4) Ralph believes that Atlantis is an underwater city. Therefore, there is something such that Ralph believes that it is an underwater city.

But the inference appears to be invalid. Its premise may well be true while its conclusion is false. Ralph may mistakenly think that Atlantis exists while being under no illusion regarding the water level of all actually existing cities (or the cityhood of all things underwater). In such a case Ralph may believe that Atlantis is an underwater city while there is nothing that Ralph takes to be an underwater city. For, what would be a plausible candidate? Certainly not Atlantis, since there is no such thing. Berlin, London or even Venice are out of the question, since Ralph does not think that either of them is underwater. And the Great Barrier Reef or the Titanic are out, too, since Ralph is well aware that they are not cities. Thus, if the reference shift thesis is true and a few further plausible assumptions

---

[4] This, by the way, allows Frege—who thinks that denotation failure is contagious—to say that (3) may well be true—depending on Ralph's state of mind—even though a free-standing occurrence of the embedded sentence 'Atlantis is an underwater city' is neither true nor false due to the lack of denotation of the unembedded occurrence of 'Atlantis'.

[5] Pautz (2008: 338) writes 'truth-value' here. But, although semantics and the world team up to determine the truth-value of a sentence, this is unnecessarily far downstream, so we opted for appeal to truth-conditions here. Nothing depends on this.

[6] The second conjunct in the antecedent is included to deal with cases such as Quine's famous Giorgione case: from 'Giorgione is so-called because of his height' we do not want to conclude 'There is someone who is so-called because of his height', but this is so, since 'Giorgione' has the *additional* function of providing the antecedent for the anaphoric 'so-called' in the sentence. Pautz (2008: 338) also includes the additional conjunct '$S(t)$ is true iff o satisfies the open sentence $S(x)$' in the antecedent. However, he never discusses why the Fregean should accept this claim in the case to be discussed presently, so we omit it here. As far as we can see, nothing in our discussion hinges on this.

are correct, either a seemingly invalid inference is valid after all or Exportation fails. Consequently, the argument concludes, the reference shift thesis is false.

We should note that various similar arguments can be run to the same effect. For instance, as Pautz (2008: 338) observes, instead of focusing on the inference in (4) that employs a term that is (ordinarily) denotationless, we could have used an example with a denoting term instead, e.g.,

(5) Ben believes that Hesperus is a planet. Therefore, there is something such that Ben believes that it is a planet, to wit: [Hesperus].

Again, the inference appears to be invalid: unless Ben mistakes a concept for a planet, the inference's premise may be true even though its conclusion is false. So, the argument does not essentially depend on the presence of denotationless terms, let alone on a certain treatment of fictional terms.

Instead of specifying a witness we may also explicitly restrict the range of the quantifier to concepts. The result is:

(6) Ben believes that Hesperus is a planet. Therefore, there is a concept such that Ben believes that it is a planet.

So, the argument does not essentially depend on the semantics of witness specifications.

We should also note that the argument may be generalisable in various respects. First, analogous arguments can be run for virtually any position that holds that singular terms in that-clauses denote anything that is not easily mistaken for their ordinary denotations. For, suppose some position says that 'Hesperus' in:

(7) Ben believes that Hesperus is a planet;

denotes anything other than the planet Hesperus, an F say, where Fs are not easily mistaken for planets. If so, the following inference is invalid, while the proponent of the semantics of that-clauses under discussion is as hard pressed as the Fregean to cope with this observation:

(8) Ben believes that Hesperus is a planet. Therefore, there is an F such that Ben believes that it is a planet.

Secondly, as Schiffer (2003: 30) argues, an analogous argument targets other syntactic positions within that-clauses, most pertinently the position of the expression that acts as a *predicate* in ordinary contexts. For, Schiffer says, any position that accepts compositionality should hold that 'is a planet' in (7) is a denoting singular term.[7] The Fregean will say that it denotes a concept, the Russellian that it denotes a property. But whatever it denotes according to some position, the proponent of this position will be hard pressed to deny the validity of the following inference:

(9) Ben believes that Hesperus is a planet. Therefore, there is something such that Ben believes that Hesperus it.

But while the premise may well be true, the conclusion of this 'inference' is not even well formed, let alone true. Thus, any position that accepts compositionality and claims that expressions within that-clauses do not have their ordinary denotation has a choice between two unpalatable options: accept the validity of a blatantly invalid inference or deny Exportation.

II. Against the Argument

Let us start by setting aside a problematic aspect of the arguments that we will not target here. On the face of it, it is rather surprising that Schiffer employs the arguments rehearsed against the reference shift thesis above. For, in the very same place—Schiffer (2003)—Schiffer spells out his view of that-clauses in propositional attitude ascriptions and speech act reports as singular terms for propositions (this is an integral part of what Schiffer calls the *face value theory* of such sentences).

Now, it is well known that the face value theory has some difficulties with substitution.[8] As a consequence, it has difficulties with quantification into the position of the that-clause. Consider the following two sentences:

(10) Ben fears that the world will end tomorrow.
(11) Ann hopes that the world will end tomorrow.

If Ben is overly fearful and Ann feels a bit blue, these sentences may well be true. But the corresponding existential quantifications appear not to be:

(12) There is something such that Ben fears it, namely the proposition that the world will end tomorrow.

(13) There is something such that Ann hopes it, namely the proposition that the world will end tomorrow.

---

[7] Let us note our doubts about Schiffer's claim and the reasons he offers for it. Since our main objection applies to the generalized argument if it applies to the original, we suppress further discussion of the former.

[8] See e.g. Bach (1997), Moltmann (2003), Rosefeldt (2008).

In order for the proposition that the world will end tomorrow to be a witness to the existential quantification (12) Ben would have to be stricken by fear of an abstract object, which he may well not be even while worrying about the continued existence of the world beyond the next twenty-four hours. And (13) does not even seem to be grammatical, let alone true. But Exportation seems to license both inferences. Instead of specifying a witness the point could also be made by explicitly restricting the quantifier to propositions:

(14)   There is a proposition that Ben fears.
(15)   There is a proposition that Ben hopes.

Again, (14) does not seem to follow from (10) for the reason given above and neither does (15) from (11).

Now, we don't think that this argument shows that Schiffer's claim that that-clauses are singular terms for propositions is false. But it suggests that at least Schiffer should agree that Exportation needs to be tweaked. This is so, for one, since—we think—the predicate 'fear' has two different (though systematically related) meanings triggered in (10) on the one hand and (12) and (14) on the other (roughly: a content-oriented vs. an object-oriented one). Because of this meaning change the two existential generalizations do not have to follow from (10) even if Schiffer's thesis is correct. Whether this requires fine-tuning of Exportation depends on how plausible it is to say that it is part of the contribution the that-clause makes to the truth-conditions of (10) to trigger one reading of 'fears' rather than the other. If so, the second conjunct of the antecedent of Exportation is subtly not satisfied, so that Exportation does not license the inferences in question. If not, Exportation needs to require that the meaning of all *other* expressions remain constant. Since we don't think there is a similar problem of meaning change in the arguments against reference shift considered here, we will not dwell on this any further.[9] The 'hope' case on the other hand would seem to suggest that we need to require grammaticality of all sentences involved in Exportation. This modification casts doubt on Schiffer's generalization of the argument to the position of predicates but leaves the other arguments unaffected.

We leave things with this observation, since our main complaint deals with all of the arguments we encountered in the last section in the same fashion. In what follows we therefore focus on the arguments that concern quantification into the position of the expression that in ordinary contexts functions as a singular term. Moreover, since we would prefer to avoid problems that result from differing opinions on seemingly vacuous fictional terms such as 'Atlantis', we focus our discussion on our second example, repeated here:

---

[9] But see King (2002), Künne (2003: 258ff.) and Forbes (2018) for discussion of substitution failures that we take to be on the right track.

(5) Ben believes that Hesperus is a planet. Therefore, there is something such that Ben believes that it is a planet, to wit: [Hesperus].

Points exactly analogous to the ones we will make presently in response to (5) could be made with respect to the other problem cases discussed in Section I, in particular to Pautz's (4).

Our complaint is rather straightforward. Pautz and Schiffer assume that 'Hesperus' acts as a singular term in:

(7) Ben believes that Hesperus is a planet.

Since the Fregean reference-shifter is committed to the claim that its semantic value in this context is [Hesperus], Pautz and Schiffer conclude that, according to the Fregean, 'Hesperus' in (7) is a singular term that refers to [Hesperus], and to which, therefore, Exportation applies. But it is open to the Fregean to deny that 'Hesperus' in (7) functions as a singular term. To be sure, 'Hesperus' does function as a singular term in free-standing uses such as:

(16) Hesperus is a planet.

But it is agreed on all sides that the function of expressions may be context-dependent: Schiffer relies on this view when he claims that 'is a planet' in (7) functions as a singular term, while in (16) it functions as a predicate. There are, of course, also less contentious examples, for instance:

(17) Yesterday was a Sunday.
(18) Yesterday I went to the lake.

In (17), 'yesterday' functions as a singular term referring to a certain day, while in (18) 'yesterday' functions as an adverb whose denotation is a particular day but which does not refer to anything.

In our opinion, the Fregean should simply claim that just like 'yesterday' functions as a singular term in (17) but not in (18), so 'Hesperus' functions as a singular term in (16) but not in (7). Consequently, Exportation is inapplicable to (7) and the Fregean can have her cake and eat it, too: she can deny that inferences such as

(5) Ben believes that Hesperus is a planet. Therefore, there is something such that Ben believes that it is a planet, to wit: [Hesperus].

are valid, and she can accept Exportation at the same time.

IN DEFENCE OF FREGEAN THAT-CLAUSE SEMANTICS 241

Pautz anticipates this reaction on behalf of the Fregean, but his retort is unconvincing. He writes:[10]

> [T]here are different types of terms with semantic values. Besides singular terms, there are predicates, connectives, and so on. Yet 'Hesperus' does not play any of these other semantic functions in (7). 'Hesperus' does not occur in (7) as a predicate. Nor does it occur there as a connective. Therefore, if the occurrence of 'Hesperus' in (7) has a semantic value at all, it must be functioning there as a singular term.

Even by his own lights, the 'Therefore' is not warranted. He acknowledges that there are various functions the occurrence of an expression can have besides that of a singular term, and gives two examples. He then correctly points out that 'Hesperus' in (7) does not have these two functions and concludes that it 'therefore' has to have the function of a singular term. If there are glaring non sequiturs this is certainly one of them.[11]

Of course, 'Hesperus' does not act as an adverb or a modal or a range of other kinds of expression with a commonly recognized function either, so Pautz's case could be strengthened if we had a complete list of possible functions expressions with denotations can have in a sentence. However, nothing in her position commits the Fregean to accept any list Pautz could offer her. In effect, there is an easy and systematic way for extending any list on offer in such a way that the Fregean can defuse Pautz's argument: for any entry on Pautz's list e, add an entry e such

---

[10] We substituted our example.

[11] Schiffer (2003: 30) also gives an argument for the claim, though it is not quite clear to us what the argument is supposed to be. On one interpretation, it is simply a version of Pautz's argument by exclusion. In this case, our reply in the main text applies. On another interpretation, Schiffer's argument (adapted to fit the case at hand) runs as follows: The Fregean thinks that a that-clause such as 'that Hesperus is a planet' refers to the concatenation of the sense of 'Hesperus' with the sense of 'is a planet', ⌈Hesperus⌉,⌈is a planet⌉ for short. Thus, the that-clause and the concatenation expression are both complex singular terms that refer to the same thing. From this, Schiffer wants to conclude that 'Hesperus' as it occurs in the former and '[Hesperus]' as it occurs in the latter both function as (co-referential) singular terms. The plausible principle that would support this conclusion eludes us. Here is one try: if t and t' are complex singular terms containing the constituents c and c' respectively, where (i) t and t' are co-referential, (ii) c functions in t as a singular term, and (iii) c denotes in t the same thing as c' denotes in t', then c' functions in t' as a singular term that is co-referential with c in t. However, the principle has false instances. Consider the complex singular terms (t_1) 'the value of the function *father of* for the argument Gottlob' and (t_2) 'the father of Gottlob'. t_1 contains the constituent (c_1) 'the function *father of*' and t_2 contains the constituent 'father of'. Now, (i) t_1 and t_2 are co-referential: they both refer to Karl; (ii) c_1 functions in t_1 as a singular term that refers to a certain function, and c_2 denotes in t_2 that very function. But this does not mean that c_2 functions in t_2 as a *singular term* that *refers* to that function. On the contrary, as Schiffer would agree, 'father of' in 'the father of Gottlob' is a general term rather than a singular term, while general terms do not have the function to refer to anything. The principle is, thus, false, and there is no obvious correct candidate in the neighbourhood. Since Schiffer does not specify the missing principle, we conclude that his argument fails on its second interpretation as well.

that the occurrence *o* of an expression functions as an *e* just in case *o* occurs in the that-clause of a propositional attitude ascription or speech act report, and in a freestanding use of the sister-clause of the complementizer 'that' this occurrence functions as an *e*. According to that view, for instance, since 'Hesperus' in (16) functions as a singular term, 'Hesperus' in (7) functions as a singular term*. Since 'is a planet' functions as a predicate in (16), 'is a planet' functions as a predicate* in (7), and so forth.[12]

Schiffer and Pautz may object that the addition of these various new functions expressions can have is an ad hoc move on the part of the Fregean. We disagree. Being a singular term is a syntactico-*semantic* classification. And, according to the Fregean, the semantic functions of the expression 'Hesperus' in (7) and in (16) are fundamentally different: in (7) 'Hesperus' contributes its *ungerade Bedeutung* in (16) its *gewöhnliche Bedeutung* to the determination of the truth-conditions of the sentence. The objection that the distinction is ad hoc fails to engage with this Fregean thesis and thus simply begs the question against the Fregean reference-shifter.

An observation that we take more seriously is the following: though inferences such as

(5) Ben believes that Hesperus is a planet. Therefore, there is something such that Ben believes that it is a planet, to wit: [Hesperus]

are invalid, closely related ones are valid:

(20) Ben believes that Hesperus is a planet. There is such a thing as Hesperus. Therefore, there is something such that Ben believes that it is a planet, to wit: Hesperus.

Our Fregean claims that in the first premise of (20) 'Hesperus' does not function as a singular term but rather as a singular term*. Consequently, Exportation does not license the inference in question. But such inferences are systematically valid. The Fregean seems unable to explain this phenomenon.

---

[12] There are two strategies for extending the list that have equivalent results for the cases that concern us here but different results for multiply embedded occurrences. Consider, for instance:

(19) Ann said that Ralph believes that Hesperus is a planet.

According to one suggestion, 'Hesperus' in (19) will be a singular term**, since in (7) 'Hesperus' acts as a singular term*. Since, in principle, 'Hesperus' may occur *n*-deeply embedded for any natural number *n*, each list of functions on offer should be extended to an infinite *-closed list. Alternatively, the Fregean could claim that the type of function of an expression depends on the function it ultimately has in the unembedded clause, so only one-starred additions are needed. This mirrors a debate between Frege scholars whether to attribute to Frege only a binary division between *gewöhnliche* and *ungerade Bedeutung* or rather potentially infinite ranks of *Ungeradheit*. Though philosophers tend to dislike the second option, at present we don't see any deep reason to go with one rather than the other. For present purposes, nothing appears to hinge on the choice.

We agree that it would be preferable for the Fregean to be able to explain *why* the inference just cited should be valid while the seemingly very similar but problematic inferences adduced by Pautz and Schiffer are invalid. We will take on this challenge in the next two sections by giving an account of the interaction of quantification with Fregean that-clause semantics.

III. A Questionable Semantic Hypothesis

According to the Fregean, the denotations of various kinds of expressions shift from their regular denotations—objects in the case of singular terms, properties in the case of predicates—to senses that determine these ordinary denotations. The problem Schiffer and Pautz isolate focuses on the behaviour of variables (or traces or pronouns in our maximally explicit natural language renderings). The key question, which Frege himself did not have the semantic resources at his disposal to ask, is therefore:[13] what is the denotation of a variable under an assignment?

Schiffer and Pautz seem to presuppose in their argument that, as in the usual case, the denotation under an assignment σ of a variable x within a that-clause is exactly what it is outside: it is simply the object that σ assigns to the variable x. That is:

$$[\![x]\!]^\sigma = \sigma(x).$$

Call this the *Simple Hypothesis*. Thus, for instance, according to the Simple Hypothesis, if σ_1 assigns the planet Hesperus to x, the denotation of x under σ_1 is that very planet, if σ_2 assigns to x the concept [Hesperus], the denotation of x under σ_2 is that concept, and so forth, even within a that-clause.

Given reasonable further assumptions about the composition of the denotation of a belief report, this hypothesis yields the problematic truth-conditions for

(21) There is something such that Ben believes that it is a planet

which would license the inference in

(5) Ben believes that Hesperus is a planet. Therefore, there is something such that Ben believes that it is a planet, to wit: [Hesperus].

---

[13] These became available through Alfred Tarski's seminal (1935).

For, suppose a that-clause denotes that proposition which consists of the concatenation of the denotations of its constituents under an assignment. For instance, the that-clause in

(7) Ben believes that Hesperus is a planet

denotes the concatenation of the sense of 'Hesperus' with the sense of 'is a planet', represented here as an ordered tuple of the concatenated items: ⟨[Hesperus], [is a planet]⟩. Given the Simple Hypothesis, that very same proposition is also denoted by the that-clause in (21) under σ_2. Accordingly, 'believes' combines with both that-clauses to yield as a denotation under σ_2 a property that an object exemplifies just in case it stands in the belief relation to ⟨[Hesperus], [is a planet]⟩. Hence, (7) and (21) are true under σ_2 just in case Ben believes the proposition in question. Finally, (7) is true simpliciter just in case Ben believes ⟨[Hesperus], [is a planet]⟩ and (21) is true simpliciter just in case there is some assignment under which 'Ben believes that x is a planet' is true, which, as we have just seen, the truth of (7) ensures with σ_2. Thus, the Simple Hypothesis yields the problematic claim that the inference in (5) is valid with [Hesperus] as a witness.

Things are even worse than this: not only does the Simple Hypothesis yield that the intuitively invalid (5) is really valid, it also does *not* ensure that the intuitively valid inference

(22) Ben believes that Hesperus is a planet. There is such a thing as Hesperus. Therefore, there is something such that Ben believes that it is a planet, to wit: Hesperus

is valid. For, assume, plausibly, that an existential quantification has an object as a witness just in case an assignment under which the embedded open sentence is true assigns that witness to the variable in question. Then, according to the Simple Hypothesis, (21) has the planet Hesperus as a witness just in case Ben believes some proposition that consists of the concatenation of *that very planet* with the sense of 'is a planet'. But that there is such a proposition is by no means ensured by the fact that Ben believes the proposition that consists of the concatenation of *the sense of 'Hesperus'* with the sense of 'is a planet'. On the contrary, given Fregean strictures against the composition of propositions out of anything but senses, the Fregean has a reason to think that there is no such proposition that is completely independent from accidental facts about Ben's mental life.[14]

---

[14] This Fregean stricture becomes obvious in his exchange with Russell (excerpt from Frege to Russell, 13 November 1904, Frege (1980), 163), where he writes that '[t]he sense of the word "moon" is a component part of the thought that the moon is smaller than the earth[, while t]he moon

One begins to wonder whether the Pautzian problem really results from the Fregean semantics for that-clauses or rather from its combination with the Simple Hypothesis. On the face of it, the Simple Hypothesis is a very strange view on the semantics of variables for the Fregean to have: according to the Fregean, the denotations of *all other* expressions shift from their *gewöhnliche* to their *ungerade Bedeutung* within that-clauses. If the Simple Hypothesis were true, the only non-shifting denotation would be the denotation of a variable under an assignment. No wonder that this imparity in the treatment of variables on the one hand and all other expressions, particularly singular terms, on the other creates semantic havoc! If the Fregean were committed to the Simple Hypothesis, this would be bad news indeed. Fortunately, there is no good reason to think that she is. In the next section we will spell out a Fregean view of the semantics of variables that is a straightforward extension of her views on singular terms, predicates and so forth. As the reader might suspect, this Fregean semantics validates (20) and invalidates (5) compatibly with Fregean assumptions about the compositional meaning of that-clauses, in particular reference shift.[15]

IV. Fregean That-Clause Semantics

The key idea of a Fregean semantics for variables within that-clauses is that, just like the denotation of a singular term, the denotation of a variable under an assignment σ shifts from the object it denotes outside of a that-clause under σ to a sense which determines that object. For instance, since σ_1 assigns the planet Hesperus to the variable 'x', $[\![x]\!]^{\sigma_1}$ within a that-clause is a sense that determines Hesperus rather than the planet Hesperus itself. Likewise, since σ_2 assigns the concept [Hesperus] to 'x', $[\![x]\!]^{\sigma_2}$ within a that-clause is a concept of the concept [Hesperus] rather than [Hesperus] itself.[16]

There is one obvious difficulty with this suggestion we make on behalf of the Fregean. There are indefinitely many senses that determine any given object. For instance, while [Hesperus] determines Hesperus, so does [Phosphorus], [Venus], [the planet which is mentioned most prominently in Frege's discussion of that-clauses] and many more. Which of these should be taken to be *the* sense denoted by 'x' under σ_1 within a that-clause? It would seem that there is no non-arbitrary way of choosing. In the case of singular terms there are some (relatively) good

---

itself [...] is not part of the sense of the word "moon"; for then it would also be a component part of that thought'.

[15] We take a broadly Tarskian perspective on the semantics of variables. An even easier case could be made by tying the semantics of variables closely to that of singular terms, e.g. via variations on interpretations of dummy singular terms. Since a Tarskian view appears to us to be the orthodoxy, we opted for the route that makes our life slightly more difficult here.

[16] Here and in what follows we use indexed double bracket notation as shorthand for talking about the denotation of the enclosed expression under an assignment.

candidates: the denotation of 'Hesperus' in (7), for instance, is the sense the word 'Hesperus' has (ideally) in the mouths of competent speakers, or in the mouth of the speaker of (7), or perhaps in the mouth of Ben outside of a that-clause.[17] But in the case of variables (or traces or pronouns) there is not obviously any sense that the variable has in the mouths of competent speakers (or this or that speaker) even under a given assignment.

There are two options for the Fregean to deal with this difficulty. On the one hand, she could argue that there is a contextually salient sense even for variables. Perhaps, whenever someone utters (21) there is a way of thinking about Hesperus that is salient in the context of utterance, and it is this sense that the variable denotes under σ_1. However, since one may utter an existential quantification like (21) without being able to specify a witness, this option is rather implausible. Moreover, something similar would have to hold for *any* object an assignment can assign to 'x', rendering the view even more implausible. For instance, with a bow to Peter Geach an assignment function may assign some particular pebble on the beach of Brighton to 'x', but there may well be no sense that anyone has ever grasped that would determine that pebble, let alone one that would be salient in some context of utterance.

We take the following strategy to be much more promising. Suppose an assignment assigns an object o to a variable x. There is an indefinite number of senses s_1, s_2,...each of which determines o. Rather than saying that 'x' within a that-clause definitely denotes exactly one out of these indefinitely many candidates, the Fregean should claim that, within the that-clause, the variable *indefinitely* denotes all of them. This indefiniteness will make its way up the semantic tree. For instance, rather than definitely denoting some proposition that is the concatenation of some s_i with [is a planet], under σ_1 'that x is a planet' will indefinitely denote all of the propositions of the kind $\langle s_i, [is\ a\ planet]\rangle$.

Since we do not want to say that 'Ben believes that x is a planet' indefinitely denotes the truth-value True (since Ben believes $\langle [Hesperus], [is\ a\ planet]\rangle$, say) and the truth-value False (since Ben does not believe $\langle [the\ heavenly\ body\ most\ famously\ appealed\ to\ by\ Frege], [is\ a\ planet]\rangle$, say) under σ_1, indefiniteness cannot be preserved all the way up the semantic tree. A plausible stopping point is the place of the propositional attitude verb, since, recall, it is only part of the Fregean reference shift thesis that reference shifts within that-clauses *in the case of propositional attitude ascriptions and speech act reports*. Following a Kaplan-inspired suggestion developed in Forbes (1990), we think it is plausible

---

[17] As Frege laments in Frege (1918/1993), there is no one sense a typical natural language proper name has in the mouths of all competent speakers, so the disjuncts are not equivalent. But this is a difficulty that need not concern us here. Interestingly, the solution we suggest for the case of variables might be applicable to the problem of variably interpreted proper names as well, as sketched in the next footnote.

that 'Ben believes that x is a planet' is (definitely) true under σ_1 just in case there is *some* sense s that determines Hesperus such that Ben believes $\langle s, [\textit{is a planet}]\rangle$. This suggests a natural semantics for 'believe' and other propositional attitude and speech act verbs that complements our semantics for variables within that-clauses: 'believes' should combine with a that-clause to denote a property (or a function from objects to truth-values) that is exemplified by an object just in case that object believes *at least one of* the indefinite denotations the that-clause has.[18]

The idea sketched in the last two paragraphs may be made more precise by using sets as semantic values for singular terms and variables. Definitely denoting terms will have unit sets as denotations, indefinitely denoting terms have sets of two or more objects as denotations.[19] Accordingly, we propose on behalf of the Fregean to replace the Simple Hypothesis with the Fregean Hypothesis of the denotation of a variable x under an assignment σ within a that-clause. Under the Fregean Hypothesis, this denotation is the set of senses that determine the object σ assigns to 'x'. That is:

$$[\![x]\!]^\sigma = \{s | s \text{ is a sense that determines } \sigma(x)\}.$$

We modify the view that denotations of that-clauses are concatenations of the denotations of their constituents in order to be able to deal with indefinite constituent denotations in the obvious way: the denotation of a that-clause is the set of concatenations of any one of the denotations of the first constituent with any one of the second with any one of the third, etc. Let's simplify by only considering that-clauses of the form 'that t is F' with only two semantically relevant constituents 't' and 'is F'. Then we have:

$$[\![\text{that } t \text{ is } F]\!]^\sigma = [\![t]\!]^\sigma \times [\![\text{is } F]\!]^\sigma$$

Finally, the denotation of 'φs that p' under an assignment σ for a propositional attitude or speech act verb φ is as described above:

$$[\![\varphi\text{s that } p]\!]^\sigma = \lambda x. \exists y (y \in [\![\text{that } p]\!]^\sigma \wedge [\![\varphi]\!]^\sigma(y)(x)).$$

---

[18] To preserve uniformity, we may treat a definitely denoting that-clause such as, perhaps, 'that Hesperus is a planet' as the limit case that has exactly one 'indefinite' denotation. The recognition of indefinitely denoting that-clauses also promises a solution to the problem mentioned in the last footnote: even though there may not be one sense every competent speaker associates with a proper name such as 'Hesperus', there may be a *range* of legitimate such senses, so that 'that Hesperus is a planet' has more than one indefinite denotation after all, which still fixes a single truth-value for propositional attitude ascriptions in which it occurs.

[19] If we wish, we can then say that a singular term t refers to an object o just in case o is an element of the denotation of t.

248 UNSTRUCTURED CONTENT

It remains to check that these proposals yield the desired truth-conditions for

(23)   There is something such that Ben believes that it is a planet

according to which the planet Hesperus and not the concept [Hesperus] is a witness whenever

(7)   Ben believes that Hesperus is a planet

is true and there is such a thing as Hesperus.

Let's work from the top down. (21) is true just in case there is an assignment σ such that

$$[\![\text{Ben believes that } x \text{ is a planet}]\!]^\sigma = \textit{True}$$

iff

$$[\lambda x. \exists y \, (y \in [\![\text{that } x \text{ is a planet}]\!]^\sigma \wedge [\![\text{believes}]\!]^\sigma (y)(x))]([\![\text{Ben}]\!]^\sigma)$$

iff

$$\exists y (y \in ([\![x]\!]^\sigma \times [\![\textit{is a planet}]\!]^\sigma) \wedge [\![\text{believes}]\!]^\sigma (y)([\![\text{Ben}]\!]^\sigma)).$$

Now, according to the Fregean, the relevant occurrences of 'Ben' and 'believes' have their *gewöhnliche Bedeutung* while those of 'x' and 'is a planet' have their *ungerade Bedeutung*. That is:[20]

$$[\![\text{Ben}]\!]^\sigma = \{\text{Ben}\}$$
$$[\![\text{believes}]\!]^\sigma = \{\lambda x.[\lambda y. x \text{ believes } y]\}$$
$$[\![x]\!]^\sigma = \{s | s \text{ is a sense that determines } \sigma(x)\}$$
$$[\![\text{is a planet}]\!]^\sigma = \{[\text{is a planet}]\}.$$

Substituting in our truth-conditions for (21) and simplifying yields that (21) is true under an assignment σ just in case:

---

[20] Recall our decision to use unit sets as the denotations of definitely denoting expressions and sets with more than one element as the denotations of indefinitely denoting expressions. Thus, for instance, the first clause states that 'Ben' definitely denotes Ben, and the third clause states that 'x' under σ indefinitely denotes those senses that determine $\sigma(x)$.

$\exists y \, (y \in (\{s|s \text{ is a sense that determines } \sigma(x)\} \times \{[\text{is a planet}]\}) \land \text{Ben believes } y)$.

We finally note that the set of concatenations $\{s|s$ is a sense that determines $\sigma(x)\} \times \{[\text{is a planet}]\}$ just is $\{\langle s, [\text{is a planet}]\rangle | s$ is a sense that determines $\sigma(x)\}$, i.e. the set of propositions that consist of a sense that determines $\sigma(x)$ concatenated with the sense of 'is a planet'. Thus, we arrive at the result that (21) is true just in case there is an assignment σ that assigns an object o to x such that there is a proposition that consists of a sense that determines o concatenated with the sense of 'is a planet' and which Ben believes.

As desired, the derived truth-conditions for (21) show that the quantification has the planet Hesperus as a witness, if there is such a thing as Hesperus and, for instance, Ben believes that Hesperus is a planet. And it does not have the concept of Hesperus as a witness, unless Ben should somehow come to believe that the concept of Hesperus is a planet. For this reason, our semantics has the result that the intuitively invalid inferences cited by Schiffer and Pautz turn out to be invalid and the intuitively valid inferences cited above turn out to be valid. Both of these results follow on the assumption that the Fregean reference shift thesis is true.

We end by noting that while our discussion leaves Pautz's Exportation principle intact but inapplicable, it offers an addition to Exportation, Exportation*, and it suggests a generalized exportation principle that underlies both Exportation and Exportation*. The addition licensed by our semantics is:

Exportation*: If t in $S(t)$ is a singular term that denotes a sense that determines o and makes no other contribution to the truth conditions of $S(t)$, then $S(t)$ entails *There is something such that S(it)*, where o is a witness to that quantification.

It should be obvious from the above discussion that this is a straightforward consequence of our Fregean semantics for that-clauses, in combination with the view that occurrences of expressions within that-clauses that are normally singular terms are singular term*s. The combination of Exportation and Exportation* systematically covers all cases Schiffer and Pautz take Exportation alone to cover, and they do so in a way that has no implausible consequences for the Fregean.

The generalized exportation principle that underlies both Exportation and Exportation* is:

Generalized Exportation: If t as used in $S(t)$ is ordinarily a singular term whose ordinary denotation (*gewöhnliche Bedeutung*) is o and that makes no other contribution to the truth conditions of $S(t)$ than its denotation, then $S(t)$ entails *There is something such that S(it)*, where o is a witness to that quantification.

Supposing that unproblematic occurrences of singular terms and those within that-clauses are the only relevant cases, Generalized Exportation is licensed by our semantics and covers all cases envisaged by Schiffer and Pautz in a single principle. The only relevant difference to Exportation is that, where Exportation speaks of the denotation the expression in question has *in the linguistic context in which it occurs*, Generalized Exportation speaks of the denotation the expression *ordinarily* has. For the opponent of reference shift there is, thus, no recognizable difference between Exportation and Generalized Exportation either in scope or prediction—after all, she thinks that the denotation an expression has in any linguistic context is always its ordinary denotation. According to Schiffer and Pautz, for the Fregean (and for reference-shifters in general), there should not be a difference in scope (since Schiffer and Pautz do not distinguish between singular terms and singular term*s) but a difference in prediction, so that the two principles are in conflict. We, on the other hand, have argued that the Fregean should take the scope of Generalized Exportation to be more inclusive than that of Exportation: it covers both ordinary occurrences of singular terms as well as those within that-clauses. Since it also yields the correct predictions, the Fregean can both uphold Exportation as a special case that does *not* apply to the problematic inferences as well as license those additional inferences that ought to be licensed via Generalized Exportation.

This concludes our limited defence of the Fregean semantics for that-clauses. There might be various worries one could legitimately have concerning the Fregean picture, but Schiffer's and Pautz's is not one of them.[21]

References

Bach, K. 1997. 'Do belief reports report beliefs?'. *Pacific Philosophical Quarterly* 78: 215–41.
Forbes, G. 1990. 'The indispensability of Sinn'. *Philosophical Review* 99: 535–63.
Forbes, G. 2018. 'Content and theme in attitude ascriptions'. In *Non-Propositional Intentionality*, ed. A. Grzankowski and M. Montague, 114–33. Oxford: Oxford University Press.
Frege, G. 1892/1994. 'Über Sinn und Bedeutung'. In *Funktion, Begriff, Bedeutung. Herausgegeben und eingeleitet von Günter Patzig*, 40–65. Göttingen: Vandenhoeck & Ruprecht. Page references are to the original publication.

---

[21] We would like to thank participants at the *Sprachphilosophie Kolloquium* 2019 in Hamburg (particularly its organizer Miguel Hoeltje), at the workshop *Language and World* in Graz and the *Research Seminar Theoretical Philosophy* in Bielefeld for helpful comments and discussion. In addition, KF would like to thank Tobias Rosefeldt for setting the question of this paper as a homework assignment, which she now somewhat belatedly hands in. AS gratefully acknowledges financial support from the University of Zurich's *Forschungskredit* (grant no. FK-16-078). He would also like to thank Wolfgang Künne for impressing on him the idea that a defence of Frege is generally well worth one's time. (He leaves it to the reader to decide whether this is one of those few false instances every worthwhile generalization allows.)

Frege, G. 1918/1993. 'Der Gedanke'. In *Logische Untersuchungen. Herausgegeben und eingeleitet von Günther Patzig*, 30–53. Göttingen: Vandenhoeck & Ruprecht.
Frege, G. 1980. *Philosophical and Mathematical Correspondence*. Oxford: Basil Blackwell.
King, J. C. 2002. 'Designating propositions'. *Philosophical Review* 111: 341–71.
Künne, W. 2003. *Conceptions of Truth*. Oxford: Oxford University Press.
Moltmann, F. 2003. 'Propositional attitudes without propositions'. *Synthese* 135: 77–118.
Pautz, A. 2008. 'An argument against Fregean that-clause semantics'. *Philosophical Studies* 138: 335–47.
Perry, J. 1977. 'Frege on Demonstratives'. *Philosophical Review* 86: 474–97.
Rosefeldt, T. 2008. ' "That"-clauses and non-nominal quantification'. *Philosophical Studies* 137: 301–33.
Schiffer, S. 2003. *The Things We Mean*. Oxford: Clarendon Press.
Tarski, A. 1935. 'Der Wahrheitsbegriff in den formalisierten Sprachen'. *Studia Philosophica* 1: 261–405.
Williamson, T. 2007. *The Philosophy of Philosophy*. Oxford: Blackwell.

General Index

Since the index has been created to work across multiple formats, indexed terms for which a page range is given (e.g., 52–53, 66–70, etc.) may occasionally appear only on some, but not all of the pages within the range.

aboutness 129–30
accuracy conditions 216 n.16, 216–17, 229–30
actual world xx, 70–1, 86, 91–2, 96–7, 173–4, 194
actuality 91–2
adjunction 11–27
   ideal 11, 11 n.7, 25, 33, 33 n.13
   internal 20
   minimal 20–1
   partial 20–1, 25, 28
alethic properties xiii–xiv
anti-actuality 91, 100
Aristotelian truth 69–70, 72–4
assertability semantics 67
assertion 65, 75, 160–1, 170, 172–3, 195
attitudes
   as evidence 196–8
   as explanation 196–8
   cognitive vs. non-cognitive 62–3
   expressing vs. describing 62–3
attitudinal objects xxi, 136, 143–7
   as primary content bearers 136
   characteristic properties of 145
   kinds of 147
austere relationalism 205–6, 211–12
austere representationalism 205–11

Bayesian epistemology 75–9
belief 193–4
   fragmentation theory of xviii, 11–12, 24, 27–8
   functionalist account of xv
   metaphysics of 47–9, 56–8
   naive conception of 52, 54
   refined concepts of 198–9
belief reports 37

causal relations 203
causal-pragmatic picture of content 47–8, 50–1
clausal complements
   as predicates 151–4
   of attitude verbs 137
closure
   ideal 5–6, 8
   minimal 6–9
   under conjunction elimination 7–9, 18–19
   under parthood 19–21
co-belief 42–56, 60
commitment xix, 42–5, 52–5, 60
   externalist conception of 44, 60
   internalist conception of 44, 60
common ground xii, 139, 160–1
communication, problem of 64
consistency
   ideal 10
   minimal 10, 21–4
   partial 22, 24
containment 98
content
   factual vs. normative 63, 66–7
   fine-grained notion of 135–6, 141–2
   unstructured 192–3
context set xii–xiii, 139, 173

deontic modals 139
dependence 110–12
disjunctivism 211, 213–14

emotivism 62
entailment xiii–xiv, 5, 98
epistemic modals 75, 150–1
epistemic norms 74–9
epistemic probability 77–8
equivalence property 46
experiential content 207–10
experiential states 202–3
exportation principle 236–7, 249–50
expressivism xix–xx
   about epistemic norms 74–9
   about truth 67–74
   contemporary versions 63
   vs. non-naturalism 71–4
extensional semantics x–xi

factual discourse 63, 66–7, 73–4
Fregean Particularism 215–27
   Advantages of 225

254 GENERAL INDEX

Frege-Geach problem xix–xx, 64
functional compositionality x–xii

gappy contents 214–15, 220–4

hallucination 201 n.2, 201, 210–15, 221–5, 227–8
harmonic modals 140, 158–60
hyperintensionality xx, 118–19

illocutionary acts xii
illocutionary products 146, 152
illusion 207–8, 215, 222, 224, 227
impossible worlds xvii–xviii, 8 n.4
inconsistency
   blatant vs. opaque 21–3
intensional phenomena xi
intensional semantics ix–xi, 11, 26–7
intentionality, problem of 69
interpretation function x–xi

logical omniscience xviii–xix

Mereology 119–20
minimal rationality xviii–xix, 3–4, 9–10, 16
minimal sufficiency xx–xxi, 111–12
minimalism about truth 71–3
modal objects 136, 145–7
modal properties xiii–xiv
modal realism 71 n.16
modes of presentation 217–19
   de dicto 217–18
   de re 218–19

naturalism 72
necessary truths xvi–xvii, xxii, 185
non-cognitivism 63, 72
non-natural realism xx
non-naturalism 71–4
normative discourse 62–3, 66–7
normative logic 64–7
normative naivete, problem of 65

object-based truthmaker semantics xxi–xxii, 136–7
   advantages of 147–51
   applications of 154–61
omniscience property 46

partial truth xx, 83, 86–7, 89–95, 98–103
particularity
   phenomenological 203–4
   relational 204–5
perception
   as relational 205–7
   as representational 205–7

perceptual capacities 215–17, 219–20
perceptual content 58–9, 208–10, 215–19, 229–30
permissions
   heavy and light 148–9
permissivism, epistemic 76–7
phenomenal character 202–3, 207–8
phenomenal sameness 202–3
possible worlds 65–70, 66 n.8, 192–3
possible worlds semantics xi–xiv, xvii
   advantages of 135, 139–40
   problems with 135–6
pragmatics 73–5, 177–81
prior probability, epistemic 77–9
propositional attitudes xiv–xv, xxi–xxiv, 137–8, 234–5
propositions 192–3, 198–9
   act-type theories of ix–x, xiv
   as sets of possible worlds xi, xiii–xiv, 65–6, 69–71
   primitivist theories of xiv
   structured 192–3
   structured theories of xi–xii, xiv, xxii, 140–1
   unstructured theories of ix–xxiv
Protagorean truth 70–1

quantification 237–9
quantificational analysis of modals 137–8
Question Mereology 14–15
quizpositions 13
quizposition conjunction 18–19
quizposition negation 21
quizpoisional updates 28–30

radical interpretation 56–9
rationality 63
reference shift xxiii–xxiv
reference shift thesis 234–5
   the argument against 235–43
relational analysis of attitude reports 137, 143–5
relationalism 205–7
representation xiv–vi
representationalism 205–7

satisfaction conditions 136, 145–6, 150–1
semantic values x–xi
semantics
   assertability 67
   compositional 64–7, 70, 73–5, 135
   for that-clauses 243–50
   of variables 245–7
   truth-conditional 64, 67
singular content 213–15
situation semantics xvii–xviii, 136, 141–2

that-clauses 234–5, 245–50
truth
  relative vs. absolute 14, 70–1
truth conditions xxii–xxiii, 136, 194–6
truthmaker semantics xvii–xviii, xx–xxii, 136, 141–3

underspecification of content 149–51

verbs
  attitude 154–7
  factive 156–7
  response-stance 154–6

Name Index

Since the index has been created to work across multiple formats, indexed terms for which a page range is given (e.g., 52–53, 66–70, etc.) may occasionally appear only on some, but not all of the pages within the range.

Aristotle 69–71, 73
Ayer, A.J. 62

Bach, K. 238 n.8
Barwise, J. xvii–xviii, 194
Bealer, G. ix–x, xvi
Berto, F. xvii–xviii, 8–9, 28
Blackburn, S. 63 n.2
Block, N. 206–7
Braddon-Mitchell, D. xviii
Brewer, B. 206–7, 211
Brown, T. xvi
Burge, T. 206–7, 221 n.21, 228
Byrne, A. 205 n.5, 206–7

Campbell, J. 205 n.4, 205 n.5, 206–7
Cattell, R. 154–6
Chalmers, D. 218, 229–31
Charlow, N. xvi
Crane, T. 204 n.3, 228–9
Cresswell, M.J. x, 8–9

Davidson, D. 151, 151 n.12
Davies, M. 201, 209–10

Evans, G. 219 n.20, 228

Felka, K. xxiii–xxiv, 144
Field, H. 63, 182–7
Fine, K. xx, 116–17, 119 n.21, 136, 141–2
Fish, W. 206–7
Forbes, G. 239 n.9, 246–7
Frege, G. xix–xx, xxiii–xxiv, 67–8, 217–18, 234, 243

Gemes, K. 119 n.21
Genone, J. 206–7
Geurts, B. 160
Gibbard, A. xix–xx, 63–76, 66 n.8, 78
Goodman, N. 19 n.11, 121 n.23
Graff Fara, D. 149–50
Grice, H.P. 176–8
Groenendijk, J.A.G. xii, 13

Hacquard, V. 140
Hajek, A. 77–8, 77 n.29
Hallett, M. 128 n.38
Hamblin, C. xii–xiii, 13
Hanks, P. ix–x, 140–1
Harman, G. 213
Heim, I. xi, xiv, 138 n.1, 139
Heller, M. xvi
Hempel, C.G. 109–10
Hill, C. 205 n.4, 206–7
Hinton, J.M. 211 n.10
Hintikka, J. 138, 149–50
Hoek, D. xviii–xix
Horwich, P. 63, 67–8
Hume, D. 113–16, 132

Jackson, F. xviii
Jago, M. xvii–xviii, 7, 8 n.4, 10
Johnston, M. 205 n.5, 206–7, 218 n.19
Jubien, M. xvi, 140–1

Kayne, R. 144 n.6
Kim, J. 112 n.6
King, J. ix–xiii, xvii, xxii
Kment, B. 111 n.5
Kratzer, A. xi, 117, 117 n.16, 124, 125 n.36, 140, 158–9
Krämer, S. 141
Kripke, S. 8, 179 n.21, 198, 215

Lewis, D. ix–x, xiii, xvi, xviii, 11, 58, 71 n.16, 77–8, 124, 153
Logue, H. 206–7
Lycan, W.G. 206–7, 228–9

Martin, M.G.F. 205 n.5, 206–7, 211 n.8
McDowell, J. 206–7, 211 n.9, 211 n.10, 213 n.11, 219 n.20, 228
McGinn, C. 208 n.7, 209 n.8
Merricks, T. ix–x, xvi–xvii
Moltmann, F. 137, 140–1, 144–6, 151 n.13, 151 n.12, 155, 157, 159–61
Montague, R. x–xi, 25
Moore, G.E. 8–9, 206–7

NAME INDEX

Moss, S. 124, 124 n.33
Muskens, R. xi–xii

Nagel, T. 69

Parikh, R. xv
Pautz, A. 235–7, 240–5
Peacocke, C. 206–7
Perry, J. xvii–xviii, xxii–xxiii
Pickel, B. xi–xii
Plantinga, A. xvi
Portner, P. 139, 160
Pranav, A. 140
Price, H.H. 206–7

Quine, W.V.O. xv–xvi, 78

Richard, M. xvii
Ripley, D. xvii–xviii
Roski, S. 114

Salmon, N. ix–xi
Scanlon, T. 72
Schellenberg, S. xxiii, 205 n.4, 206–7
Schiffer, S. xxiii–xxiv, 235, 237–40, 243, 249–50
Schlenker, P. 114 n.10
Schroeder, M. 67, 74

Searle, J. 147, 147 n.9, 150–1, 206–7, 209 n.8
Sellars, W. 121–2
Skyrms, B. 115 n.11
Snowdon, P. 211 n.10, 213 n.11
Soames, S. ix–xi, xvi–xvii, 140–1, 167
Socrates 71
Soteriou, M. 206–7, 209 n.8
Speaks, J. xvi, 231 n.26
Stalnaker, R. xii, xiv, xvii–xx, 27, 45–55, 57–9, 61, 168–80, 171 n.11, 182–6
Stevenson, C. 62
Stokhof, M.J.B. xii, 13
Strevens, M. 111 n.5

Thomasson, A. 146 n.8
Thomason, R. xi–xii
Travis, C. 205 n.5
Twardowski, K. 146, 146 n.8
Tye, M. 206–7, 209 n.8, 214 n.12

Ulrich 145–6

White, R. 77 n.27
Williams, J.R.G. xix, 56–7, 214 n.13
Williamson, T. 77–8, 118 n.18

Yablo, S. xx–xxi, 4–5, 7–8, 19, 84, 152–3
Yalcin, S. xviii, 12 n.9, 74–5, 124